Who Are Canada's Aboriginal Peoples?

UNIVERSITY OF WINNIPEG, 515 Portage Ave. Winnipeg, MB R3B 2E9 Canada

UNIVERSITY OF WINNIPEG, 515 Portage Ave., Winnipeg, MB R3B 2E9 Canada

Purich's Aboriginal Issues Series

Who Are Canada's Aboriginal Peoples?

Recognition, Definition, and Jurisdiction

Edited by Paul L. A. H. Chartrand
Foreword by Harry W. Daniels

Purich Publishing Ltd.
Saskatoon, Saskatchewan
Canada

The author gratefully acknowledges the financial contribution of the Congress of Aboriginal Peoples (CAP) towards the writing of this book. The views expressed are those of the authors and do not necessarily reflect those of CAP or any of its elected or non-elected officers, employees, or constituents.

Purich Publishing Ltd.
Box 23032, Market Mall Post Office
Saskatoon, SK Canada S7J 5H3
Phone: (306) 373-5311   Fax: (306) 373-5315
Email: purich@sasktel.net
Website: www.purichpublishing.com

National Library of Canada Cataloguing in Publication Data

Main entry under title:

Who are Canada's aboriginal peoples? : recognition, definition, and jurisdiction / edited by Paul L.A.H. Chartrand ; foreword by Harry W. Daniels.

(Purich's aboriginal issues series)
"This book emerged from a number of papers originally written for a conference held in Vancouver in 1998 by the Congress of Aboriginal Peoples"–introd.
Includes bibliographical references and index.
ISBN 1–895830–20–6 (bound)

1. Native peoples—Canada.* 2. Native peoples—Legal status, laws, etc.—Canada.* I. Chartrand, Paul L. A. H., 1943– II. Congress of Aboriginal Peoples. III. Series.
E78.C2W488 2002   971'.00497   C2002-911367-9

Cover design by NEXT Communications Inc., Saskatoon, Saskatchewan.

Editing, design, layout, and index by Roberta Mitchell Coulter, Saskatoon, Saskatchewan.

Printed in Canada by Houghton-Boston, Saskatoon on acid-free paper.

The publisher acknowledges the financial assistance of the Government of Saskatchewan through the Cultural Industries Development Fund towards the publication of this book.

Readers will note that words like Aboriginal, Native, and Indigenous have been capitalized in this book. In recent years, many Aboriginal people have argued that such words should be capitalized when referring to specific people, in the same manner that European and American are capitalized. We agree.
The Publishers

Contents

About the Authors

Russel Lawrence Barsh
Russel Barsh studied law at Harvard, and taught at the University of Washington, the University of Lethbridge, and as a Visiting Professor at Harvard and Dartmouth before accepting his present position at New York University Law School. He has acted as a spokesman for the Mi'Kmaq Grand Council at the United Nations; represented U.S. Indian tribes in litigation over sacred sites and federal recognition; and served as a consultant to institutions such as the United Nations Development Programme (UNDP) and the Royal Commission on Aboriginal Peoples. His writing has been supported by the National Endowment for the Humanities, the MacArthur Foundation, and the Harry Frank Guggenheim Foundation.

Paul L. A. H. Chartrand
Paul Chartrand is Professor of Law at the University of Saskatchewan. A member of the Canadian Indigenous Bar Association, he is a graduate of Manitoba Teachers College, the University of Winnipeg, and the law schools at Queensland University of Technology, Australia, and the University of Saskatchewan. He has held teaching and other academic appointments in Canada, the U.S.A., Australia, and New Zealand, and has been an advisor and consultant to Aboriginal and governmental organizations. His public service record includes service as a commissioner on the Canadian Royal Commission on Aboriginal Peoples (1991–1995), on the Aboriginal Justice Implementation Commission of Manitoba (1999–2001), and being a founding director of the Aboriginal Healing Foundation (1998–99).

Harry W. Daniels
Harry Daniels has been one of Canada's foremost national Aboriginal leaders. He was president of the Native Council of Canada (NCC) when it led the fight for recognition of Aboriginal rights in the constitutional amendment of 1982. A

founding member of the NCC, he has served the organization as its president, vice-president, and secretary treasurer. From 1997 to 2000, he was president of the NCC's successor, the Congress of Aboriginal Peoples. He was a director of the World Council of Indigenous Peoples in its formative years, and has extensive experience in representing Indigenous people in the international arena. He is also an accomplished actor who has performed in movies, radio, and television.

Dale Gibson

Dale Gibson graduated in Arts from what is now the University of Winnipeg in 1954, and in Law from the University of Manitoba as gold medallist in 1958. After obtaining an LL.M. degree from Harvard University, he began teaching law at the University of Manitoba in 1959, a post he held until moving to the University of Alberta in 1991. Since retiring from the latter institution in May 2001, he continues to write and practise as a consulting barrister in the area of public law. He is the author of several books and many articles, chiefly about constitutional law and legal history. He is a Fellow of the Royal Society of Canada, and was designated "Distinguished Professor" by the University of Manitoba. His public service includes a lengthy term with the Manitoba Law Reform Commission, chairmanship of the Manitoba Human Rights Commission, and service as constitutional advisor to several governments, as well as to the Royal Commission on Aboriginal Peoples.

John Giokas

John Giokas is a lawyer and policy analyst who has practised law in both British Columbia and Ontario. He has worked as a lawyer and legal writer for the federal government, two Aboriginal organizations, two federal commissions of inquiry, and the Canadian Bar Association. At present he is providing legal policy advice to the federal government under contract.

Robert K. Groves

Robert Groves is principal of *The Aboriginal Affairs Group Inc.*, an Ottawa-based consulting firm involved in Aboriginal governance, lands, and resources. He is responsible for directing negotiation agendas, public opinion studies, socio-economic research and for coordinating litigation.

He has been involved in Aboriginal policy issues since 1976, and was a participant in the drafting of section 35 of the *Constitution Act, 1982*. He has also acted as a constitutional policy advisor to the deputy minister and assistant deputy minister at the Department of Indian Affairs and Northern Development (1982–84). He was closely involved in the legislative process on Bill C–31 and other Indian legislation during the 1980s, and participated in all *Indian Act* reform efforts from 1986 to 1994. The Royal Commission on Aboriginal Peoples engaged him in 1994–95 as a member of its governance team and to advise on federal-Aboriginal institutional relationships, the results of which are reflected in the Commission's final reports relating to self-government, the *Indian Act* regime, and options for integrating Aboriginal governance within confederation.

In addition to land claims and self-government assignments for Aboriginal organizations, Mr. Groves is presently advising the minister and deputy minister of Indian Affairs and Northern Development on the federal government's First Nations' Governance initiative.

Bradford W. Morse

Bradford W. Morse is Professor of Law at the University of Ottawa, where he has been teaching since 1976. He has served as a legal advisor to a number of First Nations since 1977, as well as to the Native Council of Canada from 1984–1993 and a number of other Aboriginal associations. He has been a consultant to the Law Reform Commissions of Australia and Canada, the Canadian Sentencing Commission, the Aboriginal Development Commission, the Waitangi Tribunal, the Treaty of Waitangi Fisheries Commission, and to the governments of New Zealand, British Columbia, Ontario, and Canada. He was the director of research for the Aboriginal Justice Inquiry of Manitoba (1988–1991) and was chief of staff to the federal minister of Indian and Northern Affairs (1994–1996). He is a member of the Bar in Ontario and a graduate of Rutgers University, the University of British Columbia, and York University.

For Harry, Maria & Murray

Foreword

Harry W. Daniels

This book deals with a range of complex constitutional and legal issues that Aboriginal leaders in Canada have been struggling with for much of the last three decades. My wish is that this book will contribute to a helpful debate about the rights of all the Aboriginal peoples of Canada, and our rightful place within our homeland. Our political battles are far from over, but at the moment there seem to be few opportunities to pursue our rights directly in the domestic political arena. In these circumstances the decisions of the courts provide an avenue for some measure of justice and perhaps changes in government policy and practice that will facilitate cooperative political discussions.

The many complex legal issues surrounding the identity and rights of the various groups of Aboriginal people in Canada were often at the forefront of the agenda during the era of negotiations on Aboriginal rights in the Constitution. I was involved in these negotiations during my term as President of the Native Council of Canada (NCC), the precursor of the Congress of Aboriginal Peoples (CAP), from 1975 to 1981, and as Western Vice-President of NCC from 1983 to 1985.

The high-water mark of our negotiations with governments during that time was the inclusion of an Aboriginal rights clause in the so-called "patriation amendment" to the Constitution of Canada in 1982. The main reasons of the federal and provincial governments for amending the Constitution at that time were to provide a domestic amending formula and to introduce a *Charter of Rights and Freedoms*. This gave us a chance to make our case for the recognition of Aboriginal peoples and our rights. As one of the participants in the events that led to the adoption of that clause, I would like to recount my experience in securing an historic constitutional provision that expressly recognized the three groups of Aboriginal peoples, and specifically, the Métis people.

In January 1981, when the patriation amendment was agreed upon, the NCC represented both the Métis and unrecognized or unregistered Indians. The latter are those Indian people, commonly called non-status Indians, who are not

11

recognized under the federal definition of "Indian" in the *Indian Act*, and who consequently are not included in federal Indian policies that apply only to registered Indians, including entitlement to residence on Indian land reserves.

The following describes what happened at those crucial meetings in Ottawa in the negotiations over the Aboriginal rights clause. My recollections of those events are assisted by contemporaneous notes taken by my assistant, Janet Wightman, which are contained in the archives of CAP in Ottawa.

On January 30, 1981, a special joint committee of the House of Commons and the Senate on the Constitution met in the West Block of the Parliament Buildings in Ottawa. I received a call in the afternoon from Jean Chrétien, Minister of Justice, informing me that the committee was about to deal with the Aboriginal rights provision, which was then section 24. When I arrived, the leaders of the Inuit Committee on National Issues (ICNI), Eric Tagoona and Mark Gordon, pulled me aside and explained to me that the joint committee was prepared to recommend the inclusion of the following provision in the Constitution of Canada: "The aboriginal rights of the aboriginal peoples of Canada are hereby recognized and confirmed."

I discussed this development with Peter Ittinuar, Member of Parliament for Nunatsiaq. I said the proposal was good but not good enough. I insisted that for purposes of clarity, it must be stated that "aboriginal peoples" includes Indians, Inuit, and Métis, and that the term not be left open to interpretation at a later date.

I then spoke with Del Riley, President of the National Indian Brotherhood (NIB), Warren Allmand, and Eric Tagoona. Del stated that the NIB was satisfied with the proposed article and did not agree it should be amended as I had urged. At this point, the Minister of Justice asked the Chairman, Serge Joyal, for a fifteen minute break to discuss the Aboriginal rights amendment while the three national Aboriginal leaders were present. Chrétien immediately approached me, and upon hearing my proposal for a change, asked if I would go to London to support patriation if the proposal were accepted. I agreed, provided "Métis" was included. Minutes later, Chrétien announced he had negotiated as far as possible and could not support my proposal.

I should allow my assistant's notes to describe my reaction at this point: "HWD was angry and frustrated, with clenched fist he replied, 'Then I mobilize my people, that's the only thing we'll accept.'"

Chrétien left to confer with Jake Epp, spokesman for the Progressive Conservative Party on the Committee, and Peter Ittinuar of the New Democratic Party (NDP). Upon returning to the room, Chrétien asked my assistant where I was, and he explained that he had called Prime Minister Trudeau, and that she should "tell him I'll agree to all his points…." I had been invited to meet with Epp, who gave the support of the Conservatives. The NDP also agreed, as did Warren Allmand. The meeting was reconvened, and Chrétien asked Peter Ittinuar to read the motion in English. Allmand then read it in French. Ittinuar then thanked the committee and Chrétien and Trudeau for their efforts, and announced, "Now we can build a stronger nation." The new Aboriginal rights provision was then passed unanimously by all parties.

That is how "Métis" got into section 35 of the *Constitution Act, 1982.* It was the first constitutional provision that generally recognized the Métis and their rights, and only the second time since the recognition of the Métis in section 31, the land rights section of the *Manitoba Act, 1870,* that the Métis were expressly mentioned in the Constitution of Canada. It was an historic moment.

We knew, however, that we needed more political negotiations to agree on the meaning of the new clause, and so we also secured a promise to hold a First Ministers' conference to further elaborate the Aboriginal rights provision. This became section 37 of the *Constitution Act, 1982.*

A quick review of events following the adoption of sections 35 and 37 will explain how we came to the situation in which we now find ourselves, asking the courts to do what the politicians would not. It also teaches us some valuable lessons about the place of Aboriginal peoples and their rights in Canadian constitutional politics.

The four First Ministers' conferences that were held on the subject between 1983 and 1987 did not yield a political consensus. The meetings bogged down on the meaning of "existing" and the substantive meaning of "self-government." The result of this political impasse was that Aboriginal leaders were never presented with a proposal on the definition of our rights which could be considered. That is why we are led to the courts now. It is not our preference. We would rather reach a negotiated agreement, but what choice do we have?

The Meech Lake Accord, a proposal for constitutional amendments to respond to demands by the province of Quebec, followed the First Ministers' conferences. This was a reminder to Aboriginal people that what really concerned these national attempts at constitutional reform was the Quebec separatist agenda. Quebec's demands for greater autonomy had created a heightened sense of self-preservation among the other provinces. Provincial protectionism was another factor that worked against efforts by Aboriginal leaders to secure constitutional changes to recognize and protect Aboriginal interests.

The final national attempt at constitutional reform was the Charlottetown Accord of 1992, which was rejected in a national referendum. With the Accord's rejection went a specific agreement, a subset of the Charlottetown Accord, the Métis Nation Accord. It had been negotiated between the Métis National Council (MNC), the government of Canada, and the provinces of British Columbia, Alberta, Saskatchewan, Manitoba, and Ontario. The MNC had been created in 1983, after a split with NCC, which had until then represented the Métis.

The whole national exercise of amending the Constitution, which ended with the 1992 Charlottetown Accord, was not led by any widespread regard for the rights of Indigenous peoples in Canada. It was led by the reaction to Quebec separatism. The traditional political struggles between French- and English-speaking Canadians had changed into a new struggle between Quebec separatism and the rest of Canada, now not so English any more. The switch from a French-Canadian ethnic nationalism to Quebecois civic nationalism, based upon common civil rights within territorial boundaries and residence rather than upon ethnic identity contained an important lesson for the Métis. Quebec politicians used their power as a province to push for a new Quebecois identity, in spite of the protestations of the English minority and the Aboriginal peoples in the province.

Aboriginal people face tremendous challenges in asserting identities that transcend provincial boundaries and rely on historic ethnic identities. The Quebec experience shows the importance of a politically demarcated territory upon which jurisdiction can be asserted, and highlights the significance of Aboriginal peoples' demands for land-based self-government.

Our dreams to promote the rights of Aboriginal peoples as "nations" within Canada were dimmed by the failure of the Charlottetown Accord. In 1996 the Royal Commission on Aboriginal Peoples (RCAP) also proposed that Canada recognize the inherent right of Aboriginal nations to self-government within Canada under section 35. The government of Canada, which has yet to comment on the constitutional vision of RCAP, or to offer an alternative vision, continues its tactics of delay and obfuscation.

This recent history recalls the alternative strategies that had been identified by our people during the course of our constitutional negotiations over two decades ago. During wide consultations with our constituents, we had identified the issues that are again the subject of discussion in this book.

In a publication approved by the NCC in August 1979, a plan of action identified three ways in which the question of our rights could be approached.[1] The first and most preferable was through direct political negotiations with the government. The second idea was a joint commission of the government of Canada and the NCC. A third option was litigation, an option we are still forced to consider.

One advantage we now have is the express recognition in the 1982 *Constitution Act* of all the Aboriginal peoples, including not only the Inuit and the Métis people but also a category of "Indians" that is broader than the one imposed by the federal government through the *Indian Act*. I believe that is an important provision, one that will assist the courts now that the political process has failed to define our rights and our peoples. Perhaps our political efforts to clearly identify our rights in the Constitution of Canada were not in vain and may yet come to bear fruit.

---

[1] Native Council of Canada, *A Statement of Claim Based on Aboriginal Title of Metis and Non-Status Indians* (Ottawa: Native Council of Canada, February 1980) at 8.

Introduction

Paul L. A. H. Chartrand

Who are the "aboriginal peoples of Canada"? Who decides? How many are there, and where do they live?

These are questions of great national significance. To the extent that they involve matters of constitutional interpretation, they are questions on which we have very little judicial authority, notwithstanding the jurisprudence which has begun to map out the doctrine of Aboriginal and treaty rights. They are also the subject of controversial and disputed policy approaches.

The federal government currently recognizes over six hundred Indian bands or "First Nations" under the *Indian Act*. These account for some half a million persons, most of whom, outside the Northwest Territories, reside or are entitled to reside on Indian reserve lands. The federal government also recognizes, in policy and practice, its jurisdictional responsibilities in respect to an Inuit population exceeding thirty thousand persons in northern communities. New land claims agreements and treaties are also providing a new legislative framework of recognition outside the scheme of the *Indian Act*.

Census statistics, however, reveal that over a million persons in Canada identify themselves as Aboriginal persons. This number includes several hundred thousand non-status Indians and Métis who do not live in Aboriginal communities that are recognized as such by federal policy.

In its 1996 report, the Royal Commission on Aboriginal Peoples (RCAP) argued that section 35 of the *Constitution Act, 1982* recognizes and protects a common law right of Aboriginal self-government. That right, however, is not vested in the *Indian Act* bands, which have relatively small populations, although their members would undoubtedly be at the core of any constitutional meaning of "Indians." Drawing on the concept of "peoples" from international law, RCAP argued that the right is vested, rather, in larger "nations" which must be socially and politically reconstituted. These newly constituted entities must be accorded

15

official recognition by the government of Canada for purposes of entering into new "nation-to-nation" agreements that give practical meaning to the new constitutional protection accorded to the Aboriginal right of self-government.

According to the RCAP recommendations, the present *Indian Act* recognition system must be overhauled and new legislation passed, not only to recognize newly constituted Indian nations but also to respect and implement the constitutional recognition of Inuit and Métis peoples, with whom nation-to-nation agreements must also be concluded. A new national Aboriginal recognition framework based upon new legislation is needed to reflect the new constitutional reality.

Current federal policy also recognizes an inherent Aboriginal right of self-government. This right is considered to be vested in all Aboriginal peoples, not only in the Indian and Inuit people with whom the federal government in fact negotiates self-government agreements. Thus, the policy itself logically implies the need for fundamental changes in the current legislative and policy framework, which must include Indians and Inuit people as defined in political agreements, and also the Métis people.

Current federal policy regarding the Métis people, however, creates or compounds a constitutional anomaly. Section 35 of the *Constitution Act, 1982* expressly includes the Métis people, as well as the Indian and Inuit peoples, within the constitutional category of Aboriginal peoples of Canada. Since section 35 recognizes and protects the rights of the Aboriginal peoples, legislative and other governmental actions are required to protect these rights and to make them effective. In Canada, legislative authority is distributed, in the text of the *Constitution Act, 1867,* between provincial and federal governments. Legislative authority in respect to Aboriginal affairs is based on the grant of exclusive authority over "Indians and Lands reserved for the Indians" in section 91(24) of the *Constitution Act, 1867.* There is an apparent anomaly, which has yet to be given constitutional interpretation by the courts, between the category of "Indians" in section 91(24), and the category of "aboriginal peoples" in section 35. The category of "Indians" appears in both constitutional provisions, and requires the conclusion that the section 91(24) category is broader than the section 35 category. This is supported by the 1939 decision of the Supreme Court of Canada, which found that the Inuit people are included as 91(24) "Indians."[1]

The added anomaly found in the current federal policy is the political stance that the Métis people are not included within the federal legislative authority derived from section 91(24). Accordingly, there has been no federal Métis legislation or regulations enacted outside the federally controlled territories since the nineteenth and first half of the twentieth centuries, when the Aboriginal title of the Métis people was dealt with. The lobbying of Métis organizations has not changed this policy approach, and the Métis are not currently included in self-government negotiations, notwithstanding ambiguous statements in federal policy documents.

At the time of writing, it appears that, following an earlier era of direct national political discussions on Aboriginal constitutional reform, these significant issues will be resolved by incremental legislative reform, initiated in reaction to case-by-case decisions of the Supreme Court of Canada.

Origins and Scope of this Book

This book emerged from a number of papers originally written for a conference held in Vancouver in 1998 by the Congress of Aboriginal Peoples (CAP), a national Aboriginal political representative organization that succeeded the former Native Council of Canada. These papers have been revised to consider subsequent authoritative case law. Additional chapters were added. These are based either on papers written expressly for inclusion in this book, or, in the case of chapters 4 and 6, previously unpublished papers that were selected for their particular significance and relevance to the issues mentioned above.

The CAP conference aimed at discussing litigation strategies that might assist its constituents—"non-status Indians" and Métis—in securing the benefits of official recognition as Aboriginal people, and clearing up the jurisdictional issue described above.

CAP's non-status Indian constituents are self-identified ethnological Indians, descendants of various historic Indian nations from across Canada, who have organized politically to lobby for official recognition in Canadian legislation and policy, and generally to promote the aspirations of the members. As individuals, they do not fall within the federal definition of Indians who are officially recognized in the *Indian Act*. They are not, generally, members of the Indian bands or First Nations that are recognized in the *Act*. The federal government generally deals with Indian issues through the department of Indian and Northern Affairs Canada (INAC), with "status Indians" represented by over six hundred band chiefs who are organized nationally as the Assembly of First Nations (AFN).

CAP's Métis constituents are organised in provincial and territorial associations that assert various bases for their identity as Aboriginal people and have joined CAP, the national organization, to lobby for recognition as Métis. They share the common feature of exclusion from official recognition, and an emphasis, in their self-definition, on mixed Aboriginal and non-Aboriginal personal antecedents. The latter feature reflects the etymological origins of the French term *métis*.

One of the main issues considered at the conference was the question of jurisdiction described above, that is, the nature and scope of the federal legislative authority respecting "Indians." A closely related issue concerned the prospects for success in litigation that might require the federal government to respond to claims that Métis and non-status Indians possess Aboriginal rights protected by the Constitution. This focused discussion on identity or definition, especially on the question of Métis definition. It is not practically helpful to reach the conclusion that the Métis are included as "Indians" in section 91(24) of the *Constitution Act, 1867* if the identity or definition of the Métis community is not known.

The significance and controversial nature of the question of Métis definition is reflected in the fact that another national Aboriginal representative organization, the Métis National Council (MNC), represents the Métis of western Canada. The western Métis are well known in Canadian history for their political and military resistance against, first, the intruding British fur trade colonizers in the early 1800s, and subsequently, the Canadian government when it initially tried to annex the West in the second half of the nineteenth century. The concerted and sustained political actions of the Métis secured their official recognition, not only in military reactions, but in executive and legislative actions, including negotiations that led to the birth of the province of Manitoba in 1870, and later in legislation that purported to deal with their Aboriginal rights which was implemented only in the west and northwest from 1885 to 1921.

The controversy over Métis definition thus involves two distinct views, each promoted by a national representative organization. For CAP, Métis identity is the focus of a pan-Indian movement that emphasizes Indian ancestry and heritage. For MNC, on the other hand, the 1982 constitutional amendment that recognized and affirmed "the *existing* aboriginal and treaty rights of the aboriginal peoples of Canada," must be interpreted by reference to the pre-existing history of political relations between the ancestors of the western Métis and the Crown. Implicit in this view is the proposition that legal rights are derived from political action, and since the Métis representatives of today cannot gain these rights in direct political negotiations, the courts ought to find the source of Métis rights in past Métis-Crown relations.

This book provides scholarly analyses on some aspects of these questions in order to contribute to the continuing legal and policy debate. The approach taken is to address the general questions raised above in the context of the following particular issues:

1. The need for a principled and defensible policy of recognition of the Aboriginal peoples that extends beyond the current *Indian Act* and includes all

the Aboriginal peoples who are expressly mentioned in the Constitution, that is, the Indian, Métis, and Inuit peoples. The focus is upon the Métis and non-status Indians who are not recognized in the *Indian Act.*

2. The meaning of "the Métis people" in section 35 of the *Constitution Act, 1982.*

3. The nature and scope of the federal legislative jurisdiction respecting the Indian people who are outside the federal *Indian Act* policy regime and the Métis people. This deals with the meaning of section 91(24) of the *Constitution Act, 1867.* That original provision, which allocated exclusive federal legislative authority respecting "Indians" to Parliament, must be interpreted in light of the 1982 constitutional recognition of three categories of Aboriginal peoples and their rights.

These are controversial questions of constitutional interpretation that will be addressed by the courts in individual cases. They arise following the failure of national political initiatives conducted in an atmosphere of mistrust between Aboriginal and government representatives between the late 1970s and the early 1990s.

Outline of Topics Covered

Chapter 1 provides an account of this important political background and illuminates the analysis in the subsequent chapters. The recent constitutional and political context is described, including the First Ministers' conferences on Aboriginal constitutional reform of the 1980s and the 1992 Charlottetown Accord. The recommendations of the final report of the Royal Commission on Aboriginal Peoples of 1996 are reviewed, as well as the official federal response to these recommendations.

Canadian Aboriginal policy is characterized by slow, incremental change. The prime motivator of incremental change consists of Supreme Court decisions. This may be illustrated by reference to the *First Nations Governance Act,* which was introduced in Parliament on 14 June 2002. The proposed legislation was reintroduced on 9 October 2002 as Bill C–7. It responds to the Supreme Court of Canada's decision in the *Corbiere* case, which is fully canvassed in chapter 2. Although it proposes amendments to the *Indian Act,* it does not deal with the larger questions of recognition, definition, or membership discussed in this book. Nor does it follow the recommendations made by RCAP, which included doing away with the *Act.*

At the time of writing, the Supreme Court had agreed to hear appeals in two important cases involving Métis claims. They are expected to be heard early

in 2003. These cases, both of which are considered in chapters below, are important because the Court has no legal precedents of its own on Métis legal rights;
the issues are *res integra*.

The *Blais* case, from the Manitoba Court of Appeal, does not involve the
question of Métis definition for purposes of section 35, which is discussed in this
book.[2]

The *Powley* case,[3] from the Ontario Court of Appeal, involves a defence to
a charge under provincial game laws based upon an assertion of Métis Aboriginal
hunting rights protected by section 35. A decision in line with the reasoning of
the Ontario Court of Appeal on the concept of Métis definition would favour a
broad definition of "the Métis people" in section 35. Since the courts decide only
the law before them, on the facts presented in each case, it is important to note
that the issue of Métis definition in this book is distinct from the question at
issue in *Powley*. There, the issue of Métis definition is for the purpose of hunting
rights that are argued to be vested in a small community of people who, although
their immediate ancestors are Indians, claim a Métis identity on the basis of
remote "mixed-blood" ancestors. In this book, the question of Métis identity is
analysed for the purpose of deciding who has the Aboriginal right of self-government in section 35. Although the decision of the Supreme Court in the *Powley*
case may be expected to make a significant contribution to the question of Métis
identity in section 35, it certainly will not resolve the question of Métis definition for the purpose of self-government.

It is also certain that, whatever decision is given, the result will be politically controversial. The legal justification will be based upon legal principles, but
will be criticized on the basis of political arguments. The concept of recognition,
which is analysed in this book and which can act as a conceptual frame of reference to assess the merits of the judicial results, will contribute to the debate that
is sure to ensue from the decision. In this context, it will be useful to have a
conceptual frame of reference external to the law.

The remainder of the book can be categorized under the three headings of
recognition, definition, and jurisdiction.

Recognition

Section 35 of the *Constitution Act, 1982* expressly recognizes and affirms the
existence of three distinct categories of Aboriginal peoples, whose rights are protected by the Constitution. In contrast, federal law and policy continues to be
based largely upon the nineteenth century *Indian Act,* which contains a limited
definition of "Indian" that has not changed substantially since it was unilaterally
drafted by federal officials in 1876. In chapter 2, John Giokas and Robert Groves
examine the history and the provisions of the federal *Indian Act,* including the

1985 amendments, commonly known as Bill C–31, which recognized a large number of individuals as "Indians," and explain its operation as recognition legislation. This study explores the weaknesses of the historic and contemporary recognition policy in Canada, and makes the case for a principled and defensible recognition policy in respect to all the Aboriginal peoples included in section 35.

The recent *Corbiere* decision of the Supreme Court of Canada, which dealt with eligibility of voters in band elections, is analysed to identify the potential of judicial interpretation of the equality provisions of the *Charter of Rights and Freedoms* to dismantle the *Indian Act*, which remains the primary legislative foundation for Indian recognition in Canada. The recently introduced *First Nations Governance Act* is the federal reaction to the *Corbiere* decision. The proposed legislation deals with leadership selection, administration, and accountability of Indian bands, and makes related amendments to other *Acts,* but, as mentioned, it will not deal with questions of Indian definition, membership in Indian bands or "First Nations," or entitlements derived from membership.

The concept of recognition, which is derived from international law and practice, offers an external standard against which to assess the case-by-case development of the common law doctrine of Aboriginal rights, and the incremental shifts of Canadian Aboriginal policy. It provides a conceptual frame of reference that may be applied to both law and policy as to what is right and what works. It can in this way be used as a measure for both political and judicial accountability.

The concept of recognition has been known and applied in the American legal and policy context of U.S.–Indian relations for a long time. It is therefore instructive to have regard to the history and substance of American law and practice of Indian recognition in a Canadian situation where legislative and policy recognition must inevitably respond to the 1982 Constitutional recognition. The concept of recognition is therefore not only an external conceptual framework for measuring Canadian judicial and policy performance, but one that already offers a significant amount of historical experience in the U.S.A., and allows its application to test the performance of two countries against the same standard.

In the early historical stages of contact, Indian nations or tribes in Canada and the United States were separate and distinct, both territorially and in terms of culture and political organization. Treaties with these nations or tribes recognized the capacity of a distinct political entity with which the state wished to enter into legal and political relations. In time, however, and largely due to policies of dismantling those nations, the nature and composition of these formerly distinct nations has changed. In Canada, the changes have been particularly acute in the case of non-status Indians and Métis, who do not always live in geographically discrete communities and who may now lack many of the social institutions that characterized the historic communities from which they are descended.

Section 35 recognizes and affirms the existence of group or community rights, not individual rights. Aboriginal rights are vested in communities, and individuals may enjoy and exercise them only by virtue of their membership in a contemporary Aboriginal community. Since Aboriginal communities are essentially social and political communities, not static anthropological curiosities, there are contested claims to political representation of the descendant communities, as well as to the identity of the contemporary communities themselves. Probably most significant is the public and government response to the idea of newly recognized communities of individuals with group rights who will now be constitutionally protected in their enjoyment of rights that are not vested in all members of the public. This is especially so in the case of the right of self-government.

Recognizing a right of self-government in Canadian law and policy requires the identification of communities and their members from among Canadian citizens, and recognizing their distinct status which entitles them to enter into negotiations and political relations with the federal government, which represents all Canadian citizens. The concept of recognition is useful in the conceptualization of an appropriate constitutional theory, which the courts are doing, for the reasons explained above.

In chapter 4, John Giokas shows how, despite the many historical, political, and constitutional differences between the two countries, the American experience with recognition of Indian tribes can provide valuable lessons for Canada in the development of laws and policies that respond to the 1982 constitutional recognition of Aboriginal peoples.

The chapter begins with a review and explanation of the concept of recognition and the two distinct theories that have emerged in response to international practice. The analysis is based upon a publication of the Royal Commission on Aboriginal Peoples (RCAP) in 1993 containing the initial arguments for an Aboriginal right of self-government. This analysis traces the application of the concept of recognition to the American Indian tribes in the United States who have been viewed as "domestic, dependent nations," and assesses the implications of the RCAP model of recognition of Aboriginal peoples in Canada in comparison with the American model.

Chapter 1 reviews one of the final recommendations of RCAP, published in 1996, for federal recognition of all the Aboriginal peoples recognized in the 1982 constitutional amendment for purposes of conducting and concluding nation-to-nation agreements. While advocating a right of self-government that can, in legal theory, be exercised unilaterally by Aboriginal nations, the final report outlines a framework for a national recognition system that ultimately vests the decision to recognize an Aboriginal nation, for purposes of self-government negotiations, in the federal Cabinet. The reader should compare the final recommendations of the RCAP, which are described in chapter 1, to the initial RCAP analysis that is featured in chapter 4.[4]

The central features of a comparison between the American and Canadian situation in the context of recognition theory and practice are section 35, the 1982 constitutional provision which recognizes and affirms the Aboriginal and treaty rights of the Aboriginal peoples of Canada, and the 1934 *Indian Reorganization Act (IRA)* in the United States. In both Canada and the United States political forces will determine which subgroups have this right to self-government.

The American response to the *IRA* was the Federal Acknowledgment Procedure. An account of the twentieth-century American experience in applying a recognition policy to determine with which contemporary Indian social and political entities the American government would conduct governmental relations reveals the challenges that are now faced by Canada in designing a constitutionally valid policy that substantiates the constitutional recognition of Aboriginal peoples who are not now recognized by federal law and policy. By and large, these are the Métis and non-status Indians. In chapter 6, Russel Barsh, a leading scholar and practitioner in both the United States and Canada, provides a comprehensive review of Bureau of Indian Affairs decisions on applications by American Indian groups for federal recognition from 1935 to 1996, a valuable supplement to the Giokas analysis. He describes the weaknesses of a federal recognition policy administered by federal government officials with relatively little judicial and legislative guidance. That is exactly what Canada now faces, given the lack of federal response to the RCAP recommendations to discard the *Indian Act* and enact legislation to recognize all the Aboriginal peoples of Canada.

Definition

Questions of definition are closely related to the issue of recognition. Historically, once British and Canadian representatives had negotiated Indian treaties or had set aside reserve lands for the use and occupation of a particular Indian group, the definition of those individuals and groups who were to be the subject of continuing federal policy attention was enacted unilaterally, without Indian consultation, in the *Indian Act*.

Important questions of definition now arise as a result of the constitutional recognition and affirmation of the Aboriginal peoples and their rights. The social and political integrity of the Indian nations that were initially recognized has changed significantly. Does section 35 recognize and protect an Aboriginal right vested in Aboriginal peoples to define their own membership? If so, how is such an Aboriginal group, which must be either a "people" or a subgroup of a people, identified? Are there constitutional criteria which apply to the exercise of an assumed group right to define membership? Do individuals possess rights to membership in an Aboriginal people that are constitutionally enforceable against the group? If so, what factors give rise to the individual entitlement to membership? None of these issues were resolved in the national political process of the 1980s where the Prime Minister exercised his discretion and invited the leaders of the four Aboriginal national political representative organisations to discuss section 35 and its meaning. There is very little judicial guidance on these issues in the cases decided to date.

The question of Métis identity and definition is addressed in this book for the purpose of identifying "the Métis people" that has an Aboriginal right of self-government. The original meaning of the term *métis* evokes the idea of a "mixed" or "in-between" people. However, the notion of a mixed-blood people distinct from the Aboriginal peoples of a region is an unusual one in the international experience of Aboriginal-colonial relations. Generally, mixed-blood people are either part of the Aboriginal community or part of the new colonial society, since communities are formed not by biological but by social and political processes. The usual policy in both the United States and Canada was to settle the possessory interests of individuals or families who occupied lands ahead of surveys with a pre-emption right to the lands they occupied in their individual capacity, whether they were of mixed-blood or not,[5] and to deal with the local Aboriginal community as a group in respect to their group use and occupation of the lands.

The case of the Métis of western Canada is unique, involving a relatively large local population that was well established prior to the establishment of any significant colonial settlements or governmental authority. Having developed a group identity, they were able to assert it in political and military relations with colonial and Canadian intruders. Now that the courts have found that certain Aboriginal rights are vested not in large "nations" but in small local communities, a large number of claimants are asking the courts to recognize their contemporary communities as Métis communities, even where there is no history of prior government recognition.

In chapter 3, Giokas and Chartrand review the law and policy relating to "mixed-blood" people and those historically identified as Métis, and show that today the term *Métis* is an evolving one which shows no sign of settling into a consistent or coherent pattern. The review includes consideration of the *Indian Act* definition and its administration, and shows that much of the attempts at Métis definition have approached the question as a "boundary" issue to the definition of recognized Indians. In Canada, an arbitrary recognition system for Indians has not provided a rational basis for defining "Indians." That system cannot therefore be expected to yield a rational Métis definition at its boundary. It is concluded also that the 1982 constitutional recognition in section 35 requires a new and rational approach to the status system under the *Indian Act,* including a review of its validity and legitimacy in respect to the identification of "treaty nations" and other Aboriginal communities.

In chapter 8, the same authors draw on the conclusions in chapter 3 and undertake to explore the meaning of "the Métis people" in section 35, for the purposes of recognizing an Aboriginal right of self-government. The meaning of "the Métis people" will be developed in cases that consider the purpose behind section 35 in protecting the right that is at issue in a given case. The broadest definition will arise from the meaning of "the Métis people" in relation to the Aboriginal right of self-government, an issue that has not yet come before the courts. A review of the general principles of constitutional interpretation, principles relating to Aboriginal rights, and the purposes behind section 35, leads to the identification of the historic Métis nation of western Canada, "Riel's people," which has a well-known history of Crown-Métis relations in which is found the source of Métis constitutional rights. The test for proof of Aboriginal rights is briefly considered, and discussed in relation to the goal of identifying the proper claimants to the right of self-government today. The discussion includes consideration of the approaches to Métis definition by CAP and MNC, and of some key "open" questions in Aboriginal rights jurisprudence that leave some important aspects of the inquiry unfinished.

Jurisdiction

The central issue of jurisdiction involves the meaning of "Indians" in section 91(24) of the *Constitution Act, 1867,* which grants exclusive legislative power to Parliament in respect to "Indians and Lands reserved for the Indians."

Chapter 5, by Bradford Morse and Robert Groves, assesses alternative legal strategies for resolving the current uncertainty over the scope of federal power, and whether, as a result of jurisdiction and the recent constitutional recognition of Aboriginal rights, there are now positive obligations of the federal government to Indians within its jurisdiction. In particular, the analysis focuses on the Métis and non-status Indians who are not officially recognized in federal legislation.

A review of decisions of the lower courts identifies a tendency to look to social tests of "Indianness" to decide whether persons are within federal jurisdiction over Indians. This reflects the policy of dismantling the historic "nations" of Aboriginal peoples who were historically recognized in Canada, a policy goal that was evident in the review of both American and Canadian recognition policy in the previous chapters.

The analysis explains the need for a recognition policy for all Aboriginal peoples, which, because the rights affirmed in section 35 are group rights, must be based upon a definition of the collective boundaries between Inuit, Indian, and Métis peoples. The chapter expands on the discussion of the implications of the American and Canadian dual recognition policies for individual Indians and Indian groups, which is considered in previous chapters.

In chapter 7, Dale Gibson assumes the conclusion from the previous chapter, namely that federal legislative jurisdiction extends to all the Aboriginal peoples in section 35, and assesses the consequences of federal jurisdiction for Métis and non-status Indian persons and groups not within the current federal recognition system.

The analysis is based upon the broader view of Métis definition, referring to persons and groups descended from Indians, and whose aim is "full association with their Indian heritage." Using a *Charter*-based equality analysis, Gibson argues that federal non-recognition amounts to discrimination on the basis of race and ethnic origin. Litigation intended to secure judicial enforcement of federal recognition is recommended, with the aim of increasing the number of persons entitled to the medical and other benefits currently available to status Indians who are recognized in the federal *Indian Act*. This objective emphasizes the significance of the cost factor in the current American and Canadian recognition policy, which aims to keep those numbers down and thereby reduce the costs of a recognition policy.

In a concluding chapter, some general comments address the current circumstances in which the courts are faced with deciding cases on the fundamental issues of Aboriginal rights jurisprudence that have been considered in the book.

Notes

[1] *Re Eskimos*, [1939] S.C.R. 104.

[2] *R. v. Blais*, [2001] 3 C.N.L.R. 187 (Man. C.A.), leave to appeal to the Supreme Court of Canada granted: [2001] S.C.C.A. No. 294 n. 52.

[3] *R. v. Powley*, [2001] C.N.L.R. 291 (Ont. C.A.), leave to appeal to the Supreme Court of Canada granted: [2001] S.C.C.A. No. 256 n. 48.

[4] The original text of chapter 4 has not been disturbed, since its basic thesis and analysis have been vindicated in the final report of RCAP, and have continuing relevance for legal and policy analysts.

[5] See generally Jennifer Brown & Theresa Schenk, "Métis, Metizo and Mixed-Blood," in Philip J. Deloria & Neil Salisbury, eds., *A Companion to American History* (Walden, MA, and Oxford: Blackwell Publishers, 2002) 231–38; *R. v. Powley*, [2001] 2 C.N.L.R. 291 at 299–300 (Ont. C.A.). In Manitoba, Métis Aboriginal title was dealt with in s. 31 of the provincial constitution, while settler rights were recognized in s. 32: Paul L.A.H. Chartrand, *Manitoba's Métis Settlement Scheme of 1870* (Saskatoon: University of Saskatchewan Native Law Centre, 1991).

Chapter One

Background

Paul L. A. H. Chartrand

The immediate historical and political context from which the questions of recognition, definition, and jurisdiction arise include the First Ministers' conferences on Aboriginal constitutional reform of the 1980s, the constitutional amendments proposed in the failed Charlottetown Accord in 1992, as well as the recommendations of the Royal Commission on Aboriginal Peoples (RCAP) of 1996.

The federal policy response to the RCAP recommendations is also examined, with particular attention to the final recommendations on the recognition of Aboriginal "nations" for purposes of negotiating self-government agreements. These final recommendations may be compared with the analysis of the initial RCAP publication on the subject provided in chapter 4.

The *Constitution Act, 1982*
The *Constitution Act, 1982* was enacted primarily to "patriate" the Constitution of Canada; that is, to remove the remaining formal authority of the British Parliament over amendments to the Canadian Constitution. However, the changes, which included the addition of a new *Charter of Rights and Freedoms,* effected some other fundamental changes. The former system of parliamentary sovereignty was replaced by a constitutional democracy, where the courts would have an increased role in prescribing the limits of governmental authority and in finding positive obligations of governments to protect rights and make them effective.

In the sphere of Aboriginal rights, some very significant changes took place. Section 35 recognized and affirmed the Aboriginal and treaty rights of the Abo-

27

riginal peoples. Section 35.1, which was added in 1983, emphasized the distinct political character of the Aboriginal peoples, and their unique constitutional status as groups entitled to participate in future consultations on constitutional amendments.[1] Section 37 imposed positive obligations on the Prime Minister to call meetings of national statesmen to further consider the nature and scope of the rights mentioned in section 35. Manifestly, as the Supreme Court of Canada later observed,[2] the 1982 amendments represented a new deal in which negotiations with Aboriginal representatives concerning their fundamental rights and interests were to replace the former constitutional order in which the federal government had exercised a free hand in dismantling Aboriginal communities, taking their property and defining not only their basic interests but also their very identity.

In a sense, however, section 35 represented an empty shell for the filling.[3] It contained no definition of either the Aboriginal peoples or of the rights that were the subject of constitutional recognition. It did not resolve the question of the scope of section 91(24) jurisdiction. What follows is a brief account of three national processes that addressed these questions, questions that must now be addressed as a matter of constitutional interpretation by the Supreme Court.

First Ministers' Conferences, 1983–1987

The First Ministers' conferences on Aboriginal constitutional reform were part of a series of national attempts at constitutional reform dating from the late 1970s to the early 1990s.[4]

In 1983, acting on the authority of section 37, Prime Minister Pierre Trudeau invited the three national organizations that represented Aboriginal people in Canada—the Assembly of First Nations (AFN), the Inuit Tapirisat of Canada (ITC), and the Native Council of Canada (NCC)—to attend conferences[5] on Aboriginal constitutional reform. The AFN is made up of the chiefs of the more than six hundred federally recognized Indian bands across Canada. The ITC was invited to represent the Inuit people of the North. The NCC was initially invited to represent non-status Indians and the Métis. The representation issue grew more complicated as a new national organization, the Métis National Council (MNC) was formed from within the ranks of the NCC to represent the Métis "nation" of western Canada. The MNC was eventually invited to participate, bringing to four the number of national representative organizations appearing on behalf of the three categories of Aboriginal peoples mentioned in section 35.

Although recommendations were made by the MNC on the definition of the Métis people[6] and their constitutional rights, the government representatives did not agree to recognize them in new amendments to the Constitution. These only added provisions on sexual equality and land claims agreements in section 35, and section 35.1. Nothing that resulted from the First Ministers' conferences contributed to a resolution of the basic questions of recognition, definition, or jurisdiction, or to elaborate the nature and scope of the rights of the Aboriginal peoples. Government representatives never agreed to a proposal that could be considered by the Aboriginal representatives. There was nothing on the table for the Aboriginal peoples' representatives to take or to leave.

The disappointment of the Aboriginal representatives at the last First Ministers' conference in the spring of 1987 was exhibited in their final closing remarks.[7] The deep distrust between Aboriginal people and government representatives that had been evident in the enactment of a constitutional provision to oblige the Prime Minister to call a meeting with Aboriginal representatives on constitutional matters appeared to be warranted when, within the same year, all the First Ministers agreed on a package of reforms dealing with Quebec demands in the Meech Lake Accord of 1987.

The ratification process for this Accord, which did not contain any substantive Aboriginal provisions, failed on 23 June 1990, with an Oji-Cree member of the Manitoba legislative assembly, Elijah Harper, playing a key role in its demise.[8]

In the summer of 1990, armed conflicts flared up between Mohawk people and public security forces in Mohawk communities in the Montreal area. One person was killed. Not only were police involved, but up to 3,700 soldiers were engaged under the *National Defence Act*, amid widespread allegations of human rights abuses, including the stoning by Montrealers of Mohawk women, children, and elders. There was also destruction and loss of property and livelihoods.

Reviewing these events, the House of Commons Standing Committee on Aboriginal Affairs made a number of recommendations, including the establishment of an independent tribunal to deal with land use conflicts, and a Royal Commission to report upon relations between Aboriginal people and other Canadians, including on matters of constitutional reform, and recognition of the right of self-government.[9]

During the summer of 1990, another round of consultations and discussion on national constitutional reform, dubbed the Canada Round, began.[10]

The Royal Commission on Aboriginal Peoples

On August 27, 1991, Prime Minister Brian Mulroney announced the establishment of a Royal Commission on Aboriginal Peoples, which he declared to be a key element of the government's "Native Agenda" with the goal of "full participation in the country's economic prosperity and political life." He also declared that "the Royal Commission will complement, and not substitute for, current efforts at constitutional reform."[11]

RCAP first met in late September and began its work shortly thereafter. In February 1992, RCAP published a commentary on the Aboriginal right of self-government, intending to contribute to the Canada Round constitutional discussions on the subject. It recommended criteria for any provisions dealing with the Aboriginal right of self-government, and suggested options for constitutional amendments.[12] This document, which did not comment directly on the issues of definition and jurisdiction, is discussed by John Giokas in chapter 4.

The Charlottetown Accord, 1992

The RCAP publication was available during negotiations on a new national accord on constitutional reform reached in October 1992 between government and Aboriginal representatives. The Charlottetown Accord would have expressly recognized that Aboriginal peoples have an inherent right of self-government and clarified that section 91(24) applies to all the Aboriginal peoples of Canada. That would have settled the outstanding jurisdictional question discussed by Morse and Groves in chapter 5 and elsewhere in this book.[13]

The Charlottetown Accord did not include a definition of the Aboriginal peoples, but a separate Métis Nation Accord reached between the federal government, five provinces, and the Northwest Territories would have defined the Métis nation as the historic "nation" of the North West. The Métis definition proposed in the accord is discussed in chapter 8.

The Charlottetown Accord was subsequently defeated in a national referendum, and the Métis Nation Accord went with it. Although its provisions have not been enacted, they represent the high-water mark of national agreement on the rights of the Aboriginal peoples of Canada.[14]

RCAP Recommendations on Recognition, Definition, and Jurisdiction

Following the failure of the Charlottetown Accord, the era of constitutional reform ended in Canada, and has not shown signs of resurrection since. Having observed the failure of the political process to achieve further amendments to clarify the meaning of the recognition of the rights of the Aboriginal peoples of Canada, RCAP published an argument that the Aboriginal right of self-government is protected by section 35 as an existing common law Aboriginal right. This initial view of RCAP, published in 1993 under the name *Partners in Confederation: Aboriginal Peoples, Self-Government, and the Constitution*, argued that Aboriginal "nations," which comprise the "aboriginal peoples of Canada" or subentities of the "peoples" recognized section 35, had an inherent right of self-government which could be unilaterally exercised without government approval in certain core areas. In this view, other peripheral subject matters outside the scope of the core jurisdiction of the Aboriginal governments required agreement with national and provincial governments.

This approach is criticized in chapter 4 on the basis that Canadian governments are likely to balk at the prospect of self-defining, sub-state, self-governing entities claiming the right to come into existence by their own initiative, and to claim a particular population of Canadian citizens as being under their jurisdiction, without regard to the other governments with whom they would be in a relationship. The analysis in chapter 4 argues that RCAP ought to have developed a sound and realistic set of objective recognition criteria to guide Aboriginal peoples as well as governments, since without such criteria, the recognition of "the aboriginal peoples" in section 35 will be decided by the courts and by non-Aboriginal governments. The author draws from the relatively more lengthy American experience with the use and application of recognition criteria to American Indian tribes as a useful conceptual frame of reference against which to measure Canadian judicial and policy developments in giving meaning to the constitutional recognition of the Aboriginal peoples of Canada in section 35.

The history of the application of the Indian recognition criteria following the American *Indian Reorganization Act* "New Deal," which is analysed in chapter 6 by Russel Barsh, shows the difficulties and tribulations that arise where there is an official policy that recognizes "domestic dependent nations" but where recognition is left largely in the hands of government officials with the aid of some judicial guidance.

By 1995, a new federal government had replaced the one that had appointed the RCAP. The Liberal government issued an official policy statement which stated that "The Government of Canada recognizes the inherent right of self-government as an existing right within s.35 of the *Constitution Act, 1982*."[15] The identity of the Aboriginal peoples having this right was left as an open question, reference being made to Aboriginal "groups."

The final report of RCAP was published in 1996. While it elaborated its initial arguments based on the premise that the Aboriginal "peoples" already exist and have an inherent right to define and govern themselves unilaterally, it added new features. It argued that the authority of an Aboriginal nation to define its own membership is limited by constitutional principles derived from section 35 itself.[16] These include non-discrimination on grounds of gender, and a prohibition against rules of membership based only upon race or personal ancestry.

The need for recognition of self-governing nations by other governments in the Canadian federal system is dealt with in a series of recommendations for a "transition" period to move toward the full realization of effective government by autonomous Aboriginal nations within the constitutional framework of Canada. These recommendations include a process for identifying Aboriginal nations entitled to govern themselves, upon the recommendation to the Cabinet of an independent tribunal established under federal legislation. This tribunal would recommend recognition of "nations" which had met two basic prerequisites. First, the nation was to have drawn up a national constitution, including an acceptable membership code, measured against the constitutional principles suggested by RCAP, and second, it had applied to the tribunal for a positive recommendation.[17] The recommendation would be made to the executive government, which would not be bound by it.

The recognition process consisted of three stages.

1. An organization stage in which communities would authorize representatives to seek government recognition and assistance to organize themselves for recognition.

2. The adoption of a constitution which included a citizenship code in addition to the identification of its governing structures. In this respect RCAP restricted itself to suggesting that "Aboriginal people" with "a rational connection to a particular community or nation, whatever their current residence or circumstances, should be given a fair opportunity to acquire citizenship, should they so desire, according to fair standards fairly applied." [18]

3. The recognition decision would be made by the federal Cabinet, upon the recommendation of a recognition panel appointed by, and operating under, the proposed lands and treaties tribunal. Its authority would include applying the criteria for nation recognition established in the proposed federal *Aboriginal Nations Recognition and Government Act.*

The commission expressly refrained from commenting upon the application of its general principles to the various groups which claim Métis identity, observing that "recognition of nationhood is an essentially political function about which we commented at length [earlier]..."[19] This comment illustrates the difficulty of trying to reconcile, in practice, the argument for an inherent right of self-government held by "nations" with the fact that it will be rendered relatively meaningless without the political recognition of those nations by the Canadian government. This is the central issue addressed in chapter 4.

On the question of jurisdiction, the commission recommended an amendment to section 91(24) to remove all doubt about its application to all the Aboriginal peoples mentioned in section 35, as the federal government had agreed to do in the Charlottetown Accord.[20] Failing an amendment, RCAP recommended that the government refer the meaning of the present section to the Supreme Court of Canada in a constitutional reference.[21] This recommendation has not been adopted. In chapter 5, alternative strategies for resolving the issue in litigation are assessed.

Before reviewing the government response to these recommendations, it is instructive to outline the broad recommendations of RCAP which were thought to be necessary to implement its approach to the recognition of the Aboriginal peoples in section 35. These recommendations will show the kind of political action and policy that would be required to decide issues that, in the absence of political action, will now be decided by the courts.

RCAP recommended a policy or plan for political action that involved four distinct elements.[22]

1. The promulgation by the Parliament of Canada of a Royal Proclamation and companion legislation to implement those aspects of the renewed relationship that fall within federal authority;

2. Activity to rebuild Aboriginal nations and develop their constitutions and citizenship codes, leading to their recognition through a proposed new law, the *Aboriginal Nations Recognition and Government Act;*

3. Negotiations to establish a Canada-wide framework agreement to set the stage for the emergence of an Aboriginal order of government in the Canadian federation; and

4. The negotiation of new or renewed treaties between recognized Aboriginal nations and other Canadian governments.

Federal Policy Response to RCAP

On January 7, 1998, the federal government released its official response to the RCAP report, in which it stated that "the Action Plan responds to the Royal Commission and sets directions for a new course based on greater cooperation with Aboriginal groups and provinces." [23] The government's response was published in a policy document, *Gathering Strength,* which refers to its previous 1995 policy of recognizing the right of self-government.[24] Under the heading "Recognition of Aboriginal Governments," the policy states that consultations will be conducted with Aboriginal organizations and the provinces and territories on appropriate instruments to recognize Aboriginal governments.[25] It also states that "while the Royal Commission captured some of the key factors that must be considered, any initiative in this regard would be undertaken only in close consultation with Aboriginal and other partners."[26] In other words, the government did not accept RCAP recommendations on recognition as sufficient. Further, it states that "the federal government supports *the concept* [emphasis added] of self-government being exercised by Aboriginal nations or other larger groupings of Aboriginal people. It recognizes the need to work closely with Aboriginal people, institutions and organizations on initiatives that move in this direction...."[27]

Here are the RCAP principles that were recommended to guide the enactment of federal recognition legislation that would "formally acknowledge the existence of Aboriginal nations and establish the criteria and process for recognition":[28]

- A broad and flexible standard of Aboriginal nationhood should be embraced, emphasizing the collective sense of Aboriginal identity, shared by a sizeable body of Aboriginal people, and grounded in a common heritage.

- Aboriginal groups might assert their modern nationhood in a variety of ways, incorporating, among other things, modern political affiliations.

- Nationhood is linked to the principle of territoriality. This principle does not require exclusive territorial rights and jurisdiction for an Aboriginal nation and its government to exercise the inherent right of self-governance.

- Except for rare exceptions, Aboriginal nations are not synonymous with *Indian Act* bands or small communities.

- One formula for self-government cannot be expected to satisfy the interests and needs of every Aboriginal nation or meet the requirements for its relations with the other two orders of government.

RCAP explained that "the proposed recognition and government act would prescribe how the government of Canada would give formal recognition to Aboriginal nations and make explicit what is implicit in section 35 of the *Constitution Act 1982*, namely that those nations have an inherent right of self-government."[29]

Furthermore, "although we are proposing *recognition* legislation, Aboriginal nations do not require federal (or provincial) legislation to have the constitutional authority to function as governments. That authority, it will be recalled, has its source outside the Canadian constitution, although it is recognized and affirmed in it."[30] This statement refers to the *source* of the authority, not to its current constitutional status. Elsewhere, it may be recalled, the final report made it quite clear that the substantive right of self-government was now constrained by the Constitution.[31] The conceptual reconciliation of these apparently inconsistent positions is discussed in chapter 4, by applying the concept of recognition, and the competing declaratory and constitutive theories.

RCAP emphasized the key significance of the treaties in establishing the political relationship between Aboriginal nations and Canadian governments.

> Once recognized a nation government should receive enhanced funding to exercise expanded powers for its increased population base. In the longer term, the exercise of powers by Aboriginal nations and their governments will be dealt with through the comprehensive treaties that we see as the end products of negotiations between the federal and provincial governments and recognized Aboriginal nations.[32]

The 1998 federal policy statement adopts this view of treaties, and makes reference to non-recognized groups of Aboriginal people in the following terms.

> The federal government remains willing to enter into a treaty relationship with groups which do not have treaties. This could take the form of a comprehensive claim agreement or a self-government agreement, so long as, where required, the relevant province or territory is party to the agreement. In this case, certain provisions in self-government agreements with First Nations, Inuit, Metis and off-reserve Aboriginal people could be constitutionally protected as treaty rights under section 35 of the *Constitution Act 1982*.[33]

Treaties appear to represent, under this policy statement, the strategic route to recognition for groups of Aboriginal people outside the *Indian Act* regime. This approach is reflected, conversely, in the modern land claims agreements, including the recent Nisga'a treaty,[34] which remove the operation of the *Indian Act* to the members of the treaty group.

In respect to the historic Indian treaties signed until 1929, and the *Indian Act* groups that are descendants of these treaty nations, *Gathering Strength* states: "The Government of Canada is prepared to work in partnership with Treaty First Nations to achieve self-government within the context of the treaty relationship..."[35]

It may be emphasized that the federal policy failed to endorse the national action plan recommended by RCAP.[36] This included, it may be recalled, four elements, including negotiations called by the Prime Minister to establish a Canada-wide framework agreement to set the stage for the emergence of an Aboriginal order of government in the Canadian federation. A national policy approach of this sort is quite different from the small-scale, group-by-group approach adopted in federal policy. In addition to the advantage of creating national guidelines that have been agreed between government and Aboriginal representatives to guide "nation-to-nation" negotiations, the RCAP national approach, by identifying the scope of the possible in local negotiations, would provide the Canadian public with an appreciation of the nature and scope of the negotiations. This can reasonably be expected to garner public support and confidence.

The continuing preference of the current government for slow, incremental policy shifts may be illustrated by the following comments by the Minister of Indian Affairs. Referring to the proposed amendments to the *Indian Act,* he stated that[37] "this initiative will *not* [emphasis added] address band status and membership entitlements or Aboriginal rights and title." The federal policy response suggests that incremental change is more politically manageable than the fundamental change recommended by RCAP.

The New Jurisprudence and the Identification of "The Aboriginal Peoples"

In seeking judicial assistance in making their claims for political rights, Aboriginal organizations may look for encouragement in a new jurisprudence that is emerging on the interpretation of the Constitution. The main political purpose of the 1982 amendment of the Constitution was to "patriate" the Canadian Constitution, that is, to remove the residual formal authority of the British Parliament to amend it. The amendments, which included a new *Charter of Rights and Freedoms,* have had a significant effect upon some then well-established constitutional principles derived from British law, history, culture, and practice.

The doctrine of parliamentary supremacy, which had required the courts to give the legitimacy of law to the policy of dismantling Indian nations, has been replaced with a doctrine of constitutional supremacy.[38] The courts have been assigned a duty to decide the limits of parliamentary constitutional authority, and they have found a doctrine of positive obligations which binds the executive and legislative branches.[39]

At the same time, the Court has been assigned, by section 35 and the failure of the national political process, the constitutional role of designing a new constitutional and Aboriginal rights jurisprudence that is based upon Canadian history, culture, and experience,[40] and that accords with contemporary "appreciations" and "reassessments."[41]

In Canada, since the enactment of the *Constitution Act, 1982,* judges and lawyers are no longer allowed to look exclusively, or primarily, to British history and culture for inspiration to develop Canadian rights; the patriation of the Constitution in 1982 mandates the Court to develop a North American jurisprudence, one that recognizes and affirms the historical foundations and cultures of Canada, including the histories, cultures, and philosophies of the Aboriginal peoples of Canada.[42]

In addition to the demise of the doctrine of parliamentary supremacy, a feature of the emerging doctrine of Aboriginal rights has particular importance for the questions of recognition, definition, and jurisdiction. The Court has found that Aboriginal rights are, in their nature, group rights that are vested in communities. Individual persons are entitled to carry out particular activities protected by these group rights only by virtue of their membership in the community.[43]

The relationship between the individual member of the group and the rights-bearing community has not been directly addressed by the Court. One of the reasons for this is that in most cases, the issue before the Court involved an Indian person belonging to a recognized Indian band. Since these bands must be assumed to fall within the scope of any judicial tests that might be developed to determine the identity of an Aboriginal rights-bearing community, the parties have usually agreed not to contest the issue. Another difficulty arises from cases where the Court has found that Aboriginal rights are vested in relatively small local communities, which would not fall within the concept of a "nation" of the kind contemplated by RCAP.[44]

Although section 35 recognized the rights of the "aboriginal peoples" in 1982, there is no case law to assist the exegete in discerning the identity of an Aboriginal "people," and very little to assist the resolution of such fundamental issues as the authority of the Aboriginal groups with Aboriginal rights to decide their own membership. Given that at least some Aboriginal rights seem to be vested in relatively small communities, what is the relationship between those communities, which could not be described as "peoples," with the larger aggregations of communities that do comprise a "people"?

In chapter 8, the authors propose an approach that attempts to apply some of the principles of the emerging constitutional jurisprudence to the various open questions surrounding the question of defining an Aboriginal people.

Notes

[1] S. 35.1 provides: "The government of Canada and the provincial governments are committed to the principle that, before any amendment is made to Class 24 of section 91 of the *Constitution Act, 1867*, to section 25 of this Act or to this Part, a) a constitutional conference that includes in its agenda an item relating to the proposed amendment, composed of the Prime Minister of Canada and the first ministers of the provinces, will be convened by the Prime Minister of Canada; and b) the Prime Minister of Canada will invite representatives of the aboriginal peoples of Canada to participate in the discussions on that item." Section 35.1 was added by the *Constitution Amendment Proclamation, 1983* SI/84–102, 1983, R.S.C. 1985, Appendix II, No. 46, which also substituted new s. 25(b), adding new s. 35(3) and (4), and adding new ss. 35.1, 37.1, 54.1, and 61 of the *Constitution Act, 1982*.

[2] *R. v. Sparrow,* [1990] 1 S.C.R. 1075 at 1105–6.

[3] Ira Barkin, "Aboriginal Rights: A Shell Without the Filling" (1990) 15:2 Queen's L.J. 307. See also, Bryan Schwartz, *First Principles, Second Thoughts: Aboriginal Peoples, Constitutional Reform and Canadian Statecraft.* (Montreal: The Institute for Research on Public Policy, 1986), esp. Chapter XXIV, p. 353–64. Professor Schwartz's view is based on a spirited defence, on pp. 36–38, of what he calls "the political and philosophical advantages of liberal

individualism." Cf. Noel Lyon, "The Charter expresses the values of a liberal democracy on the European model. It favours individualism and assumes a highly organized and impersonal industrial society. To apply those values to Native societies is to destroy them…" as quoted in Barkin, *supra* this note at 311.

⁴Here, the focus is on aspects of national statecraft that directly affect Aboriginal issues, which special reference to matters related to questions of recognition, jurisdiction, and definition. Additional information on the national process of constitutional reform is provided where necessary to give the reader an understanding of the immediate context of the issues. See the series of publications on the First Ministers' conferences by the Institute of Intergovernmental Relations at Queen's University, which includes *inter alia:* David C. Hawkes, *The Search for Accommodation* (1987); David C. Hawkes, *Negotiating Aboriginal Self-Government: Developments Surrounding the 1985 First Ministers' Conference* (1985); David C. Hawkes, *Aboriginal Peoples and Constitutional Reform: What Have We Learned?* (1989).

⁵Section 37, which comprised Part IV of the *Constitution Act, 1982* provided:

> (1) A constitutional conference composed of the Prime Minister of Canada and the first ministers of the provinces shall be convened by the Prime Minister of Canada within one year after this Part comes into force.

> (2) The conference convened under subsection (1) shall have included in its agenda an item respecting constitutional matters that directly affect the aboriginal peoples of Canada, including the identification and definition of the rights of those peoples to be included in the Constitution of Canada, and the Prime Minister of Canada shall invite representatives of those peoples to participate in the discussions on that item.

> (3) The Prime Minister of Canada shall invite elected representatives of the governments of the Yukon Territory and the Northwest Territories to participate in the discussions on any item on the agenda of the conference convened under subsection (1) that, in the opinion of the Prime Minister, directly affects the Yukon Territory and the Northwest Territories.

The conference was held in March 1983, but no agreement was reached on the identification and definition of the rights of the Aboriginal peoples. S. 37 was repealed by the operation of s. 54 on April 17, 1983, but a new series of conferences were held pursuant to a new provision added by the *Constitution Amendment Proclamation, 1983*, which was repealed on April 18, 1987 by operation of s. 54.1.

S. 37.1

> (1) In addition to the conference convened in March 1983, at least two constitutional conferences composed of the Prime Minister of Canada and the first ministers of the provinces shall be convened by the Prime Minister of Canada, the first within three years after April 17, 1982 and the second within five years after that date.

> (2) Each conference convened under subsection (1) shall have included in its agenda constitutional matters that directly affect the aboriginal peoples of Canada, and the Prime Minister of Canada shall invite representatives of those peoples to participate in the discussions on those matters.

> (3) The Prime Minister of Canada shall invite elected representatives of the governments of the Yukon Territory and the Northwest Territories to participate in the discussions on any item of the agenda of a conference convened under subsection (1) that, in the opinion of the Prime Minister, directly affects the Yukon Territory and the Northwest Territories.

> (4) Nothing in this section shall be construed so as to derogate from subsection 35 (1).

⁶See c. 8, *infra.*

⁷The trenchant, bitter, yet eloquent admonitions of MNC spokesman Jim Sinclair

have been put to music and acquired iconic status in the recent annals of Aboriginal rights. See M.E. Turpel & P.A. Monture, "Ode to Elijah: Reflections of Two First Nations Women on the Rekindling of Spirit at the Wake for the Meech Lake Accord" (1990) 15:2 Queen's L.J. 345 at 349.

[8]*Ibid.*

[9]Canada. House of Commons. "The Summer of 1990" *Fifth Report of the Standing Committee on Aboriginal Affairs.* May 1991.

[10]On the process of constitutional reform in this period, see e.g. Leslie A. Pal & F. Leslie Seidle, "Constitutional Politics 1990–1992: The Paradox of Participation" in Susan D. Phillips, ed., *How Ottawa Spends: A More Democratic Canada? 1993–1994* (Ottawa: Carleton University Press, 1993) 143–202.

[11]Office of the Prime Minister, Release, "Royal Commission on Aboriginal Peoples" (August 27, 1991). The Commission was established by a federal order in council P.C. 1991–1597, pursuant to Part I of the *Inquiries Act.* It is disclosed that the author was one of the seven commissioners appointed by this order in council.

[12]Canada, Royal Commission on Aboriginal Peoples, *The Right of Aboriginal Self-Government and the Constitution: A Commentary* (Ottawa: February 13, 1992).

[13]The proposals were in ss. 54 and 55, as follows:

> S. 54. For greater certainty, a new provision should be added to the *Constitution Act, 1867,* to ensure that Section 91(24) applies to all Aboriginal peoples. The new provision would not result in a reduction of existing expenditures on Indians and Inuit or alter the fiduciary and treaty obligations of the federal government for Aboriginal peoples. This would be reflected in a political accord.

> S. 55. Metis in Alberta/Section 91(24). The Constitution should be amended to safeguard the legislative authority of the Government of Alberta for Metis and Metis Settlements lands.

[14]See Peter Hogg, *Constitutional Law of Canada,* 1998 Student Edition (Toronto: Carswell, 1998) at 596.

[15]Canada, *Federal Policy Guide, Aboriginal Self-Government: The Government of Canada's Approach to Implementation of the Inherent Right and the Negotiation of Aboriginal Self-Government* (Ottawa: Minister of Public Works and Government Services Canada, 1995) at 1.

[16]Canada, *Report of the Royal Commission on Aboriginal Peoples: Restructuring the Relationship,* vol. 2 (Ottawa, Supply and Services Canada, 1996), 237–9. RCAP explains that Aboriginal peoples are not "races" but social and political communities, the membership of which evolves and changes through time and circumstance, at 176–7.

[17]In Aotearoa/New Zealand, a similar idea has been proposed for the recognition of Maori people. See Donna Hall, "Indigenous Governance and Accountability" in Edward Te Kohu Douglas & Mark Robertson Shaw, *Ngai Tatou 2020: Indigenous Governance and Accountability: Whakahaere-A-Iwi, Whakamarama-A-Iwi* (Auckland, New Zealand: The FIRST Foundation, 1999) 23 at 29.

[18]RCAP, *supra* note 16 at 317.

[19]Canada. *Report of the Royal Commission on Aboriginal Peoples: Perspectives and Realities,* vol. 4 (Ottawa, Supply and Services Canada, 1996) at 206.

[20]*Ibid.* at 209–10. See the Charlottetown Accord provision in note 13, *supra.*

[21]RCAP, *supra* note 16 at 210.

[22]*Ibid.* These recommendations are listed on p. 311 and elaborated at 310–53.

[23]Government of Canada, News Release Communique 1–9801, "Canada's Aboriginal

Action Plan—Focused [sic] on Communities, Founded on Reconciliation and Renewal" (Ottawa: January 7, 1998).

²⁴Canada, *Gathering Strength—Canada's Aboriginal Action Plan* QS–6121–000–EE– A1 (Ottawa: Minister of Public Works and Government Services Canada, 1997) at 13.

²⁵*Ibid.* at 15.

²⁶*Ibid.* at 15.

²⁷*Ibid.* at 13.

²⁸RCAP, *supra* note 16 at 313.

²⁹*Ibid.*

³⁰*Ibid.* at 314.

³¹See *ibid.* at 32.

³²*Ibid.* at 319–20. Although the language of recognition refers to "nations" in RCAP, and to "Indian tribes" in U.S. policy, it is evident that the recognition is, in practice, extended to the government that is representative of the nation or tribe. See Barsh, *infra* c. 4.

³³*Gathering Strength, supra* note 24 at 17.

³⁴The text of the Nisga'a Treaty and related materials are available at *www.aaf.gov.bc.ca/ aaf/treaty/nisgaa/.* See also Douglas Sanders, "We Intend to Live Here Forever: A Primer on the Nisga'a Treaty" (2000) 33 U.B.C. L. Rev.; Paul Rynard, "Welcome In, But Check Your Rights at the Door: The James Bay and Nisga'a Agreements in Canada" (2000) 33 *Canadian J. of Political Science* 211; Christopher McKee, *Treaty Talks in British Columbia: Negotiating a Mutually Beneficial Future,* 2d ed. (Vancouver: University of British Columbia Press, 2000).

³⁵*Gathering Strength, supra* note 24 at 18.

³⁶See *supra* note 24 at 18.

³⁷"Speaking notes for the Honourable Robert D. Nault, P.C., M.P., Minister of Indian and Northern Affairs Canada to Launch Consultations on First Nations Governance" May 2, 2001, available at *www.fng-gpn.gc.ca/.*

³⁸*Quebec Secession Reference* case, as cited in Joffe (2000) McGill L.J. 155 at 173 and note 85. For a severe condemnation of the doctrine of parliamentary sovereignty in respect to Indian policy, see Menno Boldt, *Surviving as Indians: The Challenge of Self-government* (Toronto: University of Toronto Press, 1993) at 9.

³⁹*Hunter* v. *Southam,* [1984] 2 S.C.R. 145; *Quebec Secession Reference, supra* note 38.

⁴⁰Common law rights are included within the category of rights protected by s. 35, and common law rights are based in historical experience. *R.* v. *Sparrow,* [1990] 1 S.C.R. 1075; *Kruger* v. *The Queen,* [1978] 1 S.C.R. 104. See also Patrick Macklem, *Indigenous Difference and the Constitution of Canada* (Toronto: University of Toronto Press, 2001) c. 8 "Indigenous Difference and State Obligations."

⁴¹*R.* v. *Big M Drug Mart,* [1985] 1 S.C.R. 295 at 335. For a contemporary appeal to the idea that justice suggests that Canadians ought to adopt an image of Canada as a multinational North American country that respects its indigenous or North American foundations, see Paul L.A.H. Chartrand, "Aboriginal Self-Government: Towards a Vision of Canada as a North American Multinational Country" in J. Oakes & R. Riewe, *Issues in the North.* vol. II (Winnipeg: Canadian Circumpolar Conference and Department of Native Studies, University of Manitoba, 1997) 81.

⁴²See also Brian Slattery, "The Organic Constitution: Aboriginal Peoples and the Evolution of Canada" (1995) 34 Osgoode Hall L.J. 101, at 111, 112.

⁴³*R.* v. *Sparrow, supra* note 2.

⁴⁴*R.* v. *Cote,* [1996] 4 C.N.L.R. 26 (S.C.C.); *R.* v. *Adams,* [1996] 4 C.N.L.R. 1.(S.C.C.)

Chapter Two

Collective and Individual Recognition in Canada

The *Indian Act* Regime

John Giokas & Robert K. Groves

Introduction

The purpose of this chapter is to examine briefly the origins, nature, and effect of Canada's domestic recognition practice under the *Indian Act* as it affects Aboriginal people in Canada other than those who are recognized as "Indians" under the *Indian Act*. Some of the definition issues regarding "Aboriginal peoples" under Canadian law will be examined, and the nature of recognition in international law will be discussed. However, the primary focus will be on the existing *Indian Act* regime for the recognition of "Indians" as set out in the amendments contained in Bill C–31 of 1985. A brief review of some of the most relevant events in the long history of the *Indian Act* will be provided, along with reference to relevant judicial decisions, including the *Corbiere* case.[1]

Who Are Indians, Inuit, and Métis?

Indians

"Constitutional" Indians

Despite the spate of judicial decisions on Aboriginal rights over the past three decades, there is still a great deal of uncertainty regarding how to identify the Aboriginal peoples of Canada. Under the *Constitution Act, 1982*, three different Aboriginal peoples are recognized in section 35 as possessing Aboriginal and treaty rights: the "Indian, Inuit and Métis peoples." Under the earlier *Constitution Act, 1867*, Canada is accorded jurisdiction in section 91(24) over "Indians and Lands reserved for the Indians." The "Indians" mentioned in these two documents are often referred to as Canada's "constitutional Indians."

The question that has arisen is whether the "Indians" mentioned in section 91(24) are the same "Indians" mentioned in section 35 (thereby excluding the Inuit and Métis from the category of "Indians") or whether the category "Indians" mentioned in section 91(24) includes the Aboriginal peoples mentioned in section 35, namely the "Indian, Inuit and Métis."

In support of the first hypothesis is the constitutional use of the word "Indian." Since a constitution arguably speaks with one voice, an "Indian" for one constitutional purpose ought to be the same as for another. However, in support of the second hypothesis, the Supreme Court of Canada has previously ruled that the Inuit people are included within the term "Indians" in section 91(24).[2] Hence, many academic and other commentators have argued that the term "Indians" in section 91(24) must also include the Métis.[3]

It may well be that both constitutional provisions refer to the same group of Aboriginal people, with section 35 clarifying who is within the section 91(24) constitutional category of "Indians." This would mean that despite their separate mention in section 35, Métis are also "constitutional Indians." The federal government presently resists this interpretation.

Canada's current position is that the term "Indian" in section 91(24) refers only to Indians and Inuit. Moreover, Canada argues that it refers only to those persons of Indian and Inuit ancestry or affiliation that it has chosen to recognize, namely, status Indians and accepted members of recognized Inuit communities respectively. Canada resists acceptance of constitutional jurisdiction over Métis, non-status Indians, and persons of Inuit descent who are not accepted as members by Inuit communities.

It nonetheless seems likely that the federal government would admit to section 91(24) jurisdiction over at least some of the Aboriginal persons referred to as non-status Indians or as Métis. Bill C–31 alone is proof of that, given that over one hundred thousand persons of Aboriginal ancestry were either returned to Indian status or granted Indian status for the first time. The only way that Parliament could have done so was if its section 91(24) jurisdiction *already* extended to them prior to 1985. On this logic, many of the Aboriginal people still referred to as non-status Indians or as Métis could equally be returned to status or granted status for the first time if Parliament chose to do so, and on the same constitutional basis, namely, that Parliament's jurisdiction over "Indians" already extends to them.

Two Supreme Court decisions support the argument that Métis and non-status Indians fall within federal law-making jurisdiction over "Indians" in section 91(24). The first cases focused on Aboriginal ancestry as the basis for federal jurisdiction. In *A.G. Canada* v. *Canard* Mr. Justice Beetz declared that the section 91(24) reference to Indians was essentially racial.

> The *British North America Act*...by using the word "Indians" in section 91(24) creates a racial classification and refers to a special group for whom it contemplates the possibility of special treatment. It does not define the expression "Indian." This parliament can do within constitutional limits by using criteria suited to this purpose but among which it would not appear unreasonable to count marriage and filiation and, unavoidably, intermarriages, in the light of either Indian customs and values... or of legislative history.[4]

This line of reasoning suggests that Parliament could legislate for anyone of "Indian" race and provides a constitutional basis for the expansion of the status Indian category through Bill C–31 of 1985 mentioned above. This means that Indian ancestry (and inevitably kinship through marriage and adoption) are the determining factors. On this basis, virtually anyone of Indian descent could become amenable to federal jurisdiction. This would obviously include persons now classified as Métis or as non-status Indian.

More recently, further indirect support has been offered by the Supreme Court decision in *Delgamuukw* where Mr. Justice Lamer alludes to the possibility that section 35 protects a core of "Indianness"[5] from provincial intrusion, and that this is the same core of "Indianness" protected by section 91(24) jurisdiction.

> The extent of federal jurisdiction over Indians has not been definitively addressed by this Court.... As I explained below, the Court has held that section 91(24) protects a "core" of Indianness from provincial intrusion, through the doctrine of interjurisdictional immunity.
>
> It follows, at the very least, that this core falls within the scope of federal jurisdiction over Indians. That core, for reasons I will develop, encompasses Aboriginal rights, including the rights that are recognized and affirmed by section 35(1).... Those rights include rights in relation to land; that part of the core derives from section 91(24)'s reference to "Lands reserved for the Indians." But those rights also encompass practices, customs and traditions which are not tied to land as well; that part of the core can be traced to federal jurisdiction over "Indians."[6]

Thus, the Court seems to have opened the door to possible litigation by Métis and non-status Indians, those who are not currently recognized by the federal government as falling within section 91(24) jurisdiction. Their argument would be that since section 35 protects a core of Indianness, and since two of the section 35 peoples mentioned—Indian and Inuit—are "Indians" under section

91(24) for whom the federal government takes constitutional responsibility, then it follows that the third Aboriginal people, the Métis, are also section 91(24) "Indians" for whom the federal government ought to take responsibility. This raises the distinct possibility that a judicial finding in favour of Métis Aboriginal rights under section 35 could trigger a related finding of federal legislative authority over Métis under section 91(24).[7]

"Legal" Indians

As mentioned earlier, another complication flows from the fact that Canada has chosen to recognize only some of the "constitutional Indians" discussed above. They are the Indians referred to in the *Indian Act* and its pre-Confederation predecessors. These "Indians," according to the most recent version of the *Indian Act*, are Canada's registrable, or "status" Indians.[8] These are Aboriginal people (or non-Aboriginal people who have married or been adopted by registrable Aboriginal persons) who can meet the federal criteria for registration under the *Indian Act*. They comprise a numerically smaller group than those making up the broader category of "constitutional Indians" and are the people recognized by Canada for purposes of its constitutional jurisdiction under section 91(24). This narrower group of Indians is sometimes referred to as "legal Indians."

In short, Canada equates this group of "legal Indians" with the group of "constitutional Indians" for most purposes. The result for Métis and non-status Indians (i.e., those Aboriginal persons and groups who cannot meet the criteria for registration as an Indian under the *Indian Act*) is that Canada has not provided them with a federally protected land base, access to federal Indian programs and services, or standing to bring certain types of claims against Canada (e.g., specific treaty entitlement claims under Canada's policy of the same name) or to participate in land claims settlements on the same basis as status Indians.[9] In short, the federal position is that Métis and non-status Indians are provincial residents for most (if not all) constitutional purposes.[10]

Even under the *Indian Act*, there may be several different types of "legal Indians." Some of the distinctions made are based on law, while others are based on other criteria, including those used by Aboriginal people themselves. Thus, reference is often made to "old status" (pre-1985) Indians versus "new status" (post-1985) Indians (new status Indians are also referred to as "Bill C–31s"); "6(1)s" (persons registrable under section 6(1) of the *Indian Act*) versus "6(2)s" (persons registrable under section 6(2) of the *Indian Act*); status Indian band members versus non-status Indian band members or versus status Indian non-band members. In addition, under the *Indian Act* persons who are band members but who do not have Indian status will be deemed to be Indians for the purposes of certain sections of the *Indian Act*. These are the "deemed Indians."[11]

These distinctions will be discussed below in more detail when Bill C–31 is reviewed. They flow from the different basis upon which Indian status was granted to the 115,000 non-status Indians and Métis who did not have it prior to 1985 and from the fact that band membership and Indian status have been separated. The consequence of this new array of distinctions is that the same person may be recognized as an Indian for one purpose, but not for another.

As a result, the case law concerning entitlement to a variety of benefits under the Constitution or under the *Indian Act* is often confusing and contradictory and of little assistance to policy-makers or politicians. In addition, there is currently a great deal of litigation under way questioning the distinctions set out in the *Indian Act* or challenging the way in which the Indian status, band membership, and residency rules have been implemented.[12] This too makes it difficult for policy-makers to see their way out of the thicket of distinctions made and maintained by the federal government.

Inuit

While Canada has had an official recognition policy for "Indians" through the *Indian Act*, it has had no similar policy for Inuit. Originally (as with the Métis) they were defined by way of exclusion: they were not viewed by the federal government as being under federal jurisdiction over "Indians" and were therefore ineligible for Indian programs and services. Their needs were addressed in the federal territories on a different basis and, in the case of Quebec, they were simply assumed by the federal government to be a provincial constitutional responsibility. Since the 1939 Supreme Court decision in *Re Eskimos,*[13] however, Canada has been forced to accept its section 91(24) constitutional jurisdiction over Inuit. Since then, Inuit groups have been recognized as such by Canada, and provided with federal services, but have been explicitly excluded from the *Indian Act* since 1951.[14]

Federal policy for recognizing Inuit has evolved slowly since the 1930s and has included arbitrary blood-quantum definitions of Inuk status for certain purposes like access to food fishing permits under the *Fisheries Act* and regional fisheries regulations.[15] For purposes of general identification, in 1941 each Inuk in Canada's northern territories was provided with a four-digit number stamped on a disc for identification as being "Inuk." The identification disk system was formally abandoned in 1971.

Inuit are now identified individually through vital statistics records and uninsured benefits lists in the territories, provinces, and nationally on the basis of "self-identification and/or community recognition...."[16] Thus, Canada's overall approach with regard to Inuit recognition has become one of recognizing a regional group and permitting that group to determine membership or entitle-

..... ᴡᴏ ᴀccess to federal programs, services, and special resource access poli-cies.[17]

Métis

The first version of the *Indian Act* was passed in 1876. From the outset, Métis who were not living an "Indian" lifestyle in close association to Indian bands have been excluded from the ambit of the *Act*.[18] The exclusion of Métis from the *Indian Act* was gradual and attuned to regionally specific issues. Métis in Ontario or elsewhere out-side of the Prairie Provinces, the Northwest Territories, and northeastern British Columbia have never been formally excluded from the *Indian Act* because they are not connected to any land-grant system under federally constituted Half-breed Scrip Commissions and the *Dominion Lands Acts*.

Notable in this respect is the decision in 1875 by Canada to recognize a Métis community in the northwest angle of Ontario through a formal adhesion to Treaty 3. Despite the 1967 amalgamation of this community into the contem-porary Coochiching First Nation,[19] the survey stakes still evident today attest to the federal recognition of "Half-Breed Reserve 18A and 18C," set apart at the time for the half-breed adherents of treaty. This is the only known instance in which the federal government knowingly entered into a treaty adhesion with a community of Aboriginal persons recognized from the outset as being Métis.[20]

Aside from this one instance of treaty recognition, Métis have been recog-nized as Métis through the *Manitoba Act* and various pieces of dominion land legislation, the goal of which was to provide them with access to land other than as "Indians," i.e., as individuals rather than as members of a Métis collective.[21] There has never been a consistent or coherent national policy on Métis.[22] In-stead, federal policy for recognition of Métis began in 1870 as a prelude to, and as part of, the treaty-making process with Indians in the old North-West Terri-tory. Although there were variations in how Métis were treated outside of the North West,[23] for the most part the process involved the issuance of land or money scrip to persons described as "half-breeds."

The general assumption was that this population would become integrated into the non-Aboriginal settler population and would not require lasting com-munity-level recognition of the type accorded to Indians under treaty and via the *Indian Act*. The western Métis land and scrip process had stopped by the 1930s with the completion of the eleven numbered treaties and the transfer of control over natural resources to the Prairie Provinces through the natural resources transfer agreements concluded with each of them.

Federal preferences in relation to Métis recognition in the recent past have included the emergence in 1992 of a draft political accord supporting the Métis National Council's (MNC) definition of "Métis" in a variety of program and policy contexts.[24] The MNC core constituency is the descendants of the original Red River Métis. Although the evolving MNC definition of "Métis" goes beyond the descendants of the original Red River Métis, it is not as broad as that of the Congress of Aboriginal Peoples (CAP, the former Native Council of Canada). CAP's definition embraces virtually everyone of mixed Aboriginal and non-Aboriginal descent who chooses to self-identify as Métis. Given what it regards as the uncertainty over who the Métis are, Canada has never formally adopted either the narrower MNC definition or the broader CAP definition.

Provincial acceptance of responsibility for, or jurisdiction over, Métis groups varies. With the partial exception of Alberta, provinces with Métis populations usually maintain that Canada ought to exercise its constitutional jurisdiction under section 91(24) over the Métis and thereby relieve them of the financial burden they pose. This stance is particularly evident in the provinces with the most sizeable Métis populations, Manitoba and Saskatchewan.

In Alberta, limited recognition of Métis as a group exists through provincial legislation providing land to eight Métis collectives in that province.[25] In the face of Canada's refusal to exercise constitutional jurisdiction over Métis, Alberta is thus the only province to have stepped into the policy vacuum by establishing eight Métis settlements (basically, Métis "reserves") operating under provincial legislation. This was done originally as a temporary 1930s relief measure aimed at destitute "half-breeds."[26]

The Alberta legislation for the Métis was originally based on the *Indian Act* and used a blood-quantum definition (a 1/4-blood person not considered an Indian or a non-treaty Indian for the purposes of the 1927 *Indian Act*). Despite the recognition accorded to these Métis settlements by Alberta, there remain many other unrecognized Métis groups and individuals in Alberta outside the eight settlements.

Roots of Domestic Recognition Practice in International Law

Aside from its other functions, the *Indian Act* is also recognition legislation through which the Canadian state determines which Aboriginal individuals it will acknowledge as "Indians" and which Aboriginal groups it will acknowledge as Indian "bands." Thus it addresses both an individual and a collective dimension of recognition.[27]

Recognition is a concept of international law referring principally to the practice of states of acknowledging that another entity is also a state and therefore its equal in international law. In technical terms, recognition in contemporary international law means that the recognized state has the full legal "personality" associated with international law and is therefore capable of carrying out the duties of a state and enjoying the privileges of statehood, such as immunity from legal actions in the courts of another state. To be considered a state by other states, the entity seeking recognition must generally have all of the following characteristics: a permanent population; a defined territory; a government; and the capacity to enter into relations with other states.[28] Importantly, even where all these conditions are met, there is no obligation on states to confer recognition. State recognition is an executive function that is as inspired as much by political considerations as by purely legal ones.[29]

Recognition in international law brings important obligations and benefits:

1. Standing to make claims before international tribunals to have their international rights vindicated;

2. Subjection to some or all international duties;

3. Capacity to enter into binding international agreements, i.e., treaties, conventions, etc.;

4. Enjoyment of some or all of the immunities from the jurisdiction of domestic tribunals available in international law.[30]

The notion of recognition was imported during the colonial period from international law into domestic American and Canadian law to deal with the fact that North America was already populated by peoples organized into distinct political units referred to by the settlers as "tribes" and "nations." The *Royal Proclamation of 1763*, for instance, refers explicitly to "the several Tribes or Nations with whom We are connected, and who live under Our Protection...."[31]

The later acknowledgment through treaties and other forms of government-to-government relationships by early settlers and the colonial authorities of the status of Aboriginal peoples were also acts of recognition equivalent in their spirit to international acts of recognition between states. The Supreme Court of Canada noted as much in the 1990 *Sioui* decision, concluding that with respect to Imperial and colonial relations with those tribes and nations "it was good policy to maintain relations with them very close to those maintained between sovereign nations."[32]

The *Indian Act* as Recognition Legislation

Under international law, states are normally not concerned about how other states determine their citizenship. As mentioned above, this is not the case in Canada's domestic scheme. The Canadian state is very concerned with how recognized groups determine their membership and has imposed restrictive rules that it enforces primarily through funding formulae based on the number of status Indians or accepted Inuit community members in the recognized group.

In other respects, however, it is easy to see how the essential characteristics of a state are paralleled by the band system established by the federal government under the *Indian Act*. In the first place, Canada is under no legal obligation to afford recognition to groups of Aboriginal persons. It is a purely political decision inspired by many factors. There are still many "unrecognized" Indian bands in Canada.[33]

Those groups of Aboriginal persons recognized as such by the Canadian state tend to show the characteristics set out in the international context. For example, a "band" is defined in section 2 of the *Indian Act* as a "body of Indians" (permanent population) "for whose use and benefit in common lands... have been set apart" (defined territory). A band operates through a "council of the band" that is either elected pursuant to section 74 or operates through "custom" (a government).

The fourth criterion—capacity to enter into various types of agreement with other governments—has posed some challenges which are being met outside the formal structure of the *Indian Act*. This gap in the *Indian Act* has been the subject of repeated attempts at reform and has been addressed by the courts on a case-by-case basis in favour of band legal capacity to conduct business within Canada.[34] Federal policy, furthermore, has evolved a wide range of instruments through which band councils conduct their intergovernmental affairs for purposes of administering funds in the form of funding arrangements with Canada,[35] service purchase agreements with provinces and municipalities, etc. Thus, by dint of repeated court decisions, administrative arrangements, and current legislative efforts, it can be argued that Indian bands also met the fourth criterion for recognition.

The international benefits and obligations have their domestic parallels. For instance, recognition as a "band" under the *Indian Act* gives a group of Indians the standing (under federal policy) to lodge a specific claim against Canada on behalf of its members. Enfranchised bands (enfranchisement is discussed below), non-recognized groups, and individual Indians without a band affiliation cannot do this.[36] The federal and provincial governments also try to restrict the benefit of accessing constitutionally protected Aboriginal and treaty rights under section 35 only to those people recognized by Canada as being Indian or Inuit.[37]

In the same way that internationally recognized entities are subject to international duties, bands of Indians are subject to the constitutional power of the federal government under section 91(24) of the *Constitution Act, 1967*. Internationally recognized entities enjoy immunities. Similarly, bands of Indians (as well as individual Indians, in the case of tax entitlements) enjoy certain immunities from domestic legal processes in the form of exemptions from income tax for income earned within the defined territory of the reserve and exemption from seizure of goods on reserve in sections 87 and 89 respectively of the *Indian Act*.

As mentioned above, international law deals with group recognition: a state (comprised of many individual citizens) recognizes another state (equally comprised of many individual citizens). States ordinarily have no interest in how the citizens of another state may have acquired their citizenship. It is enough that they are citizens according to the internal rules of that other state.

It is different with Canada's *Indian Act* recognition regime, for it goes beyond merely recognizing groups known as "bands." It is not a true group recognition instrument because in its definition of "Indian" it also concerns itself with the question of who is a "citizen" of the recognized group. It is instructive to note that the *Act* is singular: it is the *Indian Act*, not the "Indians Act" or the "Bands of Indians Act."

The modern *Indian Act* is based on the definitions in section 2 of "Indian" and "band." An Indian is someone who is registered or entitled to be registered as an Indian. This is a circular definition. The *Indian Act* closes that circle arbitrarily. In keeping with the individualistic focus, "band" is defined in section 2 as a "body of Indians" and not as, for example, a successor entity to the "several Nations or Tribes of Indians" referred to in the *Royal Proclamation of 1763*. In 1763, those nations or tribes (like states now do under international law) decided who they were and who their members were and these decisions were respected by the British imperial authorities (as noted above in the *Sioui* case).[38]

While recognition of new bands is possible under the *Indian Act*, in one respect this process is based on the identity of the individuals who will comprise the band. For example, under section 17 the Minister may amalgamate existing bands or "constitute" new bands. However, in the latter case the new band will only be constituted from existing band lists or from the Indian Register of persons already registered as being Indians. In short, only if the individual members of a potential new band are already recognized either as band members or as status Indians will the Minister exercise this power.[39] This is thus not a true group recognition policy of the type found in international law.

The second way to recognize new bands is through the power of the Governor in Council—essentially, the federal cabinet—to declare that a band exists. This power is referred to in section 2(1) and in section 6(1)(b) of the *Indian Act*. The former provision notes that "band means a body of *Indians*... (c) declared by the Governor in Council to be a band...." This provision would seem to require that any new band be made up of persons who are already "Indians," since, by its very wording, a band cannot be other than "a body of Indians." Thus, only if the persons who will be declared to be a band are *already* Indians can the declaration be made. However, the Minister already holds such a power.

A proper reading of the prerogative power of the Governor in Council under section 2 is that it affords the Crown the capacity to recognize or establish "bands" within the meaning of the *Indian Act* that had not formerly met the legislative definitions otherwise provided for at section 2 or in section 17. In other words, this aspect of the *Indian Act* is the sole basis for a full-blown recognition policy of the type recommended by RCAP. This clause allows the Crown to bring a group of previously unrecognized persons who are "Indians" within the ambit of section 91(24) of the *Constitution Act, 1867*. This ability is affirmed in section 6(1)(b) of the current *Act* by defining an Indian as "a member of a body of *persons* that has been declared by the Governor in Council... to be a band...." On this wording, the persons declared to be band do not already have to be Indians pursuant to the *Indian Act* definition before the declaration—they need only be "persons." In short, on this interpretation of the wording, they become Indians within the meaning of the *Indian Act* only after the declaration that they are a band. This allows the Governor in Council to avoid the otherwise "fact-based" definition of a "band" and the circular definition of "Indian" established in section 2. On this reading, the declaratory power becomes a true recognition power allowing Canada to recognize any Aboriginal group as being an Indian band.

In short, from Canada's perspective and for the reasons discussed earlier in this chapter, "legal Indians" have tended to be what Canada regards as "constitutional Indians." Yet the plain reading of the *Indian Act* itself, together with Canadian practice in recognizing previously unrecognized groups as Indian bands (though they do not otherwise meet the fact-based definition now concretized in the current *Indian Act)*, leads clearly to the conclusion that a recognition capacity is legislatively available to Canada—it is only absent a recognition policy.

A Short History of the *Indian Act*[40]

The first full version of the *Indian Act* was passed in 1876 as a consolidation of colonial legislation and previous Canadian and British imperial policies dating back to the 1700s. These policies were originally developed in response to the increasing social and commercial contact between traders and settlers and Indian nations and reflected the official belief that Indian people were unable to deal with persons of European ancestry without being exploited.

Protection and Civilization

One of the main goals of the imperial authorities was to recognize Indian land rights and to protect Indians against loss of their lands to squatters and unscrupulous speculators. Thus, Crown superintendents were appointed to manage relations with Indian nations and to ensure Royal protection of Indian lands. A clear line was drawn between Indian-occupied territory and the colonial settlements. Through a series of official pronouncements culminating in the *Royal Proclamation of 1763,* the rule was established that Indian lands could only be purchased for settlement after they had been publicly surrendered to the Crown by the Indian nation concerned. This rule is now reflected in the surrender provisions of the *Indian Act* in sections 37–41.

As the settler population increased, it became necessary to create reserves where Indians could pursue their traditional economies and make the necessary adaptations to the colonial societies growing rapidly around them. Many Indians also started farming on their reserves and began to learn the trades that were common at that time. The colonial authorities and the churches were enthusiastic about assisting Indians in these "civilizing" efforts, and initially there was a relatively high degree of cooperation in this respect between Indian and colonial societies.[41]

The protective policy of the *Royal Proclamation* was first put into legislative form by a colonial assembly in 1839 as a result of settler encroachments on Indian land in Upper Canada. In 1839 the *Crown Lands Act*[42] solidified the Crown role as guardian of Indian lands. It was emulated in Nova Scotia, New Brunswick, and Lower Canada by mid century and later supplemented by more detailed legislation in 1850 authorizing Crown officials to directly manage Indians lands to better protect them from trespassers and squatters. For the first time, an attempt was made to define the term "Indian" for purposes of government jurisdiction. "Indians" for these purposes were band members or reserve residents *of Indian blood* as well as all those, male or female, married to, adopted by, or living amongst such persons.[43]

The 1850 definition of Indian was narrowed in amendments to Lower Canada legislation in 1851,[44] so that non-Indian men who married Indian women would no longer acquire Indian status and with it the right to reside on reserve. The status of their Indian spouses and mixed-blood children was not affected. This was apparently to prevent non-Indian men from gaining access to reserve lands. However, the converse was not true, as non-Indian women who married Indian men would still be considered to be Indian and permitted to reside on reserve with their husbands. Thus, for the first time Indian status (and with it band membership and reserve residency rights) began to be associated with the male line.

Assimilation

By the 1850s new currents of thought began sweeping through the British Empire. No longer content to assist Indian communities to adapt at their own pace, reformers began to press for their rapid absorption into colonial society and the ending of the protected status of reserve lands. Rather than abandon the prior policies of protection and civilization, however, imperial authorities simply added assimilation to the earlier policy goals and began searching for ways of encouraging Indians to renounce Indian status and to leave their reserve communities.

The *Gradual Civilization Act*[45] was passed in 1857. Its premise was that Indian men would be encouraged to assimilate into colonial society through the offer of an individual allotment of 50 acres of land (which would be removed from the reserve land base) and a share of the band's treaty annuity moneys. It was hoped that Indian communities and reserves would slowly disappear as Indians became "enfranchised"[46] and as reserve lands were reduced in 50-acre increments. Any Indian man who met the qualifications for enfranchisement could do so, and his wife and children would be enfranchised with him. This was the first attempt to encourage Indians to freely abandon their Indian status.[47] In many ways, this legislation was one of the most significant events in the long history of imperial and colonial Indian policy as it foreshadowed many of the elements that would later find their way into the *Indian Act*.[48]

In 1860 new legislation was passed transferring the protective role of the imperial authorities to the united province of Canada.[49] At Confederation that role was inherited by the federal government through the allocation of responsibility for "Indians and Lands reserved for the Indians" in section 91(24) of the *Constitution Act, 1867*. The next year Canada passed legislation giving the federal government direct control of Indian lands and creating the position of Chief Superintendent of Indian Affairs (later renamed Superintendent-General, a role now discharged by the Minister of Indian Affairs).[50]

In 1869 the federal government renewed the assimilation policy through the *Gradual Enfranchisement Act*.[51] Aside from the enfranchisement provisions, the *Act* introduced a system of individual property-holding through a "location ticket" (now known as a certificate of possession) to be obtained from the Superintendent-General. The new legislation also authorized the Governor in Council to impose an elective system for chiefs and councillors with a three-year term of office.

Federal Powers Over Indians

The *Gradual Enfranchisement Act* also contained other provisions that reflect the Victorian values of the day. For instance, only men were permitted to vote in band elections. Moreover, where an Indian woman "married out" by wedding a non-Indian man, she would lose Indian status and band membership, as would any children of that marriage. However, Indian men were not subject to the same measures for marrying non-Indian women. Their wives would actually acquire band membership, as would any children of the marriage. All these provisions made their way into the *Indian Act* seven years later.

The first version of the *Indian Act* in 1876[52] consolidated and continued the provisions in the previous legislation. It was very detailed and added new provisions empowering federal officials to control the daily activities of Indian communities. For instance, the Governor in Council could order a band to abandon its traditional political system in favour of municipal-style band council elections. The restrictive definition of Indians from earlier Indian legislation was continued.

Reform Efforts

As the years went on, the powers of the Governor in Council and the Superintendent-General were regularly expanded. By the turn of the century the *Indian Act* had nearly doubled in size, from its original 100 sections to an unwieldy 195. The effort to cut it down to more manageable proportions over the following decades was unsuccessful and by the end of the Second World War it had become clear that fundamental changes were needed. After several years of study, public hearings, and consultations by a joint committee of Parliament, the *Indian Act* was substantially revised in 1951.[53]

Although considerably shorter, the 1951 *Indian Act* was still highly detailed and contained most of the paternalistic and assimilative provisions already described. Terms of office for chiefs and band councillors were reduced to two years, with the Minister replacing the Governor in Council for purposes of supervising the band council by-law making powers. The Governor in Council (and after 1956, the Minister), continued to have the power to order bands to abandon their traditional forms of government and to adopt the elective band council system. Several hundred bands experienced this transition in the 1950s, including the Batchewana Band, which became the subject of the Supreme Court's *Corbiere* decision in 1999.

Although Indian women could now vote in band elections, as will be discussed in more detail below, the marrying-out provisions were actually strengthened. Indian men could still marry whomever they wished without fear of loss of status or band membership. Importantly, the definition of Indian and control of band membership remained in non-Indian hands, and the definitions were actually tightened for fiscal reasons by introducing an Indian Register as a centralized record of those entitled to registration as an Indian (and to the receipt of federal benefits). Prior to this development, federal government officials had kept treaty pay lists and records of band elections, estates administration, band membership commutation, and "half-breed" scrip, but had attempted no comprehensive listing.[54]

While the powers of the Governor in Council and the Minister were reduced in the 1951 revision, they still directly administered over half the *Act*. This remains the case with the current version of the *Indian Act*: the Governor in Council has 25 specific powers, while those of the Minister are found in 87 separate provisions.[55]

By the late 1950s the *Indian Act* was increasingly perceived as being out of date. Another joint parliamentary committee held hearings over a two-year period before delivering a report in 1961 calling for more equality of access by Indians to social services, voting rights for non-resident band members, more research on the real needs and problems of Indian people, and more federal-provincial cooperation in tackling the social problems confronting reserve communities. In 1960, in the midst of the joint committee's hearings, reserve-based Indians were given the right to vote in federal elections.

A few technical amendments were brought forward in the 1950s and 1960s, and in 1969 the federal government introduced a White Paper proposal to repeal the *Indian Act*. It was withdrawn two years later in the face of Indian opposition.[56] In 1970 the *Indian Act* was revised without significant change, and during the ensuing years little was done to remedy problem areas because of the search for broader constitutional solutions that culminated in the *Constitution Act, 1982*.

Nonetheless, in the face of pressures that will be described below, some of the problematic areas of the *Indian Act* were changed. In 1985, sexism in the *Act* was addressed through amendments that, among other things, restored Indian status to the many thousands of Indian women and their children who had lost it as a result of the marrying-out and enfranchisement rules referred to earlier.

Bill C–31: An Overview

On April 17, 1982 the *Canadian Charter of Rights and Freedoms* became part of the supreme law of Canada with the advent of the *Constitution Act, 1982*. In order to allow the federal and provincial governments time to bring their legislation into conformity with its requirements, section 15, the equality provision, did not become operative until April 17, 1985. The *Indian Act* would have been greatly affected by section 15 had the latter been operative in 1982.

In June 1985 Bill C–31 was given Royal Assent (and given retroactive force as from April 17, 1985). It amended the *Indian Act* to accomplish three primary purposes:

1. To eliminate the gender and gender-related discriminatory effects of the

status and band membership provisions in the *Act*, as well as several non–sex based forms of discrimination (e.g., the bar against descendants of those who received half-breed scrip);

2. To reinstate several classes of persons (primarily those suffering sexual discrimination and their first generation descendants) who had lost Indian status or been enfranchised over the years; and

3. To permit bands to take control of band membership by drawing up membership codes.

Indian status was to remain in the hands of the federal government, however. It remains there, presumably for fiscal reasons: the federal government is thereby able to control the number of people for whom it has primary constitutional responsibility.

Background

Discriminatory Provisions

The distinction between what the editors of the *Felix S. Cohen's Handbook of Federal Indian Law* refer to as Indians in an "ethnological" sense (Indians by virtue of ancestry[57]) and Indians in a "legal" sense (Indians by virtue of recognition in law as such)[58] has become a well-established one in Canadian law. From this perspective both status and non-status Indians are "ethnological Indians," but only status Indians are "legal Indians."

The distinction between status and non-status Indians evolved through the gradual imposition by the colonial and later federal government of legal standards whereby ancestry, common culture and language, membership in an Indian community, and a subjective sense of being "Indian" no longer determined whether or not a person was an Indian for official purposes.

To briefly review the historical record, amendments to Indian land protection legislation in Lower Canada in 1851[59] required, for the first time, that a non-Indian man who married an Indian woman be denied membership in the woman's band and with it the right to reside on reserve. A non-Indian woman who married an Indian man faced no barrier to membership in the band.

Six years later the *Gradual Civilization Act*[60] became law in both Canadas. Any Indian man who met the qualifications for enfranchisement could do so. His wife and children were automatically enfranchised with him. In 1869, the *Gradual Enfranchisement Act*[61] went farther than previous mixed-marriage legislation in terms of the consequences for Indian status. Henceforth when an Indian woman married a non-Indian man, not only would he be denied Indian band membership, she and any children of the marriage would also lose theirs.

These provisions were carried forward into the first *Indian Act* in 1876.

Amendments in 1920 transferred to the Superintendent-General the band council power to decide whether Indian women who "married out" would continue to receive their entitlements to treaty annuity and band money distributions or whether they would receive a lump sum settlement.[62]

As mentioned earlier, the notion of "Indian blood" and group membership that had been features of the definition of Indian were replaced by the notion of "registration." The initial Indian registry system was to "consist of Band Lists and General Lists."[63] Band lists were based on whatever lists were then available to develop a register, including the informal band and treaty pay lists. Prior to 1951 there was no well-organized or rigorously maintained manner of compiling band lists. There were many persons who may have been missed when the required band lists were developed in 1951 but who were considered (and considered themselves) to be members of a particular band.[64] One factor may have been the wide definitions and loose departmental supervision prior to 1951.

> These terms ["Indian," "Irregular band," "non-treaty Indian"] were so imprecise that agents had difficulty in sorting out conflicting claims concerning eligibility to reside on a reserve, to receive treaty benefits, and to obtain government social assistance. The situation was compounded by the lack of verifiable band membership lists, poor supervision of isolated reserves, and by Depression era conditions, which encouraged Indians to move from band to band seeking relief, or to return to the reserves from the city after years of absence.[65]

The net result was that many persons who ought to have been included on the new band lists for purpose of status in 1951 were not.[66]

The 1951 *Indian Act* went farther than earlier versions in attempting to sever the connection between Indian women who married out (and their children) and their reserve communities. A good example is the so-called "double mother" rule in former section 12(1)(a)(iv) under which a status Indian could lose status at age 21 if his or her mother and grandmother had obtained their own status only through marriage to a status Indian man. The double mother rule applied to all women without Indian status under Canadian law, regardless of whether or not they were ethnological Indians. Thus it included those who might have been involuntarily enfranchised earlier or who might have been left off the post-1951 band lists for the reasons described above.

The double mother rule could lead to ridiculous results in situations like that of the Mohawk reserve at Akwesasne that straddles the border between Canada and the United States. If the grandmother and mother of a Mohawk child were both from the American side of the reserve they would not be considered to be status Indians in Canada except through having married a Canadian status Indian man. Thus, the 21-year-old grandchild would lose Indian status in Canada automatically, even though he or she might be Mohawk by descent, culture, and group affiliation.

After 1951 the marrying-out provisions in the *Act* were strengthened. Formerly, an Indian woman who married a non-Indian man lost her Indian status and with it her right to hold or reside on reserve land and to pass on status to her children by that marriage. Despite that, if she had refused commutation of her band moneys benefits, she would have been able to retain her band membership and the right to participate in band money and treaty annuity distributions and could even have continued to reside on reserve for as long as no one chose to have her evicted.[67]

The 1951 amendments changed this so that such a woman would be enfranchised as of the date of her marriage to the non-Indian man by order of the Governor in Council.[68] This meant loss of status and band membership and the compulsory disposal of any reserve lands she held.[69] These provisions were later characterized by Mr. Justice Laskin (in dissent) in the *Lavell and Bedard* case as a "statutory excommunication" and "statutory banishment."[70]

Indian men could not be forcibly enfranchised. The figures for enfranchisements for the twenty years between 1955 and 1975 when forced enfranchisements of women were in effect illustrate this: 1,576 men voluntarily enfranchised along with another 1,090 family members (wives and children); whereas 8,537 women were forcibly enfranchised along with 1,974 of their children.[71]

The 1951 *Indian Act* did not refer to the children of such women who were forcibly enfranchised. Prior to 1956 their children were enfranchised too despite the lack of legislative authorization to do so. Although further amendments in 1956 restored the Indian status of the children, they also clarified that children could also be enfranchised upon the mother marrying out.[72] In practice, a woman's off-reserve children would usually be enfranchised, while those living on reserve would retain their Indian status.[73]

The 1956 amendments also allowed for challenges to the Indian status of any illegitimate children of an Indian woman if it could be shown that the father was not an Indian.[74] There was no corresponding challenge provision regarding the illegitimate children of Indian men.

Pressure for Reform

The manifest unfairness of these rules led to many legal challenges that drew adverse publicity to their discriminatory nature both domestically and internationally. The *Lavell and Bedard* case was the most prominent example. Two Indian women who had lost status automatically upon marrying non-Indians argued that they had been discriminated against contrary to the guarantee of "equality before the law" in section 1(b) of the *Canadian Bill of Rights*.[75]

At the request of the Minister of Indian Affairs and as a result of the strenuous urging of the national status Indian organizations, the *Lavell* case (which Mrs. Lavell had won on appeal to the Federal Court) was appealed by the federal government to the Supreme Court of Canada. The National Indian Brotherhood (now the Assembly of First Nations) intervened on the side of the federal government, while a number of smaller Aboriginal women's organizations and the Native Council of Canada (now the Congress of Aboriginal Peoples) intervened on the side of Mrs. Lavell and Mrs. Bedard.

A bare majority of the Supreme Court (5 to 4) held against the two women on the basis that there was no impermissible discrimination. Writing for the majority, Mr. Justice Ritchie distinguished the Court's earlier ruling in *Drybones*[76] (striking down a provision of the *Indian Act* on equality grounds) because it had involved a sanction levied against Indians that would not be levied against non-Indians in similar circumstances.

> The impugned section [in *Drybones*] could not be enforced without denying equality of treatment in the administration and enforcement of the law before the ordinary courts of the land to a racial group, whereas no such inequality of treatment between Indian men and women flows as a necessary result of the application of section 12(1)(b) of the *Indian Act*.[77]

Commentators have been confused by this passage since it was first written, but it may refer to the fact that Indian women have a choice regarding whom they will marry.[78] Thus, the loss of status under section 12(1)(b) attendant upon marrying a non-Indian man does not become a factor for Indian women as a necessary result of being an Indian woman. It only becomes a necessary result if she exercises her power of choice and marries a non-Indian man.

The reasoning is not convincing because Mr. Drybones could not be convicted of being an Indian intoxicated off a reserve as a necessary result of being an Indian. He would have to have exercised his power of choice to become intoxicated first. In any event, the Court's decision in *Lavell and Bedard* seems in retrospect to have been a policy decision by the Court to prevent the *Indian Act* in its entirety from being overturned on equality grounds. The controversies generated by this case animated public discussion and created strong pressure for reform.

Pressures for reform increased with the *Lovelace* case in 1981.[79] Canada was criticized by the Human Rights Committee, which was established pursuant to the International Covenant on Civil and Political Rights under which individual complaints may be brought to the committee.[80] Canada is a signatory to the Covenant, and it is one of the documents that influenced the development of the *Canadian Charter of Rights and Freedoms*. The Covenant contains many human rights provisions similar to *Charter* protections.

The Human Rights Committee found the marrying-out provisions of the *Indian Act* to unjustifiably deny Sandra Lovelace her right as a member of an ethnic minority to enjoy her culture and language in community with other members of her band.[81] The committee did not find the loss of status attendant upon her marrying out to be reasonable or necessary to preserve the identity of the Tobique Band to which she belonged.

Reform Efforts

The pressure on the federal government for reform resulted in the Minister of Indian Affairs announcing in June 1980 that the government would suspend the operation of the most discriminatory sections of the *Act*: those dealing with loss of status on marrying out and the "double mother" rule. Most bands, however, apparently saw little advantage in preventing women from being expelled from their communities under these provisions. By 1983, only 41 bands had requested suspension of the former provision and only 105 had requested suspension of the latter.[82]

In 1983, the Standing Committee on Indian Affairs and Northern Development (the Penner Committee) issued its reports on Indian women and the *Indian Act* and on Indian self-government.[83] It recommended a two-tier approach where there would be a general list of status Indians eligible for federal benefits, and individual Indian First Nation membership lists. The two would not necessarily coincide. Thus status would have remained under federal government control, with Indian First Nation citizenship under Indian control.

Bill C–47 followed in 1984, in which the government proposed reinstating former members of bands and their first- and second-generation children. However, Bill C–47 died in the Senate after the federal government called an election later that summer. Similarly, Bill C–52, the *Indian Nation Recognition Act* which proposed a formal statutory recognition policy for Indian nations on a basis that was nominally free from the "status" regime of the past, also died on the Order Paper in 1984, although this bill was clearly intended to launch a debate rather than conclude one.

Bill C–31 of 1985 was built on the foundations of C–47, but with a caveat. While Bill C–31 sought to correct some of the deficiencies of Bill C–47 and to bring finality to the lingering injustices associated with the administration of the *Indian Act* as regards Indian status and band membership, it also sought to rein in the scope of reinstatements and the related fiscal complications for government.

The result, compounded by a late attempt to add in new powers for bands over membership, is a complex compromise that has produced a number of anomalies based on the division of status Indians into two categories: section 6(1) Indi-ans and section 6(2) Indians, as well as introducing the notion of non-status band members and status non-member Indians.

The C–31 Regime and Indian Status

Subsection 6(1)(a) of the *Indian Act* recognizes that all those persons who were already registered or entitled to registration as "Indians" when Bill C–31 came into force on April 17, 1985 will continue to have Indian status. These are the "old status" Indians, those who were status Indians under the old rules.

In addition, subsection 6(1)(b) recognizes that anyone who is a member of a group that is declared to be a band under the *Indian Act* after April 17, 1985 will also have status. There have been no new bands created since 1984,[84] how-ever, and the effect of this latter provision is minimal.

Subsections 6(1)(c)(d)(e) and (f) and 6(2) register a number of subcatego-ries of people who had earlier lost or been denied status through operation of the *Indian Act*. These are the "new status" Indians, also known as the "Bill C–31s." There are two types of new status Indians: those who re-acquired status after having lost it prior to 1985, and those who acquired status for the first time as a result of Bill C–31. Of the 115,000 new status Indians reinstated at the end of 1999, around 23,000 fall into the first category, with the remaining 92,000 fall-ing into the latter.[85]

Subsection 6(1)(f) and 6(2) also serve to define who will be a status Indian in future. Thus, subsection 6(1) registers those who lost or were denied status as a result of:

- the "double mother" rule;

- having married a non-Indian man;

- having been the child of a non-Indian man and a woman who was a status Indian at the time of birth;

- enfranchisement, voluntary and involuntary; and

- the first-generation children of the above.

The overall effect of these amendments, aside from the reinstatements to Indian status, was that henceforth no one would gain or lose status through marriage. Non-Indian women who gained status through marriage prior to 1985 will nonetheless retain their acquired status. Enfranchisement as a concept was entirely abolished—there is now no apparent way for a status Indian to renounce status. Status may yet be lost as a result of marriage, however, since it is clear under the new rules that for status to be passed on, marriages must produce children who fit into the definition section for status in section 6.

Since there is no difference in this respect between status Indian men and women, the visible sex discrimination that was a feature of the pre-1985 rules has been removed. However, residual discrimination remains because the children of women who married out of the *Indian Act* prior to 1985 will be disadvantaged in their capacity to transmit status entitlements to their children, in contrast to the children of male Indians, who are assured both status and acquired rights to membership under the legislation.

This results from the distinction between those persons falling into subsections 6(1) and those who fall into subsection 6(2). Subsection 6(1)(f) registers all those persons whose parents (living or dead) were both registered or entitled to be registered under *either* subsection 6(1) or (2). Subsection 6(2) registers the child of *one* parent (living or dead) who was registered or entitled to registration under *only* subsection 6(1). As will be illustrated below, this will usually be the child of an Indian woman who married out prior to the 1985 amendments. The differences between 6(1) and 6(2) status Indians lies in their relative abilities to pass that status on to future generation, and it is here where the effects of the prior discrimination are felt.

For the grandchildren of the present generation of "old status" or "new status" Indians, the manner in which one's parents and grandparents acquired status will be important determinants of whether they will have status themselves.[86] The net result of the new rules is that by the third generation, the effects of the 6(1)/6(2) distinction will be most clearly felt. The following diagram shows how transmission of status works under these categories:

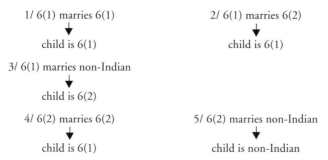

1/ 6(1) marries 6(1)
↓
child is 6(1)

2/ 6(1) marries 6(2)
↓
child is 6(1)

3/ 6(1) marries non-Indian
↓
child is 6(2)

4/ 6(2) marries 6(2)
↓
child is 6(1)

5/ 6(2) marries non-Indian
↓
child is non-Indian

Thus, it is clear that the children of a 6(2) parent are penalized immediately if the 6(2) parent marries out, while the children of 6(1) parents are not. Thus, who the children marry will be crucial in determining whether status will be passed on to future generations, since there is a definite disadvantage to falling into the 6(2) category.

If one assumes that a status Indian brother and his status Indian sister both marry non-Indians, the example becomes clearer. The children of the sister who married out prior to the 1985 amendments will be "new status" since they all fall into the 6(2) category at the outset because they will only have one parent (their mother) who was registered or entitled to registration under Bill C–31. The children of the brother who married out prior to the 1985 amendments will be "old status" because both their parents already had status on April 17, 1985. They will therefore be 6(1)s and will start off with an advantage over their similarly situated 6(2) cousins in terms of status transmission.

But, it must be recalled, this has nothing to do with actual Indian ancestry, since the 6(1) and 6(2) children discussed above will have exactly the same degree of Indian ancestry. They will each have one ethnological Indian parent and one non-ethnological Indian parent. At the root of it is the legal fiction whereby the children of the status Indian man who married out had status, while the children of the status Indian woman who married out did not. Thus, the effect of the pre-1985 discriminatory status rules continue to discriminate against Indian women, but the effects are simply postponed to the subsequent generations unless the 6(2) child marries someone within the 6(1)/6(2) categories.

In short, this aspect of Bill C–31 means that for 6(1) Indians, after two consecutive generations of marrying out, Indian status will be lost. For 6(2) Indians, only one generation of out-marriage will do the trick. As Harry Daniels, former president of the Congress of Aboriginal Peoples notes, "The new rules obviously place tremendous pressure on existing Status Indian communities to take steps to maintain the 'racial' purity of their community and to discourage unions with Non-Status Partners."[87]

There is another and related anomaly in the new rules with respect to how illegitimate children are treated. In 1983 the Supreme Court held in *Martin* v. *Chapman*[88] that the illegitimate child of a status Indian man and a non-Indian woman would also have status. The illegitimate children of a status Indian woman and a non-Indian, however, would not. Although the child of the latter union will now have status, it will be "new status" as a 6(2), while the child of the former union will be "old status" as a 6(1).

Some Indian communities have maintained that as a result, children of non-Aboriginal ancestry adopted by "old status" Indians—and therefore 6(1)s—have greater rights than children of Indian ancestry reinstated or registered under Bill C–31. In short, children with no Indian ancestry whatsoever will have greater rights to pass on Indian status than children who may have a high degree of Indian ancestry.

Another problem lies in the unequal treatment of members of the same family. For example, in an "old status" family where a non-Indian wife gained s through marriage to a status Indian man prior to 1985, if the husband enfranchised under the pre-1985 rules she and any children of the marriage would also have been enfranchised. Under the post-1985 rules, the husband and those children would have regained their Indian status under section 6(1)(d). Those children would therefore be 6(1)s.

The non-Indian wife, however, would not regain Indian status under the 1985 rules because section 7(1)(a) specifically bars women who had gained status only through marriage under former section 11(i)(f) from regaining their status if they had lost it prior to the 1985 amendments. Nonetheless, any children born to her and her husband during the period when the family was without Indian status would gain Indian status. However, unlike the children born prior to enfranchisement, the later-born children would be first-time registrants. Since only one of their parents (the father) is registerable under the post-1985 rules, they would be 6(2)s. Thus, siblings could have different abilities in law to pass on status, despite being from the same family and with exactly the same degree of Indian ancestry.

It is plain that the 1985 status rules are complex. The many problems associated with their implementation have been well-documented and will not be repeated here except to note that the financial and other aid necessary for existing bands to be able to accommodate the new registrations under Bill C–31 has not necessarily been forthcoming. Bands are left, therefore, with little incentive to admit these potential new members to their reserve communities.

Band Membership

From 1951 to 1985, status and band membership went hand in hand, with only a very few exceptions. Bill C–31 also changed the band membership rules in the *Indian Act* by separating status from band membership so that one may now have Indian status without band membership or band membership without Indian status. Bill C–31 grants automatic band membership to some classes of status Indians, but not to others. Subject to what the bands do with regard to band membership rules, eight classes of persons have automatic band membership while another five classes of persons have conditional band membership.[89]

A band may now take control of its own membership from the Department of Indian and Northern Affairs (INAC) by following the procedures set out in Bill C–31. These procedures call for band membership rules that respect the rights of those reinstated persons with acquired rights to membership prior to the band taking control of its membership. Band membership rules must be adopted by a majority vote of the band's electors.

Band membership rules take effect from the date that notice is sent to the Minister, who must approve it if it is in proper form. That date could be any time after Bill C–31 entered into force on April 17, 1985. Those with an automatic right to band membership in a particular band will be members if they have been reinstated to status prior to the date the band takes control of its membership. If they are reinstated to status after that date, they must then apply to the band for membership, since *Indian Act* rules will no longer apply and their automatic right will no longer be operative.

Persons with conditional band membership, however, had to wait two years before knowing whether they would become members of a particular band. Bill C–31 gave bands until June 28, 1987 to adopt band membership rules that might exclude conditional members. If a band had not done so by that date, then conditional members became band members automatically on the date they had been entitled to status. The mere adoption of restrictive band membership rules prior to that date is insufficient to exclude conditional members if the Minister has not been notified in accordance with the *Act*.[90]

The gist of the new band membership provisions in Bill C–31 is that there is really only one class of status Indians who had no doubts about their band membership after 1985: old status Indians who were band members immediately prior to Bill C–31 coming into force in 1985. Whether Bill C–31 Indians acquired band membership depended on when they acquired or re-acquired their Indian status in relation to when the band may have adopted its own band membership rules. As Harry Daniels put it: "The thrust of the legislation was clear: Bands, if they so chose, could exclude C–31 Indians—and above all the children of formerly "enfranchised" Indians—from membership in their Band."[91] There are several cases ongoing in which reinstated Indians are challenging their bands' refusal to admit them to membership.[92]

There is no requirement that band membership rules be published or otherwise made available for inspection, although they can be obtained by application under the federal *Access to Information Act*.[93] A bill to require publication was put forward in 1988 but died on the order paper when Parliament was dissolved in 1988, and a second effort to provide notice of such enactments through the *First Nations Gazette*, now published under the authority of the Indian Taxation Advisory Board, lapsed in 1997. It is therefore not easy to get information about band membership rules.

The Bill C–31 band membership provisions are as problematic as the Indian status rules. First, they do not deal with every person who has Indian status. For example, those on the pre-1985 General List of Indians without a band affiliation are not provided for. There were about one hundred persons on that list prior to Bill C–31. Such persons have no right to band membership, automatic or conditional, and must therefore apply to the council of a particular band for membership.

In addition, where a band has taken control of its membership, the only appeals from band decisions regarding membership are to whatever review mechanism the band has set up under its membership rules. The only judicial review of band decisions is for failure to follow the dictates of Bill C–31 or on general constitutional law principles. What this means is that unfairness may be built into the system so long as the formalities of Bill C–31 are followed. For this reason, the possibility that a band may wish to replicate the discriminatory features of the pre-1985 status and band membership rules cannot be discounted.

From this perspective, what the amendments in Bill C–31 have done is to transform the question of band membership from one of departmental control and sexual discrimination to one of band control and sexual discrimination. This assessment is borne out to some extent by a 1992 study commissioned by the Assembly of First Nations of the population impacts of Bill C–31. Of the 236 bands that had taken control of their membership, 49 had adopted membership codes with *Indian Act* status provisions. A further 97 had codes with eligibility criteria based on a specified blood quantum (normally 50 percent) or on the requirement that both parents have Indian blood. Only 90 had codes based on single-parent eligibility criteria.[94]

This puts the issue of membership firmly in the hands of the band council governments and, since most bands are small and rural, removes it from the daily scrutiny of the press and hence from public view. In a contest between Indian self-government powers and sex discrimination, it is not clear that the rights of individual women will be protected by the federal government or by the courts, since to do so might be viewed as interfering with the general trend in favour of Indian self-government. In at least one recent case where a woman had been automatically reinstated to band membership, the Department of Indian Affairs did nothing to assist her when the band council subsequently refused to allow her to vote in band elections.[95]

The American case of *Santa Clara Pueblo* v. *Martinez*[96] offers one example of how Canadian courts might deal with a contest between Indian self-government and Indian women's rights. In the *Martinez* decision, the adult children of Julia Martinez, whose husband was Navajo, were disqualified from membership in the Santa Clara Pueblo under a tribal membership ordinance that denied membership to the children of women (but not to the children of men) who married outside the tribe. Julia Martinez and one of her children sued the Pueblo, alleging sexual discrimination, and the United States federal courts took jurisdiction under the equal protection of law provision of the *Indian Civil Rights Act*[97] (federal legislation applying certain procedural rules to tribal government behaviour).

At trial, the judge applied a balancing test, finding that the tribal ordinance was a custom of long date to which he felt bound to defer. Judgement was granted for the Pueblo on the basis that it was best suited to arrive at the proper balance of interests between Pueblo cultural values and the protection of individual rights under the *Indian Civil Rights Act*.

On appeal, the court also applied a balancing test and found the opposite: the ordinance was of more modern origin and therefore not entitled to the same judicial deference. The balance was struck by the court in favour of Julia Martinez and her daughter and the trial decision was reversed.

The Supreme Court avoided the merits and decided on narrower procedural grounds. It refused to interfere because the sovereign immunity of tribes as extra-constitutional self-governing entities meant that such issues were for the tribal, not the federal, courts to decide.

The *Martinez* case is not in any way determinative of how such an issue would be handled in Canada. In American constitutional theory tribes are not bound by U.S. constitutional strictures, having never ratified the Constitution and being neither states nor federal territories or agencies. They are bound only by congressional legislation that applies to them, explicitly or implicitly, and by state legislation that Congress allows to apply in the absence of federal regulation of a particular area. Nonetheless, the *Martinez* case offers at least a hint about how Canadian courts may choose to deal with band or Indian First Nation sex discrimination issues should they arise in an approximately similar context.

As the U.S. Supreme Court did in *Martinez*, Canadian courts might choose to return an issue arising out of a band membership code that on its face is discriminatory to whatever Indian-controlled forum will exist in the future under whatever self-government regimes eventually emerge in Canada. This is likely not a prospect to which large numbers of Indian women in Canada look forward with enthusiasm. Nor is bringing such issues into the wider Canadian court system a prospect that the federal government necessarily regards with enthusiasm. To do so would bring into sharp relief two competing paradigms that have yet to be reconciled in the United States after more than 150 years of tribal self-government. Indian collective self-government and individual liberal democratic notions of sexual equality are somewhat ill-matched partners. The intertwining of these issues will pose an enormous challenge in the Canadian Aboriginal self-government context in the future.

Continuing Injustice

With the passage of Bill C–31 the federal government argued that it had addressed injustice by restoring Indian status and band membership to those unjustly deprived of them in the past. But injustice remains. First, not all persons of Indian ancestry were included. There are still many thousands of such persons—unrecognized "constitutional Indians" who are not registered as "legal Indians" under the *Indian Act* and who do not belong to recognized "legal Indian" communities. Many of these people have never been registered as Indians, while others may have been registered but have lost that registration for one reason or another and are challenging those decisions.[98] Many are the constituency of the Congress of Aboriginal Peoples.[99]

Second, the "two generation cut-off" effect may actually lead to decline in the number of registered Indians, despite the initial result of Bill C–31 of adding 115,000 people to the total population of registered Indians. This gain may soon be offset by the effects of the subsection 6(1)/6(2) distinction because Indian status may be lost after two successive generations of marriage between Indians and non-Indians. This is borne out by a 1992 study of band membership codes in which the authors conclude that their projections "suggest a declining Indian Register population beginning in roughly fifty years or two generations."[100]

Third, sex discrimination has not been eliminated by Bill C–31 because the effects of the earlier sex discrimination fall harder on Indian women and their descendants than on Indian men. Since "C–31 Indians" are drawn mostly from the ranks of formerly enfranchised Indian women and their descendants, they are also the ones bearing the brunt of the refusal of a considerable number of bands to accord them band membership and/or residency on the reserve.[101]

Fourth, band membership codes do not deal with every person who has Indian status. For example, those on the pre-1985 General List of Indians without a band affiliation are not provided for. There were about one hundred persons on that list prior to Bill C–31. There are now thousands of such persons. They have no right to band membership, automatic or conditional, and must therefore apply to the council of a particular band for membership.

Fifth, even where bands have been unable to exclude the new band members that Bill C–31 has added, other ways are sometimes found to exclude them from the benefits of band membership. In one case, a band discontinued per capita distributions to new members through an administrative arrangement with DIAND whereby the band operating budget was transferred from the capital to the revenue account. The revenue account was already under band control pursuant to section 69 of the *Indian Act*. Thus, using its section 69 power, the band simply stopped paying the new members after the administrative transfer.[102]

Finally, there are the injustices regarding how children are treated. Prior to 1985 the illegitimate child of a status Indian man and a non-Indian woman would have Indian status, while the illegitimate child of a status Indian woman and a non-Indian man would not. Although the latter will now have status, it will be under section 6(2), while the former will be under section 6(1). The anomaly is that non-Indian children legally adopted by "old status" Indians—who are therefore section 6(1) status Indians after 1985—may have greater rights than pre-1985 illegitimate children of Indian ancestry reinstated or registered under Bill C–31.

Moreover, adoptions are not treated equally under the new rules. Only pre-1985 legal, not custom, adoptions qualify according to a DIAND interpretive guideline issued in 1991. Thus, if a child, whether of Indian ancestry or not, was adopted by a registered Indian prior to 1985 under a custom adoption procedure, he or she will not be recognized under Bill C–31 as having any entitlement to Indian status.[103] The result is that legally adopted children with no Indian ancestry whatsoever may have greater rights to pass on Indian status than children who may have a high degree of Indian ancestry but who may have been illegitimate or adopted by way of custom prior to 1985.[104]

The *Corbiere* Case[105]

The Batchewana Band is located near Sault Ste Marie, Ontario and is a signatory to the Robinson Huron Treaty of 1850. The band received reserve lands, most of which it surrendered in 1859. Until 1952 the overall remaining reserve land base was too small for the band population, and a majority of band members was forced to live off the reserve. In 1952 a larger reserve was established, and by 1985 upwards of 68 percent of the band's members were on-reserve residents. However, the increase in band population from 543 to 1,426 due to Bill C–31 meant that after 1985, 68 percent of the membership was living off reserve.

From 1899 onward, Batchewana Band council elections have been governed by the *Indian Act* and its regulations. Prior to 1951, there was no requirement in the *Act* that members be reserve residents in order to vote. In 1951 the *Act* was revised to require that all "electors" be "ordinarily resident" on the reserve in order to be legally entitled to vote. Nonetheless, for several years non-resident band members continued to vote in band elections. After 1962 the residency requirement began to be enforced and off-reserve members were no longer able to participate in Batchewana Band elections or other procedures restricted to electors.

Although section 77(1) restricts voting rights to persons 18 years of age "ordinarily resident on the reserve," other provisions of the *Indian Act* make it clear that all band members, not just electors, are entitled to the benefits of band membership. This includes the right to reside on reserve and to share in band assets such as the proceeds of disposition of reserve lands and Indian monies held by the Crown for the band.

However, only electors may participate under section 39 in reserve land surrenders and designations or elect the band council that makes decisions under sections 64 and 66 of the *Act* to distribute band capital and revenue monies respectively. Bands operating under custom pursuant to section 2 of the *Indian Act* need not restrict voting rights to on-reserve band members. About 60 percent of the 609 bands in Canada are custom bands, to which section 77 does not apply.[10] However, the Batchewana Band is not a custom band.

The *Corbiere* action began in 1990 in Federal Court and the judgement was released in 1991, upholding the plaintiff's challenge to the voting restriction in section 77(1) and the related provisions of Indian Band Election Regulations. The trial judge found that in so far as the asset management function of the Batchewana Band council was concerned, the voting restriction in section 77(1) breached the equality provision in section 15 of the *Charter* because it discriminated unjustifiably against off-reserve band members. His reasoning rested on the fact that off-reserve band members constituted a historically disadvantaged group meriting the protection of section 15 and that the residence of band members was an irrelevant personal characteristic upon which to base a distinction in voting rights. The imposition of a residency requirement for local government matters was upheld, but finding it impossible to sever the local government from the asset management functions, he was forced to strike down section 77(1) in its entirety. However, this decision was restricted to the Batchewana Band. Finally, he suspended the effect of his ruling until July 1, 1994 to give Canada time to make the appropriate modifications to the *Indian Act*.

This decision was appealed, and in 1996, the Federal Court of Appeal upheld the finding of general invalidity, but did not endorse the trial judge's distinction between local government and asset management functions because band councils serve all the band members, wherever they are located. The Court of Appeal also enlarged the grounds of discrimination from merely denying off-reserve members a say in asset management to denying them a right to participate in band life more generally.

Instead of striking down the subsection as the trial judge had done, the Federal Court of Appeal then used the doctrine of constitutional exemption so that the words in the subsection "and is ordinarily resident on the reserve" would not apply to the Batchewana Band. They would therefore continue to apply to all other bands (unless they brought separate actions to invoke *Charter* rights the way the Batchewana Band had done).[107] In sum, the Court of Appeal's remedy was to exempt a single band from section 77(1) while avoiding having to guide Parliament to legislate for a "split governance" model and simultaneously leaving it open to off-reserve members of other bands to apply for similar exemptions on a case-by-case basis or on the basis of section 35 Aboriginal or treaty rights.

An appeal by the Crown and Batchewana Band and a cross-appeal by the original plaintiffs was filed with the Supreme Court of Canada, which delivered its judgment in 1999. The Supreme Court was unanimous[108] in finding the words "and is ordinarily resident on the reserve" in section 77(1) of the *Indian Act* to be invalid for infringing the *Charter* section 15 equality rights of off-reserve band members. The Court also agreed that the federal government had not demonstrated that the complete denial of their voting rights was necessary to carry out the goal of this part of the *Indian Act* to restrict governance decisions to those most affected by them.[109] Thus, the offending words were struck down so that henceforth, section 77 should be read as if these words were not present.

Moreover, and unlike the lower courts, the Supreme Court did not confine its ruling only to the Batchewana Band. Instead, the Court ruled that the words were invalid across the board. What this means is that they will not apply to any band in Canada that uses the *Indian Act* election provisions for its band council elections. This involves some 269 bands, representing almost 50 percent of the total registered Indian population. However, the legal effect of the ruling was suspended by the Court for a further 18 months in order to allow the federal government to amend the *Indian Act* to reflect the Court's judgment by "developing an electoral process that will balance the rights of off-reserve and on-reserve band members."[110]

Initially, the federal government moved to meet the Court-imposed deadline in two ways. First, it introduced amendments to the Indian Band Council Election Regulations and the Indian Band Referendum Regulations. The proposed amendments provide for all band members to participate in referenda or in elections for the positions of chief and, with some exceptions, councillor. However, the regulations have not been able to address the issue of entitlement to nominate or run for the position of councillor since these are statutory matters that are not amenable to regulatory alteration and, moreover, are set out in provisions that were not directly held to be invalid in the Supreme Court's judgement in *Corbiere*.

The second way in which the government has announced its intention to respond to the *Corbiere* decision is by mounting a "longer-term" overhaul of the *Indian Act* election regime that would include either amendments to the *Indian Act* or the passage of alternative legislation. In the second session of the 37th Parliament, Bill C–7 was introduced (first reading) on October 9, 2002, in the same form as Bill C–61 of the first session, at date of prorogation.

On 14 June 2002, the Minister of Indian Affairs introduced Bill C–61 (the *First Nations Governance Act)* to meet this commitment. The *Act* (which technically died on the Order Paper on 16 September 2002 at prorogation) has been re-tabled as Bill C–7 on 9 October 2002. It empowers bands to establish their own leadership selection codes, financial management codes, and government administration codes in accordance with basic legislative standards. In this respect, ministerial and Governor in Council powers are considerably reduced, although fallback provisions including regulatory powers are provided where bands choose not to act. The *Act* also permits bands to aggregate for purposes of common governance, a feature that represents a new flexibility in Canada's official policy towards "subra-band" entities, and one not limited to already recognized Indian groups. At time of writing, the Bill was just entering the committee process prior to second reading, which signals in advance the tolerance of the government for substantive amendments before it reaches final approval in the House of Commons.

This process began in early 2001 with the goal of consulting with First Nation members and with national representative organizations, including the Assembly of First Nations, Congress of Aboriginal Peoples, National Aboriginal Women's Association, Native Women's Association of Canada, regional First Nation (band-based) groups, and affiliates of other national groups.

Regardless of the federal response, the legal situation is clear. At the expiry of the eighteen-month period, as of November 20, 2000, the ruling took effect and off-reserve band members across the country have been able to participate in band council elections under the *Indian Act*. It is likely that this will meet with significant resistance from some bands, particularly those that have relatively large off-reserve band membership.

The potential implications of the *Corbiere* decision on other areas of the *Indian Act* cannot be ignored. Electors participate directly in decisions other than band council elections such as surrenders and reserve land designations (section 39). Moreover, the band council elected by the electors also makes important decisions that affect the financial resources of the band (distribution of capital and revenue band monies in sections 64 and 69[111]). In the same way, the band council passes the by-laws that regulate reserve residence.[112] In these and other ways the issue of who is an elector is crucial to decisions that will ultimately affect all band members, whether they are able to vote in band council elections or not.

Another generation of *Charter* section 15 legal challenges may be expected in the wake of *Corbiere*. Those who may have been denied status, band membership, or reserve residency rights as a result of the passage into law of Bill C–31 in 1985 may be encouraged to continue the dismantling of the *Indian Act* structures that have been built on such fragile policy foundations. The sheer volume of equality issues tied up in the *Indian Act* may be such as to prevent limited amendments of the type called for by the Court in *Corbiere*. If so, the administrative regime established by the *Act* and financed through INAC may well begin to crumble in the ensuing decades in the face of this anticipated litigation. Ironically, if the population projections referred to earlier are accurate,[113] by then there may be few status Indians left and the entire landscape of federal government/First Nations relations that has been built on the basis of the status–non-status distinction so carefully maintained through Bill C–31 will have changed beyond recognition.

In conclusion, this canvassing of the *Indian Act* regime for recognition of Indian people, as collectivities and as individuals, underscores the challenge yet to be grappled with in Canada: to design a principled and defensible recognition policy or statutory regime that extends to all three of the Aboriginal peoples of Canada, Indian, Inuit, and Métis.

Notes

[1] *The Queen and Batchewana Band* v. *Corbiere et al.,* [1999] 3 C.N.L.R. 19 (S.C.C.). As discussed later, the recently tabled *First Nations Governance Act* (Bill C–7, introduced on 9 October 2002, see *infra* note 34) will not alter the basic *Indian Act* scheme of collective or individual recognition.

[2] *Re Eskimos*, [1939] S.C.R. 104. This is why the Inuit were explicitly excluded from the *Indian Act* when it was revised in 1951. Otherwise they would be required to be organized in bands and would have to conform to the definition of Indian under the *Act*.

[3] See Canada, *Report of the Royal Commission on Aboriginal Peoples: Restructuring the Relationship,* vol. 4 (Ottawa, Supply and Services Canada, 1996) at 295 and sources cited in notes 62–64 therein for the argument that the term "Indians" in s. 91(24) refers to the same peoples called "Indians, Inuit and Métis" in s. 35. The federal Department of Justice is reported to have sought a number of legal opinions on the matter in the early 1980s in the course of constitutional talks required under s. 37 of the *Constitution Act, 1982.* According to sources known to both authors, opinion among Justice Department lawyers was divided. Ultimately, Canada chose to accept the view that Métis are not "Indians" for constitutional purposes. At the time of preparing this paper, this is the position maintained by the federal government.

[4] *A.G. Canada* v. *Canard,* [1976] 1 S.C.R. 170 at 207.

[5] The term "Indianness" has arisen through a series of cases dealing with the extent to which Indians living on federally protected Indian reserves may be regulated by the laws of the province in which the reserves are located. Indianness refers to "the essential characteristics of a people as Indian people": Jack Woodward, *Native Law* (Toronto: Carswell, 1989) at 122. Unlike the case in American constitutional theory, under Canadian constitutional law Indian reserves are not enclaves of exclusive federal jurisdiction: *Cardinal* v. *The Queen,* [1974] S.C.R. 695. The modern rule about the extent to which provincial laws of general application that are not referentially incorporated into federal law may affect Indianness was authoritatively stated in *Dick* v. *The Queen* (1985) 23 D.L.R. (4th) 33 at 57: "[provincial] laws which had crossed the line of general application were laws which, either overtly or colourably, single out Indians for special treatment and impair their status as Indians." On this basis, only if a generally applicable provincial law impairs the status of an Indian is it constitutionally invalid. Beyond these kinds of statements, the essential characteristics of Indians, their

"Indianness," have yet to be authoritatively set out by the courts and remain the subject of speculation.

[6]*Delgamuukw* v. *British Columbia*, [1998] 1 C.N.L.R. 14 at 83.

[7]That being said, it is arguable that the mere finding of federal legislative jurisdiction means very little since traditional approaches to constitutional interpretation note that Parliament is not compelled to exercise its constitutional jurisdiction. Thus, Canada has never treated Inuit as it has treated Indians, and has dealt with them largely as northern residents. They have never been subject to the *Indian Act*, have not been organized in bands of "status Inuit," and have never been provided with reserves. Moreover, even if Parliament does choose to exercise jurisdiction, it is not necessarily required to exercise it to the fullest possible extent or in exactly the same way with regard to all those that fall under its legislative authority. *Charter* s. 15, with its guarantee of equal treatment before the law, provides a strong challenge to this line of reasoning, however. Current understandings of s. 15 indicate that it may well be necessary that the federal government treat similarly situated Aboriginal persons in similar ways. Thus, if Métis and non-status Indians were found to be within s. 91(24) federal constitutional jurisdiction, it may well be necessary to extend a similar range of federal programs and services to them. Of even more significance is the possibility that the federal government may be obliged to provide a similar range of programs and services to Métis and non-status Indians who are similarly situated to status Indians and bands even in the absence of a finding of s. 91(24) constitutional jurisdiction over the former. For fuller discussions of this point, see *infra* c. 5 and 7. The SCC will hear the appeal in the *Powley* case in 2003, in which the existence of Métis Aboriginal rights protected by s. 35 is in issue.

[8]*Indian Act*, R.S.C., 1985, c. 6., see s. 6–7. Under s. 5(1) of the *Indian Act*, an Indian is a person "who is entitled to be registered as an Indian under this Act." Thus, a person need not be registered to be an Indian—it is sufficient if he or she is entitled to be registered.

[9]This is not to say that *individual* Aboriginal persons who identify themselves as either non-status Indian or as Métis may not access these programs and services or participate in rights-based policies. No matter how an Aboriginal person is identified, he or she may nonetheless be eligible for Indian-specific programs and services if they are able to meet the current definition of Indian under the *Indian Act*. Moreover, since rights-based policies and processes under s. 35 have their origins in Imperial common law, the presence or absence of federal recognition under the *Indian Act* is constitutionally irrelevant. If a non-status Indian or Métis person can show a substantial connection to a rights-bearing Indian or Inuit community, he or she may participate in the policy or process as a member of that community regardless of eligibility for Indian status under the *Indian Act* or for formal membership in the federally recognized Inuit community.

[10]It cannot be for all purposes since the federal government provides an array of pan-Aboriginal programs and services to off-reserve Aboriginal peoples either directly or indirectly through the provinces. Whether these programs and services constitute federal recognition of at least an obligation to Aboriginal people more generally, and whether they leave the federal government open to equality challenges under *Charter* s. 15 are open questions.

[11]S. 4.1. This informal use of the term "deemed Indian" should not be confused with the technical use in s. 6(3) of the *Indian Act* in connection with deceased Indians.

[12]This litigation is managed by the Department of Indian Affairs through the Litigation Management Branch. Precise information about the nature, scope, and amount of litigation is not readily available to the public.

[13]*Supra* note 2.

[14]The provision in the current version of the *Indian Act* [R.S.C. 1985, c. I–5] reads as follows:

> s.4(1) A reference in this Act to an Indian does not include any person of the race of aborigines commonly referred to as Inuit.

[15]The current *Northwest Territories Fishery Regulations,* C.R.C. 1978, c. 847, refers to "an Indian, Inuk or person of mixed blood." In previous versions, however, the reference to Inuk blood was much more direct: an Inuk had to be someone of at least one-quarter Inuk blood.

[16]Department of Indian Affairs and Northern Development, "Identification and registration of Indian and Inuit People," information document provided to RCAP, June 1993, at iv.

[17]This may mean that only the beneficiaries of Inuit claims settlements will in the future be accorded "Inuit" status. In Labrador, for instance, the Labrador Inuit Association (LIA) restricts access to certain federal program benefits to its membership. However, LIA membership is a sub-group of the potential land claim beneficiary population of Inuit descendants which includes a geographically distinct group of mixed-blood persons. This group styles itself the Labrador Métis Nation (LMN) and its members live in two dozen communities in central and southern Labrador. Many LMN members would be entitled to LIA beneficiary entitlements but for their residence in these southern communities. The provincial government has recently recognized LMN members as being "Métis," including changes to their Museums policy and signing a forestry management agreement, while earlier administrations had argued that as Inuit descendants their entitlements under s. 35 are entirely up to the LIA.

The federal position has yet to solidify. Since 1995, successive Ministers of Fisheries and Oceans have been unable to conclude an Aboriginal fisheries management arrangement with the LMN, despite having done (and doing) so with other non-status and/or Métis in Atlantic Canada, and despite treating the LMN as an Aboriginal organization for other purposes, including representative organizational funding, Aboriginal Human Resources Development Strategy delivery agreements, membership as an Aboriginal body on the Board of the federally mandated Labrador Environmental Monitoring Institute, etc.

[18]S.C. 1876, c. 18, s. 3(e):

> Provided also that no half-breed in Manitoba who has shared in the distribution of half-breed lands shall be accounted an Indian; and that no half-breed head of a family (except the widow of an Indian or a half-breed who has already been admitted into treaty) shall, unless under very special circumstances, to be determined by the Superintendent-General or his agent, to be accounted an Indian, or entitled to be admitted into any Indian treaty.

[19]The amalgamation of this Métis community near Fort Frances into an existing Indian band has had the legal effect of recognizing that the individual members of the community are status Indians since, by definition under s. 2(1) of the *Indian Act*, a band is a "body of Indians."

[20]Many persons who might have been identified or have self-identified as being Métis did enter into a treaty relationship with Canada, but they did so as members of Indian bands due to their close association with the band and their choice to "take treaty" as an Indian and not to "take scrip" as a Métis. See Alexander Morris, *The Treaties of Canada with the Indians of Manitoba and the North-West Territories* (Toronto: Belfords, Clarke & Co., 1880; reprint Saskatoon: Fifth House, 1991). An argument has been made repeatedly since 1870 that s. 31 of the *Manitoba Act* is the memorial of part of a treaty made by Canada with the Métis. See Paul L.A.H. Chartrand, *Manitoba's Métis Settlement Scheme of 1870* (Saskatoon: University of Saskatchewan, 1991). The federal government resists this interpretation.

[21]For a fuller description of this process as well as a discussion of who the modern Métis may be, see Bradford Morse & John Giokas "Do The Métis Fall Within Section 91(24) of the *Constitution Act, 1867*" and Don McMahon & Fred Martin, "The Métis and 91(24): Is Inclusion the Issue?" in Royal Commission on Aboriginal Peoples, *Aboriginal Self-Government: Legal and Constitutional Issues* (Ottawa: Supply and Services Canada, 1995) 140, 282.

[22]See c. 3 for a full discussion of this issue.

[23]In Ontario, Métis were dealt with in three distinct ways. The Métis community at Fort Frances (now part of the Coochiching First Nation) signed an adhesion to Treaty 3 in 1873 as "half-breeds," not as Indians. However, at Fort Albany, other persons known to be "half-breeds" signed Treaty 9 as Indians. In another instance from Treaty 9, an established "half-breed" community at Moose Factory demanded Métis scrip and were then promised 160 acres each by the province, a promise that has yet, after over a century, to be implemented. See Shin Imai, *Aboriginal Law Handbook,* 2d ed. (Toronto: Carswell, 1999) at 86–97.

[24]The draft Metis Nation Accord and its approach to defining Métis is described in both Morse and Giokas and in McMahon and Martin, *supra* note 21.

[25]See Morse & Giokas, McMahon & Martin, *ibid.*, for a description of the legislation and the definitions of Métis in them. The Alberta approach to the eight Métis collectives it has recognized as settlements under provincial legislation has been similar to that employed by the federal government with respect to status Indian bands: the provision of a protected, collective land base with local, municipal-style government for members of the collective.

[26]A good description of the problem and process followed in the 1930s in Alberta regarding the Métis issue is provided by Fred Martin, "Federal and Provincial Responsibility in the Metis Settlements of Alberta" in David C. Hawkes, ed., *Aboriginal Peoples and Government Responsibility* (Ottawa: Carleton University Press, 1989) 243.

[27]International concepts of recognition are more fully considered later in this book, particularly in c. 4 and 6. It is convenient, however, to review some key points that are important to the discussion in this chapter.

[28]1933 Montevideo *Convention on the Rights and Duties of States.* For a discussion of these elements see Martin Dixon, *Textbook on International Law* (London: Blackstone Press Ltd., 1990) at 54–57.

[29]Thomas Buergenthal & Harold Maier, *Public International Law,* 2d ed. (St. Paul: West Publishing Co., 1990) at 196. One has only to think of the failure of the United States to formally recognize Communist China until many years after most other states had done so to see the truth in this statement. Buergenthal and Maier note (at 198) in this connection that "[r]ecognition has been used as a political tool by the United States government in the past...."

[30]Martin Dixon, *supra* note 28 at 52–53.

[31]R.S.C. 1985, appendix II, no. 1.

[32]*R.* v. *Sioui,* [1990] 1 S.C.R. 1025 at 1053.

[33]For example, the unrecognized Blackwater Band was discussed in the case of *The Queen* v. *Thomas Chevrier,* [1989] 1 C.N.L.R. 128.

[34]See Woodward, *Native Law, supra* note 5 at 395 *et seq.* for a review of these developments over the years. The government of Canada is also attempting to close the gap through its First Nation Governance legislation (tabled on 14 June 2002 as C–61 and reintroduced as Bill C–7 on 9 October 2002), which at s. 15 clarifies the legal capacity of bands as natural persons (but not as constituent or constitutional entities), a status that has been provided to date for Indian groups in optional legislative initiatives *(First Nations Lands Management Act)*

or in self-government agreements protected as treaty rights (as in the Nisga'a Final Agreement).

[35]For a description of these instruments see John Giokas, "The *Indian Act:* Evolution, Overview and Options for Amendment and Transition," Royal Commission on Aboriginal Peoples, *For Seven Generations: An Information Legacy of the Royal Commission on Aboriginal Peoples* (CD-Rom by Libraxus Inc., Ottawa, Canada, 1997) at 271–80.

[36]The Michel Band of Alberta (which enfranchised as a group in 1958) is prevented from filing a specific claim against Canada with regard to land surrenders that took place before the band enfranchised. See *10 Indian Claims Commission Proceedings* (1998) at 69: "Friends of the Michel Society Inquiry 1958 Enfranchisement Claim." The government tabled a bill on June 14, 2002 (C–60) to provide a validation, mediation, and negotiation alternative for *Indian Act* or former *Indian Act* bands seeking a resolution of claims for entitlement for lost lands, moneys, or treaty entitlements. It is not clear whether or not the Michel Band would be included in this definition.

[37]For the reasons discussed in note 9 *supra*, this restrictive approach to access to constitutional rights is likely doomed.

[38]The current Indian bands that are recognized through the *Indian Act* are nonetheless the successors (of fragments) of those Nations. The tribes and Nations mentioned in the *Royal Proclamation* were the original charter groups from which the contemporary bands are descended.

[39]For example, in 1972 the Big Trout Lake Band in northern Ontario was split into eight bands to recognize the fact that the band members had formed "satellite" bands in the region. See Imai, *supra* note 23 at 102.

[40]The matters dealt with in this portion of the chapter are considered in more detail in John Giokas, "The *Indian Act,*" *supra* note 35 at 14.

[41]A brief description of this period is provided by J.R. Miller, *Skyscrapers Hide the Heavens* (Toronto: University of Toronto Press, 1989) at 99–115.

[42]S.P.C. 1839, 2 Vict., c. 15.

[43]S.P.C. 1850, c. 42, s. V; S.P.C. 1850, c. 74, s. X.

[44]S.P.C. 1851, c. 59, s. II.

[45]S.C. 1857, c. 6.

[46]"Enfranchisement" referred, initially, to gaining full rights of a British subject, and the commensurate abandonment or loss of the "protection" associated with being an Indian under that statute.

[47]Compulsory enfranchisement for any Indian who became a doctor, lawyer, teacher, or clergyman was introduced in the *Indian Act* in 1876: S.C. 1876, c. 18, s. 86. Four years later an amendment removed the involuntary element: S.C. 1880, c. 28, s. 99. In 1884 another amendment removed the right of the band to refuse to consent to enfranchisement: S.C. 1884, c. 27, s. 16. Further amendments in 1918 allowed off-reserve Indians to enfranchise: S.C. 1918, c. 18, s. 6. In 1920 further amendments once again allowed compulsory enfranchisement: S.C. 1919–1920, c. 50, s. 3. This provision was repealed two years later (S.C. 1922, c. 26, s. 1) but reintroduced in modified form in 1933 (S.C. 1932–1933, c. 42, s. 7) and retained until 1951 when a modified form of compulsory enfranchisement was introduced: S.C. 1951, c. 29, s. 108(1). This was retained until 1961: S.C. 1960–1961, c. 9, s. 1. Compulsory enfranchisement of Indian women who married non-native, Métis, or unregistered Indian men was introduced in 1951: S.C. 1951, c. 29, s. 108(2). It was retained until repealed in 1985 by Bill C–31: R.S.C. 1985 (1st supp) c. 32, s. 20.

[48]The *Gradual Civilization Act* had a number of effects. First, it created a major inconsistency regarding the protection of Indian land by allowing the allotment of reserve land without going through the surrender procedure set out in the *Royal Proclamation of 1763*. Second, it marked a clear change in Indian policy since "civilization" was code for the eradication of Indian communities. This would occur with the gradual enfranchisement of the entire population and the erosion of the reserve land base in 50-acre increments. Third, it created a political crisis in colonial-Indian relations in Canada when the cooperative relationship between band councils and missionaries and humanitarian Indian agents broke down in acrimony and political action by Indians to see this *Act* repealed. Fourth, it was another step down the road of non-Indians determining who would be recognized as being an "Indian" because it set in motion a process by which persons of Indian descent, culture, and group affiliation could be removed from Indian communities and from the protected status that Indians enjoyed under imperial and colonial policy. Fifth, the *Act* reinforced the sexist definitions of "Indian" in the earlier 1850 Lower Canada legislation since enfranchisement of a man automatically enfranchised his wife and children. Sixth, the tone and goals of the *Act*, especially the enfranchisement provisions that asserted the presumed superiority of Euro-Canadian cultural traits, also accelerated the process of devaluing and undermining Indian identity and cultural values.

[49]S.C. 1860, c. 151.

[50]S.C. 1868, c. 42.

[51]S.C. 1869, c. 6.

[52]S.C. 1876, c. 18.

[53]S.C. 1951, c. 29.

[54]The 1951 *Indian Act* and its national "Registry" was rooted in part in the philosophy that racial or sub-national minorities could or should be defined legislatively, an idea that was motivated by both administrative pressures (e.g., to maintain financial accounts for minors and orphans alienated from their nascent groups) and then-prominent theories about the genetic grounding of enduring social/cultural boundaries (i.e., racism). The main architect of the 1951 *Indian Act* (Canada's first "Registrar" of Indians) was renowned for his self-proclaimed ability to "spot a half-breed at a quarter mile," and indeed his facility in this regard was tested after he ejected over 2,000 individuals from band lists in Alberta in the late 1930s, only to be overturned in some two-thirds of the cases by the courts.

[55]Woodward, *supra* note 5 at 153. The recently introduced *First Nations Governance Act* would remove many Governor in Council and ministerial powers, but not in relation to the statute's determination of status or membership entitlements.

[56]See Sally Weaver, *Making Canadian Indian Policy: The Hidden Agenda 1968–1970* (Toronto: University of Toronto Press, 1981).

[57]According to *The Concise Oxford Dictionary* (Oxford: Clarendon Press, 1964) ethnology is "the science of races and their relations to one another."

[58]R. Strickland *et al.,* eds., *Felix S. Cohen's Handbook of Federal Indian Law* (Charlottesville: The Michie Co. Law Publishers, 1982) at 19.

[59]*Supra* note 44.

[60]S.C. 1857, c. 6.

[61]S.C. 1869, c. 6.

[62]S.C. 1919–20, c. 26, s. 2.

[63]S.C. 1951, c. 29, s. 5.

[64]Linda Rayner writes as follows in "The Creation of 'Non-Status' Indian Population

by Federal Government Policy and Administration" (research paper prepared for the Native Council of Canada, 1978) at 6:

> ...It is believed that the band lists which formed the Indian register in 1951 were created in an apparently *ad hoc* manner. Such lists were to be based upon the band lists already in existence in the Department. The lists were to be posted "in a conspicuous place in the Superintendent's offices that serves the band or persons to whom the list relates and all other places where band notices are ordinarily displayed." The lists already in existence would presumably be treaty pay lists, band fund lists, and other lists of this type. Non-treaty areas (the Maritimes, northern Quebec, most of British Columbia, the Yukon, and the Northwest Territories where Treaties 8 and 11 remain unfulfilled) could very well have lacked adequate lists on which to base band lists. Further, in remote regions, or in regions where people still maintained a highly nomadic mode of subsistence, many could have been absent or simply never saw the lists posted in such "conspicuous" locations as the superintendent's office.

[65]John Leslie, *Assimilation, Integration or Termination? The Development of Canadian Indian Policy, 1943–1963* (Ottawa: Ph.D. Thesis, Carleton University, 1999) at 80.

[66]See Canada, *Report of the Royal Commission on Aboriginal Peoples: Looking Forward, Looking Back,* vol. 1 (Ottawa: Supply and Services Canada, 1996) at 312.

[67]Thus, although such a woman was no longer an *Indian Act* Indian, she could continue to receive some of the benefits associated with Indian status in so far as band benefits were concerned. For these purposes, prior to 1951 it had been the practice in some Indian agencies to issue so called "red tickets" to these women to identify them as entitled to share in band and treaty moneys. This practice was ended by amendment to the *Indian Act* in 1956 whereby these women were paid out in a lump sum and in that way put in the same situation as other Indian women who married out: S.C. 1956, c. 40, s. 6(2). See RCAP, *supra* note 66 at 301–2.

[68]S.C. 1951, c. 29, s. 108(2).

[69]*Ibid.,* s. 25. However, she would receive a portion of any treaty moneys to which her band might have been entitled as well as one per capita share of the capital and revenue moneys held by the federal government for the band.

[70]*A.G. Canada* v. *Lavell, Isaac* v. *Bedard*, 1974 S.C.R. 1349 at 1386.

[71]These figures are drawn from statistics obtained from the Department of Indian Affairs and reproduced in Kathleen Jamieson, *Indian Women and the Law in Canada: Citizens Minus* (Ottawa: Supply and Services Canada, 1978) at 64.

[72]*An Act to amend the Indian Act*, S.C. 1956, c. 40, cl. 26.

[73]Jamieson, *supra* note 71 at 62.

[74]*Supra* note 72, s. 3(2).

[75]S.C. 1960, c. 44.

[76][1970] S.C.R. 282. Joseph Drybones was acquitted of the charge under s. 94(b) of the 1952 *Indian Act* for being "intoxicated...off a reserve" because the *Indian Act* imposed a penalty on an Indian for doing something that would not necessarily have been an offence in the Northwest Territories for non-Indians.

[77]*Supra* note 70 at 1372.

[78]See *e.g.,* Ian Greene, *The Charter of Rights* (Toronto: James Lorimer & Co., 1989) at 28–29.

[79][1981] 2 H.R.L.J. 158, 68 I.L.R. 17. The case is discussed in A. Bayefsky, "The Human Rights Committee and the Case of Sandra Lovelace" (1982) 20 Can. Y.B. Int'l L. 244.

[80]The *Covenant on Civil and Political Rights* and the *Optional Protocol* entered into force in Canada on August 19, 1976. The Human Rights Committee established under the

Covenant is not a court, although its decisions may well have similar force to those issued by a court. See Martin Dixon, *supra* note 28 at 228–9.

[81]S. 27 reads as follows:

> In those states in which ethnic, religious or linguistic minorities exist, persons belonging to such minorities shall not be denied the right, in community with the other members of their group, to enjoy their own culture, to profess and practice their own religion, or to use their own language.

[82]Reported in Douglas Sanders, "The Renewal of Indian Status" in Bayefsky & Eberts, eds., *Equality Rights and the Canadian Charter of Rights and Freedoms* (Toronto: Carswell 1985) 529 at 549.

[83]Parliament of Canada, *Special Committee on Indian Self-Government: Indian Self-Government in Canada* (Ottawa: Ministry of Supply and Services, 1983).

[84]The Conne River Micmac community of Newfoundland was declared to be a band under the name Miawpukek Band on June 28, 1984 by order in council.

[85]*Bill C–31: The Abocide Bill*, online document of the Congress of Aboriginal Peoples (www.abo-peoples.org/programs) at 5–6. See also c. 3 note 91 *infra*. The total in September 2002 was 127,000.

[86]This was most graphically illustrated in *Landry* v. *Canada* (1996) 118 F.T.R 184, where the applicants, registered Indians, sought to prevent the DIAND Registrar from removing their names from the Indian register. They were the grandchildren and great grandchildren of Antonio Landry and Clothilde Metsalabanlette, and had regained status through their descent from them on the basis that they were both Indians. After it was discovered that Antonio Landry could not have been an Indian, the children of Antonio and Clothilde were reclassified as registerable under s. 6(2), not s. 6 (1). Therefore, they could not pass on Indian status to their own children, the grandchildren of Antonio and Clothilde. As the grandchildren and great-grandchildren of Antonio and Clothilde, the applicants therefore could not be registered as Indians under any provision of the *Indian Act*.

[87]*Bill C–31: The Abocide Bill, supra* note 85 at 5.

[88]*Martin* v. *Chapman*, [1983] 1 S.C.R. 365.

[89]The eight classes are:

- "Old status" band members, i.e., those already on a band list prior to 17 April 1985;
- "New band" members, i.e., members of groups declared to be bands after 17 April 1985;
- Persons regaining status under Bill C–31 who lost or were denied it due to:
  - the "double mother" rule,
  - marriage to a non-Indian,
  - illegitimate children of an Indian mother and non-Indian father,
  - involuntary enfranchisement due to marriage to a non-Indian, and
  - any children involuntarily enfranchised due to the involuntary enfranchisement of the mother;
- Children born after 17 April 1985 both of whose parents are members of the same band.

The five classes are:

- Anyone enfranchised voluntarily;
- Anyone enfranchised involuntarily for living outside Canada without permission for more than five years;

- Anyone enfranchised involuntarily for acquiring a university degree, or becoming a doctor, lawyer, or clergyman;
- A child whose parents belong to different bands;
- A child, only one of whose parents is, or was, entitled to be a member of a band.

[90]This is illustrated by *Gros-Louis* v. *Nation Huronne-Wendat* (1988) 24 F.T.R. 244 where the band adopted a restrictive band membership code on a band vote on June 18–20, 1988. The effect of the membership code was to exclude from membership children register-able as Indians only under s. 6(2). Because the Minister was not notified prior to June 28, 1988, their conditional band membership became absolute, however, despite the band membership code. In law, there was no band membership code prior to June 28, 1988.

[91]*Bill C–31: The Abocide Bill*, *supra* note 85 at 6.

[92]For example: *Poitras* (active), *Noade* (inactive), *Krahenbil* (active), *Huzar* (active), *Prince* (inactive), *Courtereille* (inactive), *Hodgson* (two cases, both active), and *Ward* (active).

[93]R.S.C. 1985, c. A–1, as confirmed in *Twinn* v. *Canada*, [1987] 3 F.C. 368 (F.C.T.D.).

[94]Stewart Clatworthy & Anthony Smith, "Population Implications of the 1985 Amendments to the Indian Act: Final Report," prepared for the Assembly of First Nations, December, 1992.

[95]*Scrimbatt* v. *Sakimay Indian Band Council*, [2000] 1 C.N.L.R. 205 (F.C.T.D.). Prior to the Sakimay Band taking control of its band membership in 1987, Ms. Scrimbatt was reinstated to Indian status and became a band member automatically. When the band took control of its membership on September 17, 1987, her name appeared on the list of members forwarded to the Department of Indian Affairs by the band. She moved onto the reserve some time later and participated in band council elections in 1991, but was not permitted to vote in subsequent elections because the band council adopted a policy excluding Bill C–31 members from voting. She brought the band to court on a judicial application review and the band was forced to rescind its policy and allow her to vote because of her automatic band membership. During the years in which she attempted to resolve the matter, she wrote at least twice to the Department and to the Minister and was advised each time to pursue the matter with the band because "Sakimay had exclusive control [and] DIAND and the Minister could not make changes to the membership list." (p. 211).

[96](1978) 436 U.S. 49.

[97]25 U.S.C. ss. 1301–1341. This legislation was passed by Congress in 1968. Among other things, it applies the language of the U.S. Bill of Rights—including the equal protection and due process provisions—to Indian tribes. This gives the U.S. federal courts a supervisory role regarding the functioning of tribal governments in much the same way that the Canadian Federal Court is able to supervise the functioning of band councils as was done in the *Scrimbatt* case, *supra* note 95.

[98]E.g., *Grunerud* (inactive).

[99]This could well be the situation of the descendants of Antonio Landry and Clothilde Metsabanlette, referred to in the case of *Landry* v. *Canada*, *supra* note 86. They are clearly descended from at least one Indian person and by their actions in bringing their legal action appear to believe themselves to be Indians.

[100]Clatworthy & Smith, *supra* note 94 at ii. They go on to note that "some First Nations, whose out-marriage rates are significantly higher than the national norms, would cease to exist at the end of the 100 year projection period."

[101]This is also shown by cases such as *Courtois* v. *Canada*, [1991] 1 C.N.L.R. 40, a

Canadian Human Rights Tribunal decision requiring the Minister of DIAND to ensure that the child of a reinstated female band member received an on-reserve education. In this case, two women had married non-Indian men prior to 1985 and lost their Indian status as a result. Following reinstatement under s. 6(1), they enrolled their children, registered under s.6(2), in the reserve school on the reserve where they were residing. The band subsequently decided to exclude all the s. 6(2) children from the school. As it turned out, these were all children of reinstated women who had married non-Indian men before 1985.

[102]*Martel* v. *Omeasoo* (1992) 58 F.T.R. 231. This case involves the Samson Band. The *Martel* case is now inactive as the band is making offers to the reinstatees offering them band membership provided they agree to relinquish their claims to any per capita distribution moneys owed to them. *Courtois* v. *Canada, ibid.,* is another example of the same tendency to use administrative means to deny band membership benefits to new members.

[103]This is the case with Graham Tuplin, whose father was adopted at infancy prior to the 1985 amendments that recognized custom adoptions from that point forward. Mr. Tuplin has been attempting to have himself registered as an Indian by virtue of the prior adoption of his father by the Lennox Island Band but has consistently been refused by the Registrar. Recently, the P.E.I. Supreme Court ruled that he was entitled to have the matter heard by way of *trial de novo: Graham Tuplin* v. *Registrar, Indian and Northern Affairs Canada,* [1999] 1 C.N.L.R. 268. Another case in which a child was adopted in accordance with custom but enfranchised by his father is going forward under the name of Johnson.

[104]The Samson Band is currently litigating to challenge the addition of adopted children to the band membership on the basis that the *Indian Act* definition of "parents" in s. 6(1)(f) does not include adoptive parents and the reference to "child" in s. 2 means infants or minors.

[105]*Supra* note 1.

[106]On the distinction between custom bands and other bands, see Shin Imai, *The Annotated Indian Act* (Toronto: Carswell, 2001).

[107]One of the reasons given by the Court for using the constitutional exemption approach was to preserve the ability of other bands to bring future actions based on their particular individual histories advancing a claim to exclude off-reserve band members as an Aboriginal right protected by s. 35 of the *Constitution Act, 1982.* This reasoning was based on recent Supreme Court jurisprudence on the assumption that such an argument might succeed if the claimant band could show that the right of excluding off-reserve members flowed from a pre-contact practice, custom, or tradition integral to the distinctive culture of the band.

[108]The Court split on the issue on how the legal analysis under *Charter* s. 15 should proceed. A majority (Justices McLachlin, Bastarache, Cory, Major, and Lamer) took one approach, while a minority (Justices l'Heureux-Dubé, Gonthier, Iacobucci, and Binnie) took another. However, all judges agreed with the result and so on this aspect the judgment is unanimous.

[109]*Supra* note 1 at 28–30 (the majority).

[110]*Ibid.* at 31.

[111]Although s. 69 refers explicitly to the band, in practice it is the band council that makes the revenue distribution decisions.

[112]S. 81(1)(p.1)

[113]Clatworthy & Smith, *supra* note 94.

Chapter Three

Who Are the Métis in Section 35?

A Review of the Law and Policy Relating to Métis and "Mixed-Blood" People in Canada

John Giokas & Paul L. A. H. Chartrand

> Nature has special blessings for hybrid people, the offspring of interracial procreation,... It will be seen, ... that conduct and lifestyle will be noted in terms of "halfbreeds[1] living the 'Indian way of life,'" in this dismally racist subject of litigation.
>
> Muldoon J. in *Sawridge Band* v. *Canada,* [1995] 4 C.N.L.R. 121 at 147

> Aboriginal peoples are not racial groups; rather they are organic political and cultural entities. Although contemporary Aboriginal groups stem historically from the original peoples of North America, they often have mixed genetic heritages and include individuals of varied ancestry. As organic political entities, they have the capacity to evolve over time and change their internal composition.
>
> *RCAP final report: Restructuring the Relationship,* vol. 2, part 1, c. 3 at 177

These two quotations illustrate the wide gulf that separates the views of Canadians about the identity of the Métis people. The judge's opinion reflects one broadly held view, even among Métis people themselves. The question of defining "the Métis people" has become very significant in Canadian law and policy since the enactment of section 35 of the *Constitution Act, 1982,* which expressly recognized the Métis people as one of the Aboriginal peoples of Canada. The RCAP quotation was meant to explain that the Constitution recognized the rights of a people, not the rights of a racial minority, which is the work of section 15 of the *Charter of Rights and Freedoms.*

At the policy and political level, the issue of defining the Métis for section 35 purposes illustrates the negative aspect of having secured constitutional recognition for a group of people with no formally defined or recognized land base[2] or territorial rights, and with few if any subsisting social or political institutions to maintain and define their group identity and interests. The high degree of personal integration by Aboriginal persons into general Canadian society adds to the challenge of definition. In effect, the newly recognized but undefined rights of the Métis people constitute a recently discovered interest or resource which is bound to attract competing claimants in the courtrooms of Canada.

A recent study revealed confusion about Aboriginal definitions, shifting identities over time, and a wide range of functional definitions used by government departments and organizations dealing with Aboriginal people. This study examined the results of the 1996 census[3] and reported the following:

- Just over a million (1,101,955) persons reported at least one Aboriginal ancestor.

- 779,790 persons identified themselves as an Aboriginal person.

- 451,000 registered Indians declared both Aboriginal origin and identity, while the 1996 Indian register contained 610,000 persons.

- 208,605 persons reported an Aboriginal mother tongue.

- Of persons who declared Aboriginal ancestry, 178,000 who are not recognized as status Indians identified as Métis.

- Within the last group, a further 26,000 status Indians also identified as Métis.

Law and Policy Relating to Métis and Mixed-blood People

The term "Métis" is generally viewed in Canada as referring to "in-between people"—those within neither of the two racial categories of Indian or White. Hence we have the English term "Half-breed"—half this and half that, and not enough of either to move into one or the other category.[4] The French term *métis* is "semantically more accurate because it does not carry the freight of a phony and damning folk biology...."[5] Nonetheless, meaning "mixed," it equally implies being in neither one nor the other category.

The challenge of definition is well set out by Judge Swail in *Blais*, a recent Manitoba case dealing with a descendent of the historic Red River Métis Nation who asserted hunting rights under section 35 of the *Constitution Act, 1982* and the *Natural Resources Transfer Agreement (NRTA).*

> The question of exactly who is a Métis within the meaning of this section of the *Constitution Act* is a difficult one. It is complicated by the fact that the term "Métis" has been used in different ways at different times. Even today, there is dispute as to the correct meaning of the term at any given period of history. It is further complicated by the fact that there are at least two distinct cultural backgrounds for the mixed blood people known today as Métis. There are the descendants of British (English and Scottish) "half-breeds" as they were originally known, who were the children of Hudson's Bay Company employees; and there were the original French Métis who, for the greater part, were the children of North West Company employees from Quebec.
>
> Another complicating factor is the evolution in the use of the term "Métis," which saw the government of Canada adopt a protocol by at least 1870 whereby all mixed-blood descendants of European and Indian people were referred to in official documents in English as "half-breeds," and in official documents in French as "Métis." Beyond this, the question of who is or is not a Métis has been highly politicized by some fairly disparate organizations claiming to speak for the Métis of today.
>
> A further, final complicating factor has been the change by the Government of Canada of the criteria for status as an Indian under the *Indian Act* in 1985. This apparently has resulted in a substantial number of people, who might otherwise have claimed status [sic] as a Métis, now taking status as Indians.[6]

As the foregoing passage notes, the central problem is that "the term Métis has been used in different ways at different times." Three of the ways in which the term has been used over time are mentioned. They are:

1. Associating English and French mixed-ancestry groups (from Rupert's Land) as if they were the same group;

2. Including other mixed-ancestry persons whose origins may have been far removed from the Red River and Rupert's Land Métis Nation;

3. Referring loosely to persons of mixed ancestry who may never have had Indian status, or who, having had status, may then have lost it through the status and enfranchisement rules in the *Indian Act*.

Each of these topics will be examined in order to illustrate the dilemma facing contemporary judges, policy makers, and politicians.

Associating English and French Mixed-ancestry Groups

There were two primary mixed-ancestry groups in the Red River area prior to the events that led to the entry of Manitoba into Confederation in 1870. The English-speaking Half-breeds or "country born" were largely Protestant, politically more conservative, more sedentary, more agriculture-oriented, and more closely attached to the Hudson's Bay Company as a governing and commercial entity. The largely Roman Catholic, French-speaking Métis, or *métif*,[7] on the other hand, were politically more independent and more inclined to trading and to buffalo hunting than to full-time agriculture.[8]

This is not to say that the Half-breeds did not participate in the buffalo hunt or that the Métis did not farm, for clearly both groups did both. Nor is it to say that there were not elements in each of the two groups that spoke each other's language and had other close social and commercial associations.[9] It is simply to say that despite the many shared cultural elements, the differences between the two mixed-ancestry groups were as obvious to outside observers as to the two groups themselves.[10] In fact, it is equally well-known that the resistance of the Métis to Canada's takeover of Rupert's Land was largely inspired, led, and carried out by the French-speaking Métis under Louis Riel.[11]

Nonetheless, the concessions given by Canada to the provisional government in the form of the *Manitoba Act* in 1870 applied to all the residents of the original province of Manitoba, including all mixed-ancestry persons.[12] The self-definition of these two groups as a "nation," and their ability to form a provisional government, establish civil order, and defend their territory through arms, as well as the fact that they obtained diplomatic recognition from Canada and constitutional recognition in the *Constitution Act, 1871,* fuels the perception both inside and outside the historic Red River and Rupert's Land Métis/Half-breed community that they were a single people.[13]

This was the beginning of the confounding of the terms Half-breed and Métis. Thus, in the English version of section 31 of the *Manitoba Act,* the reference is to "the Half-breed residents," while in the French version it is to "des Métis residants."[14] From that point on, references in Canadian legislation do not distinguish between what had at one time appeared to be two distinct groups of mixed-ancestry people. Thus the versions of the *Dominion Lands Act* passed subsequently, for instance, all referred to land grants to satisfy the claims of "Half-breeds" of Manitoba and the North-West Territory.[15]

As a result of this terminological protocol, no distinction is made today between the original Half-breeds and Métis. In *Blais,*[16] for instance, the accused descendent of the historic French-speaking Métis was referred to as being "Métis," as was the accused descendant of the English-speaking "Half-breeds" in the more recent *Howse* case[17] from British Columbia.

It should also be observed that, in any event, most of the western Canadian Métis now speak English. On this basis alone the original linguistic distinction no longer seems useful. Accordingly, all further references to Métis in this chapter will include both historic groups—those originally referred to as Métis, and those originally referred to as Half-breeds. However, the term Half-breed will also be used in reference to legal definitions, as this was the English term employed in much of the legislation and orders in council of the day.

Including Other Mixed-Ancestry Persons in Western and Northern Canada

The Métis of Red River and Rupert's Land developed their identity within economic niches of the fur trade system,[18] and by the mid nineteenth century lived a lifestyle involving elements drawn from both Indian and European cultures. They lived in settlements along the rivers in much the same way that the European and Canadian settlers did, farmed their river lots, traded, and worked as clerks or at other occupations associated with the settled communities in that part of Rupert's Land. They often received European education and religious instruction. They spoke European languages, English and French, along with Aboriginal languages, including *Michif* languages and *Bungi*.[19]

They, and particularly the French-speaking Métis, also used and occupied the plains freely on both sides of the border between Canada and the United States.[20] They engaged in great buffalo hunts, sometimes wintering far from their settlements. Many continued to intermarry with Indians and to engage in other aspects of the "Indian lifestyle." The result was a variety of styles of life and modes of commerce.

Writing in 1880, Manitoba Lieutenant Governor Alexander Morris noted three types of mixed-ancestry persons in Rupert's Land based on their lifestyles, cultures, and sense of who they were.

> The Half-breeds in the Territories are of three classes—1st, those who, as at St. Laurent, near Prince Albert, the Qu'Appelle Lakes and Edmonton, have their farms and homes; 2nd, those who are entirely identified with the Indians, living with them and speaking their language; 3rd, those who do not farm, but live after the habits of the Indians, by the pursuit of the buffalo and the chase.[21]

Red River and Rupert's Land Scrip-Takers

Because of these differences in lifestyle, culture, and self-identification among those of mixed ancestry, when the treaty commissioners entered Manitoba in 1871 to negotiate the first of what would become the eleven numbered treaties, "Half-breeds... entirely identified with the Indians, living with them and speaking their language" were allowed to take treaty as Indians. An amendment to the *Indian Act* in 1876 aimed to guard against individuals acquiring status in both Métis and Indian groups, by preventing recipients of Métis lands or scrip from registering as Indians.[22]

Those who had "their farms and homes" as well as those who lived "after the habits of the Indians" were offered scrip.[23]

In short, those who thought of themselves as Indian and lived the Indian lifestyle were treated by Canada as being Indians. Those who thought of themselves as different from Indians and who lived either the more settled European farming lifestyle or the more nomadic and seasonal Métis lifestyle were treated more in the way that the non-Aboriginal inhabitants were dealt with, at least as far as their land rights were concerned.[24]

Scrip was a certificate by means of which the federal government distributed Crown land on an individual basis to members of particular groups such as the original non-Aboriginal settlers in Manitoba, veterans of the 1885 Northwest Rebellion and the Boer War, officers of the North West Mounted Police, and mixed-ancestry persons.

The scrip offered to mixed-ancestry persons was of two types: land or money. The former was expressed as a certain amount of land denominated in acres, whereas the latter was expressed in a dollar amount that could then be exchanged for land.[25] In 1874 scrip was offered to the heads of the Métis families under the 1874 *Dominion Lands Act*[26] to supplement the land distribution scheme in the *Manitoba Act*.

In 1876, the *Indian Act* definitions of "Indian" and "non-treaty Indian" each required Indian blood. Non-treaty Indians, defined as members of an "irregular" band or those following an "Indian mode of life," were those who belonged to groups that had not entered into a treaty relationship with Canada.[27] The treaty-making process would continue until 1921, and afterwards in the form of adhesions, and Indian Branch officials needed some term with which to refer to those of Indian blood with whom Canada had not established a formal relationship.[28]

However, Indian blood alone was not the distinguishing characteristic of those Aboriginal people officially classified as being "Indians" and "non-treaty Indians," for by definition, Métis also possessed Indian blood. A legal distinction was required for official purposes, for otherwise Métis would arguably fall within the definition of Indian or non-treaty Indian.[29] Thus, the *Indian Act* also provided that "no half-breed in Manitoba who has shared in the distribution of half-breed lands shall be accounted an Indian."[30] And so began the second association, that connecting the term Métis with a land distribution scheme as opposed to descent from a particular socio-political group or historic nation.

There were problems with the administration of the land allotment provisions for Métis children in section 31 of the *Manitoba Act* as well as with the issuance of scrip to Métis heads of families after 1874.[31] The Royal Commission on Aboriginal Peoples (RCAP) refers to this process as a national disgrace, for reasons that increasingly well known.[32] In any event, within a relatively short time the Manitoba Métis were swamped by the tide of new arrivals from Ontario and elsewhere.[33] Many left Manitoba prior to receiving their land or their scrip, while others sold or otherwise disposed of theirs.[34] In this regard Chairman Street of the first Half-breed Scrip Commission reported:

> The scheme was to give each half breed head of a family 160 acres, and to each half breed child 240 acres, the intention being that they should settle upon the land and become farmers. There were long delays, however, in making the allotments and preparing the Crown grants of the land and in the result, the majority of the half breeds received little benefit from their allotments. Being poor and improvident, numbers of them sold their rights to speculators for a trifling sum and had spent the proceeds long before the grants were issued.[35]

The result was that by 1886, only about 15 percent of the approximately 10,000 Métis persons resident in Manitoba in 1870 had received and retained their land.[36] Those who left established themselves for the most part on the three areas mentioned by Alexander Morris: the Cypress Hills and Batoche-St. Laurent areas of Saskatchewan and in Alberta around Edmonton, Lesser Slave Lake, and in other smaller communities. With Canada's westward expansion, they too demanded that their land rights be dealt with, which Canada undertook to do beginning with the Street Commission mentioned above in 1885.

After 1885, Half-breed commissions devoted entirely to issuing land or money scrip to mixed-ancestry persons became a regular feature of the treaty-making process in western and northern Canada. Money scrip, which was instantly transferrable, was often issued in western and northern Canada in place of land scrip.[37] Between 1885 and 1921 a total of twelve Half-breed commissions allowed more than 13,200 scrip claims, two-thirds of which were for money scrip.[38]

Having taken land or money scrip, these mixed-ancestry persons and their families and descendants were explicitly barred from being considered to be Indians within the meaning of the *Indian Act* through successive versions of the *Act* until the 1985 revision, when the scrip bar was removed.[39]

The procedure was for the commissioners to examine the applicants to ensure that they were of mixed ancestry and had not already received scrip either in Manitoba or elsewhere in the North-West Territory.[40] As in the case of the earlier Manitoba Métis heads of family scrip issuance, many of the scrip certificates were disposed of quickly, leaving the original recipients landless. For instance, Mr. Justice Street reported that the very first person to receive scrip from his commission sold it on the spot for one-half its face value.[41]

Other Scrip-Takers

Not everyone who took scrip after 1885 was a member or descendant of the Métis of Red River or the other Métis communities in Rupert's Land mentioned by Lieutenant Governor Morris. Many were persons of mixed ancestry unconnected to the Red River and Rupert's Land Métis who were following what the *Indian Act* referred to as the "Indian mode of life."[42] Nor was mixed ancestry a characteristic that distinguished them from Indians. In an inquiry into this very issue a number of decades later, Alberta Justice MacDonald later commented:

> It is well-known that among the aboriginal inhabitants there were many individuals of mixed blood who were not properly speaking Halfbreeds. Persons of mixed blood who became identified with the Indians, lived with them, spoke their language and followed the Indian way of life were recognized as Indians. The fact that there was white blood in their veins was no bar to their admission into the Indian bands among whom they resided.[43]

As had occurred in Manitoba earlier, these mixed-ancestry persons were offered the choice of taking treaty as Indians or of taking Half-breed scrip. In defiance of any interpretation of the *Indian Act* that would have required "pure" Indian blood in order to be considered to be Indian, the courts recognized the legal consequences of having opted for Indian identity via the treaty process.

For example, in the 1894 North-West Territory case of *R.* v. *Howson*, a band member of mixed ancestry was convicted of being an Indian in possession of intoxicants contrary to the 1886 *Indian Act* alcohol prohibition in section 96. The *Indian Act* definition of an Indian as someone possessing "Indian blood" was held by the Court "to mean any person with Indian blood in his veins, and whether that blood is obtained from the father or mother." Going on, the Court noted that:

> It is notorious that there are persons in those bands who are not full blooded Indians, who are possessed of Caucasian blood, in many of whom the Caucasian blood largely predominates, but whose associations, habits, modes of life and surroundings generally are essentially Indian....[44]

However, other currents of thought were conspiring to overturn Canada's focus on lifestyle and self-identification with a view to cost-cutting and accommodating philosophies of assimilation. This was generally a period in the development of Canadian Indian policy when, after the North-West Rebellion, the emphasis was on reducing expenses in the Indian Branch, and of more actively promoting Sir John A. Macdonald's long-standing program of "civilizing" Indians by encouraging them to learn farming and trades, send their children to residential schools, and adopt local municipal-style band council government in reserve communities.[45]

In keeping with this approach, individual enfranchisement and assimilation was promoted, and the out-marriage rules of the *Indian Act* were permitted to disrupt the cohesiveness of Indian reserve communities in an attempt "to do away with the tribal system and assimilate the Indian people in all respects with the inhabitants of the Dominion, as speedily as they are fit for change...."[46]

Part of doing away with the tribal system and promoting individual economic self-sufficiency was to encourage mixed-ancestry persons who had taken treaty as Indians to withdraw and to take Half-breed scrip instead. With this in mind, the *Indian Act* was amended twice. The first amendment in 1879 would have required applicants for scrip to repay treaty annuity money received.[47] The second in 1884 removed this condition.[48] The 1885 Street Commission reported that, out of a total of 3,446 scrip claims allowed, over one-third (1,292) were issued to persons withdrawing from treaty. Another Half-breed commission one year later reported that of 349 claims allowed, fully 321 represented people leaving treaty to take scrip.[49]

The treaty and Half-breed commissions did not deal with everyone in western and northern Canada who was eligible either for treaty or scrip, and applications for both continued after 1921. At a certain point, the Indian Branch became concerned about the number of mixed-ancestry persons taking treaty as Indians. As a result of the late treaty adhesions in the Lesser Slave Lake area, for example, the local band lists were examined and over 600 people were discharged on the sole basis that they were of mixed ancestry.

The resulting furore led to an inquiry by Judge W. A. Macdonald of the Alberta District Court, who found that only around 200 of the discharged persons had taken scrip earlier and therefore merited discharge under *Indian Act* rules. The rest, in his view, ought to have been reinstated on the basis of the long-standing policy of giving mixed-ancestry persons who lived an Indian lifestyle the choice of taking treaty. Nonetheless, the Department reinstated only about a third of those that he recommended be returned to band membership.[50]

The net result of the issuance of scrip to mixed-ancestry persons living an Indian lifestyle who were not connected to the historic Red River Métis Nation or to the related Rupert's Land Métis communities mentioned by Lieutenant Governor Morris was to create a large population of persons of Aboriginal descent, culture, and lifestyle who were not recognized by Canada as being Indians and who therefore had no legal right to live as members of bands on Indian reserves.

Many of these people were found in the more northerly portions of the Prairie Provinces and in the Northwest Territories, where they continued to pursue a traditional wildlife-harvesting lifestyle in smaller family groups or as part of Aboriginal communities outside the formal reserve system. They might otherwise self-identify as, and be called, non-status Indians or non-treaty Indians. However, they are now often called Métis because they are associated with the land distribution system reflected by the use of scrip for money or alienable land.

Their essential "Indianness" and poor socio-economic conditions inspired Saskatchewan in the 1930s to press the federal government to reverse its policy and to reinstate these so-called Métis to Indian status.[51] Just the opposite approach was taken in Alberta. During the Ewing Commission hearings regarding the "Half-breed population" of the province of Alberta in 1935, Aboriginal witnesses made it clear that the majority of the most destitute "Half-breed/Métis" were "Indian through and through, except for the names, they are still Indian."[52] The Commission agreed, and took as its working definition of Half-breed/Métis "a person of mixed blood, white and Indian, who lives the life of the ordinary Indian...."[53]

The definition of Métis adopted in the 1938 *Metis Betterment Act* establishing the Métis colonies was somewhat broader,[54] but reverted in 1940 to a narrower definition requiring one-quarter Indian blood. The quarter-blood requirement remained in the *Act* until 1990[55] and effectively excluded the descendants of the Red River and Rupert's Land Métis whose Indian ancestors were usually too far removed in time to meet this requirement.[56]

The issue of Indian versus Métis identity has now re-emerged in a judicial context in a series of hunting and fishing cases from the Prairies. For example, in the recent *Morin and Daigneault* case from Saskatchewan the accused were the descendants of mixed-ancestry persons who took scrip and were characterized by counsel and by the Provincial Court as being Métis. Both accused persons had been charged with fishing without a licence. However, both were pursuing a traditional lifestyle as members of a northern Saskatchewan Aboriginal community that continued to live off the land. In discussing the heritage and self-description of the accused, the Court noted the following:

> Louis Morin... is the father of the accused Bruce Morin. While he is of mixed white and Indian blood, fitting the definition of Metis, he both called himself and considered himself to be a non-status or non-treaty Indian. All of the Metis witnesses, including the accused consider themselves as non-treaty Indians.[57]

The Provincial Court also noted that those who took scrip were virtually indistinguishable from those who took treaty. Furthermore, they took scrip to avoid being confined to reserves or restricted in how they lived their lives—in order to be "the boss of themselves"[58] as one of the accused put it, and not because of any sense of being markedly different from the Aboriginal people living the same lifestyle who took treaty as Indians.[59] On appeal, the lower court's finding was echoed by the Court of Queen's Bench.[60]

Similar observations emerge from other commentators[61] as well as in other cases from western Canada. In the *Ferguson* case from Alberta, for instance, the accused was descended from persons who took scrip, referred to by the Provincial Court as "half-breeds." However, Mr. Ferguson, who had been charged with hunting without a licence, was born and raised in an isolated northern Alberta Cree-speaking community that continued to follow what the Court referred to as "the Indian mode of life." In upholding his right under the *NRTA* to hunt as an Indian, the Court rested its conclusion on the fact that the accused's Indian lifestyle made him a "non-treaty Indian" under the 1927 *Indian Act,* notwithstanding that all four of his grandparents had taken scrip.[62]

The result of this and similar cases is that it is not entirely clear how people who were never part of the historic Red River or Rupert's Land Métis Nation would choose to describe themselves were they faced with the option to do so by official policy. Although often described by judges, government officials, and other Canadian citizens as being "Métis," it seems clear that this is a loose description based only on their mixed ancestry and a history of having taken scrip.

A good example is provided by the situation of the mixed-ancestry persons now resident in the area of Grande Cache in western Alberta. They are not descended from the Red River and Rupert's Land Métis; rather, they are the descendants of Iroquois, French Canadian, and other freemen who intermarried first with the local Aboriginal people and then increasingly among themselves.[63]

Living in a relatively isolated part of Alberta, this group was never confronted with the necessity of defining itself. Under the influence of Christian missionaries, a large number of these people established themselves at religious missions near Edmonton in the nineteenth century, adopted farming, took treaty as the Michel Band of Indians, and were assigned a reserve.[64] The others, many of whom took scrip, continued with their hunting and trapping lifestyle in the Grande Cache area until relatively recently.[65] Although usually described by outsiders as being Métis, in a famous incident in the early 1970s, Alberta Lieutenant-Governor Ralph Steinhauer "found them without a ready answer when he asked them if they were treaty Indians, non-status Indians or 'métis.'"[66] Since then, however, the increased contact between this group and outsiders has caused them to seek assistance by joining the Alberta Métis Association. However, commentators have stated that the Métis label has been something of a "flag of convenience" for them.

For the Grande Cache people, adopting a métis identity does not mean that they have lost sight of themselves as a distinct social group. Identifying themselves as métis achieves quite the opposite effect—it ensures their continued distinctiveness in a social, political and economic environment now dominated by Euro-Canadian immigrants. Of all possible identities, métis most closely fits the perceptions which outsiders have historically had of the group and is thus easily accepted by newcomers and government as a basis for interaction. It also perpetuates the distinctiveness from Indian social groups which characterized the freemen of the nineteenth century.[67]

It seems clear in retrospect that the legal distinction between the Grande Cache Métis and their relatives who became the Michel Band cannot have had anything to do with their relative degrees of Indian blood. Nor could their lifestyle have had much to do with the issue, for the group described as being Métis followed a more traditional "Indian" hunting and trapping lifestyle than did those who took treaty as Indians. The latter appear to have adopted farming as their primary means of livelihood.[68]

Thus, the only distinction between Metis and non-status Indians appears to be a legal one based on how Aboriginal people of mixed ancestry chose to address their Aboriginal land rights.[69] Nevertheless, this distinction can no longer be one in which federal authorities are able to repose much confidence. Increasingly scrip-takers and their descendants are challenging their characterization as "non-Indians" for *NRTA*[70] and related purposes and are finding judicial support.

In fact, if the trend of judicial rulings continues in this direction, it can no longer be assumed that scrip-takers do not have an actionable claim to restoration of Indian and band status as well as treaty and reserve land rights. This is shown by cases such as the recently consolidated actions in Federal Court by scrip-takers or their descendants in *Desjarlais, Gill, Malcolm, Pulliam,* and *Parenteau.* Scrip-takers and their descendants are now challenging the legality of the issuance of scrip and the resultant loss of status and treaty rights on the basis that Canada's actions in enticing them to take scrip were in breach of their treaty rights as well as instances of duress, undue influence, fraud, bribery, and *non-est factum.*[71]

Moreover, it also seems possible that scrip-takers and their descendants may be able to challenge the Indian status system on the basis that some scrip-takers and their descendants have been granted Indian status while others have not. There are many reasons why scrip-takers or their descendants may have been able to acquire band membership and, after 1951, Indian legal status, despite the *Indian Act* provision explicitly excluding them from Indian legislated status. One reason which is discussed below may have to do with the relatively lax record-keeping of the Department of Indian Affairs prior to the 1951 *Indian Act* revision.

In any event, in 1952 it became a matter of some notoriety across Canada that many persons with a history of scrip-taking had acquired Indian status despite the statutory bar mentioned earlier. That year the Samson Band of Alberta attempted to have 103 of its members removed because they or their ancestors had taken scrip. In 1954 these persons were ordered to be expelled from the band but, due to the resulting nation-wide furore, their band membership and Indian status were confirmed in 1957.[72]

Nor was this an isolated incident: other bands also attempted during this period to expel members they claimed were scrip-takers or their descendants.[73] Ultimately, the *Indian Act* was amended in 1958 to clarify that the statutory bar to scrip-takers having Indian legal status would not apply to anyone who already had Indian status as of August 13, 1958.[74]

This effectively ended the wave of attempted expulsions, but it created two classes of scrip-takers: those who were band members and status Indians prior to that date, and those who were not. Nor are the numbers of the latter insignificant. One commentator notes that "there is ample evidence that many of the First Nations across the prairies include people or descendants of people who took scrip."[75]

Including Persons Who Never Had or Who Lost Indian Status

As mentioned earlier, the requirement of Indian blood was part and parcel of the definition of "Indian" and "non-treaty Indian" from the first version of the *Indian Act* in 1876. The major exception was for non-Indian women who married Indian men and thereby acquired Indian status.

Over time, a variety of status and enfranchisement provisions found their way into the *Indian Act,* where they would remain in one form or another until the 1985 amendments in Bill C–31.[76] Their net effect was to cause large numbers of persons of Indian descent to lose Indian status and the right to reside in band communities on reserve land. The effects of these provisions fell more severely on Indian women and their children than they did on Indian men, especially after the 1951 revision of the *Act* and the renewed emphasis on enforcing the marrying-out and enfranchisement provisions.[77]

Many of the persons characterized as Métis or as non-status Indians in the hunting and fishing cases from the Prairies were persons with a clear Indian lifestyle, culture, and sense of self-identity whose mother had lost status through the marrying-out provisions in the *Indian Act*. In the *Laprise* case, for example, the accused, a "native of Chipewyan origin [who] lives in a predominantly Chipewyan community" (that was not a reserve) was not a status Indian because his "treaty Indian" mother had married a "non-treaty Indian."[78]

Persons Who Never Had Indian Status

By 1951 it was clear that reliance on an Indian blood requirement had been overtaken by events, as there were by then such large numbers of people of Indian blood who were not officially recognized as being Indian that the logic of the blood requirement had been undermined.[79] Nor was lifestyle, what the *Indian Act* referred to as following the "Indian mode of life,"[80] a determining criterion for Indian status. As the Prairie hunting and fishing cases cited earlier illustrate, there were, and continue to be, large numbers of scrip-takers and others who were not recognized as being "Indian" under the *Indian Act* despite the fact that they were of Indian descent, spoke Indian languages, and often lived on or adjacent to Indian reserves or in isolated wilderness areas where they pursued traditional Aboriginal lifestyles.

Thus, the *Indian Act* references to "Indian blood" and the Indian "mode of life" were replaced in 1951 by a new approach to defining who was and who was not an Indian. The new criterion became "entitlement" to be registered as an Indian on a central Indian registry to be maintained by the Department of Indian Affairs in Ottawa. Entitlement was based on meeting a number of criteria that essentially recapitulated the *status quo,* favouring descent through the male line, but with a greater degree of formality than had been the case earlier.[81]

The actual Indian registry was to consist of "Band Lists and General Lists."[82] Band lists were based on whatever lists were then available to develop a register, including informal band lists, treaty pay lists, and Indian census records, among others.[83] Prior to 1951 there was no well-organized or rigorously maintained manner of compiling such lists. The result was that the names of many Aboriginal persons who were considered by others and who considered themselves to be members of a particular band may not have been inscribed on the more informal band, treaty, and other lists when it came time to use them as the basis for drawing up the legislatively mandated band lists in 1951.

Two factors contributing to the imprecise record-keeping prior to 1951 may have been the very broad definitions of "Indian," "Irregular band," and "non-treaty Indian" in earlier versions of the *Indian Act*[84] and the loose supervision exercised by departmental officials in the field.

> These terms were so imprecise that agents had difficulty in sorting out conflicting claims concerning eligibility to reside on a reserve, to receive treaty benefits, and to obtain government social assistance. The situation was compounded by the lack of verifiable band membership lists, poor supervision of isolated reserves, and by Depres-

sion era conditions, which encouraged Indians to move from band to band seeking relief, or to return to the reserves from the city after years of absence. In many cases, government officials turned a blind eye to these practices out of humanitarian and other considerations.[85]

Another factor may have been the haste and attendant lack of diligence accompanying departmental efforts to compile formal band lists after 1951. Local Indian agents were required by law to post the new lists in a "conspicuous place"[86] where band members would be likely to see them so as to be able to comment on or correct them before they became official. As RCAP and others have noted, "The names of many people who ought to have been on the band lists or the general list were never added."[87]

Persons of Indian descent, culture, and lifestyle who considered themselves to be Indians and who, prior to 1951, were viewed as Indians either because they were members of "irregular bands" or were "non-treaty Indians" following an "Indian mode of life," often also found themselves unable to register as Indians for technical reasons. In the first place, they could not have their names entered on a band list for registration purposes because, under previous versions of the *Indian Act,* they were not "bands" as such. Rather, they were, as the name attests, "irregular" bands, and officials were not required to maintain up to date or accurate lists of the members of irregular bands.

Accordingly, there was no necessary list from which an irregular band list could have been drawn up. That did not mean, however, that these people could not be registered as Indians under the new system. They should have been able to be registered as status Indians on the general list.[88]

However, the term "General List" was not defined in the 1951 *Indian Act.* Thus there was no necessary statutory guidance to the registrar about whose names ought to be included on it. At that time it contained fewer than twenty names.[89] By the time the *Indian Act* was next revised to abolish the general list, thirty-four years later in 1985, it only had about a hundred names on it.[90] These relatively low numbers appear to give substance to RCAP's conclusions that all the eligible persons who ought to have been registered as Indians in 1951 were not included.

In short, irregular band members and non-treaty Indians do not appear to have been considered by the registrar in 1951 for inclusion on the band lists or on the general list and appear to have been largely ignored. The failure of the Indian Branch to include everyone of Indian descent had the effect of creating the category of persons loosely referred to as "non-status" Indians, that is, a population of people of Indian blood, affiliation, and often of Indian lifestyle who simply could not register as being Indian within the meaning of the *Indian Act.*

Persons Who Lost Indian Status

To this initial population of non-registered persons of Indian descent must be added the many thousands who had already lost, or who later lost, Indian status or were enfranchised pursuant to the provisions of the *Indian Act*. As mentioned earlier, large numbers of these people were Indian women who married out, or their descendants. After examining the available records, RCAP observed that "the number of enfranchisements, which had been relatively small in the century following the passage of the Gradual Civilization Act jumped markedly after 1951."[91]

Thus, by the time of the Bill C–31 *Indian Act* amendments in 1985, there was a large population of Aboriginal people who either had never had Indian status or, having at one time had status, had lost it under the pre-1985 rules in the *Indian Act*. As a result of the changes to the definition of eligibility for Indian legal status brought about by Bill C–31, approximately 112,500 people were returned to status or had received status for the first time by the end of 1999.[92]

It is to be noted, however, that scrip-takers and their descendants are not explicitly mentioned in the new criteria for registration as an Indian under the *Indian Act*.[93] This has created a large pool of status claimants who are currently classified as either non-status Indians or as Métis. The basis for their claim to Indian status lies in the absence after the 1985 amendments of any provision in the *Act* explicitly barring scrip-takers or their descendants from acquiring Indian status. This would suggest that they need only establish their eligibility for registration under one of the current registration provisions in section 6.[94] However, the Department of Indian Affairs registrar continues to apply the pre-1985 status rules.[95] It is impossible to estimate the numbers of potential status claimants affected by the continuing bar to status based on this interpretation of the new status entitlement provisions.

The Indian status rules are set out in subsections 6(1) and (2) of the 1985 version of the *Indian Act,* and are reviewed in chapter 5. Despite the addition of 112,500 people to the total population of registered Indians as a result of Bill C–31, it is generally accepted that the two-generation cutoff discussed earlier will inevitably lead to decline in the registered Indian population. This will likely mean a corresponding increase in the population of Aboriginal persons generally described as Métis or non-status Indian.

In short, the one-time status Indian population gain may soon be offset by the effects of the subsection 6(1)/6(2) distinction because Indian status may be lost after two successive generations of marriage between persons eligible for registration and persons who are not eligible for registration, whether or not these persons are of Aboriginal descent. As RCAP and other observers have noted, the

Bill C–31 status provisions, "like their historical predecessors, ...appear to continue the policy of assimilation in disguised but strengthened form."[96]

This is supported by a 1992 study of band membership codes whose authors conclude that if out-marriage rates increase at a moderate rate of 10 percent over forty years, their projections "suggest a declining Indian Register population beginning in roughly fifty years or two generations."[97] Evidently, this will mean an increased number of non-status Indians and a reduced number of status Indians. These conclusions are supported by more recent Department of Indian Affairs statistical data.[98]

It is evident from the above review that mixed ancestry, far from being the exception, is now the norm among the Aboriginal population of Canada. Historical policy decisions based on blood quantum, patrilineal descent, and a supposed connection between Indian lifestyle and membership in a recognized Indian band have created a large population of Aboriginal people in Canada who are not recognized as being Indian within the meaning of Canada's Indian-recognition system.

Unable to acquire Indian status and group recognition under the *Indian Act*, these are the people who often self-identify as Métis, as the mixed-ancestry groups from Grande Cache and Labrador have done, but not on account of descent from a group that historically identified itself and was recognized as Métis, but rather as a political vehicle for realizing their rights claims and related aspirations.

Mixed Ancestry Elsewhere in Canada

This review of the use of the term "Métis" has to this point concentrated on issues of identity arising in the West and North, the homeland of the Métis Nation associated with Louis Riel, because it was here that Canada's policies of recognition of Aboriginal peoples produced the best recorded and judicially examined results to date. RCAP devoted only a scant few pages to its consideration of what it referred to as the "other Métis" in its final report. It noted that "the history of Métis people who are not part of the Métis Nation is not easy to relate."[99]

The phenomenon of mixed Aboriginal and non-Aboriginal ancestry is common across Canada. However, due to the less structured and consistent Indian recognition and reserve-creation approach in Quebec and the Maritimes prior to Confederation, it is not possible in the absence of further research to know with clarity what official attitudes were to mixed-ancestry persons and how such persons may have organized and described themselves in the past.

Nor is it possible to know with certainty the extent to which identifiable communities of mixed-ancestry persons existed as communities as such as opposed to groupings of frontier families and were accorded some form of communal recognition as being Métis. Many commentators are of the view that it was only in the upper Great Lakes and Red River/Rupert's Land area that collective Métis social organizations with a sense of Métis national consciousness as such took hold. The editors of a special Métis edition of *Canadian Ethnic Studies* observe that:

> In eastern Canada communities distinct from both Indians and Euro-Canadians did not arise, and mixed-race people were defined as either Indian or White. Only in the fur trade areas of Rupert's Land and in the region of the Great Lakes did the "mixed-bloods" assume a distinctive ethnic identity—or, to be precise, two identities [English "Half-breed" and French "Métis"].[100]

Thus, although there were reserves in New France from 1637 onwards, there were only six until 1851, and as late as the 1970s most of the James Bay Cree were without reserves. Those that were created in Quebec after 1851 were often not inhabited until much later and had to be augmented by additional lands under Quebec legislation passed in 1922. From 1851 onwards there were various attempts by government and by the churches to persuade many Quebec Indian bands to move onto the reserves created for them instead of continuing their more nomadic harvesting lifestyles north of the St. Lawrence River.[101]

As a result of the sporadic and inconsistent approach and the reluctance of many Indians to conform to official desires to establish them on reserves, little is known about how mixed-ancestry people were defined, and whether and to what extent they were considered to be Indians. Some evidence of official attitudes is provided by an *Indian Act* amendment in 1880 confirming the right of "Half-breeds who are by the father's side either wholly or partly of Indian blood" to reside and hold property on the Kanawake reserve if they had been resident there for the prior twenty years.[102] Beyond scanty bits of information such as this, though, much remains to be discovered in connection with mixed-ancestry persons and groups in Quebec.

In the same way, reserve-creation policies in Nova Scotia, New Brunswick, and Prince Edward Island followed their own logic different from the model followed in Upper Canada prior to Confederation and the post-1867 national model imposed by Canada in the Prairies. Although official inquiries into Indian affairs were carried out in the three Maritime provinces, and while efforts were made to protect and to "civilize" the Indians there, the situation in those colonies was somewhat different.

Never protected by imperial authorities to the same extent as the western Indians, the relatively small Maritime Indian population was scattered and isolated and viewed by officials as being on the road to extinction. Moreover, Indian administration was decentralized and had no Indian department. There were therefore no allocations of imperial monies for Indians and their needs. Reserves were established for Indians by colonial authorities, according to one commentator, as a result of their petition or their sorry circumstances rather than from the policy of a central authority.[103]

As with Quebec, little is known about past policies regarding mixed-ancestry persons, although testimony collected by RCAP indicated that in New Brunswick at least, mixed-ancestry persons were included in treaties on an individual basis as beneficiaries until 1870.[104] After that, as elsewhere in Canada, the imposition of the *Indian Act* system led to the apparent marginalization of persons of Aboriginal ancestry who could not obtain band membership and Indian status.

Newfoundland and Labrador present a special case, insofar as there were no status Indian communities in the province until the 1985 recognition by the federal government of the Miawpukek Band at Conne River.[105] While it is clear that mixed-ancestry persons have been present, especially in Labrador, since contact, it also seems that these persons and communities have not historically identified themselves or been recognized as being Métis people. They live in about twenty communities in southern Labrador and are of mixed Inuit, Innu, and non-Aboriginal ancestry and have pursued traditional wildlife harvesting lifestyles, what the early versions of the *Indian Act* called the "Indian mode of life," since they first arose.

As with the Grande Cache mixed-ancestry group discussed earlier, RCAP notes that the people who now call themselves Labrador Métis have not been consistent in their use of the term.

> As the Labrador Métis Association brief suggests, communities of mixed-ancestry Labradorians did not always refer to themselves as Métis. That term has come into use recently in Labrador, chiefly since the inclusion of the word "Métis" in section 35 of the Constitution Act, 1982. Some members of the Métis Nation think it is not appropriate for the Labradorians to call themselves Métis now when they did not do so in the past. The position of the Labrador Métis Association and its members is that what counts is not the expression used—then or now—but the substance of their ancestry and identity.[106]

In Ontario, mixed-ancestry people were dealt with in several ways. The Métis community at Fort Frances, which is now part of the Coochiching First Nation, signed an adhesion to Treaty 3 in 1875 as "half-breeds."[107] It is not known why this mixed-ancestry group was allowed to enter treaty on a group basis while others in Ontario were prevented from doing the same. One commentator concludes that it was simply because federal government policy was to confine Métis land grants to the North-West Territory where the federal government had title to the ceded lands and therefore needed no provincial concurrence in land-related dealings with Aboriginal people.[108]

For instance, other mixed-ancestry persons and groups had been deliberately excluded from the earlier Robinson-Huron and Robinson Superior treaty processes and appear to have disappeared as identifiable mixed-ancestry communities. Some of their original members moved west into what is now Manitoba to form part of the Red River and Rupert's Land Métis Nation discussed earlier.[109] Others took treaty as members of Indian bands. The ancestor of the accused in *Powley,* for example, along with other members of the local community now claiming a Métis identity in court, became a member of the Batchewana Band following the signing of the Robinson-Huron Treaty in 1850.[110] Others joined the nearby Garden River Band.[111] Similarly, in the Treaty 9 area of northern Ontario, when the treaty commissioners visited Fort Albany, "they admitted 375 native people into treaty. Among these were over thirty "Half-breeds," who thereby gained Indian status.[112]

In another area of Treaty 9, however, the "Half-breeds" of Moose Factory were deliberately excluded from treaty rights on "grounds they were not living the Indian mode of life."[113] They demanded Métis scrip and were then promised 160 acres each by the province. This promise is yet to be fulfilled.[114] Another mixed-ancestry community at Burleigh Falls appears to have been comprised mainly of former members of the Curve Lake Mississauga First Nation who ran afoul of the status provisions in the *Indian Act*.[115] They seem to have been largely ignored until the 1985 *Indian Act* amendments, by which most have regained Indian status.[116]

In summary, and with the possible exception of parts of Ontario, what eastern Canada seems to show is a history of White-Indian relations that is much longer and marked less by the type of clear demarcations between groups that was demonstrated by the visible collision between peoples and cultures that occurred in western Canada. As Olive Dickason notes:

> The métis of the "Old Northwest" [Ohio Valley and Great Lakes area] were a short step away from the "New Nation." But it was a step that was never taken, as it was forestalled by the rush of settlement.
>
> Instead it was in the Far Northwest that a sense of separate identity finally crystallized. It was only there that appropriate conditions were found: isolation, slowness of settlement and the enduring importance of the fur trade. In this context, French-English rivalries encouraged the new spirit, contrary to what their effect had been in

the East. The fur trade allowed it to be born; the isolation, far from the pull-and-haul of intercolonial warfare... allowed it to develop. When settlers finally arrived at Red River in 1812, they were too few to overwhelm this spirit; instead their presence was the catalyst which transformed mild awareness into conviction. From that point, the métis knew they were a distinct people with a way of life that was worth defending.[117]

Other commentators share her assessment.[118] Nonetheless, as in western Canada, there were and are in eastern Canada what might be referred to as "boundary people" of mixed ancestry. Across Canada, people of mixed ancestry are reclaiming an Aboriginal identity from the assimilationist pressures of Canada's Indian recognition policies.

The special Métis edition of *Canadian Ethnic Studies* referred to earlier includes a case study of a non-status Alberta woman of Cree descent who gradually redefined herself as Métis under these pressures.[119] The editors note that "these enfranchised persons of Indian background, not having a distinct identity of their own, have gravitated towards the Métis, finding in their cultural and political organizations the identity they seek."[120]

There is more than a question of personal identity. There is a clear rights and entitlement component to the issue. Unable to get through the "Indian" door, people of mixed ancestry who consider themselves entitled to constitutional rights and program benefits despite their lack of Indian status will consciously attempt to access their rights through other avenues, including Métis organizations.[121]

Everywhere we look in Canada, especially since 1982, Aboriginal people and organizations can be seen to be jostling and shifting their identities to try to conform with the expectations of what are guessed to be official policies and constitutional meanings in order to try to get what they ask for from the government.[122]

Summary: Métis Identity

From the foregoing it seems clear that the term "Métis" is an evolving one that shows no sign at the moment of settling into a consistent or coherent pattern. In western Canada, for example, judges and others refer to persons who took scrip or who ran afoul of the *Indian Act* marrying-out provisions as Métis, regardless of how they may describe themselves. In Ontario, people of mixed ancestry living in the area of an original community of mixed-ancestry persons at Sault Ste Marie call themselves Métis as part of their political and social efforts to re-establish a community. In Newfoundland, persons of mixed ancestry who cannot get Indian status as the community at Conne River did, also clamour for the designation "Métis." In Labrador, mixed-ancestry persons call themselves Métis because their less numerous and more northerly Inuit relatives refuse them entry into the political process designed to settle the Inuit land claim. Politically, the Congress of Aboriginal Peoples allows anyone, no matter how they may have lost Indian status or whether they ever had it, to call themselves Métis if they wish. Meanwhile, the people who were historically recognized politically by the government of Canada and legislatively in the *Manitoba Act* as Métis have formed their own political organization, the Métis National Council, in a bid to recover the designation "Métis" for themselves.[123]

As some Prairies cases show, Aboriginal persons are also inconsistent in how they define themselves, and shift categories depending on the context or call themselves by multiple names. This semantic overlap is in part inevitable, given that the issue of Métis definition is a boundary issue of the larger question of who is an Indian—an issue itself related to Canada's long-standing policies of assimilation and restricted access to Aboriginal rights. In this context, both Métis and non-status Indians are in the same leaky boat.

> Metis claims and the claims of non-status Indians are historically separate. Many Metis and non-status Indians find themselves today in similar situations. They are members of groups that are supposed to have been assimilated. They are conscious of a distinct identity but the politicians tell them that they are simply part of the national population. They may be part of the multicultural mosaic, but they have no special rights.[124]

The real issue for the future seems to be whether the term "Métis" will continue to be a boundary issue influenced by the numbers of people moving out of, or into as in the case of Bill C–31, the "Indian" category. It can be anticipated that, given the potential impact of the 6(1)/6(2) distinction discussed earlier, within less than a century the category of "Métis" will be numerically the largest. In this light, perhaps the question is not so much "Who is a Métis?" as "Who is not a Métis?" Framing it that way puts the issue squarely in the lap of Canada's status system under the *Indian Act.*

The above question assumes that the term "Métis" has a positive as opposed to a negative meaning. It also assumes that the term "Indian" has a positive meaning. However, there is no consistent basis for Canada's approach to recognition of Indians. Rather than recognizing the institutions that maintained the identity of the original Indian "nations" or groups with which treaties were entered into, or in some other way establishing a functional relationship with Indian communities, Canada instead unilaterally legislated one general definition of "Indian" for all its purposes, without regard for membership in distinct "nations" or other communities.

It is this legislated system of Indian definition that has been reviewed here, not the meanings of Indian identity that might have resulted had the Indian nations been free to decide their own membership, or the meanings of Indian identity that a national policy of free national reconstitution as recommended by RCAP might develop.

The lack of consistency in the federal administration of Indian definition may be measured against the usual factors that are available to create a definition system to maintain the corporate identity of an original "charter" group, namely blood, kinship, and lifestyle.

Indian legal status under this system cannot be a function of blood quantum, for example, because many of Canada's registered Indian population are of mixed ancestry, and out-marriage rates ensure that the "mixing of blood" will continue into the future. In any event, after so many generations of intermarriage between Indians, Métis (however defined), and non-Aboriginal people, mixed ancestry alone is no longer (if it ever was) a characteristic that distinguishes one category of Aboriginal people from another since "mixed blood peoples were not excluded from Indian status when membership lists were first prepared and could not now be excluded without purging the Indian reserve communities of at least half their population."[125]

Nor, as discussed earlier, was blood quantum historically the sole or determining criterion for Indian status. If it had been, mixed-ancestry persons could never have taken treaty. White women could never have become Indians through marriage, and their children equally could never have had Indian status.

Nor can it be kinship, for the scrip, marriage-out, and enfranchisement provisions have had the effect of splitting families. Moreover, as the previous discussion has illustrated, the way the 6(1)/6(2) distinction works, families will continue to be split because status is not equally transmissible between siblings who married out prior to 1985. Nor can the determining criterion be lifestyle, for, as the Prairies cases show, status and non-status Indians in some parts of Canada live in similar if not identical ways in communities that are different only because of legal distinctions. This is, of course, why *Charter* section 15 is such a threat to Canada's current policies relating to the three categories of Aboriginal peoples expressly recognized in the *Constitution Act, 1982*, recognizing some and refusing to recognize others.

Nor can Indian identity even be tied to self-identification, for the simple reason that many Aboriginal people self-identify as Indian but cannot obtain entitlement to registration. The converse is also true, for many people self-identify as non-treaty Indians or as Métis but now find themselves eligible for registration under the *Indian Act*. Others are registered as Indians but find that the

Indian Act will not allow them to opt out. In any event, given that entitlement to registration leads to benefits not available to those not so entitled, there are powerful incentives for people to self-identify as Indian even if they have little or no connection to their Indian roots or heritage.

What Canada has is an increasingly arbitrary recognition system for Indians. Like so much of Canada's historic Aboriginal policy, the basis for its recognition of Aboriginal peoples seems less a question of conscious design than of haphazard and shifting policies influenced by fiscal pressures, changing currents of social and anthropological thought, and even the personalities of federal and provincial politicians and policy-makers. Since there is no consistent basis for designating persons as falling into the category of Indians, it should not be surprising that little or none is present in the case of those who fall between the categories into the boundary group called Métis.

There seems little logic or utility to trying to define "Métis" in the absence of a serious, sustained, and rational approach to the status system under the *Indian Act*, including a review of its validity and legitimacy in respect to the identification of "treaty nations" and other First Nation communities.

Trying to define the term "Métis" at the boundary of Canada's increasingly irrational approach to defining "Indian" is a fool's errand. It is necessary to abandon the idea that "Métis" can be defined negatively as those Aboriginal persons who are not Indians, and to adopt instead a principled approach which moves towards the positive core of Métis identity.

Problems at the Boundary of Indian Identity

It has been concluded that the boundary of legislated Indian identity is uncertain and cannot provide a rational foundation for a Métis definition for constitutional purposes. Yet the aspirations of many individuals and communities for recognition as Indians, as reflected in the analysis by Gibson in chapter 7, have been cloaked in a Métis identity, resulting in arguments that tend to merge the two identities.

It is a thesis of this work that the just response to the claims and aspirations of those who wish to be identified and recognized as Indians is, in appropriate cases, to recognize them as Indians. Descent from Indians ought to lead to recognition as Indians, not as something else. The well-known concept of "passing" describes the process whereby an individual attempts to take on an identity that does not match the claimant's personal and community heritage. This process is *prima facie* a doubtful foundation upon which to build new Aboriginal nations, who will doubtless use all the community solidarity they can muster. It is easy to speculate that many individuals who take on a Métis identity on account of descent from a family within a First Nation do so because they are now excluded from the official recognition system that applies to Indians.

It has been proposed by RCAP that First Nations ought to be recognized as having the authority to decide their membership. Policies that respect the right of Indian nations to decide their own membership can be expected to provide an avenue for the unfulfilled aspirations of individuals who aspire to their Indian heritage.

The conclusion that it is better, as a matter of law and policy, to move away from the uncertain boundary of Indian definition as administered by the federal government is supported by the identification of conceptual and practical problems that arise from attempts to define "the Métis" at the boundary.

Two main concerns have arisen in scholarly and judicial discussions about the concept of Métis definition. The first is the notion conceived by some commentators that the Métis people have no rights themselves, but only rights derived from their Indian ancestors. This is the "derivative rights" or "trace" theory.[126] A second result of the uncertainty at the boundary of Indian definition is the idea that a Métis identity can be legally nurtured and maintained *within* Indian groups. That idea was canvassed by the Court of Appeal of Ontario in the *Powley* case.

Derivative Rights Notion

The notion of derivative rights suggests that the rights held by the Métis people are held on account of their descent from Indians. The derivative rights invention seems to disregard the constitutional recognition of the Métis as an Aboriginal people in section 35, seeing only Indians and Inuit as legally relevant, or according them primary significance. The Métis Society of Saskatchewan explained its view in 1970 of the idea that a person is either an Indian or White: "The Metis nation in Saskatchewan, ...find ourselves in the unsavoury position of being non-people...."[127] The idea of derivative rights recalls the notion behind the doctrine of *terra nullius,* which denies the existence of Indigenous people, in the sense that they do not legally matter when Europeans arrive, and who therefore have no history that matters. The derivative rights invention cannot be reconciled with the express reference to "the Métis people" in section 35 as a people distinct from Indian and Inuit peoples.

Those Indian persons who aspire to associate fully with their Indian heritage can do so within their families and communities. Those among them who aspire to be recognized in law and policy as part of an historic Indian nation may do that, too. Pursuit of the aspiration to fully associate with one's Indian heritage has no rational association with identification with an historic nation that was distinct from Indians. So if this is the idea that attracts claims to the boundary of Indian definition, then logic, experience, and justice all suggest they ought to stay at the boundary or enter the fold, but as Indians, not as Métis.

The idea that the Métis people have no rights of their own can be expected to arouse an extreme reaction from members of the Métis nation, whose ancestors have fought since the early nineteenth century to distinguish themselves from both Indians and Europeans. The idea that the Métis have "derivative" Indian rights proposes that the Métis owe their rights, not to their ancestors who fought for them, but to individual members of Indian groups who were at times their military enemies.[128] The merits of that approach might be tested by asking if Canadians and Americans would be happy to have only rights derived from their British ancestors. Presumably, the Americans, who waged military campaigns against the British, might find the idea even more repellent than the gentle Canadians, who emancipated themselves peacefully over a long period of time but who are now made up of persons with diverse heritages from all over the world.

Aboriginal rights law and policy ought not only to be developed with the legitimate interests of its ostensible beneficiaries in mind; it ought also be such as to attract the political support and confidence of these beneficiaries. The notion of derivative rights provides no useful conceptual tools for an understanding of Métis rights and identity and cannot be expected to be accepted by the descendants of the Métis who fought for their distinct identity.

The kind of rights that are generally being asserted in cases where the claimants assert a Métis identity relate to small-scale primary harvesting of natural resources such as fishing and hunting moose or deer for the family larder. In these cases the courts have not had to consider the question of Métis identity in the broader context of political rights and the implications raised by the discussion of recognition theory in earlier chapters.

In particular, the courts have not generally pondered the meaning of "the Métis people" in light of the generally understood international law meaning of "peoples." Neither have the courts been required to address the meaning of "the Métis nation" for the purposes of securing federal recognition in order to negotiate self-government, as recommended by RCAP.[129] That meaning is the subject of analysis in chapter 8. The derivative rights notion seems to conflict with the norms behind the right of self-determination, which is a human right that requires that each "people" be seen as equally entitled to respect and rights. The same principles, it is suggested, ought to inform the construction of section 35 in domestic constitutional law. Section 35 requires that each Aboriginal "people" be equally respected in its identity and rights. Finally, the derivative rights idea seems to run afoul of the requirements of the *Charter of Rights and Freedoms* because it requires the interests of the Métis people, a distinct "people" recognized as such by the Constitution, to be merged with the interests of Indian people. This is contrary to the constitutional values in section 15, which prescribe respect for the distinct identity and history of all the Aboriginal peoples recognized in section 35.[130]

'Métis' Identities within Indian Bands or First Nations

The second problem at the boundary of Indian identity is the idea that a Métis identity can be maintained and constitutionally protected *within* Indian groups. This notion owes its origins to the *Powley* case in the Ontario Court of Appeal.[131] The plaintiff, who was the respondent on appeal, was from Sault Ste Marie. Historians have identified a community of "mixed-blood" persons in the area, which had either been merged into the local population in the mid-nineteenth century or joined the local Indian bands. The respondent's ancestor had joined the Batchewana Band in the 1850s, with the result that his descendant's membership in the band was subject to the membership rules in the *Indian Act*.

In time, Powley's ancestor was "enfranchised," or lost Indian status. Rather than challenging the provisions of the *Act* which had resulted in the enfranchisement of his ancestors, and consequently his "non-status" as an Indian, Powley asserted a Métis identity. He joined two political representative organizations, both of which purport to represent the Métis people in the area. One is affiliated with CAP, the other with MNC.

The Court agreed that he could identify himself as Métis for purposes of proving hunting rights protected by section 35. The Court rejected Crown arguments that Powley's ancestors had ruptured their continuity with a Métis community.[132] Instead, the court took the view that a Métis identity, with attached Métis rights, survived the abandonment of the Métis community by Powley's ancestors, and his adoption of the Batchewana Indian Band as his home community.

The implications of this view deserve scrutiny. As mentioned earlier, there are some 26,000 persons who identified themselves as status Indians in the 1996 census, but who also claimed a Métis identity.[133]

On the view expounded by Justice Sharpe in *Powley*, an Indian band could harbour some constitutional black sheep who claim membership in two distinct constitutional categories, Indian and Métis. It also follows from Sharpe's view that a band becomes an incubator of a dormant Métis identity vested in individuals, harbouring the seeds of social disunity. The Métis in the Indian band

participates in the life of the Indian community and contributes to its maintenance and its legal continuity. The Métis resides in the community, and is recognized in federal legislation as an Indian. The Métis attracts the burdens and benefits of Indian legislation and of the Crown-Indian fiduciary relationship. If the
band is a member of a treaty nation, the Métis is a member of an historic Indian
treaty group recognized by the Crown. And yet, on this view, the Métis has the
ability at any time to rupture the bonds of community within the Indian band by
declaring a preference for a new Métis identity and insisting on the enjoyment of
new rights that are not enjoyed by the other members of his community.

Without casting doubt on the intention of the Court of Appeal to do justice to new claimants to a Métis identity, it seems that allowing Indian bands to
incubate Métis personal identities for generations, with the results that have just
been described, seems to run counter to the view expressed by the same court
many years ago: "...Although it is not possible to remedy all of what we now
perceive as past wrongs... it is essential and in keeping with established and accepted principles that the Courts not create, by a remote, isolated current view of
events, new grievances."[134] Justice requires that Indian communities be secure in
the identity upon which the group rights of the members depend.

The federal Parliament has already unilaterally decided who belongs to
Indian bands. The review in this chapter showed that one effect was to rupture
the bonds of Indian community life over generations. Justice may demand that
individuals who suffer the effects of the enfranchisement provisions of federal
Indian legislation have an actionable claim against the Crown in respect to the
rupturing of their relations with the Indian band or treaty nation to which they
belong. A legal challenge may be possibly be made against the authority of Parliament and the Crown to decide the membership of treaty nations. However, the
proposition that individuals who have accepted membership in Indian bands
may contribute to the rupture of Indian communities by declaring a new Métis
identity does not appear to be based upon any considerations of justice. If Indian
bands are viewed as the core groups through which original Indian societies or
nations may exercise their treaty and Aboriginal rights, then, in principle, the
social composition or membership of such Indian groups ought to be decided by
the expression of the legitimate political will of the Indian group, and ought not
to be subject to judicial dismemberment on the basis of gossamer concepts related to personal sentiment, or to the fact that members have mixed-blood personal antecedents.

With respect, the view of Justice Sharpe seems also to conflict with existing
judicial authority. In the *Blueberry River Band* case, which the Supreme Court
refused to hear on appeal, the Federal Court of Appeal held that Aboriginal rights

are held collectively by members of an Aboriginal group; the rights are held by virtue of membership in the group, and not by virtue of personal antecedents. In *Blueberry River*, the rights at issue were rights to land, but the analysis reflects the general principle applicable to rights vested in Aboriginal groups.[135] This view is supported by the persuasive weight of American decisions where descendants of Canadian Métis have been recognized as Indians and members of American Indian tribes.[136]

The effects of judicially recognizing the capacity of Indian bands to incubate Métis personal identities suggest the potential for infringing Indian rights and identity. It seems preferable to define "the Métis people" by moving away from the boundary of Indian definition and identifying the positive core of Métis identity.

It appears that many cases that are argued as "Métis" cases might properly be argued as "Indian" cases. One of the difficulties faced by the courts, which leads to confusion about Métis identity, is that in most of the cases in which the issues arise, the court is asked to deal with an individual defendant who claims to be a Métis, and who raises an Aboriginal right as a defence to a prosecution, often under provincial game and fish legislation. This frequently leads the courts to an unhelpful inquiry into the personal antecedents of the defendant, rather than an inquiry into the identity and history of the Aboriginal community to which the defendant belongs. It is established law that Aboriginal rights are vested in Aboriginal communities, although some of them are exercised by individuals, and may be raised as a defence by individuals entitled to exercise them.[137] Proof of Aboriginal rights requires proof of continuity between a contemporary and an historic Aboriginal community, not proof that an individual is descended from an historic individual. Aboriginal rights are not inherited by individuals, like personal property; nor are they inherited as genetic traits according to racist notions. A community is a social and legal fiction maintained through generations by social institutions. A successful defence based upon an Aboriginal right requires proof of membership in the Aboriginal community in which the Aboriginal right is vested.[138]

A cautious judicial approach in dealing with individual claimants to Métis identity will allow the courts to develop principles to recognize the inherent right of "Indian nations" as well as of "the Métis people" to define their membership, and to respect the free choice of association that Canadian citizens ought to have in deciding with which Aboriginal community they belong, subject to the group's membership rules.

Notes

[1]The word "halfbreed" has pejorative connotations and is not acceptable in modern usage. It is used in this book in the interests of historic and analytical accuracy.

[2]Exceptionally, Alberta has legislated the establishment of several Métis settlements, but ironically, the residents, who are descendants of Cree people enfranchised by scrip, and the settlements are not represented as such in the Métis National Council. See generally, on the settlements' history and legislation, Catherine E. Bell, *Contemporary Metis Justice: The Settlement Way* (Saskatoon: University of Saskatchewan Native Law Centre, 1999). S. 31 of the *Manitoba Act, 1870* provided for a Métis land base, but the constitutionality of the means whereby the Métis were deprived of that land is currently the subject of an action for a declaration of constitutional invalidity: *Dumont* v. *Canada (A.G.) sub.nom. Manitoba Metis Federation* v. *Canada (A.G.)*, [1987] 2 C.N.L.R. 85 (Man. Q.B.); rev'd [1998] 3 C.N.L.R. 39 (Man. C.A.), rev'd [1990] 2 C.N.L.R. 19 (S.C.C.).

[3]Andy Siggner, Jeremy Hull, Annette Vermaeten, Eric Guimond & Lorna Jantzen, "Understanding Aboriginal Definitions: Implications for Counts and Socio-Economic Characteristics." Paper presented at the Canadian Population Society Annual Meetings at Laval University, Quebec City, Canada. June, 1, 2001, in the possession of the authors.

[4]The author of the leading anthropological study of the Métis of the Canadian West took the view that the Métis did not, at the time of his studies in the 1930s, fit into either the Indian or the non-Indian society of Canada. See e.g., Marcel Giraud, "A Note on the Half-Breed Problem in Manitoba" (1937) *The Canadian Journal of Economics and Political Science* 541.

[5]Jacqueline Peterson & Jennifer S.H. Brown, eds., "Introduction," *The New Peoples: Being and Becoming Metis in North America* (Winnipeg: University of Manitoba Press, 1985) 3 at 5. The "folk biology" that equates genetic composition with social, cultural and political identity is explored in more detail by Jennifer S.H. Brown in "The Presbyterian Métis of St. Gabriel Street, Montreal," *ibid.*, 194 at 196:

> *Métissage*, or the process by which this population arose, is a term that has generally been used with two meanings which need to be carefully distinguished. Biologically, it is the creation of persons of mixed Indian-white parentage and the mingling of groups characterized by distinctive traits such as blood group, gene O. so widely distributed in New World aboriginal populations. For the purposes of this discussion, however, it is the social, cultural and political creation of persons who accept or decide to affirm that "we are métis," taking that dual aspect of their ancestry and affiliation as central fact of life.

[6]*R.* v. *Blais* [1997] 3 C.N.L.R. 109 (Man. Prov. Ct.) per Swail J. at 114–15. The Supreme Court of Canada made a similar observation in *Lovelace* v. *Ontario*, [2000] 4 C.N.L.R. 145 at 150 in the context of Ontario per Iacobucci J.: "The two Be-Wab-Bon appellants did not advance a common definition of "Métis," and in this respect, I note that the issue remains politically and legally contentious." For similar explorations of the range of possible definitions of Métis see Don McMahon & Fred Martin, "The Métis and 91(24): Is Inclusion the Issue?," Royal Commission on Aboriginal Peoples, *Aboriginal Self-Government: Legal and Constitutional Issues* (Ottawa: Minister of Supply and Services, 1995) 277, 290–94; and Robert K. Thomas, "Afterword," *The New Peoples, supra* note 5, 243 at 250.

Nor is the issue of Métis definition solely for outside commentators. The Metis Association of Alberta makes a similar observation in *Metis Land Rights in Alberta: A Political History* (Edmonton: Metis Association of Alberta, 1981) at 8:

A note must be made about the terms Metis, Half-breeds, Status and Non-Status Indians, and Treaty and Non-Treaty Indians in this book. The terminology we have used to refer to the Metis people has of necessity varied from chapter to chapter, depending on the historical period and geographic location under consideration. For general use in the text, we have used the term Metis. This term has come to include all people of mixed Indian-white ancestry in the prairie provinces, and in recent years, elsewhere in the country. The term, when used in this way, includes Non-Status Indians....

[7]"Métis" is derived from the old French term *métif* that means simply "mixed." The traditional pronunciation of the term *métif* by Métis speakers is *michiss* or *michif*. This pronunciation results from the influence of the Cree and Saulteaux languages which do not contain the sounds required to pronounce *métif* as a French speaker would. See Paul L.A.H. Chartrand, "Aboriginal Rights: The Dispossession of the Métis" (1991) 29:3 Osgoode Hall L.J. 457, n. 8; and Robert A. Papen, "Quelques rémarques sur un parler francais méconnu de l'Ouest Canadien: Le Métis" (1984) 14 *Revue Québécoise de Linguistique*, 1, 113–39. For a discussion in the context of the Michif speakers in the Turtle Mountain Chippewa of Montana see John C. Crawford "What is Michif?: Language in the Métis Tradition" in *The New Peoples, supra* note 5, 231.

[8]See e.g., W.L. Morton, *Manitoba: A History* (Toronto: University of Toronto Press. 1957) at 78–79; and W.L. Morton, "Introduction," *Eden Colville's Letters 1849–50* (London: XIX Hudson's Bay Record Society, 1956).

[9]In "The Métis and Mixed-bloods of Rupert's Land before 1870" in *The New Peoples, supra* note 5, 95, Irene M. Spry notes (at 99) that "many métis and mixed-bloods, at least among the elite, spoke both French and English, as well as one or more of the Indian languages... It is evident that many marriages spanned the alleged gulf between the mixed-blood and métis groups," going on to list a number of other areas where the between the two groups may have been more apparent than real. A similar conclusion is reached by Hal Pruden, *The Prudens of Pehonanik: A Fur-Trade Family* (Winnipeg: Rinella Printers Ltd., 1990) at 69:

> Far more striking than these differences are the commonalities that the mixed-blood people of Red River shared in 1869. Not the least of these were common languages. Cree, Assiniboine and Saulteaux were spoken as were bastard languages Michif and Bungay. Many mixed-blood persons were multilingual, speaking indigenous languages plus English and French. Prior to 1818, religion was not an issue and it certainly remained a non-issue for those Métis who did not move to Red River after the union of the Hudson's Bay Company and the Northwest Company but who stayed near the posts in Métis communities.

[10]One of the major differences between the two groups lay in their different approaches to identifying with the European cultures from which they traced part of their descent. The English "half-breeds" on the whole were more inclined to attempt "assimilation into the British, Protestant world of their fathers," at least until the events of 1869 forced them to forge a common destiny with their French Métis counterparts in Red River: Sylvia Van Kirk, "What if Mama is an Indian?: The Cultural Ambivalence of the Alexander Ross Family" in *The New Peoples, supra* note 5, 207 at 207.

[11]Raymond Huel, ed., *The Collected Writings of Louis Riel*, vol. 1 (Edmonton: University of Alberta Press, 1985) at 31. That being said, Hal Pruden, *The Prudens of Pehonanik, supra* note 9 observes (at 69) that this did not mean that the gulf between the two groups in 1869 was a wide one: "Intermarriage is also an underappreciated fact... It is impossible to ignore the powerful meaning of James McKay's observation that the mixed-bloods who were not actually participating in the resistance were related to the resisters."

[12]See Paul L.A.H. Chartrand, *Manitoba's Métis Settlement Scheme of 1870* (Saskatoon:

University of Saskatchewan Native Law Centre, 1991) at 26–32.

[13]The Metis Association of Alberta notes that the two identities, "Half-Breed" and "Métis" remained separate, but only until 1869–70: *Metis Land Rights, supra* note 6 at 8.

[14]33 Vict., c. 3, reprinted in R.S.C. 1985, App. II, No. 8.

S. 31. And whereas it is expedient, towards the extinguishment of the Indian title to the lands in the Province, to appropriate a portion of such ungranted lands, to the extent of one million four hundred thousand acres thereof, for the benefit of the families of the Half-breed residents, it is hereby enacted, that, under regulations to be from time to time made by the Governor General in Council, the Lieutenant Governor shall select such lots or tracts in such parts of the Province as he may deem expedient, to the extent aforesaid, and divide the same among the children of the Half-Breed heads of families residing in the Province at the time of the said transfer to Canada, and the same shall be granted to the said children respectively, in such mode and on such conditions as to settlement or otherwise, as the Governor General may from time to time determine.

[15]The *Dominion Lands Act*, S.C. 1879, c. 31 had similar language:

125(e) To satisfy any claims existing in connection with the extinguishment of the Indian title, preferred by half-breeds resident in the North-West Territories outside of the limits of Manitoba...

[16]*Supra* note 6.

[17]*R.* v. *Howse*, [2003] 3 C.N.L.R. 228 (BC Prov. Ct.).

[18]Heather Devine, "Les Desjarlais: The Development and Dispersion of a Proto-Metis Hunting Band, 1785–1870," in T. Binnema, G.J. Ens & R.C. Maclead, eds., *From Rupert's Land to Canada* (Edmonton: University of Alberta Press, 2001) 129 at 152; and John Foster, "Wintering, The Outsider Adult Male and the Ethnogenesis of the Western Plains Metis," in *ibid.,* 179 ; John Foster, "The Problem of Metis Roots" in Peterson & Brown, *supra* note 5, 73, at 81; and Diane Payment, *"The Free People—Otipemisiwak": Batoche, Saskatchewan 1870–1930.* (Ottawa: Minister of Supply and Services, Minister of the Environment, Parks Service, 1990).

[19]Michif is described in note 7, *supra*. Bungi was a hybrid of Orkney Scottish and Cree and is reported to be spoken by a declining number of speakers in a few Manitoba communities: Donald Purich, *The Metis* (Toronto: James Lorimer and Co., 1988) at 11.

[20]A short account of the history of the Métis in the United States is provided by Verne Dusenberry, "Waiting For the Day That Never Comes: The Dispossessed Métis of Montana" in *The New Peoples, supra* note 5, 119. Historically the Métis now in the several states near the border with Canada are descended from two main groups of mixed-blood people: those centred in Pembina, North Dakota and those later arrivals from Canada after the events of 1869 and 1885. See also *Turtle Mountain Band* case, note 136 *infra*.

[21]Alexander Morris, *The Treaties of Canada with the Indians of Manitoba and the North-West Territories* (Toronto: Belfords, Clarke & Co., 1880, reprint Saskatoon: Fifth House, 1991) at 294.

[22]At least until 1876, when the first version of the *Indian Act* prevented those who had yet to take treaty in Manitoba from doing so: S.C. 1876, c. 18, s. 3(e):

Provided also that no half-breed in Manitoba who has shared in the distribution of half-breed lands shall be accounted an Indian; and that no half-breed head of a family (except the widow of an Indian, or a half-breed who has already been admitted into a treaty) shall, unless under very special circumstances, to be determined by the Superintendent-General or his agent, be accounted an Indian, or entitled to be admitted into any Indian treaty.

[23]Not all the Métis "who lived after the habits of the Indians" were attracted by the idea

of individual scrip and one group applied to be given a Métis reserve near the Cypress Hills of Saskatchewan in 1878: *Metis Land Rights in Alberta, supra* note 6 at 114–15.

[24]The policy is evident in the Indian legislation of Upper Canada upon which the *Indian Act* enfranchisement model is derived. Individuals who were considered capable of protecting their private lands in the open market were "enfranchised" with individual lands, while others living in traditional communities turned into Indian reserves, had their interest in the group's lands recognized, but the Crown interposed between Indian communities and others to prevent alienations of lands without the surrender of the Indian lands to the Crown, which has a fiduciary duty to safeguard the corporate interests of Aboriginal peoples. See Chartrand, *supra* note 12 at 80–84; see also John S. Milloy, "The Early Indian Acts: Developmental Strategy and Constitutional Change," in A.L. Getty & A.S. Lussier, eds., *As Long As The Sun Shines and Water Flows: A Reader in Canadian Native Studies* (Vancouver: University of British Columbia Press, 1983)

[25]Land scrip was redeemable for the number of acres appearing on its face, while money scrip could be redeemed for the number of acres corresponding to the dollar amount on its face. For a fuller description of the scrip system see *Metis Land Rights in Alberta, supra* note 6, 87 *et seq.* and *The Metis, supra* note 19, 106 *et seq.*

[26]*An Act respecting the Appropriation of Certain Dominion Lands in Manitoba,*, S.C. 1874, c. 20:

> Whereas…it was enacted as expedient towards the extinguishment of the Indian title to the lands of the Province of Manitoba to appropriate…lands for the benefit of the children of the half-breed heads of families residing in the province at the time of the transfer thereof to Canada.
>
> And whereas no provision has been made for extinguishing the Indian title as respects the said half-breed heads of families residing in the province at the period;
>
> Therefore Her Majesty, by and with the consent of the Senate and House of Commons, enacts as follows:
>
> 1. To effect the purpose above mentioned, each half-breed head of family resident in the Province…shall be entitled…to receive a grant of 160 acres of land or to receive scrip for $160, the latter to be receivable in payment for the purchase of Dominion Lands.

[27]The *Indian Act*, S.C. 1876, c. 18 contained the following definitions that would be repeated in every revision of the *Act* until 1951 when they were dropped in favour of a registry approach to defining Indians.

> 2. The term "irregular band" means any tribe, band or body of persons of Indian blood who own no interest in any reserve or lands of which the legal title is vested in the Crown, who possess no common fund managed by the Government of Canada, and who have not had any treaty relations with the Crown.
>
> 3. The term "Indian" means
>
> First. Any male person of Indian blood reputed to belong to a particular band,
>
> Secondly. Any child of such a person,
>
> Thirdly. Any woman who is or was lawfully married to such person.
>
> 4. The term "non-treaty Indian" means any person of Indian blood who is reputed to belong to an irregular band or who follows the Indian mode of life, even if such person is only temporarily resident in Canada.

[28]For example, in 1876 there were groups such as the Sioux in southern Manitoba and Saskatchewan who had emigrated from the United States. They were clearly Indians, but not Indians with whom Canada had a treaty relationship. The arrival of the Sioux in Canada is

described in Alan D. McMillan, *Native Peoples and Cultures of Canada* (Vancouver: Douglas & McIntyre, 1988) at 141–43. The first encounters of colonial and later Dominion authorities with these groups is related in *The Treaties of Canada, supra* note 21 at 276–84.

[29]It was the view of the Court in *R. v. Howson* (1894) 1 Terr. L.R. 492 (N–WTSC en banc) at 495 that the *Indian Act* was framed in the way it was, with explicit inclusions and exclusions of half-breeds in various sections "show that it was the intention of the Legislature that there are half-breeds who must be considered Indians within the meaning of the Act; because if the word [sic] "of Indian blood" in paragraph (h) of section 2 meant "of full Indian blood," then these provisions…were entirely unnecessary."

[30]*Supra* note 27.

[31]The scrip provided to heads of families *(supra* note 26) must be distinguished from the land patents issued to children pursuant to s. 31 of the *Manitoba Act, 1870,* and with scrip that was later invalidly distributed to children after all the 1.4 million acres provided for under s. 31 had been distributed. Most of the s. 31 lands were distributed as land patents and not by scrip issues: Chartrand, *supra* note 12. Land allotments totalling 1,448,160 acres were distributed for 6,034 claims of s. 31 lands, whereas 993 claims were dealt with by issue of $240 scrips.

[32]"Appendix 5C: Métis Nation Land and Resource Rights," Canada, *Report of the Royal Commission on Aboriginal Peoples: Perspectives and Realities,* vol. 4 (Ottawa: Supply and Services Canada, 1996) at 333. There is a great deal of historical writing on this subject now. For a comprehensive review of the process with legal criticisms see *Manitoba's Métis Settlement Scheme, supra* note 12.

[33]Sir John A. Macdonald confided to a colleague at this time that "[t]he impulsive Half-breeds have got spoiled by their emeute, and will have to be ruled by a strong hand until they are swamped by the influx of settlers": Public Archives of Canada, Macdonald Papers, J. A. Macdonald to J. Rose, February 23, 1870, reported in D.N. Sprague & R.P. Frye, *The Genealogy of the First Métis Nation* (Winnipeg: Pemmican Publications, 1983) at 24.

[34]Robert K. Thomas in *The New Peoples, supra* note 5, identifies (at 248–49) three groups of Red River and Rupert's Land Métis after the events of 1869 and 1885: first, those who stayed in roughly the areas of southern Manitoba and Saskatchewan where they were resident; second, those who moved farther north in Manitoba, Saskatchewan, and the Northwest Territories; and third, those who moved onto Indian reserves or reservations in Canada and the United States respectively.

[35]*Manuscript of Mr. Justice W.P.R. Street when he was made chairman of a commission to settle the claims of the Half Breed Indians in the North West Territories* [The *Street Report*] (Toronto: Royal Canadian Institute) (copy in the possession of the writers) at 5. For a discussion of the problems see *RCAP: Perspectives and Realities, supra* note 32 at 333 *et seq.* For more detailed accounts see D.N. Sprague, "Government Lawlessness in the Administration of Manitoba Land Claims, 1870–1887" (1980) 10 Man. L.J. 415; Chartrand, *supra* note 12.

[36]Purich, *supra* note 19 at 70, says it was 20 percent, while the Manitoba Metis Federation said it was 15 percent: *Manitoba Metis Federation Inc. v. A.G. Canada,* [1998] 3 C.N.L.R. 39 at 44.

[37]Money scrip was considered to be personal property and therefore assignable without the safeguards associated with land scrip, which was considered to be real property. See *Metis Land Rights in Alberta, supra* note 6 at 96.

[38]*The Metis, supra* note 19 at 111–12.

[39]The 1951 version of the *Indian Act*, R.S.C. 1951, c. 29 had a provision that read as follows:

12(1) The following persons are not entitled to be registered, namely,

(a) a person who

(i) has received or has been allotted half-breed lands or money scrip,

(ii) is a descendant of a person described in subsection (I),

Despite removal of this or any equivalent bar to registration based on scrip, the Department of Indian Affairs Registrar apparently still applies the pre-1985 rules: Larry Gilbert, *Entitlement to Indian Status and Membership Codes in Canada* (Toronto: Carswell, 1997) at 37, n. 54.

[40]Gilbert, *ibid.* at 112–16. See also the *Street Report, supra* note 35 at 17.

[41]*Street Report, ibid.*

[42]*Supra* note 27.

[43]"Excerpts from the Report of the Honourable W.A. MacDonald of the Alberta District Court on the Exclusion of Half-Breeds from Treaty Lists, August 7, 1944" in P.A. Cumming & N.H. Mickenberg, eds., *Native Rights in Canada* (Toronto: General Publishing Co. Ltd., 1972) at 325.

[44]*R. v. Howson* (1894) 1 Terr. L.R. 429 (NWT S.C. *en blanc)* at 494. See also *R. v. Mellon* (1900) 5 Terr. L.R. 580 (N–WTSC) at 581 in connection with a similar issue. The accused was found guilty under s. 94 of the *Indian Act* R.S.C. 1886 of selling intoxicants to "any Indian or non-treaty Indian" notwithstanding that the purchaser of the alcohol had none of the apparent indicia of being "Indian." The judge noted (at 582) with regard to the accused's demeanour and appearance that "Pepin speaks English fluently and dresses better than many ordinary white men; there is no indication whatsoever in his appearance, in his language, or in his general demeanour, that he does not belong to the better class of half-breeds."

[45]Indian and Northern Affairs Canada, *The Historical Development of the Indian Act*, John Leslie & Ron Maguire, eds. (Ottawa: Treaties and Historical Research Branch, 1978) at 90.

[46]Sir John A. Macdonald, commenting on the goals of Canada's Indian legislation: Return to an Order of the House of Commons, May 2, 1887, in Canada, *Sessional Papers (No. 20b) 1887*, 37. See in addition the Royal Commission on Aboriginal Peoples, "The Indian Act" in Canada, *Report of the Royal Commission on Aboriginal Peoples: Looking Forward, Looking Back*, vol. 1 (Ottawa: Supply and Services Canada, 1996) 255.

[47]S.C. 1879, c. 34, s. 1.

[48]S.C. 1884, c. 27, s. 4.

[49]The figures are cited in Percy Hodges & E.D. Noonan, *Saskatchewan Metis: Brief on Investigation into the Legal, Equitable and Moral Claimes [sic] of the Metis People of Saskatchewan in Relation to the Extinguishment of the Indian Title* (Saskatchewan Archives Board, Premier's Office, R–191, Box 1, P–M2) (Regina, July 28, 1943) at 121–22 [The *Hodges and Noonan Report*].

[50]Richard C. Daniel, *A History of Native Claims Processes in Canada* (Ottawa: Department of Indian Affairs, 1980) at 24–25.

[51]Letter from Saskatchewan Attorney General T.C. Davis to federal Minister of the Interior T.C. Crerar, December 11, 1935, extracted in *RCAP: Perspectives and Realities, supra* note 32 at 357:

> These non-treaty half-breeds constitute a considerable problem. The Indian strain predominates and they are to all intents and purposes Indians in their habits and their outlook upon life...
>
> We would therefore suggest that they be given the opportunity of becoming Treaty Indians, moving onto the Indian Reserves and coming under the jurisdiction of the Indian Department.

[52]Testimony of Jim Brady, Ewing Commission Proceedings at 54, reported in *Métis Land Rights, supra* note 6 at 190. Brady's comment was as follows:

> Well, there is one thing you have to remember, the original Half-breed, the Red River Metis, the majority of these people are still carrying on, they are still more or less able to hold their own. The majority of the destitute people today among the Metis were formerly treaty Indians, they are Indian through and through, except for the names, they are still Indians.

A similar comment was offered by Joe Dion, who noted that "[t]he most destitute amongst the Metis today are the descendants of those who left treaty to take scrip...": Testimony of Joe Dion, Ewing Commission Proceedings at 14, reported in Murray Dobbin, *The One-and-a-Half Men* (Vancouver: New Star Books, 1981) at 95.

[53]Ewing Commission Report, reported in Fred Martin, "Federal and Provincial Responsibility in the Metis Settlements of Alberta" in David C. Hawkes, ed., *Aboriginal Peoples and Governmental Responsibility* (Ottawa: Carleton University Press, 1991) 243 at 260.

[54]S.A. 1938, c. 6, s. 2(a): "Metis means a person of mixed white and Indian blood, but does not include either an Indian or a non-treaty Indian as defined in the *Indian Act....*"

[55]R.S.A. 1970, c. 233. s. 2(a): "Metis means a person of mixed white and Indian blood having not less than 1/4 Indian blood, but does not include either an Indian or a non-treaty Indian as defined in the *Indian Act....*" In 1990 the *Metis Settlements Act*, c. M–14.3, S.A. 1990, s. 1(j) replaced this with a definition requiring simply that Metis be "a person of Aboriginal ancestry who identifies with Metis history and culture."

[56]As a further reflection of the Indian-oriented slant of the colony scheme the eight colonies were organized and run by the Alberta government in much the same paternalistic way as Indian reserves were administered by the federal government: *The Metis, supra* note 19 at 145.

[57]*R. v. Morin and Daigneault,* [1996] 3 C.N.L.R. 157 at 169.

[58]*Ibid.* at 171.

[59]This judicial finding is consistent with historical evidence that the original decisions regarding who was provided with scrip or admitted to treaty were often inconsistent and arbitrary. See for example, *Entitlement to Indian Status, supra* note 39 at 3 where Larry Gilbert notes on the basis of his examination of the evidence that "bureaucrats and politicians decided that treaty entitlement was limited to a certain class of Indians. However, the definition of that class was fluid and the decisions were often arbitrary as some bureaucrats and politicians would admit half-breeds while others would not."

[60][1998] 1 C.N.L.R. 182 at 203:

> The evidence at trial, both oral and documentary, established that in northern Saskatchewan, historically and now, there was very little, if any, distinction between the Indian and Metis Aboriginal people. The distinction has always been primarily a legal one based on whether ancestors opted for Scrip or Treaty.

In the result, the accused were acquitted on the basis of a Métis Aboriginal right under s. 35.

[61]Larry Gilbert makes a similar observation, *supra* note 39 at 39: "The evidence discloses that the Government of Canada had a difficult time distinguishing between Indians

and persons of mixed blood. Perhaps it was the nomadic way of life shared by both populations, identical clothing, intermarriage, sharing of languages and sometimes customs."

[62]*R*. v. *Ferguson,* [1993] 2 C.N.L.R. 148 (Alta. Prov. Ct.), upheld [1994] 1 C.N.L.R. 117 (Alta. Q.B.). It should be noted that not all the cases go in favour of mixed-ancestry accused in the *NRTA* context. In Saskatchewan in particular the trend has been mixed. For example, in *R*. v. *Genereux,* [1982] 3 C.N.L.R. 95 at 103 the Provincial Court found that the accused was not an Indian for *NRTA* purposes because of his lack of Indian status under the *Indian Act*—and this despite the fact that his "family were half-breeds but had lived on the reserve and adhered to the same lifestyle for three generations."

[63]"Freemen" were Indian, Métis and French Canadian persons who may at one time have been employed by the fur trade companies. Subsequently they set themselves up in the business of supplying meat and furs to their former employers. See John E. Foster, "The Problem of Métis Roots" in *The New Peoples, supra* note 5, 73 at 81. The origins and history of the Grande Cache group (which includes Iroquois, Ojibway, and Cree antecedents) is discussed in *Metis Land Rights, supra* note 6, 215 at 216–22. The Cree term for "freemen" is, according to some sources, *otipemsiwuk,* and this term continues to be used by some people in reference to Métis people.

[64]Trudy Nicks & Kenneth Morgan, "Grande Cache: The Historic Development of an Indigenous Alberta Métis Population" in *The New Peoples, supra* note 5, 163 at 176–77. The branch that moved to the Edmonton area under their leader Michel Calehouis became known as the Michel Band. In 1958 the entire band purported to enfranchise, an action that the descendants now contest. See Indian Claims Commission, *Friends of the Michel Society Inquiry 1958 Enfranchisement Claim*, March 1998.

[65]The part of the group formerly resident at Jasper House moved to the Grande Cache area in 1910 when they were evicted from Jasper Park: *Metis Land Rights, supra* note 6 at 218.

[66]*The New Peoples, supra* note 5 at 177.

[67]*Ibid* at 178.

[68]*Ibid* at 176.

[69]One of the historical ironies associated with the Grande Cache mixed-ancestry group division into the Michel and the Grande Cache groups respectively has to do with the various federal policy vacillations over the years. Over time the vast majority of Michel band members lost their Indian status through enfranchisement and were then characterized as being Métis. Those who remained in the Grande Cache area were characterized as Métis from the outset. However, since the 1985 changes to the Indian status provisions, large numbers of Grande Cache persons have attempted to acquire Indian status despite their adoption of the Métis label for political and other purposes. See "Identification and Registration of Indian and Inuit People," 1993 document in the possession of the authors that was supplied by the Department of Indian Affairs (DIAND) to the Royal Commission on Aboriginal Peoples at 12. DIAND notes with regard to their attempt to acquire Indian status (at 13) that "[m]ost persons were denied registration because of the extensive instance of scrip-taking in their ancestry...."

[70]In the "game laws paragraph" of the *NRTA*s in the three Prairie Provinces, which are part of the *Constitution Act, 1930,* the province guarantees "Indian" hunting and fishing rights for food. The Agreements were negotiated with the Prairie Provinces only, when Canada transferred control of resource rights to the Prairie Provinces via the *Natural Resource Transfer Agreements* of 1930. See Peter Hogg, *Constitutional Law of Canada,* 1998 Student edition.

(Toronto: Carswell, 1998) at 571–72.

[71]Federal Court Action No. T–165–0. Larry Gilbert agrees that there may well exist a good claim on the part of many scrip-takers: *Entitlement to Indian Status, supra* note 39 at 40: "Often the person receiving the scrip was vulnerable either because of age, language barriers or the inability to read or write."

[72]The incident is related in John Leslie, *Assimilation, Integration or Termination? The Development of Canadian Indian Policy, 1943–1963,* (Ottawa: Ph.D. Thesis, Carleton University, 1999) at 290–96.

[73]See for example *Re Poitras* (1956), 20 W.W.R. 545 in which the Muscowpetung Band tried to have Joseph Poitras expelled from the band for having himself taken scrip. Mr. Poitras had been a band member and reserve resident for thirty-six years and had raised a family there prior to this incident. Poitras was successful in maintaining his band membership and Indian status because it was not proved that he was the Joseph Poitras whose name appeared in the scrip records.

[74]S.C. 1958, c. 19.

[75]*Entitlement to Indian Status, supra* note 39 at 41, note 57.

[76]See for example *RCAP: Looking Forward, Looking Back, supra* note 46, especially the sections on enfranchisement, Indian women, and Indian status and band membership, at 286, 300 and 303 respectively and the sources referred to therein.

[77]*RCAP, ibid.* at 300 refers to Indian women in this context as being "doubly disadvantaged" and describes the effect of certain provisions of the *Indian Act* as a "sustained assault on their ability to be recognized as 'Indian' and to live in recognized Indian communities...."

[78]*R. v. Laprise,* [1978] 6 W.W.R. 85 (Sask. CA).

[79]Those, as discussed earlier, who had lost status, been enfranchised, taken scrip or, like the Red River and Rupert's Land Métis never been considered to be Indians in the first place. To this list might also be added the Newfoundland and Labrador Aboriginal people, most of whom have yet to be brought in under the *Indian Act.*

[80]The definition of non-treaty Indian remained in the *Indian Act* until 1951, when it was dropped.

[81]Under s. 11 of the revised *Indian Act,* S.C. 1951, c. 29, Indian status would be granted to: (a) someone who would have been considered an Indian under post-confederation Indian legislation predating the 1876 *Indian Act*; (b) current band members; (c) direct male descendants in the male line of persons falling into either of the preceding categories; (d) legitimate children of males falling into the preceding categories; (e) illegitimate children of Indian women unless the father was not himself an Indian; (f) Indian women who were married to Indian men or the widows of Indian men.

[82]*Ibid.,* s. 5.

[83]"Identification and Registration of Indian and Inuit People," *supra* note 69 at 5 and 6. DIAND notes that the following documents were used as the basis for the band lists and general list: local agents' informal band lists; treaty pay lists; Indian moneys interest distribution lists; Indian census records; *Indian Act* election, estates administration and membership commutation lists and scrip records.

[84]The 1927 *Indian Act,* R.S.C. 1927, c. 98 definitions of these terms in s. 2 were virtually the same as those contained in the original 1876 *Indian Act.*

[85]*Assimilation, Integration or Termination?, supra* note 72 at 80.

[86]S.C. 1951, c. 29, s. 8.

[87] *RCAP: Looking Forward, Looking Back, supra* note 46 at 312:

They may, for example, have been away from the reserve when band lists were posted. In remote places, especially where people still practised a subsistence lifestyle, people could have been away on hunting parties, fishing or on their traplines. Such people were also the least likely to have been able to read in the first place. Some people were opposed to any form of registration, seeing it as a derogation from the historical status of Indian nations. Sometimes, it has been argued, the "conspicuous place" called for in the *Indian Act* was less conspicuous than it ought to have been. In any event, and for whatever reason, many people claim that they or their parents or grandparents were never included on those lists when they should have been and that they were prevented from obtaining Indian status.

[88] *Entitlement to Indian Status, supra* note 39 at 15: "As the terms 'non-treaty Indian' and 'irregular band' are omitted from the 1951 *Act,* it is abundantly clear that those terms were subsumed by the purpose and function of the general list." In this regard, the author is more explicit (at 48), noting as follows: "In 1951 the concept of a general list is introduced to ensure that those Indians whose history did not include membership in a band are nevertheless included on the Indian Register."

[89] *Ibid.* at 131.

[90] Native Women's Association of Canada, "Guide to Bill C–31" (Ottawa: Native Women's Association, 1985) at 29.

[91] *RCAP: Looking Forward, Looking Back, supra* note 46 at 302. In *Indian Women and the Law in Canada: Citizens Minus* (Ottawa: Supply and Services Canada, 1978), Kathleen Jamieson concludes (at 63–65) that between 1955 and 1975 there were a total of 13,150 enfranchisements. A total of 10,484—80 percent—were involuntary enfranchisements of Indian women who married out and their children.

[92] Canada, Indian and Northern Affairs, *Basic Departmental Data 2000* (Ottawa: DIAND Information Management Branch, March, 2000) at 6. The precise figures as of December 31, 1999 were 112,482. The statistics are available upon request from the Registrar. On September 1, 2002, the number was 127,000.

[93] R.S.C. 1985, c. I–5 as am. Subsection 6(1) makes the following categories of people eligible to be registered as Indians:

(a) those entitled to registration under the pre-1985 rules

(b) members of bands created after 1985

(c) those who lost entitlement to registration as a result of
  - the "double mother" rule (mother and grandmother not entitled to registration)
  - marrying a non-status man
  - illegitimate child whose father was not entitled to registration
  - woman and children enfranchised because the mother married a man not entitled to registration

(d) Indian men who voluntarily enfranchised along with their wives and children

(e) those enfranchised for having lived abroad for 5 years or for having acquired higher education

(f) those whose parents (both) are (or were, if dead) entitled to registration under any of the prior subsections.

Subsection 6(2) entitle those with a single parent entitled to registration under any of the prior subsections.

[94] "Guide to Bill C–31," *supra* note 90 at 11.

[95]*Entitlement to Indian Status, supra* note 39 at 39, n. 54. This is illustrated by the rationale provided by DIAND for failing to register the applicants for Indian status from the Grande Cache mixed-ancestry group discussed earlier. See note 65 *supra.*

[96]*RCAP: Looking Forward, Looking Back, supra* note 46 at 304.

[97]S. Clatworthy and A. Smith, "Population Implications of the 1985 Amendments to the *Indian Act*: Final Report" (research paper prepared for the Assembly of First Nations, 1992) at ii. They go on to note that "some First Nations, whose out-marriage rates are significantly higher than the national norms, would cease to exist at the end of the 100 year projection period."

[98]Indian and Northern Affairs Canada, *Registered Indian Population Projections for Canada and Regions: 1998–2008* (Ottawa: Minister of Public Works and Government Services, 2000) at 7:

> In 1998, an estimated 2% of births to Registered Indians on reserve were ineligible for status. This is estimated to increase to 4% by 2008. For the off-reserve population, the rate was 20% in 1998 and is projected to reach 27% by 2008.
>
> Because of the 1985 changes to the *Indian Act*, there may be an increasing number of individuals living on reserve who are children of Registered Indian (sic), but who are not eligible for registration under the *Indian Act*. Therefore, they will not appear on the Indian Register. This will have an impact on the future composition of the on-reserve community.

[99]*RCAP: Perspectives and Realities, supra* note 32 at 255.

[100]Vol. XVII, 2 (1985) *Canadian Ethnic Studies* at iii per T. Flanagan & J. Foster, eds.

[101]The history of Quebec reserves is discussed in the *Rapport de la Commission D'étude sur l'Integrité du Territoire du Québec* (The *Dorion Report*) and in Richard Bartlett, *Indian Reserves in Quebec* (Saskatoon: University of Saskatchewan Native Law Centre, 1984).

[102]S.C. 1880, c. 28, s. 14 (2).

[103]See, in regard to the history of the Maritime provinces, Leslie F.S. Upton, *Micmacs and Colonists: Indian-White Relations in the Maritimes, 1713–1867* (Vancouver: University of British Columbia Press, 1979).

[104]*RCAP: Perspectives and Realities, supra* note 32 at 257.

[105]The Conne River Micmac community of Newfoundland was declared to be a band under the name Miawpukek Band on June 28, 1984 by order in council P.C. 1984 2773.

[106]*RCAP: Perspectives and Realities, supra* note 32 at 256. The short section (255–57) on the Labrador Métis in the RCAP report notes that the mixed-ancestry families and groups result originally from the presence of non-Aboriginal fishermen who chose to live off their vessels on shore bases. Called "livyers" or "settlers," they seem to be the ones who married into the resident Inuit and Innu population of what is now Labrador.

[107]Wendy Moss, "Metis Adhesion to Treaty No.3," unpublished paper, March 16, 1979. For the text of the Adhesion to Treaty 3 at Fort Frances, see *Native Rights in Canada, supra* note 43 at 319–20.

[108]Douglas Sanders, "Metis Rights in the Prairie Provinces and the Northwest Territories: A Legal Perspective" in Harry Daniels, ed., *The Forgotten People: Metis and Non-status Indian Land Claims* (Ottawa: Native Council of Canada, 1979) 3 at 14–15. The federal government continues this practice, negotiating land claims with "Metis" groups in the Northwest Territories while refusing to do so in the provinces. Duke Redbird, former director of a Métis and non-status Indian land claim research for the Native Council of Canada agrees with Sanders's assessment: *ibid.* at 48. He goes on to explain why the distinctly Métis reserve adjacent to the Indian reserve was merged with it:

The major exception to this policy of ignoring a distinctly Metis claim [in Ontario] was the Half-breed adhesion to Treaty 3 in 1875. Through the adhesion reserve land was set aside for Half-breeds in their name but in later discovering that the adhesion could set a "dangerous" precedent for recognizing Metis claims, the federal government over the years moved to amalgamate the Half-breed lands with Indian reserves while at the same time supervised the discharge of many Half-breeds from treaty.

[109]See in this context Jacqueline Peterson, "Many Roads to Red River: Métis Genesis in the Great Lakes Region, 1680–1815" in *The New Peoples, supra* note 5, 37. In *The Queen v. Powley*, [2001] 2 C.N.L.R. 291, for example, the Ontario Court of Appeal notes as follows in this regard (at 300): "Between 1800 and 1885, some Sault Ste Marie Métis migrated to Red River Area. Others moved to the United States."

[110]*Powley, ibid.* at 332.

[111]*Ibid.* at 300.

[112]John S. Long, "Treaty No. 9 and Fur Trade Families," *The New Peoples, supra* note 5, 137 at 146.

[113]Jacqueline Peterson & Jennifer S. Brown, "Introduction," *The New Peoples, ibid.,* 3 at 10.

[114]John S. Long, *The New Peoples, ibid.* See also John Long, *Treaty No.9: The Half-Breed Question 1902–1910* (Cobalt, ON: Highway Book Shop, 1978).

[115]"Specific Case Studies: Burleigh Falls" in *The Forgotten People, supra* note 108, 49 at 49–50.

[116]*RCAP: Perspectives and Realities, supra* note 32 at 270, n. 62.

[117]Olive Dickason, "A Look at the Emergence of the Métis" in *The New Peoples, supra* note 5, 19 at 30–31.

[118]This conclusion is supported by Jacqueline Peterson, "Many Roads to Red River: Métis Genesis in the Great Lakes Region, 1680–1815," *The New Peoples, ibid.,* 37. She notes (at 64) that "the 'new people' of Red River...sprang only metaphorically from the soil" in the sense that their antecedents lay in the Métis communities around the Great Lakes that never coalesced into a true Métis nation. Douglas Sanders, *The Forgotten People, supra* note 108 agrees (at 7) that it was only in the Northwest that a true Métis political consciousness emerged.

> While Canadian Indian policy had its roots in colonial experience in New England and eastern Canada, Canadian Half-breed policy developed in response to the specific situation in the North-west. While there are mixed-blood populations in other colonized areas, the Canadian experience is unique. There are no other examples of a mixed-blood population becoming a regional political community which could successfully assert political and rights, for a period at least, against the national government. The Metis in Canada were recognized not simply as members of the general population nor simply as having partial Indian descent. There were distinct Metis claims, and unique governmental responses to those claims.

[119]Trudy Nicks, "Mary Anne's Dilemma: The Ethnohistory of an Ambivalent Identity," *Canadian Ethnic Studies, supra* note 100 at 103. Clem Chartier, a member of the Board of Governors of the Métis National Council who participated in its creation in 1983, writing in 1999 about membership of non-status Indians in Métis organizations, stated: "Hundreds of Indian people lost their Indian Status and treaty rights during the 1960s and 1970s, thus becoming Non-Status Indians. Many of them joined Métis organizations. Perhaps they did so because both groups faced similar economic, social, and political conditions. Because of that relationship, the terms Métis and Non-Status Indian were used interchangeably for many years.": John H. Hylton, ed., *Aboriginal Self-Government in Canada* (Saskatoon: Purich Publishing Ltd, 1999) at 113. See in addition the similar observations of the Alberta Métis Asso-

ciation in *Métis Land Rights, supra* note 6.

[120]*Supra* note 100 at iv.

[121]Individuals whose identity ought not to be disclosed have explained to the authors their personal experiences where, in the case of employment opportunities that are made available only to Aboriginal people, some employers will hire any person on their mere declaration that they have Aboriginal ancestry, without regard to the question of membership or belonging to any Aboriginal community, and that such declarations are sometimes invited without regard to the truth of the statement. Of course, these discretionary "affirmative action" program benefits are not the same as constitutionally protected rights, which are generally not acted upon by governments before they are found by the Court.

[122]This statement was made by one of the authors a number of years ago: Paul L.A.H. Chartrand, "Contemporary Métis Rights and Issues in Canada" (speaking notes for an opening address at the Aboriginal Law in Canada conference, Vancouver, Native Investment and Trade Association, 1995) at 5.

[123]However, they also appear to admit anyone of mixed ancestry into their organization and recently supported the Powleys in their quest to be recognized as the possessors of as Métis Aboriginal rights. The debate about who the real Métis may be continues in this organization.

[124]Douglas Sanders, *The Forgotten People, supra* note 108 at 21. The Manitoba Metis Federation formerly took the same view.

[125]Douglas Sanders, "Prior Claims: Aboriginal People in the Constitution of Canada," in S.M. Beck & I. Bernier, eds., *Canada and the New Constitution: The Unfinished Agenda,* (Montreal: Institute for Research on Public Policy, 1983) 227 at 255.

[126]Larry Chartrand calls the derivative rights concept the "trace" theory and criticizes it as "illogical and inappropriate" in "Are We Metis or Are We Indians? A Commentary on *R. v. Grumbo,* [1999–2000] Ottawa L. Rev. 267 at 278. In *R. v. Van der Peet,* [1996] 2 SCR 507, 4 C.N.L.R. 177 at 201, the Chief Justice made some obiter comments, which appear to have been given undue weight. He stated that "It may or may not be the case that the claims of the Metis are determined on the basis of the pre-contact practices, traditions and customs of their Aboriginal ancestors; whether that is so must await determination in a case in which the issue arises." Clearly, these are obiter comments indicating the decision not to consider the issue, and ought not to be given any weight in support of the derivative rights theory. There seems to be ambiguity about the status of obiter dicta in the Supreme Court of Canada and superior courts, and their significance in binding the rulings of lower courts. The confusion seems to be attributed to the courts' interpretations of the Supreme Court of Canada decision in *Sellars v. The Queen,* [1980] 1 S.C.R. 527. See the analysis of the Honourable Mr. Justice Douglas Lambert in "Ratio Decidendi and Obiter Dicta: Some Observations about *Sellars* v. *The Queen* (1993) 51 *The Advocate* 689.

[127]As quoted in Joe Sawchuk, *The Metis of Manitoba: Reformulation of an Ethnic Identity* (Toronto: Peter Martin Associates Limited, 1978) at 33.

[128]Accounts of the battles between the Sioux and the Métis include W.L. Morton, "The Battle at Grand Coteau" in A.S. Lussier & D.B. Sealey, eds., *The Other Natives: The Métis* (Winnipeg, Manitoba Métis Federation Press, 1978) at 47; W.L. Morton, *Manitoba: A History* (Toronto: University of Toronto Press, 1957) at 62, 80; Alexander Ross, *The Red River Settlement: Its Rise, Progress and Present State* (reprint Edmonton: Hurtig Publishers, 1972) at 324ff.

[129]In *R.* v. *Powley,* [2001] 2 C.N.L.R. 291, the Ontario Court of Appeal refers to the Métis people, but the question dealt with by the court involves a small community in Ontario, far from the western plains in which Riel's people, the western Métis, made their mark on Canadian history.

[130]See *Corbiere* v. *Canada,* [1999] 3 C.N.L.R. 19 (S.C.C.) at 46, per L'Heureux-Dubé J.

[131]*Powley, supra* note 129 at 332–333 C.N.L.R. para. 136–39. The court seems to have been motivated by a desire to provide remedial justice. *Accord,* Catherine Bell, "Metis Constitutional Rights in Section 35(1)" [1997] 36 Alberta Law Rev. 180, at 188. S. 35 cannot be properly seen as a receptacle for all claims based on considerations of justice. Some claims belong in the *Charter.* For example, racial discrimination may offend s. 15 principles and require the remedial assistance of discretionary government laws and programs.

[132]*Ibid.* at 332 C.N.L.R.

[133]Siggner *et al., supra* note 3 at 27.

[134]In *R.* v. *Taylor and Williams* (1981) 34 O.R. (2d) 360; [1981] 3 C.N.L.R. 114 (Ont. C.A.), where it is stated "…although it is not possible to remedy all of what we now perceive as past wrongs…it is essential and in keeping with established and accepted principles that the Courts not create, by a remote, isolated current view of events, new grievances."

[135]*Blueberry River Band* v. *Canada,* [2001] 3 C.N.L.R. 72 (F.C.A.) at 78–82.

[136]*Turtle Mountain Band of Chippewa Indians* v. *U.S.* 490. F. (2d) 935, (Jan. 23, 1974) where descendants of Canadian Metis were accepted as "Indians" and members of an American Indian tribe.

[137]*R.* v. *Sparrow,* [1990] 1 S.C.R. 1075.

[138]It is beyond the scope of this chapter to elaborate the distinctions between group rights and individual rights. For immediate purposes, a right exercisable by an individual is not an individual right if the right is only exercisable on account of group membership. For a discussion on the various kinds of Aboriginal rights, see Brian Slattery, "Making Sense of Aboriginal and Treaty Rights" (2000) 79 Can. Bar Rev. 196. Cf. C. Bell, *supra* note 131 at 354–55.

Chapter Four

Domestic Recognition in the United States and Canada

John Giokas

Introduction

The approach set out in *Partners in Confederation*[1] focuses on the inherent right of self-government that the Royal Commission on Aboriginal Peoples (RCAP)[2] views as being an Aboriginal or treaty right guaranteed and affirmed in section 35(1) of the *Constitution Act, 1982.*[3] RCAP proposes that this right be exercisable by Aboriginal groups in two stages. First, on their own initiative, Aboriginal groups may undertake unilateral action to realize their inherent self-government right in core areas of jurisdiction. Second, they may take action outside their core jurisdictional areas through agreements with the federal and provincial governments.[4]

In terms of the first stage (unilateral Aboriginal group action) two key elements of group initiative are the inherent capacity of an Aboriginal group to establish its own governing structures and to define its own membership. Both may be undertaken without the necessity of any kind of concurrence from either the federal or provincial governments because they belong to the core area of inherent Aboriginal jurisdiction.

However, the practical reality is that Canadian governments will likely balk at the prospect of self-defining, sub-state, self-governing entities that claim the right to come into existence and to claim a particular population of Canadian citizens as being under their jurisdiction without regard to the other governments with whom they will be in a relationship. In particular, they will likely wish to retain for themselves the prerogative of having some say in whether or not they wish to deal with the new entities. In other words, they will wish to decide for themselves whether, or to what extent, they may wish to recognize the self-defining Aboriginal group as a nation capable of interacting with them on the basis of rough governmental equality in certain areas.

If this assumption is correct, RCAP will have to develop a sound and realistic set of objective recognition criteria to guide Aboriginal peoples as well as the federal and provincial governments. The risk of alienating Aboriginal peoples by calling for objective standards to which they must conform are outweighed by the dangers of allowing the courts and the non-Aboriginal governments to develop their own recognition criteria. Since *Partners in Confederation* does not explore in any detail the potential problems that emerging Aboriginal nations may encounter, the relatively more lengthy American experience may be useful as a starting point for discussion on how to avoid the problems and complications that have arisen there in a similar context.

Aside from these practical difficulties of implementing the *Partners* vision of Aboriginal self-government, recognition is an important concept to examine for another reason. Embedded in the approach espoused by RCAP in *Partners* are notions of recognition that would benefit from closer examination in any event.

Recognition is a legal concept imported during the colonial period from international law into domestic American and Canadian law to deal with the fact that North America was already populated by peoples organized into distinct political units referred to by the settlers as "tribes" and "nations." *Partners in Confederation* takes the view that modern Aboriginal communities and nations are the successors to the historically distinct Aboriginal political units that occupied North America at contact.

Partners assumes that Aboriginal communities and nations already constitute a third order of government within the Canadian federation, albeit a hitherto forgotten one that has yet to fully re-emerge. The theory upon which *Partners* is based asserts that the Aboriginal peoples encountered by the settler society were "political units that became associated with the Crown at definite historical periods whether through treaties or other less formal arrangements,"[5] the net effect of which was the recognition at common law of their self-governing capacity.

The prime challenge posed by the *Partners* approach is that it does not account for the fact that treaty-making and other forms of nation-to-nation or government-to-government relations inevitably involve the notion of recognition. From the perspective of international state practice, "recognition" means acknowledgment as a state distinct from the recognizing state. In the international and domestic Aboriginal context, treaties have been the prime means of reflecting the distinct nation-to-nation relationship implied by recognition.

How, in conceptual terms, an Aboriginal nation can at one and the same time be distinct and yet be embraced by the political unit from which it is distinct through some form of "association" (that neither settler governments nor Aboriginal peoples may have been aware of at the time) is an issue that will have to be faced in more detail and with a higher degree of analytical precision if the *Partners* vision is to gain wide acceptance. Simply describing the process as "organic" is insufficient.[6]

The position adopted by *Partners* thus speaks to recognition theory, but in an indirect way. In effect, *Partners* assumes that Aboriginal communities are already to this extent "domestic dependent nations" within Canada and entitled to the prerogatives of nations, namely, the capacity to be self-governing within the norms of the Canadian federation. This largely unspoken assumption in *Partners* deprives any discussion of recognition in Canada of a domestic standard or point of reference against which to measure the proposal.

In the United States, by way of contrast, the concept of domestic recognition has always been referred to by that name and has evolved over time to accommodate the many fluctuations and course changes that have characterized American Indian policy. The result has been the recognition of tribes (including Alaskan Native villages) as self-governing "domestic dependent nations." Canadian recognition practice is most apparent in the special status afforded to "bands" under the *Indian Act* and to certain other Indian and Inuit groups that have achieved a measure of self-government by specific legislation.

In the beginning, Indian tribes or nations in what is now the United States were separate and distinct entities, both territorially and in terms of culture and political organization. They were regarded as distinct political units. Recognition was a relatively straightforward political decision that was largely analogous to the practice in international law. However, removal to new territories, confinement on reservations, the imposition of non-Indian municipal-style tribal councils, individual allotment of reservation land, the influx of non-Indians onto reservations and tribal reorganization along corporate lines have all served to change the nature and composition of the formerly distinct nations making up the Aboriginal tribes, bands, and nations with which the settler societies entered into relations.

All this has affected the notion of recognition and led to a modification of the concept over the years in the United States. Tribes and tribal territories are no longer as distinct, geographically or jurisdictionally, as they were in the beginning. There are large numbers of non-Indians who own land within reservation boundaries, and there has been a high degree of intermarriage between Indians and non-Indians. In the same way that federal and provincial law do in Canada, American federal and state law often compete with or override tribal law on tribal territory. American-style political institutions have replaced traditional tribal forms of governance in many, if not most, cases. More and more, the institutions, processes, and problems of tribal self-government often resemble those of the dominant American society.

There are also large numbers of persons who are "Indians in an ethnological sense"[7] (by virtue of racial descent and kinship links) but who do not belong to federally recognized tribes. These persons correspond to those referred to in Canada as "non-status Indians" or as "Métis." In the United States they may be members of state-recognized tribes or other groups of Indians who claim tribal status but who have yet to be recognized by the federal government. They are often to be found in urban centres throughout the United States. Generally they are not recognized as entitled to federal services because of their lack of tribal affiliation.

Recognition is now a complex and contentious issue in the United States that is based not only on the separateness and distinctiveness of tribes as political units, but also on the race of those making up tribal membership. Thus, there are two recognition policies in operation in the United States. One is for tribes, while the other is for Indians who are members of tribes. In short, not all tribal members will be recognized as Indians. This is roughly parallel to the distinction in Canada between band members and status Indians, categories that do not necessarily refer to the same persons.

Recognition is a contentious issue in Canada as well. Controversies over the recognition of individual status Indians culminated in *Indian Act* amendments in 1985 that "re-recognized" large numbers of ethnological Indians. Controversies over recognizing groups of Indians in Canada are ongoing, as the federal government has refused to recognize new bands since 1984 (the Conne River Micmac). In the same way, the federal government continues to refuse to recognize Métis communities as such for purposes of special constitutional status under section 91(24) of the *Constitution Act, 1867*.

As mentioned above, the thesis of this paper is that despite the many historical, political, and constitutional differences between Canada and the United States in terms of overall Aboriginal self-government policy and practice, there are important lessons to be drawn from the American experience. A related subthesis is that the vision in *Partners* bears striking resemblances to the 1934 *Indian Reorganization Act*[8] proposals that led to a resurgence in American tribal self-government. Another related sub-thesis is that the tripartite analysis offered in *Partners* that distinguishes between the source (inherent), scope (circumscribed), and status (subordinate) of Aboriginal self-governing powers leads directly to a view of Aboriginal nations in Canada that closely resembles the American doctrine of the "domestic dependent nation."

In short, the approach proposed in *Partners* may lead not only to Aboriginal nations in Canada having the same dependent status as American tribes, it may also lead Canada into the same type of self-government litigation that has characterized American Indian policy since 1958, when the U.S. Supreme Court decided in *Williams* v. *Lee*[9] that state jurisdiction over tribal lands was invalid if it infringed on a tribe's self-government rights. This case effectively inaugurated the modern era of jurisdictional battles on reservation lands.

For all of these reasons, it is proposed in this chapter to undertake to clarify the concepts underlying or embedded in the vision of Aboriginal self-government set out in *Partners in Confederation* in the hope that this may be of some assistance to policy-makers and to others who may be interested in the long overdue, complex, and challenging task of making Aboriginal self-government a reality in Canada.

International Law Roots

International Legal Personality: Recognition in International Law

The subjects of modern public international law are entities recognized as international legal persons (or as possessing what is referred to as international legal personality). There are four main hallmarks of international legal personality:

1. Standing to make claims before international tribunals to have their international rights vindicated;

2. Subjection to some or all international duties;

3. Capacity to enter into binding international agreements, i.e., treaties, conventions, etc.;

4. Enjoyment of some or all of the immunities from the jurisdiction of domestic tribunals available in international law.[10]

In practice it is only states and certain international organizations such as the United Nations that have full international legal personality. Other bodies may have a greater or lesser number of the attributes of international legal personality for different purposes. Non-governmental organizations—bodies recognized for certain purposes under the international system—are a good example.

A number of Aboriginal organizations currently enjoy the status of non-governmental organizations in the international system.[11]

Recognition in its most visible form in international law is the practice between states of formally acknowledging the existence of the other as a full-fledged actor entitled to exercise its legal capacity as a state under international law. This is generally done by the establishment of diplomatic relations. In short, recognition is the acknowledgment by one party that the other has international legal personality.

Recognition is above all a political act left to the executive of most states. The importance of recognition is that it is normally a precondition to the establishment of full, optional, bilateral relations between states. Recognition need not be formal, but may be implied by various acts taken by one state towards another. There are many ways in which recognition may be implied. One way is by entering into international agreements that accord mutual rights and impose mutual duties.

The important point is that this has little to do with the functional capacity of a state to exercise the rights and duties of international legal persons. An emerging state may well have the objective attributes of statehood according to the Montevideo Convention (a permanent population on a defined territory that is subject to its government and has the capacity of entering into relations with other states[12]) and yet be denied formal recognition. For example, communist China had the legal capacity for statehood in this sense long before it received official acknowledgement from the United States of its capacity in this regard through the formal recognition process.

The distinction between capacity on the one hand and acknowledgment of that capacity on the other has generated two basic theories of recognition.

1. Declaratory—This is a functional approach that holds recognition to be the formal acknowledgment of a pre-existing state of affairs that is not affected by the act of acknowledgment. In short, formal recognition is not required in order for a state to have international legal personality and therefore to be able to exercise international rights and discharge international duties. If a body has the attributes of a state, it has the legal capacity of a state and is therefore implicitly recognized by automatic operation of international law. The ultimate test is a factual one.

   The declaratory theory corresponds best with the prevailing practice of states in international law. For example, the fact that many Arab states did not formally recognize Israel did not mean they did not make claims against Israel in international forums despite refusing to enter into formal diplomatic relations or agreements.

2. Constitutive—This is a normative approach that holds recognition to be essential for the full conferral of international legal personality, i.e., to "constitute" in law the body being recognized as a state in the international system. In short, if a body is not formally recognized as having the legal capacity of a state, it does not have it and cannot enter into binding international relations with other states. From this perspective, there is no such thing as implicit recognition—an explicit act of acknowledgment is required to confer recognition.

Although this theory does not always conform to actual international practice, it highlights the fact that states are not obliged to enter into bilateral relations with each other. This theory corresponds to the ability of states to choose which entities they will treat as equals to themselves and with which they will agree to be bound by agreements and by the norms of international law. This is an important point when one considers that international agreements are often mutually agreed-upon limitations of sovereignty.

In summary, these theories appear to deal with different aspects of international law. The declaratory theory deals with functional legal capacity to act under international law. The constitutive theory deals with the normative exercise of bilateral relations. It addresses the fact that states interact with states and this is a matter that requires some degree of consent from the other states. From this perspective the legal capacity of a state means nothing if it doesn't mean establishing bilateral relations. In short, legal capacity without someone with whom to act out that capacity is a nullity. Thus, these theories do not disagree so much as put the emphasis on different aspects of what it means to be a state in a world made up of other states.

In this sense, their application to the domestic context highlights what it means to be a political unit in a federal system made up of other political units. From the declaratory viewpoint, a distinct Aboriginal political unit has the legal capacity to act as a political unit regardless of any formal act of recognition by any other political unit in the federal system. It is implicit in the fact of being a distinct Aboriginal political unit. This is the implicit theory at the root of the first self-government stage proposed by RCAP: unilateral Aboriginal action in core areas of inherent Aboriginal self-government jurisdiction.

From the constitutive viewpoint, however, the other political units in the federal system must "constitute" the Aboriginal political unit by formal acts (such as entering into formal agreements regarding how the Aboriginal political unit will exercise its legal capacity) before the Aboriginal political unit will have domestic legal personality. Before a "constitutive" act of recognition is made, actions by the Aboriginal political unit in the federal system may be in breach of the legal norms of the federal system, i.e., they may be unconstitutional or against the law as defined by the existing federal actors. This is the implicit theory lying behind RCAP's proposals regarding the second stage of Aboriginal self-government: formal agreements between the federal and provincial governments and Aboriginal groups in areas of inherent Aboriginal jurisdiction outside the core.

As a final point before leaving the international realm, it is evident that states in international law are legally independent of each other (one of the criteria of statehood) unless they have entered into other arrangements whereby they agree to limit or share sovereignty. Legal independence means the ability to pass one's own laws. Laws passed under a state's sovereign law-making power are made to be applied by a group of people who are gathered into a single political unit for the purpose of governing themselves. Under normal principles their laws do not have extra-territorial effect, i.e., they do not invade another state's domain so as to govern people gathered into a different political unit. This is, of course, unlike the situation in a federation, where the political units are permeable because membership is shared between them. Thus, analogies with international law must be applied carefully to domestic situations.

Domestic Legal Personality for Tribes in the United States

Federal recognition as a "tribe" in the United States brings with it the following elements that parallel the elements of international legal personality as described above.

1. Standing to make claims before domestic tribunals on the basis that a group of persons is a "tribe" capable of vindicating whatever rights it may have *vis-à-vis* the United States;

   Historically, the United States (as a sovereign immune to suit) would pass special legislation permitting tribes to pursue legal action against it for land and related claims. Relatively recently, a group of persons descended from ethnological Mashpee Indians in Massachusetts were refused standing to pursue a land claim on the basis that they did not constitute a "tribe" because they had long ago abandoned their tribal organization.[13] In short, as a group of persons without tribal status, they had no standing to vindicate domestic rights accruing to tribes.

2. Subjection to some or all of the duties of tribes, such as vulnerability to congressional "plenary power" (virtually unlimited federal legislative power over tribes);

   The judicial finding recognizing that the Pueblo peoples of the southwestern United States were "Indians" in this sense despite their claim of

U.S. citizenship and full ownership of their lands in fee simple is a good example. Prior to that, they had not been considered federal subject matter Indian tribes and had been exempted from United States federal Indian legislation.[14] They are now subject to congressional power over them and have mobilized on numerous occasions to lobby against congressional Indian legislation they believed to be harmful to their interests.

3. Capacity to enter into binding domestic agreements, i.e., treaties, executive agreements, land claims settlements, etc.;

In 1972, despite an absence of any specific act of federal recognition of their tribal status, the Passamaquoddy Indians of Maine brought an action against the United States to compel the Secretary of the Interior to sue the state for failure to respect early federal land surrender legislation modelled on the *Royal Proclamation of 1763*. The Federal Court of Appeal held that the Passamaquoddies were a "tribe" for these purposes[15] (followed by Department of the Interior confirmation of their federally recognized status). A land claim settlement ensued in 1980.

4. Enjoyment of some or all of the immunities from the jurisdiction of domestic tribunals available in domestic law, since recognized tribes have sovereign immunity.

The most powerful and controversial example is provided by *Santa Clara Pueblo* v. *Martinez*[16] where the Pueblo was found to be immune from judicial review by the federal courts on this basis, despite having on the face discriminated (contrary to the provisions of the *Indian Civil Rights Act* of 1968) against the mixed-blood children of a Pueblo woman who had married a Navajo man. In short, Julia Martinez, a Pueblo woman, could not sue the Pueblo in non-Pueblo tribunals.

Implicit Recognition in *Partners in Confederation*

Partners in Confederation outlines an implicit vision of recognition that in many ways resembles the position in international law with respect to the recognition of foreign nations. The *Partners* vision was prefigured by the earlier discussion in RCAP's 1992 publication, *The Right of Aboriginal Self-Government and the Constitution: A Commentary*.[17] In that publication, a distinction was introduced at the outset between the source, scope, and status of the inherent right of self-government.

To recall that argument and to translate it into the concepts of recognition, the "source" discussion differentiates between inherent and created rights of self-government. It notes that, with or without constitutional recognition, the right exists in law; it "springs from sources within the Aboriginal nations, rather than from the written Constitution"[18] (where it is merely "recognized and affirmed"). In other words, section 35 does not create or "constitute" the self-governing capacity of Aboriginal nations. They have that capacity regardless of what is contained in section 35 or in any other constitutional document. It is implicit in the very fact that they are distinct political communities. Section 35 is thus a reminder of the breadth and depth of Canadian constitutional history, but is not in itself the source or authority for what is contained in that history.

The "source" discussion implicitly refers to a declaratory theory of recognition: functional legal capacity to act exists from the moment a body has the attributes of a state whether or not that capacity is explicitly and formally recognized. It does not depend on the actions of the other actors in the international world—they confer nothing on another state in this respect except the formal acknowledgment of pre-existing legal capacity. Thus, in the domestic Canadian context, whether other governments in Canada choose to make explicit what is implicit by entering into formal agreements with Aboriginal political units around the exercise of their inherent legal capacity is irrelevant. Recognition of their capacity to act as distinct political units is implied by the fact they possess an inherent source of self-governing authority, i.e., one that is not dependent on other governments or on the Constitution that regulates how those other governments interact.

The scope and status arguments in *Commentary* maintain that inherent self-governing legal capacity is circumscribed and subordinate to federal and provincial law under general constitutional principles and pursuant to the *Sparrow* justification test.[19] In terms of recognition theory, these arguments reflect the notion that the exercise of bilateral relations is involved whenever legal capacity to act is involved. In short, no one's legal capacity is absolute in a world made up of other actors: it must accommodate itself to their existence. The argument in the *Commentary* goes in this direction, subjecting the inherent right of Aboriginal self-government to the norms of the Canadian constitutional framework, much as the exercise of state capacity to act in the international sphere would be constrained by the norms of international law. There can be no unilateral exercise of legal capacity to act that will not impact on other bodies that also have legal capacity to act.

However, the norms of international law (like the norms of Canadian constitutional law as described in the *Commentary*) are not always clear, nor can they address all contingencies. Thus bilateral and multilateral relations and mutual accommodations are required to harmonize actions, otherwise there may be disputes or even war to resolve the effects of state actions on other states. In the domestic context, disputes and war translate into federal and provincial court challenges or to Aboriginal civil disobedience and the resultant application of force through police action to prevent any unilateral exercise of the legal capacity of an Aboriginal nation to act as a separate political unit. In short, to avoid disputes and war between the distinct political units in the federal system, self-government, finance, and other agreements are the preferred way to go. *Commentary* explores this aspect in its recommendations for a constitutional recognition clause and a treaty process.[20]

As mentioned earlier, the analogy with international law is obviously not complete since the norms of the federal system are much more constraining than the norms of the international system. For example, the powers of a state in the international system might well be circumscribed and subordinate externally, but would rarely be so with regard to purely internal matters. It cannot be so in a federal system, where boundaries are less absolute than those between states in the international arena, where (in the absence of dual citizenship) the citizens of one state are not normally the citizens of another. In short, states as separate political units have separate members. In a federal system the same people will belong to different political units in different degrees.

In any event, the analogy with international law is clearer and more fleshed out in *Partners in Confederation*, where the language explicitly recalls the international analogy and leads more directly to the declaratory theory of recognition. For example, *Partners* refers to international law by implication in its reference to the origins of the inherent right "within Aboriginal communities, as a residue of the powers they originally held as autonomous nations."[21] *Partners* adds that the ultimate origins of the inherent right are "in the communities themselves rather than in the Crown or Parliament."[22] In short, the legal capacity of Aboriginal communities or nations to act as such resides in the fact that they are "political units that became associated with the Crown at definite historical periods, whether through treaties or other less formal arrangements."[23]

Thus, the Aboriginal political units are not created (constituted) as political units by the act of any political unit outside of themselves. They have the present status of political units because they are, and always have been, distinct political units in a political relationship with the larger political unit represented by the Crown. *Partners* goes on to note that section 35 "guarantees their status as distinct constitutional entities."[24] Thus, the Constitution does not "constitute" Aboriginal communities as political units: it merely guarantees that status.

The "political units" language is repeated throughout *Partners*. If for "political unit" one were to substitute "state" the analogy with international law becomes more apparent: states according to the declaratory theory derive their legal capacity from themselves and not from any other states in the world community. The many international instruments and agreements (such as the United Nations *Charter*[25]) "guarantee" their present status as states but do not confer it.

As mentioned earlier, the distinction between functional legal capacity to act and the normative exercise of bilateral relations finds another conceptual vehicle in *Partners* in the distinction between an "actual" and "potential" right of self-government. The former clearly refers to functional legal capacity to act in terms of a declaratory theory of recognition.

> As such, it can be implemented immediately to its fullest extent by unilateral Aboriginal initiatives, even in the absence of self-government agreements or court sanction.[26]

Partners in Confederation confirms that its vision is based on the declaratory theory of recognition. For example, it concludes by noting that while self-government agreements "would generally be preferable," there is no legal requirement for such agreements to be concluded with the federal and provincial governments in order for Aboriginal peoples to implement their inherent right to self-government.

> However, in the final analysis, there are persuasive reasons for thinking that in core areas Aboriginal peoples may implement their right of self-government at their own initiative, without the concurrence of federal and provincial authorities.[27]

Under the *Partners* vision the absence of such formal acts of recognition by the federal and provincial governments will no more hinder the Aboriginal nations than the absence of formal recognition by western European states hindered the Soviet Union immediately after the Russian Revolution.

In short, explicit acts of recognition in the form of agreements between political units only make it easier to act as political units *inter se*. They are not required in order that they be and act as distinct political units. While the declaratory theory conforms to the actual practice of states in the international arena, it does not conform to recent Canadian self-government practice. *Partners* attempts to deal with this by noting the practical advantages to negotiated agreements between Aboriginal nations and the federal and provincial governments. Those same arguments might be applied to the international arena as well.

For example, and by way of further analogy, there is no question that it is preferable that Israel and the majority of Arab states enter into diplomatic arrangements whereby the latter formally recognize Israel's right to exist as a state on lands they currently claim as Arab lands. But it is not necessary that they do so in order that Israel have the legal status as a state and govern the lands it occupies as its own sovereign territory.

Thus, while *Partners in Confederation* has many sound practical arguments against unilateral actions by Aboriginal political units, its implicit endorsement of the declaratory theory renders those arguments merely persuasive rather than compelling.

Recognition Practice Regarding Indians

United States Indian Recognition Policy

Who the United States will recognize as an "Indian" for official purposes is important because tribal decisions about their own membership are not necessarily accepted by the federal government. In short, federal recognition of the tribe does not mean federal recognition of all its members. Thus there may be two separate lists of tribal members: one maintained by the tribe, and another maintained by whatever federal department is providing a particular service to Indians. This corresponds to Canadian practice differentiating Indian status from band membership under the *Indian Act*.[28] The obvious motivation in both countries is to control the Indian service population.

Until the advent of the 1934 *Indian Reorganization Act*[29] *(IRA)*, federal services were generally provided to Indians in the context of fulfilling treaty or related statutory obligations. Except for certain limited purposes such as congressional Indian appropriations,[30] the issue of who was or was not an Indian in strict blood quantum or definitional terms was not a major issue because most tribes, especially in the West, were still relatively homogeneous. Thus tribal membership was viewed as the key to Indian-specific service delivery. This changed for a number of reasons, most of them having to do with the downgrading of the treaty relationship and the concomitant desire of the federal government to control its Indian-specific expenditures.

The *IRA* was the first legislation to attempt precise definitions of "tribe" and of "Indian." Under the *IRA* and other legislation such as the more recent *Indian Self-Determination and Education Assistance Act* of 1975,[31] the federal government continues to insist on membership in a "tribe" as a prerequisite for federal Indian benefits and services. At the same time, however, the government also insists on being able to determine who the "Indians" are to whom benefits and services will be provided. Now both tribal membership and blood quantum criteria are imposed. There is no universal standard for recognized Indian status as there is in Canada.

Since tribes in the United States are separate political units with the sovereign capacity of controlling their own membership, tribal constitutions contain membership codes with criteria for enrolment. There is always a blood quantum requirement (although it may be minimal). The feature that counts is tribal acceptance of someone as a member. A person who would probably be classified as Métis or non-status Indian in Canada will often be accepted as a tribal member in the United States.

For the federal government the inquiry usually begins with the tribe. The key, of course, is federal recognition. There are many Indians belonging to the estimated 130 unrecognized and 109 terminated tribes[32] who, although "Indian" from the viewpoint of racial ancestry, are not recognized as such for most federal purposes. In general, for most federal services through the Bureau of Indian Affairs (BIA) an "Indian" is someone of at least 1/4 Indian blood and is a member of one of the nearly 550 federally recognized tribes and is living on or near a reservation.[33] Enrolled tribal members who meet the federal blood quantum requirements and who live in urban centres are still recognized as Indians but are generally unable to obtain the same benefits and services.

Other federal legislation may simply defer to tribal practice, follow BIA practice, impose a higher or lower blood quantum requirement, or impose other related requirements. Thus, federal government practice is neither consistent nor uniform. Only the U.S. Census accepts self-definition by Indians. "Federal, state and tribal definitions have wide variations," notes one commentator, and "the legal definition of Indian-ness is complexly contextual."[34]

As a result of these varied practices, the editors of the latest edition of *Felix S. Cohen's Handbook of Federal Indian Law* have concluded that to be recognized as an "Indian" by the United States an individual must meet two basic criteria:

1. Racial ancestry—the individual's ancestors were present in North America before "discovery" by Europeans;

2. Tribal practice—the individual is recognized as an Indian by his or her community.[35]

It is to be noted that self-identification as such plays no role in whether or not a person will be accorded official recognition as an Indian. In any event and as mentioned above, the shift in emphasis from tribes as self-defining bodies to tribes composed of Indians recognized as Indians by the federal government began with the *IRA* in 1934. Its definition of "Indian" has been influential in the subsequent evolution of federal tribal recognition policy and is important to understand for that reason.

19. The term "Indian" as used in this *Act* shall include all persons of Indian descent who are members of any recognized Indian tribe now under Federal jurisdiction, and all persons who are descendants of such members who were, on June 1, 1934, residing within the present boundaries of any Indian reservation, and shall further include all

other persons of one-half or more Indian blood. For purposes of this *Act,* Eskimos and other Aboriginal peoples of Alaska shall be considered "Indians."[36]

This definition breaks the category of recognized "Indian" down into three subcategories:

1. Tribal membership plus racial ancestry—("The term 'Indian' as used in this *Act* shall include all persons of Indian descent who are members of any recognized Indian tribe now under Federal jurisdiction");

2. Racial ancestry plus residence on reservation lands ("and all persons who are descendants of such members who were, on June 1, 1934, residing within the present boundaries of any Indian reservation");

3. Racial ancestry alone ("and shall further include all other persons of one-half or more Indian blood").

Thus, the more distant any particular individual is from actually being accepted by the group as a member, the greater are the other objective requirements: from simple tribal membership based on descent from the original tribe one moves in the case of non-member descendants to a more stringent test requiring residence as at a certain date, to an even more restrictive pure blood quantum test for non-descendant non-members.

Canadian Indian Recognition Policy and *Partners*

The government of Canada has a long tradition of making the kind of distinctions between Indians that have been a feature of American policy since 1934 by differentiating status Indians from non-status Indians and Métis. For reasons of fiscal control it is not likely that the federal government will relinquish the power of distinguishing between "recognized" and "unrecognized" Indians.

Partners in Confederation endorses the view that the term "aboriginal peoples" in section 35 "does not refer to groups characterized by their racial make-up" but instead "designates historically defined political units."[37] In the same vein, *Partners* proposes that Aboriginal political units decide their membership according to their own citizenship rules, not on "genetic characteristics."[38] It should be noted that the term used in *Partners* is "citizenship," a notion closer to international law analogies with states than the term "membership." Evidently, states under international law control their own citizenship and need not base it on race.

In any event, under the declaratory theory of recognition it is evident that there ought to be no externally imposed constraints on who will be considered a member of an Aboriginal nation. If a distinct political unit accepts certain persons as its members and they voluntarily accept membership, other political units should not question this. It is a matter internal to the political unit in question. However, the federal government is likely to adopt a constitutive theory whereby as the "constituting" nation it may choose not to accord formal recognition to Aboriginal political units that have certain citizenship practices. Alternatively, it may accept that the political unit in question exists in law, but refuse to recognize certain persons or categories of persons as members of that political unit for particular purposes.

If the example of the United States is anything to go by, the latter scenario is likely if Aboriginal nations in Canada choose to include persons not recognized as sufficiently "Aboriginal" by the federal government. A situation like that which exists in the United States may well emerge, prompting Aboriginal nations to require a degree of Aboriginal blood quantum sufficient to attract federal government recognition of their members for purpose of program funding and federal services. If this were to happen, the vision in *Partners* would be defeated, and many Aboriginal persons would be excluded from membership in the "historically defined political units"[39] from which they are descended. This is already happening in the United States under tribal membership codes, as has been dramatically demonstrated by cases such as *Santa Clara Pueblo v. Martinez.*[40]

A scenario whereby Aboriginal nations were responsible for excluding potential members from membership on purely racial criteria incorporated into membership rules would transfer the locus of discriminatory behaviour from one government (federal) to another (Aboriginal). If the experience so far with band willingness to admit new members as a result of the impact of Bill C–31 of 1985 is any indication, the problem may already be present in Canada.[41]

Thus, the potential for discrimination by existing Aboriginal political units lends force to the notion that objective recognition criteria ought to at least be contemplated, if only for discussion purposes. If this were contemplated by RCAP as a recommendation to be made to Aboriginal communities or nations or as a mandatory recognition criterion under a constitutive theory of recognition, there is some merit to using an adapted version of the *IRA* criteria as a starting point for discussion and analysis. For example, the initial or "start-up" membership for any Aboriginal group that was contemplating self-starting inherent self-government initiatives might be:

1. All persons of Aboriginal descent or related by kinship (legitimate marriage or adoption, etc.) to such persons, who are members of a self-defining Aboriginal community or nation, whether formally enrolled as members or not and whether normally resident in the community or nation or not (to account thereby for non-*Indian Act* or other groups that may not keep formal records of membership or whose membership practices are customary or

implicit but otherwise knowable and demonstrable by the group itself);

2. All persons of Aboriginal descent who are descended from or can trace a kinship connection to members of the original historically defined Aboriginal political unit now represented by the Aboriginal group in question and who, while not currently members under the criteria referred to immediately above, are resident within a reasonable distance of the group in question (to take account of the fact that Canadian reserves and other lands set aside for Aboriginal peoples are generally considerably smaller than Indian reservations in the United States.

Any persons of Aboriginal descent who do not fall into the above two categories (such as those in urban settings, for example, or the Canadian equivalent to "lost tribes"—groups that have always existed as cohesive groups and still do but who do not have a reserve) but who nonetheless wish to organize as a distinct political unit might be required to demonstrate a degree of direct Aboriginal descent along the lines in the third prong of the *IRA* definition (some specified blood quantum, etc.).

It is here, of course, that the real difficulties lie, for the very fact that individuals live in urban environments means that the "out-marriage" phenomenon will be most pronounced. To insist on a high blood quantum as the *IRA* did (50 percent) would preclude many urban residents from acquiring membership in a recognized Aboriginal group. While 50 percent blood quantum may have been reasonable in 1934, when most Aboriginal people still lived in relative isolation from surrounding non-Aboriginal communities, it would seem to be unreasonable in the twenty-first century.

Tribal Recognition by Treaty

Historic United States Tribal Recognition Policy
The President has constitutional authority to make treaties with foreign nations, subject to ratification by the Senate,[42] as well as the power to regulate commerce with foreign nations, states, and with "Indian Tribes."[43] Most of the early American treaties contained language whereby the tribes with which the United States made treaties acknowledged the superior sovereignty of the United States. Often in these treaties the tribes also pledged themselves as allies.

Treaty-making by the executive branch was later justified by the Supreme Court beginning in 1831. That year, in an action to enjoin Georgia's encroachment on tribal lands, the Court in *Cherokee Nation* v. *Georgia* denied that the Cherokee were a "foreign nation," characterizing them instead as "domestic dependent nation."[44] The Court noted the change in their original status from a "people once numerous, powerful and truly independent"[45] to that of a people "acknowledging themselves in their treaties to be under the protection of the United States" in a state of "pupillage" that resembled the relationship of "a ward to its guardian."[46]

The protection and wardship policy described by the Court in *Cherokee Nation* appears tantamount to the protectorate enjoyed by Great Britain and France over the remnants of the Ottoman Empire after the First World War. However, unlike the situation of what are referred to in the United Nations *Charter* as "non-self-governing territories" under international mandate (where U.N. members states pledge to assist in the development of self-government[47]), the Cherokees were acknowledged by the Court to be self-governing and to have the attributes of a state in their own right.

> They have been uniformly treated as a state from the settlement of our country. The numerous treaties made with them by the United States recognize them as a people capable of maintaining the relations of peace and war, of being responsible in their political character for any violation of their engagements, or for any aggression committed on the citizens of the United States by any individual of their community. Laws have been enacted in the spirit of these treaties. The acts of our government plainly recognize the Cherokee nation as a state, and the courts are bound by those acts.[48]

Unlike international states, however, under the "domestic dependent nations" formula the Cherokees could never again exercise the full independence they formerly enjoyed. Thus, recognition through domestic treaty meant that the protectorate relationship would continue indefinitely. In modern times this view was confirmed in a dramatic way in 1978 in *Oliphant v. Suquamish Indian Tribe,* where the Supreme Court held that the exercise by the tribe of criminal jurisdiction over non-Indians was, in the absence of federal delegation to it of that power, "inconsistent with their dependent status" and therefore no longer among their inherent tribal powers.[49]

This is, of course, a position that resembles to some extent the view in *Partners in Confederation* that "historically defined political units" only have certain "core" areas of their original and inherent tribal jurisdiction available to them as a result of having become "associated with the Crown at definite historical periods whether through treaties or other less formal arrangements."[50] In other words, in both the United States and Canada these "historically defined political units" have been "implicitly divested" of aspects of their original and inherent self-governing capacity, albeit under different legal and constitutional theories.

The protectorate mandate described by the Court in *Cherokee Nation* was bilateral in form, thereby preserving its international nation-to-nation character despite the assumption of continued protection. This is critical to understanding why tribes generally accepted these arrangements and why treaties as such are still regarded by American tribes as the cornerstone of their nation-to-nation relationship with the United States.

The following year in *Worcester* v. *Georgia* the Court followed up on the international analogy by finding that as a nation in its own right, the Cherokee tribe enjoyed complete immunity from state jurisdiction.[51] The courts have continued to accept (in modified form) this theoretical framework and have explicitly approved the analogy between tribes and foreign nations.[52]

Worcester also set out some of the elements that differentiate tribes as domestic dependent nations from foreign nations. Many of these features are present in the historical Canadian framework as well.

- Aboriginal title instead of fee simple ownership of land;

- Alienation of land only to the federal government;

- Internal tribal government subjected to federal supervision via the treaty process;

- No capacity for conducting foreign affairs;

- A special protectorate (guardian to ward) relationship with the federal government.

In continuing the characterization of tribes as domestic dependent nations the *Worcester* Court also recognized the concept of tribal territory physically separate and jurisdictionally apart from that of the states around them. For the states, "Indian country" was to this extent like the territory of a foreign state, immune from their domestic tribunals and law-making bodies.

Between the first U.S. treaty in 1778 (with the Delaware Nation) and the formal ending of domestic treaty-making in 1871, the United States established bilateral treaty relations with a large number of tribes. Indian treaties were kept by the State Department along with treaties with foreign nations, and relations with the tribes were conducted through the War Department. As with recognition of foreign nations, the United States did not normally inquire into the citizenship practices of Indian tribes. Tribes that had members of mixed Indian and non-Indian blood or which had non-Indian citizens who may have married in or been adopted were rarely challenged by the United States unless American citizens who may have been captured in wars or raids were involved.

Moreover, since the President was operating in an essentially political capacity, neither did the courts challenge executive decisions around recognition issues, treating them as political questions largely beyond judicial review. Nonetheless, some judges did indicate a willingness to "de-recognize" tribes (although they did not use this terminology) that had lost their political cohesion. For example, in *Worcester v. Georgia,* Mr. Justice McLean (concurring) stated as follows:

> If a tribe of Indians shall become so degraded or reduced in numbers, as to lose the power of self-government, the protection of the local [state] law must, of necessity, be extended over them.[53]

The issue was put directly to the Supreme Court thirty-five years later in *The Kansas Indians*[54] when the state of Kansas attempted to extend state tax laws over the Shawnee, Wea, and Miami tribes. The state argued that the allotment of reservation lands to individual Indians, the sale of "surplus" reservation lands to non-Indians, and the fact that individual Indians had become through this process state citizens with rights under state law meant that the separate political status of these tribes had ceased. In short, the state argued that these people were no longer separate and distinct political units.

The Supreme Court rejected this argument on the facts, noting that despite whatever loss of distinctive tribal culture may have occurred, they were still tribes recognized as such in law so long as they met two conditions: (1) retention of internal political cohesion; and (2) maintenance of political relations with the United States.[55] The Court was clear, however, that recognized tribal status could yet be lost by "a voluntary abandonment of their tribal organization."[56] In short, if tribal members decided to cease maintaining the tribe as a separate political unit, it would merge into the larger political unit of the state and forfeit its political relationship with the United States federal government. The test of "voluntary" abandonment of tribal organization has resurfaced in recent court rulings to this effect[57] and has ripened into something of an administrative presumption that will be discussed below in the context of the Federal Acknowledgement Procedure of 1978.

There is an obvious parallel between the concept of "voluntary abandonment" and what happens in the international sphere when a country begins to disintegrate. For example, if a state such as the former Yugoslavia loses its internal political cohesion—its capacity to possess and exercise international legal personality—it will gradually lose recognized status in the world community no matter what many of the citizens of the disintegrating state may wish. In short, to continue to enjoy recognized status in the world community, the third element of the test in the Montevideo Declaration must be satisfied: effective governance of the territory.[58]

To this extent, the Court in *The Kansas Indians* remained true to the international law roots of American Indian law. However, as subsequent events were to demonstrate, Congress had designs on control of Indian policy, believing that it was time for Indians to be absorbed into the American body politic. Thus Congress was prepared to assist and even to force tribes to abandon "voluntarily" tribal status and thereby forfeit the protectorate relationship as they gradually assimilated into larger American society.

Canadian Recognition Policy and *Partners in Confederation*

It is clear that there are strong parallels between early American and Canadian treaty recognition practice. The comments of the Supreme Court of Canada in *R. v. Sioui* affirm this where the Court notes that "the Indian nations were regarded in their relations with the European nations which occupied North America as independent nations."[59] In both countries the various Indian nations encountered were in many ways treated as being roughly equivalent to "states" in the sense that bilateral relations were conducted through treaties and diplomatic protocols of various kinds to ensure good relations between them as separate political units.

The members of tribal nations were therefore "alien" to the political units represented by the United States and to the British colonies that united to form Canada. Thus, they were not considered citizens of either country. It is important to note that the acknowledgment in both countries that members of recognized tribal groups on protected land bases are also citizens of the United States and Canada respectively cannot in and of itself be said to have brought Indians into the respective constitutional frameworks of the United States and Canada. In short, the grant of membership in one political unit does not disentitle the possessor *ipso facto* of membership in the other. This is especially the case of members of political units that pre-date and stand outside the larger political unit in a constitutional sense.

In any event, although never espousing the concept of voluntary abandonment as clearly as the American courts, it seems evident in retrospect that a similar concept has animated much of Canadian Aboriginal policy. For example, Indian women who married non-Indian men, Indian men who acquired higher education, and Métis and Indian persons who took land scrip instead of "taking treaty" as Indians could all be viewed as having in one sense "voluntarily abandoned tribal organization" in terms of *The Kansas Indians* ruling. However, "voluntary abandonment" is a construction imposed from the outside that does not necessarily coincide with the motivation of the Aboriginal persons concerned. The Canadian federal government seems to be aware of this, hence, for example, the 1985 *Indian Act* amendments to restore persons removed from Indian status and band membership by measures such as those mentioned above.[60]

However, to return to the treaty process as such, it is noteworthy that there is a vital difference between Canadian and American treaty recognition practice that is reflected in *Partners in Confederation*. In the United States tribal nations are still considered to be outside the formal constitutional arrangements entered into by the settler society represented by the United States. Relations between the political unit represented by the United States and those represented by the tribal nations are therefore still conducted in principle on a nation-to-nation basis on the theory that tribes are under federal protection. Tribes and reservations, therefore, are presumptively not part of the states in which they are found except in a physical sense. They and their members are "alien" and theoretically immune to state jurisdiction while within tribal territory. In short, "Indian country" is still (in theory) foreign territory to the individual states unless the United States has permitted other arrangements under its plenary power over tribes.[61]

This is not the case in Canada, where British and Canadian policy has been to view tribal nations as somehow forming part of the colonies that united to form Canada in a jurisdictional as well as a physical sense. There has, however, been no definitive justification for this assumption beyond the standard rationales equating discovery and settlement with implicit conquest. Hence the assertion formerly common in official federal government discourse that Aboriginal sovereign powers and rights had been "superseded by law." This is a verbal formula that conceals more than it reveals because it fails to state why non-Aboriginal laws have the legitimacy to supersede those made by Aboriginal peoples for themselves.

Partners in Confederation offers a rationale for the standard Canadian assumption that Aboriginal peoples are legitimately within Canadian constitutional jurisdiction unlike the American treaty recognition model.

> In effect, section 35 serves to confirm and entrench the status of Aboriginal peoples as original *Partners in Confederation*. The rights guaranteed in section 35 are largely collective rights, held by groups rather than individuals. These groups are political units that became associated with the Crown at definite historical periods, *whether through treaties or other less formal arrangements.*[62] [emphasis added]

There is no question of treaty-recognized tribes in the United States becoming part of the United States through treaty or otherwise. In fact, the contrary is true in legal theory, the whole premise of United States Indian law as set out in *Cherokee Nation* being that tribes are nations apart from the United States with which it was necessary to enter into formal bilateral relations in order to avoid disputes or war. In terms of recognition theory, tribal nations in the United States had the legal capacity to act as nations (confirmed by the dicta cited earlier from *Cherokee Nation)* so that formal recognition by treaty was a mere confirmation of this fact.

Tribal nations in Canada had the same initial legal capacity that the tribes did in the United States—this is confirmed by *Sioui* and is reflected in the "political units" language in *Partners*. Paradoxically, however, *Partners* concludes that by the very act of formally recognizing that tribal nations were separate political units, the political unit represented by the Crown somehow incorporated them into itself. This is not only largely contrary to the views of the treaty nations in Canada, it also poses difficult conceptual problems even from the constitutive point of view. If by recognizing tribal nations the Crown thereby "constituted" them as independent nations, how could it by the very fact of constituting them also effectively "de-constitute" and incorporate them?

Partners in Confederation itself indicates one way out of this difficulty that still preserves the integrity of the treaty recognition process and the nation-to-nation relationship. In the passage cited above and elsewhere, *Partners* notes that the relationship between Aboriginal nations and the Crown is one of association. Aboriginal nations were not obliterated as distinct political units: in effect, they "federated" with the Crown. The difficulty with this theory is that it does not necessarily accord with historical reality or with the current views of treaty nations. Aboriginal peoples often view their arrangements with the settler societies as an agreement to share the land, but not necessarily to participate in the same political unit. The strongest image of this conception is the "Two Row" wampum of the Six Nations Confederacy.[63]

The *Partners* theory also discounts the political acumen and experience of Aboriginal peoples in North America. They already had long histories of treaty relations of all kinds with each other, ranging from informal and *ad hoc* defensive alliances to loose confederacies to more highly structured relationships such as that embodied in the Covenant Chain of alliances forged by the Six Nations in the seventeenth and eighteenth centuries to true confederal relationships such as those of the Six Nations or the Creek Confederacy.

Leaving these concerns aside for the moment, what the *Partners* theory amounts to, however, is that by the act of making a treaty or by the "less formal arrangements" referred to in the passage cited above (presumably the setting aside of reserves and other acts demonstrating an awareness of the distinctiveness of Aboriginal political units) a rough sort of "recognition" federalism was created. Under this theory, the Métis and the Inuit could also claim to have been recognized even in the absence of a treaty.[64] In both cases, the Crown set land aside in much the same way as has been done with regard to Indians, thereby confirming their status as recognized and separate political units.

Moreover, this view accords with the declaratory theory of recognition that *Partners* appears to endorse. Historically defined Aboriginal political units had the legal capacity to act as political units. They required no "constituting acts" by the Crown to create them as political units. That is why their powers of governing themselves as distinct political units is inherent, finding their "ultimate origins in the communities themselves rather than in the Crown or Parliament."[65] Since self-governing powers were not granted and Aboriginal political units were not "constituted" by the Crown, they have been able to survive the passage of time and changes in their size, nature, and location as a result of the historical process and Crown actions.

Thus, many of the Aboriginal political units have endured and they continue to "exist" in the sense in which the term is used in section 35 of the *Constitution Act, 1982*. In short, there has been no voluntary abandonment of tribal organization that would entitle a court to "de-recognize" them. This is most evidently the case with regard to Indian reserve band communities under the *Indian Act*. There are other "historically defined political units," however, that appear to have ceased to exist as distinct political units in this sense. The Red River Métis communities that scattered over the prairies and the north after Manitoba gained provincehood offer a good example. But can it be said that they "voluntarily" abandoned their political cohesion so as to lose their access to the right of self-government that inheres in distinct Aboriginal political units? Perhaps they lost their cohesion involuntarily as a result of historic and destructive Crown policies that undermined their political cohesion. In such cases, there may be a fiduciary obligation on the Crown to undo what it has done by assisting those "historically defined political units" to reconstitute themselves. At the very least it cannot be said that forcing certain persons to abandon their membership in the distinct Aboriginal political unit from which they are descended is in keeping with upholding the honour of the Crown pursuant to the *Sparrow* ruling.[66] Moreover, creating "refugees" from these historically defined political units under policies consciously intended to force assimilation also deprives such persons of easy or guaranteed access to the Aboriginal and treaty rights that accrue only to groups as such.

Eclipse of Treaty Recognition

Congress Assumes Control of Indian Policy in the United States

From the beginning of the American republic a struggle had been going on between executive and legislative branches for control of Indian policy. In 1871 the House of Representatives gained temporary ascendancy and in a rider to an appropriations bill ended the domestic treaty-making power of the President. The specific language shows once again the extent to which tribes were still recognized as political units distinct from the United States.

> Provided, That hereafter no Indian nation or tribe within the territory of the United States shall be acknowledged or recognized as an independent nation, tribe, or power with whom the United States may contract by treaty....[67]

Existing treaties were not repudiated, and thus tribes already recognized as "nations" by treaty would remain so. Although it is not clear in hindsight that it is possible for Congress to legislatively abridge presidential powers (some commentators refer to this event as a congressional "coup d'état"[68]), henceforth the President was limited to "executive agreements" with tribes, and power over Indian policy passed to Congress. While respecting the nation-to-nation relationship in theory, in practice Congress has tended to treat tribes as disadvantaged racial minorities rather than as citizens of separate political units. In effect, tribes that had been recognized by the President through the treaty relationship were partially de-recognized as semi-independent political units by Congress. Thus, tribal government,[69] land holding patterns,[70] and cultural practices[71] were systematically undermined to such an extent that tribes had to be assisted to reorganize again in 1934 through the Indian Reorganization Act.

Domestic Indian policy in the United States from this point on began to be dominated by an emphasis on "Indians" rather than on tribes. The distinction is crucial. Despite the formal trappings of the treaty relationship, tribes after 1871 were often treated as if they enjoyed no collective self-governing capacity— the first criterion from the decision in The Kansas Indians.[72] In other words, Congress behaved as if tribes were in the process of "voluntarily" abandoning their tribal organization. It is apparent that the international protectorate analogy no longer applied except in theory. The relationship became more classically a colonial one as the United States interfered directly with internal tribal affairs, undermined traditional practices at odds with the needs of the larger American society, and distributed tribal resources and lands to non-Indians following individual allotment of reservation lands under the 1887 Dawes Act.[73]

In this sense, American policy may be likened to French policy in Algeria prior to the latter gaining independence. France undermined Algerian culture, planted European settlers among the Arab and Berber populations, and essentially declared Algeria a part of France when it was made a département. All the while Algerians themselves were treated as second-class citizens to the extent they continued to adhere to non-French cultural norms.

The new American policy thrust was aided by the courts, which in relatively short order articulated the "plenary power" doctrine ascribing virtually unlimited power over tribes to Congress. In the leading case the language demonstrates the Court's view that while the tribes continued to exist in an ethnological sense, their political power and independence had been overtaken by events (and to this extent "voluntarily abandoned").

> These Indian tribes are the wards of the nation. They are communities dependent on the United States. Dependent largely for their daily food. Dependent for their political rights....
>
> The power of the Central Government over these remnants of a race once powerful, now weak and diminished in numbers, is necessary to their protection....[74]

Thus, having "abandoned" in some ways their capacity to conduct themselves as distinct political units, tribes had of necessity to be brought more tightly into the embrace of the United States as the only power capable of continuing to protect them. According to the courts, congressional plenary power was even capable of being exercised in compete derogation of specific treaty provisions to the contrary—a startling affirmation of the downgrading of treaties as acts of recognition and further judicial support to congressional "de-recognizing" of tribes as separate and distinct political units.[75]

Tribes did not cease to be tribes in a sociological sense even though Congress was busy undermining their capacity to act as tribes in a political sense. They were still peoples separate and apart from the settler societies and were judicially acknowledged as such. For example, in *Montoya* v. *The United States* the Supreme Court set out the most complete judicial definition of "tribe" to date (albeit in the limited context of specific federal legislation).

> By a "tribe" we understand a body of Indians of the same or a similar race, united in a community under one leadership or government, and inhabiting a particular though sometimes ill-defined territory; by a "band," a company of Indians not necessarily, though often of the same race or tribe, but united under the same leadership in a common design. While a "band" does not imply the separate racial origin characteristic of a tribe, of which it is usually an offshoot, it does imply a leadership and a concert of action.[76]

This definition is revealing of future developments in American domestic recognition policy because it clearly establishes a focus on "race" in priority to the political aspect of tribal organization. This racial emphasis was not necessarily part of early treaty recognition policy. The essence of the distinction between tribes or nations and settler society had been the concept of separate and distinct political units, between which relations were conducted by analogy with foreign affairs by nation-to-nation agreements in treaty form. The distinction between the "races"—Indian and Caucasian—had been less important than the fact that tribes and the settler society were separate and distinct political units. In fact, in *dicta* unnecessary to the decision in this case, the *Montoya* Court went some distance to indicate the new attitude in the United States towards the tribes with which the country had entered into treaty relationships.

> The North American Indians do not, and never have constituted "nations" as the word is used by writers upon international law, although in a great number of treaties they are designated "nations" as well as "tribes." ...As they had no established laws, no recognized method of choosing their sovereigns by inheritance or election, no officers with defined powers, their governments in their original state were nothing more than a temporary submission to an intellectual or physical superior.
>
> ...In short, the term "nation" as applied to the uncivilized Indian is so much a misnomer as to be little more than a compliment.[77]

The emerging focus on race as a determining criterion for recognizing tribes would remain. It would reinforce the transition to a focus on "Indians," i.e., individuals of the Indian race that has become a factor in modern recognition policy and practice. Race as a factor in distinguishing tribes and nations of Indians would eventually create distinctions based on blood quantum that are all too familiar to Canadians in connection with the controversy over the origins and current status of the Métis and the former "marrying out" provisions in the *Indian Act* that led to the changes in Bill C–31 of 1985.

This trend towards focusing on racial descent as a criterion for Aboriginal group membership may now be an irreversible one for historical, fiscal, and political reasons. In any event, it is not a criterion that either the United States federal government or the tribes themselves are likely to dispense with easily. One suspects that the same is true in Canada.

Parliamentary Control of Indian Policy and *Partners in Confederation*

There are obvious parallels between these American developments and Canadian history. In Canada, control of Indian policy passed from the British Crown to the colonial legislature in 1860 and has been with Parliament since 1867. The systematic undermining of the distinct Aboriginal political units began before the advent of the *Indian Act* in 1876 and continued. The many destructive policies engaged in by Parliament are well known and will not be repeated here.[78]

The important point is that, as in the United States after 1871, Canadian Indian policy from around 1850 onwards began to focus on race as a determining criterion for the recognition of distinctly "Indian" communities. This was one justification for undermining the Métis as a distinctly Aboriginal political unit—they were simply not "Indian" enough in the eyes of federal politicians and government leaders.[79]

As mentioned earlier, *Partners in Confederation* is clear that the Aboriginal peoples referred to in section 35 "designate historically defined political units" as opposed to "groups characterized by their racial make-up." It is not clear, however, that there exist other easily accessible objective criteria beyond racial descent by which to distinguish Aboriginal from non-Aboriginal persons after so many years of intermarriage and cultural adaptation by Aboriginal peoples to the dominant Canadian society. That being said, and in view of the proposal made earlier in this paper to use a modified version of the *IRA* Indian definition for discussion purposes, there are cogent reasons for beginning the search for such objective criteria now. Otherwise, the federal government or the courts may impose similar criteria to those applied in the United States and insist on a certain Aboriginal blood quantum.

It is important to note that in the United States the courts labour mightily to differentiate between race-based distinctions and those based on political criteria in Indian matters. In *Morton* v. *Mancari,*[80] for example, the Indian hiring preference under the *IRA* in the United States civil service was upheld by the Supreme Court even though it appeared to give preference on racial criteria contrary to the United States Constitution. The Court noted that it was tied rationally to the discharge of Congress's unique trust responsibilities to Indians as members of distinct political units—federally recognized tribes—and that it was therefore a political and not a racial preference.

The unique extra-constitutional status of tribes in the United States makes such a finding at least plausible in law. However, in fact, after so many years of racially based official policy in the United States, "race" and "tribe" are now co-extensive since both tribes and the federal government have Indian blood quantum requirements for tribal membership.

Re-recognition: Recognized Tribes of Recognized Indians

Indian Reorganization in the United States

After more than fifty years during which tribal organizations were almost totally undermined and tribal self-government replaced for all practical purposes by BIA directives, American policy changed again. Sometimes referred to as the "Indian New Deal," the 1934 *Indian Reorganization Act* sought to reverse the effects of the *de facto* de-recognition that the post-1871 policies had brought about.[81] Although not well-known at the time, the *IRA* also recognized the inherent self-governing powers of the tribes that had been held in abeyance by congressional policies.[82] In this respect, the *IRA* and *Partners* are similar, since in the United States at that time and until recently in Canada, what *Partners* refers to as "the residue of the powers they originally held as autonomous nations"[83] were not accorded any official respect or recognition in domestic law.

The *Indian Reorganization Act* allowed "any Indian tribe, or tribes, residing on the same reservation"[84] to organize under it. This is, of course, analogous to what *Partners* refers to as "the central case" regarding implementation of the inherent right of self-government: "a group that constitutes a distinct entity and possesses its own lands...."[85] The *IRA* went on to define "tribe" as "any Indian tribe, organized band, pueblo, or the Indians residing on one reservation."[86] Evidently, the definition is circular. The question of which groups of Indians were tribes was no longer an easy one to answer, for the following reasons.

In the first place, treaty-recognized tribes had been politically and culturally undermined for so long that many had all but lost their original tribal cohesion and were riven by factionalism, often between traditionalists and those advocating greater accommodation with the dominant American society.

Second, many different tribes had been forced to share the same reservation or, conversely, had been broken up and scattered over several reservations.

Third, the allotment of most reservations had led to much increased contact and resultant intermarriage between Indians and non-Indians and had created large groups of persons of mixed racial ancestry who were descendants of original tribal members and who did not necessarily wish to assimilate into larger American society but who nonetheless did not adhere to traditional tribal cultural practices or even speak the tribal language.

In addition, allotment had also led to great losses of tribal lands—from 138 million acres to 48 million[87]—and to a patchwork or "checkerboard" of landholding patterns ranging from communal tribal ownership, allotted trust lands held by individual Indians, fee simple lands held by individual Indians, fee simple lands held by non-Indians, federal public land, and state and county land including state-chartered towns and state highways cutting through the reservations.

As a result of the breaking up of the reservations through the checkerboard landholding patterns and the competing tribal, state, and federal legal framework applicable to modern reservations, "Indian country" had become a notional rather than a geographic concept. One Indian commentator notes that "Indian country" had become "about as provisional as 'Marlboro country' ...an image, or a state of mind...."[88]

Because it had become somewhat difficult to determine what now constituted a "tribe," the Interior Department developed a number of recognition criteria that were later synthesized in the 1941 edition of *Felix S. Cohen's Handbook of Federal Indian Law.* The five "Cohen criteria," jointly or singly, have been considered to be of particular relevance by the Interior Department for recognizing particular groups of Indians as entitled to organize as tribes under the *Indian Reorganization Act.*

1. The group has had treaty relations with the United States.

2. The group has been called a tribe by congressional legislation or by executive order.

3. Even if not expressly designated as a tribe, the group has been treated as a beneficiary of lands or moneys held in trust for it by the United States.

4. The group has been treated as a tribe or band by other Indian tribes.

5. The group has exercised political authority over its members through a tribal council or other governmental forms.[89]

Tribes recognized during the earlier era of treaty relations were obviously included within the criteria. Those that opted into the *IRA* were then effectively "re-recognized" in the *IRA* context. However, recognition as a tribe in law was also afforded to new groupings and divisions, not all of which corresponded to historic tribes. Nor is it apparent that all these new "tribes" had any historical relationship with the United States by treaty or otherwise as tribes prior to recognition under the *IRA*.

For instance, recognition as a tribe was granted to a number of ethnological tribes that reorganized as a single *IRA* "consolidated" or "confederated" tribe on the basis that they were sharing the same reservation. These were usually tribes that had enjoyed recognized status during the earlier treaty-making period.

In other cases, a single ethnological tribe spread out over several reservations would reorganize under the *IRA* as several different tribes. That is why there are now many Chippewa, Sioux, Apache "tribes" despite the fact that from an ethnological viewpoint they are all part of the larger Chippewa, Sioux, and Apache linguistic and cultural tribes respectively.

Yet another scenario permitted groups of Indians of one-half Indian blood quantum to organize as a group and petition for the purchase and setting aside of lands to be held in trust for them as a reservation. Upon the establishment of a reservation, they would then adopt the *IRA* and acquire recognition as a tribe. In a number of cases groups of Indians declared to have earlier voluntarily abandoned tribal status were permitted to use this latter procedure.[90] It is not clear that these new *IRA* tribes are able to access powers of inherent self-government since they are not recognized by the federal government as a historic tribe. This is a continuing political issue that at the time of writing has yet to be resolved.[91]

There were many other problems associated with tribal reorganization under the *IRA*. Some tribes, for example, simply feared putting so much power over them into the hands of the Secretary of the Interior, who had veto and other powers under the tribal constitutions that were required by the *IRA*. Many tribes had more principled objections. They asserted an unbroken line of self-governing authority despite the intervening reservation era and refused to bring themselves within the *IRA*. Their fear was that it would diminish what they saw as their recognized and treaty-protected nation-to-nation relationship with the federal government if they opted into what appeared at the time to be a vehicle that might actually limit their sovereignty. In short, they saw no need for reorganization along lines established by the federal government and distrusted the intent of the *IRA*.

The question of ratification of the *IRA* also proved to be divisive and sowed the seeds of many future tribal internal political problems. Only resident tribal members who had some legal interest in reservation land were entitled to vote for or against accepting the *IRA*.[92] However, after adoption, voting on the accompanying tribal constitution required to access the self-government powers was open to all Indians in the vicinity of the reservation who could trace their ancestry back to the original tribe pursuant to the *IRA* definition of "Indian" reviewed earlier. This allowed large numbers of non-traditional persons of mixed Indian and non-Indian ancestry to participate in tribal voting and to run for tribal office under the *IRA*. Eventually, these people assumed political control on many reservations. The factionalism on many modern U.S. reservations can often be traced back to this aspect of the implementation of the *IRA*.

In 1953, after less than twenty years during which tribal reorganization was promoted, Congress changed course again, embarking on another round of de-recognition with the passage of *House Concurrent Resolution 108*. It marked the formal enunciation of the tribal termination policy. Federal recognition was withdrawn from a total of 109 tribes and bands on the basis that they no longer needed the protection of tribal status. Some of these groups have since been re-recognized; others have not. In a number of cases the courts refused to accept that the withdrawal of federal recognition could have any effect on treaty rights.[93] This, of course, highlights the extent to which the three branches of the United States government pursue different and sometimes competing recognition policies, and offers another warning to Canada about the need for a single and widely acceptable standard.

United States policy changed again around 1968. Since then, tribal domestic self-determination has once again been paramount. The standard for recognition as a self-determining tribe now focuses on the extent to which the individual members of the tribe are recognized as "Indians" under the applicable legislation. The legislation that most strongly reflects the new policy, the *Indian Self-Determination and Education Assistance Act* of 1975, is typical in this regard. It recognizes the following as entitled to access its provisions:

> ...any Indian tribe... which is recognized as eligible for the special programs and services provided by the United States to Indians because of their status as Indians.[94]

Evidently, the definition is somewhat circular. Nonetheless, similar provisions exist in many other pieces of federal legislation, the effect of which has been to change the terms of the debate somewhat. Now, U.S. federal departments will inquire into whether a group of Indians has received services as a tribe in the past before offering services. In practice this does not greatly affect the over five hundred established federally recognized tribes. It does, however, have an impact on ethnological tribes that may or may not have been recognized historically and whose recognized status is presently denied or ambiguous.

In conclusion, if one thing is clear it is that due to the twisting and turning of U.S. policy that has been described, the American Indian "tribe" is not always easy to define for official purposes. Over the years a number of different criteria for recognition have evolved from the changes in U.S. Indian policy and as a function of different legislative and administrative contexts.[95] As a result, the editors of *Felix S. Cohen's Handbook of Federal Indian Law* note that it is not always possible to draw up two neat lists of recognized and unrecognized tribes for all purposes. The best that can be said is that a group of persons claiming Indian status and federal recognition as a tribe must generally meet the following two criteria (there are exceptions):

1. Congress or the executive has created a reservation for a group of Indians by treaty, executive agreement, executive order, or administrative action (validly undertaken); and

2. The United States has some continuing political relationship with the group as through, for example, the provision of services to Indians.[96]

Aboriginal Reorganization in Canada and *Partners in Confederation*
As mentioned earlier, the situation facing the United States in 1934 was in many ways similar to that now facing Canada. After years of being undermined by policies of assimilation similar to those operative in the United States, Aboriginal peoples in Canada have experienced similar effects destructive of their continuity as "distinct political units."

In the first place, treaty-recognized Indian nations have seen their treaty rights ignored, downgraded, or overridden by paramount federal legislation, and their status as "historically defined political units" eroded through the *Indian Act* and related Indian policies in the same way that Congress downgraded the treaty relationship with tribes in the United States.

Second, although not broken up by "checkerboard" landholding patterns like reservations in the United States, Indian reserves in Canada have been subjected to surrenders and to expropriations by public authorities and to individual landholding in the form of certificates of possession, which coupled with ministerial powers allow leasing of Indian lands to non-Indians.

In addition, like unrecognized and landless tribes in the United States, Canada has a large population of Métis and non-status Indians who have lost their lands and membership in their original and "historically defined political units" by various means including involuntary enfranchisement.

Fourth, although on a lesser scale than in the United States, entire communities of Aboriginal peoples in Canada have been forcibly relocated to suit the convenience of non-Aboriginal governments and commercial interests.

Finally, intermarriage with non-Aboriginal persons and various degrees of acculturation to the dominant Canadian society have led to relatively large numbers of persons of mixed racial ancestry and differing degrees of adherence to traditional Aboriginal culture and have contributed to factionalism in many Aboriginal communities.

The evident result of these and other effects of historic Canadian policy has been to undermine the cohesion of the remnants of the "historically defined political units" now represented by *Indian Act* reserve bands and by Métis, Inuit, and non-status Indian communities. There is factionalism within many communities and competition between them for financial and other resources. In addition, there is a growing area of tension between resident members of *Indian Act* reserve bands and those persons who may wish to return to their original communities but cannot due to limited space, inadequate infrastructure, and insufficient band financial resources.

Moreover, the Aboriginal territory remaining under even the nominal control of Aboriginal political units is no longer intact in a jurisdictional sense. Federal, provincial, and territorial laws regulate Aboriginal people as Canadian citizens and provincial and territorial residents respectively on normal constitutional grounds irrespective of Parliament's powers over Indians under section 91(24) of the *Constitution Act, 1867.* "Indian country" in Canada is even more jurisdictionally permeable than in the United States, hence the distinction in *Partners* between "core" and "peripheral" Aboriginal inherent powers (i.e., peripheral areas will involve concurrency and overlap). Even core powers, despite being "matters of vital concern to the life and welfare of the community,"[97] are capable of being overridden under the *Sparrow* justification test.[98]

Partners, like the *IRA* sixty years ago in the United States, proposes to reverse historic policy through the reorganization of the Aboriginal peoples of Canada into functioning and effective political units. *Partners* speaks of "group initiative" in terms of "community initiative" and as "the practical dimension of the concept that self-government is an inherent right."[99] Thus, it is the community that comprises the basic political unit for *Partners* as opposed to the *IRA* "tribe." Like the *IRA*, however, which fostered the reorganization of many different groups and ethnological tribes under the banner of a single *IRA* "tribe," *Partners* allows for new forms of organization, but without being in any way prescriptive.

> It lies with each group to determine the character and timing of any moves to enhance its own autonomy. Nevertheless, it goes without saying that communities may decide to join with one another in tribal, regional or larger groupings for purposes of self-government or to participate in public governments that represent all the residents of a certain territory.[100]

Partners in Confederation calls upon the federal and provincial governments to respond to any group initiative by Aboriginal communities and in particular focuses upon the possibility of "framework legislation by the federal Parliament under section 91(24) of the *Constitution Act, 1867...*."[101] The *IRA*, of course, was framework enabling legislation passed by Congress in discharge of its unique trust responsibilities towards Indians. It too was designed to respond to the initiatives of groups of Indians and to facilitate their reorganization.

Partners calls upon Aboriginal political units wishing to implement their inherent right of self-government to do two things: draw up a constitution, preferably in written form, and develop a citizenship code to identify its members "in a reasonably definite way."[102] The *IRA*, it will be recalled, called for drawing up a written constitution and was premised on the reasonable identification of tribal members by way of the membership rolls and residency within reservation boundaries.

However, through the 50 percent blood quantum definition of "Indian," the *IRA* also made provision for "landless" tribes whereby groups of such persons could organize under its auspices. *Partners* is silent on the issue of groups that may not be "distinct entities" and which do not possess their own lands, noting that this "poses a range of complex problems."[103]

The main difference between the *IRA* approach and that proposed in *Partners* resides in the fact that the former was based on a constitutive theory of recognition and therefore imposed objective criteria for recognition in the form of the definition of "Indian" and "tribe," and the need for various votes for opting into the *IRA*, adopting the constitution, etc. In this respect, the *IRA* was recognition legislation that reflected and incorporated many of the changes in Indian policy and Indian conditions that had occurred in the United States since the original treaty recognition period. *Partners* focuses on group self-identification and disregards any necessary distinctions based on racial characteristics or on the current conditions of the former historically defined Aboriginal political units. Perhaps this is deliberate, but it opens the door for a number of potential problems, all but one of which will be discussed later.

One of the real differences between the *IRA* and the *Partners* approach is that *Partners* proposes that the "initial group" of members of the distinct political units possessing their own land would meet first to decide whether and to what extent to open up the membership or to join with other units.[104] The *IRA* opened up the membership by the second prong of its definition of "Indian": any non-member descendent who was resident within reservation boundaries.[105] Thus there are at least two areas in *Partners* that appear on the basis of this analysis to require more thought: landless Aboriginal people who do not make up a distinct political unit at present; and descendants of members of the distinct political unit who may not now be members. If these matters are not thought through, the federal government may impose rules for recognition of such entities and persons for self-government purposes. The United States has such a set of recognition criteria in the form of the Federal Acknowledgement Procedure.

Federal Acknowledgement Procedure in the United States[106]

As a result of the problems and confusions described, pressure to reform the recognition process had been building over the years. The sometimes vague Cohen criteria referred to earlier had come to be supplemented by BIA internal practices, but the gaps and inconsistencies in recognition policy became highly visible in the 1970s.

For example, officially unrecognized New England tribes like the Passamaquoddy were recognized by the courts for purposes of bringing suit against the federal government for failure to enforce early federal legislation applicable to tribal land surrenders.[107] Official recognition soon followed. The opposite occurred in Washington, where five tribes already receiving BIA benefits and services lost them following the decision of the Court in *Washington* v. *Washington State Commercial Passenger Fishing Vessel Association* denying them intervener status in the action. According to the Court they had not maintained their tribal organization and therefore could not participate to vindicate tribal rights against the United States.[108]

In 1977 the American Indian Policy Review Commission (AIPRC) noted that of the more than 400 tribes in the United States, only 284 were receiving services from the BIA. AIPRC also identified 133 unrecognized tribes (exclusive of terminated tribes) with a total population of 121,000. Of these tribes, 27 held land, 37 had colonial treaties, 32 were mentioned in treaties with the United States, and a further 30 were referred to in BIA's historical records. Describing the recognition process in terms of "murky precedents," "quirky administration," and "indefensible" BIA practices, AIPRC called for the creation by legislation of an independent agency to recognize the eligibility of such groups for recognition as tribes and for access to federal programs and services.[109]

But while Congress was preparing legislation containing recognition standards, BIA announced in 1978 that it had devised a procedure to implement this recommendation, and Congress acquiesced. The set of regulations promulgated by BIA are known as the Federal Acknowledgment Procedure (FAP) for unrecognized groups. Their application is considered in detail in chapter 6 by Russel Barsh.

In general, an applicant Indian group must submit extensive evidence of its ethnographic, genealogical, and cultural and political history along with proof of its current socio-political organization, including the racial ancestry of its current members. All seven of the required criteria must be met with evidence appropriate for each criterion.

1. Identification from 1900 until the present "on a substantially continuous basis" as an American Indian entity.

2. A predominant portion of the group comprises a distinct community and has existed as a community from historical times until the present.

3. There is maintenance of tribal political influence or authority over its members as an autonomous entity from historical times until the present.

4. There is information from the group's governing document or a statement setting out full membership criteria and procedures governing members.

5. The membership consists of individuals descended from a historical Indian tribe or historical tribes that combined to form an autonomous entity.

6. The bulk of the tribal members are not members of any acknowledged North American Indian tribe.

7. There is no congressional legislation expressly terminating or forbidding the "federal relationship."

The procedure is for a group to prepare a petition and to submit it to the BIA Branch of Acknowledgment and Research (BAR) for evaluation against the criteria described above. BAR then sends back a letter of "obvious deficiencies and significant omissions apparent in the documented petition," to which the petitioner is expected to respond with better information. Sometimes there will be considerable correspondence between BAR and the applicant group at this stage of the proceedings.

At some point BAR will then issue a "proposed finding" published in the *Federal Register* (the equivalent of the *Canada Gazette*). At the same time BAR prepares a report summarizing its appreciation of the evidence and submits that to the petitioner, who has 120 days to respond formally. After reviewing any response or rebuttal, BAR will issue its recommendation to the Assistant Secretary of the Interior, who will issue the "final determination." Aside from the exchange of correspondence, the process is not an open one and there is no appeal except by bringing legal action or by lobbying Congress for recognition by statute. The overall process may take several years before a final determination is made.

The members of BAR are professionals, primarily historians, anthropologists, and genealogists whose specialty has been termed "public ethnohistory" by a former BAR staff member.[110] This is not a recognized area of social science inquiry but seems instead to be a response to government policy needs. This has led to criticisms that these BAR professionals often tailor their reviews more to satisfy policy needs than in response to the strict practices and standards of their respective professions. The closed process and the failure of the government experts to develop a collegial approach to information sharing with colleagues in their professions outside government contribute to this criticism.

There have been many other criticisms of the FAP over the years. For example, the procedure is extremely burdensome due to the bureaucratically enforced requirement that applicant groups meet each of the seven criteria in the most minute and detailed way. This places heavy intellectual and financial burdens on groups, particularly the requirement to prove identification as Indian "on a substantially continuous basis." As has been discussed, many tribes were under extreme pressure to abandon aspects of their tribal structure (especially between 1871 and 1934) and to assimilate into American society, and documentary proof sufficient to satisfy distant government experts that they have maintained their tribal identity is often difficult to obtain.

Also, the FAP is not necessarily consistent with the Cohen criteria, court rulings, and congressional statements regarding recognition. For instance, while the BIA accepts the relevance of the Cohen criteria, it asserts that meeting them merely proves tribal existence at a certain time in history. This must be supplemented with evidence of continuity. The fact that the BIA itself appears to have recognized tribes by providing services to its members (as in the case of the five Washington tribes discussed above) is not considered by BAR as sufficiently cogent evidence to support a recognition recommendation. In short, what BIA gives with one hand, it may take away with the other.

Moreover, the threshold of proof in terms of quality and quantity for meeting the FAP criteria is vague. BIA has responded to criticisms in this regard by calling for proof on the basis that "the available evidence establishes a reasonable likelihood of the validity of the facts relating to the criterion."[111] BIA has refused to adopt a legal standard such as "more likely true than not" or "on a preponderance of proof" because it asserts that such known standards are inappropriate to this procedure. The need for flexibility to respond to the unique situation of each group ("the character of the group, its history, and the nature of the available evidence"[112]) is the official rationale for this lack of comparability. This has led to charges of inconsistent application of the criteria to petitions. For example, what will be accepted as evidence of tribal political activity as a tribe is not subject to a uniform standard. Petitioning groups simply do not know what will be accepted as proof in a given situation.

The difficulties of meeting the acknowledgement criteria are also due to the vague language (e.g., "substantially continuous Indian identity") which leaves considerable scope for subjective interpretation. To a considerable extent, the FAP criteria for recognition appear to be based on a definition of "tribe" and "band" from the *Montoya* case[113] and focus on non-Indian definitions of what is supposed to constitute a tribe. One critic notes a review of successful petitions supports the suspicion that BAR seems to have an "ideal tribe" in mind when interpreting the FAP criteria. This idealized tribe of Indians would appear to have two primary characteristics:

1. It holds land already, privately or otherwise, in a relatively isolated location that allows it to be fairly easily distinguished as a "distinct" community of Indians.

2. It is endogamous (intragroup marriage).[114]

Thus, BAR appears to discriminate against landless and urban groups that marry outside the tribe. Moreover, it also seems to rule out smaller groupings whose political organization might be clan- or family-based and which might not therefore appear to be distinct enough because it is less recognizable as a political organization.

If these charges are true, BIA policy is probably behind such a practice.

Recognition would permit the tribe to petition for the purchase and setting aside of lands to be held in trust for it by the Secretary of the Interior. Federal Indian benefits and services would follow. BIA, like the Department of Indian and Northern Affairs Canada (INAC), is attempting to stabilize the Indian service population. It would prefer not to deliver services in the city that could be delivered by the state or municipality, especially to a population that would increasingly include persons of non-Indian ancestry.

A more telling criticism is with respect to the "historic" criterion. Some critics have recommended that a showing of continuous tribal existence should be dated only from 1934, the date of the *IRA*. BIA disagrees, noting that this "would provide no basis to assume continuous existence before that time."[115] When one recalls that the 1934 *IRA* allowed many non-historic tribes to reorganize, or that it permitted individuals to petition for organization under it, it becomes clear that a double standard is at work in the FAP. *IRA* tribes were not required to demonstrate historic continuity prior to 1934, but tribes seeking recognition now must do so. It seems clear that some tribes now recognized under the *IRA* could not be recognized under the FAP were they required to re-qualify.

In summary, the problems of bureaucratizing an essentially political and adjudicative process are made evident by the short but troubled history of the FAP. Perhaps the best statement of the problems is provided by one critic who notes that it is the "small inconsistencies with large cumulative impact"[116] in the BIA decision-making process that make this such a dangerous procedure for tribes seeking recognition. The same could be said of any matter administered by a bureaucracy: of necessity it will apply its own rational and procedurally oriented standards to whatever issues it must deal with.

In the final analysis this is less a criticism than a warning about leaving so important a matter as recognition as what *Cherokee Nation* referred to as a "state" and a "nation" in the hands of civil servants. If recognition is to mean anything, it must be a matter carried out with solemnity and according to legislated and widely acceptable standards and appropriate executive protocols.

Explicit References to Domestic Recognition in Canada

The Penner Committee Report

Between the first and second Aboriginal constitutional conferences, in October 1983, a parliamentary committee chaired by Liberal Keith Penner tabled its report, *Indian Self-Government in Canada,*[117] in the House of Commons. Because of the extensive efforts made to include Indian representatives on the committee and to canvass Indian views across the country, the recommendations are considered to reflect to a great extent the perspective and priorities of Indian people (even to the point of adopting the term "first nations").[118] The report has, however, been criticized as containing an obvious bias in favour of on-reserve status Indians.

The basic thrust of the *Penner Report* was to condemn the existing *Indian Act* band-based structure of delegated authority in favour of a new relationship. Like the proposals in *Partners*, this relationship would be based on the recognition of Indian self-government as an inherent Aboriginal right. However, the *Penner Report* also called for it to be explicitly entrenched constitutionally as a distinct third order of government. In this respect, the *Penner Report* crosses back and forth over the line between the declaratory and the constitutive theories of recognition.

In line with the submission of the Assembly of First Nations, the committee recommended taking the *Indian Act* band as the starting point "to begin the process leading to self-government,"[119]—the "central case" in the *Partners* approach. Similar to *Partners*, it also recommended that while membership decisions are for Indian First Nations to make, a procedure should be adopted by Indian First Nations to allow "all people belonging to that First Nation" (presumably this would include all those who had lost status and membership by operation of the *Act* earlier) to participate in the process of forming a government without regard to the status and membership restrictions in the *Indian Act.[120]*

In another parallel with *Partners*, it also encouraged Indian First Nations not to restrict themselves to *Indian Act* bands, recommending that they be able to "combine for various purposes—administrative, economic or cultural" and that they be able to merge, separate, and regroup over time.[121]

Although it mentioned them, the committee did not go so far as to actually recommend either federal legislation reinstating people to Indian status and band membership or a particular procedure to permit such people to participate in the membership decision-making process. It called instead for the federal government to consider a general list of status Indians for purposes of federal benefits for Indians who may not be members of First Nations. This proposal, the committee believed, "has the merit of meeting the concerns of some witnesses without imposing anything on Indian First Nation governments."[122] As is now well-known, however, the federal government subsequently did impose new members on existing bands via Bill C–31 of 1985 as a result of its assessment of its legal obligations under section 15 of the *Charter.*

In any event, it is clear that from the committee's perspective, *Indian Act* bands were generally considered as constituting the initial Indian First Nations, and nonmember "ethnological Indians" (like those in the United States who are not members of recognized tribes) would have to rely either on the goodwill of existing bands to devise a participation procedure to include them as members or on the federal government to reinstate them or to continue to provide services to them outside the proposed First Nation framework. Thus, the Penner Committee basically advocated a "two-tier"[123] system of Indianness, with one tier made up of Indian First Nation members and the other comprised of unaffiliated Indians without First Nation membership.

This was in many ways simply a more elegant version of the system since 1951 whereby DIAND maintained both band lists and a general register of Indians. Although everyone on the band lists was registered on the general list, the reverse was not true, and there were always persons without a particular band affiliation.[124]

Unlike *Partners*, the *Penner Report* did not use the terms "inherent right of self-government" or "inherent sovereignty" except in reference to briefs presented to it. Nonetheless, it is clear that the Penner Committee viewed "the origins and rights of Indian First Nations in Canada"[125] as meaning inherent sovereignty. For instance, it explicitly cited submissions and testimony from Indian associations to this effect. Thus, like *Partners*, the *Penner Report* hinted strongly that *Constitution Act, 1982* section 35 already referred to self-government as a protected Aboriginal or treaty right.

> Many Indian witnesses asserted that rights implicitly recognized in the *Royal Proclamation of 1763* and in the treaties provide a basis in law for true Indian governments to be recognized by the Canadian government and for Indian people to exercise their inherent right to self-government.[126]

Hence the further proposal that, pending the constitutional entrenchment of self-government, the federal government should occupy the field of "Indians and Lands reserved for the Indians" under *Constitution Act, 1867* section 91(24) and then vacate it in favour of Indian First Nations who would fill the vacuum with their own laws.[127] This occupying and vacating legislation would oust competing provincial laws and would assure that no provincial law could apply to an Indian First Nation without its consent.

In the absence of a constitutional amendment entrenching Indian First Nations as another order of government in Canada, the committee proposed interim federal legislation—an *Indian First Nations Recognition Act*—authorizing the Governor in Council to recognize by order-in-council an Indian First Nation that had met criteria such as:

1. Demonstrated support for the new government structure by a significant majority of all the people involved in a way that left no doubt as to their desires;

2. Some system of accountability by the government to the people concerned;

3. A membership code, and procedures for decision-making and appeals, in accord with international covenants.[128]

The requirement for accountability systems were in response to concerns expressed by Indian witnesses to the committee and were conceived of as including such items as financial information and annual and audit reports, etc., the reservation of certain "rights and areas of interests"[129] requiring the people's approval for action (i.e., presumably a band/Indian First Nation referendum provision not unlike those in the present *Indian Act*), a system for removing officials from office, an appeals system for government decision, and the protection of individual and collective rights.

A new department, a Ministry of State for Indian First Nations Relations, linked to the Privy Council Office, was recommended to replace DIAND. A recognition panel composed of persons appointed by the new ministry and representatives of Indian First Nations was proposed. Recommendations for recognition would go to the Governor in Council whose order-in-council would empower the Governor General to affirm the recognition thereby accorded.

Indian First Nations would not have to accept or exercise full jurisdiction over all matters to which they were entitled by the recognition process. It was an optional approach whereby they could decide "in consultation with the federal government, on the jurisdiction to be exercised."[130] Thus, additional federal legislation would authorize negotiated agreements between the federal government and Indian First Nations as to jurisdiction and funding. These agreements would be amended from time to time to reflect evolving Indian First Nation jurisdictional competency, with negotiations to be conducted with the assistance of an independent secretariat (whose members were to be jointly appointed) along the lines of the Indian Commission of Ontario or the Intergovernmental Conference Secretariat that coordinates federal/provincial meetings.

Thus, while awaiting constitutional entrenchment of Indian First Nation government, three pieces of federal legislation would be necessary:

1. A "recognition" act;

2. An "occupying and vacating" act;

3. A "negotiation authority" act to allow the federal government to enter into jurisdictional agreements with Indian First Nations.

Thus, despite implicitly endorsing a declaratory theory of recognition along the lines proposed in *Partners* (by strongly hinting at inherent sovereignty as an historically recognized part of Canadian law), the *Penner Report* explicitly advocates an approach in line with the constitutive theory by setting out criteria that an Indian First Nation would have to meet to be recognized by the federal government. Although the *Penner Report* does not call for one, Indian First Nations would presumably have been required to draft a document setting out their government structure—a "charter" or "constitution"—for examination by the recognition panel. Such a requirement is not mentioned, but it is difficult to conceive how the panel would be able to assess the extent to which the Indian First Nation had met and would continue to meet the recognition criteria in the recognition act. Of course, it is possible that the Penner Committee intended these matters to be set out in the jurisdictional agreements between the federal and Indian First Nation governments. But that too is not clear from the discussion in the report.

It is important to note that the powers of Indian First Nation governments were not delegated federal powers despite the federal occupation and vacation of the field. Any Indian First Nation governments constituted as described above would therefore have been able to operate as governments even without formal constitutional protection due to the committee's assumption that Indian First Nations already had the sovereign powers necessary for their existence and functioning as governments. Federal legislative recognition would merely have confirmed that along the lines of the declaratory theory of recognition. Provincial approval and agreement to be bound by these arrangements would have been obviated by ousting any jurisdiction they enjoyed over the areas that Indian First Nations wish to govern through federal occupation and vacation of the field of "Indians and Lands reserved for the Indians." Thus, the "protector" political unit would have used its protectorate mandate under the Constitution to clear the field of jurisdictional enemies beforehand.

In terms of jurisdiction, the Penner Committee did not see any inherent limits: "Self-government would mean that virtually the entire range of law-making, policy, program delivery, law enforcement and adjudication powers would be available to an Indian First Nation within its territory."[131] This would mean full jurisdiction over all persons, Indian or not, on Indian First Nation territory, including the power to tax "individuals, transactions, land and resources within their territorial boundaries."[132]

In the interim, while Indian First Nations were fleshing out their respective jurisdictions, a cooperative attitude would be required by all parties, Indian, federal, and provincial, to ensure workable power-sharing arrangements and "ensure recognition in Canadian law of Indian values."[133] Even after full Indian First Nation jurisdiction had been attained, a similar attitude of cooperation would be required to cope with shared areas of concern like zoning of land, environmental matters, etc., on adjoining Indian and non-Indian territory. Cooperative joint regulation of shared use areas in the case of treaty harvesting rights, for example, would also be necessary.

Even after agreements had been worked out, implementation issues would likely still arise, especially around questions of funding. The Penner Committee called for a specialized tribunal to resolve these matters, with its structure, powers, and procedures to be worked out by the federal government and representatives of Indian First Nations. There is no indication that any sort of appeal to the courts would be permitted from this specialized tribunal, meaning that its rulings would likely be final ones.

In terms of land and resources, the committee proposed a radical break with the tradition of Crown protection of Indian land by recommending that an Indian First Nation "have full rights to control its own lands in the manner it sees fit...."[134] This would include the right to "exchange, sell, or otherwise alienate their interest in lands or non-renewable resources,"[135] including the ability to mortgage those lands to raise money. In keeping with their recommendations of self-government, the committee called for shared use and joint decision-making on adjoining lands based on treaty or Aboriginal rights to them, and on sharing revenues from the resource exploitation on these lands.

In this vein, the Penner Committee noted that full Indian First Nation government control of land "poses a special problem in regard to non-Indians living on Indian lands, who might feel that, as residents, they have a right to participate in the government of the community."[136] Citing the fact that as non-Indians they do not share in the assets administered by the Indian First Nation government, the committee reiterated their earlier conclusion that membership is a question for Indian First Nations to decide, notwithstanding *Charter* protections: "Aboriginal rights should predominate over any claims of nonmembers to protection under the *Charter of Rights.*"[137]

In order to provide for an adequate land base for Indian First Nations, the committee called for a new legislatively based claims process, the elimination of the requirement for extinguishment in claims settlements, and the provision of a land base to bands without one. Significantly, and foreshadowing the problems that would arise with Bill C–31 of 1985, the *Penner Report* also recommended that in the case of legislatively reinstated band members, a review should be conducted and a mechanism established to ensure that bands have the resources necessary to address the anticipated strains of limited reserve housing that reinstatement would entail.

The trust relationship between Indians and the federal government was recast by the committee from one based on the guardian-ward relationship to one based more on the concept of the equality of nations and roughly analogous to the protectorate model of Article 73 of the United Nations *Charter* regarding "non-self-governing territories" in which the "peoples have not yet attained a full measure of self-government" and over which members states have assumed responsibility.[138]

One of the duties of the proposed Minister of State for Indian First Nations Relations was to act as the internal federal government advocate for Indian First Nations interests. In addition, an independent office similar to that of an ombudsman was to be created after federal–Indian First Nation negotiations to serve as a monitoring and reporting body to Parliament regarding the discharge by the federal government of its obligations to Indian First Nations. Also, a federally funded advocacy office was recommended to permit Indian First Nations to adequately represent their interests in disputes concerning their rights.

Bill C–52 of 1984[139]

The official response of the federal government to the *Penner Report* was delivered in March 1984. In general, it was unwilling to acknowledge an inherent Aboriginal right to self-government of the type proposed, noting that "this matter can only be resolved through agreement with Provincial Governments in the context of ongoing constitutional discussions involving First Ministers' conferences."[140] In short, a constitutive recognition theory was embraced.

The government response was short (seven pages) and carefully crafted so as not to give the appearance of outright rejection of the *Penner Report*. However, the language used and the emphasis on certain aspects of the proposals indicates that the federal government perspective on the many matters covered in the *Penner Report* was far different from that of the committee members. A few examples will give the flavour of the government response.

In its General Commentary, for example, the federal government notes that the *Penner Report* called for a new relationship that would allow "Indian First Nations and their governments… to set their own course within Canada *to the maximum extent possible*"[141] [emphasis added]. This statement simply shows the difference in emphasis between the two approaches. The government response focused indirectly on jurisdictional limits, but the *Penner Report* had not focused on limits. It preferred to emphasize empowering and assisting Indian First Nation governments rather than limiting them from the outset.

Moreover, the government response emphasized Indian needs rather than rights (breaking the "dependency cycle"), stressed the importance of cultural rather than political integrity ("cultural heritage and integrity of Indian First Nations"), and avoided the issue of present and immediately actionable self-government rights by focusing on the past ("Indian communities were historically self-governing").[142] The government response was able to agree with the Penner Committee recommendation that it should not adopt either an incremental approach to *Indian Act* amendments or a band-based subject matter opt-in approach of the type proposed by DIAND in 1982 under the title "The Alternative of Optional Indian Band Government."

The most important point of difference between the *Penner Report* and the government response involved the nature of provincial participation in Indian self-government initiatives. Unlike the Penner approach, which called for a federal jurisdictional "ousting" of the provinces from all Indian matters (on a federal protectorate or trust model), the federal government stressed the need to consider the provincial perspective.

> The Government, therefore, is prepared to acknowledge that effective movement toward self-government will require substantial restructuring of the current relationship between Indian people and the Government of Canada. Changes are clearly needed. However, it is important for us to recognize that any change in the relationship will affect not only the Federal Government and Indian peoples but also Provincial Governments and others.[143]

Thus, the federal government proposed to leave the constitutional aspects of the *Penner Report* to the ongoing series of federal/provincial/Aboriginal First Ministers' meetings and to concentrate on the other aspects: general Indian self-government framework legislation; related legislative proposals such as the 1985 reinstatement amendments to the *Indian Act;*[144] and improvements under existing legislation such as the subsequently announced community-based self-government policy,[145] alternative funding arrangements,[146] and joint policy-making initiatives.[147]

Moreover, throughout the government response the emphasis is on bilateral and tripartite consultations rather than on unilateral federal action in the many areas highlighted by the *Penner Report*. Thus, despite the strong message of the *Penner Report*, the federal government seemed to be saying that it was more or less "business as usual" regarding Indian self-government and that a slower, more cautious process would be followed "in concert with Indian First Nations and in consultation with the provinces."[148]

Bill C–52, *An Act relating to self-government for Indian Nations*, followed that same year as the self-government framework legislation which the federal government response had characterized as "the primary thrust" of the Penner

Committee recommendations.[149] It was largely in keeping with the tenor of the initial government response described above. One of the most striking features of the Bill was its length and detail (65 sections) in which Indian Nation powers were defined precisely and narrowly. Also of significance was the fact that it used the term "Indian Nations" rather than "Indian First Nations." Perhaps this was in response to the politically charged nature of the claim to inherency implied by the term "First Nation."

The Penner Committee had called for a federal recognition act that would have been relatively straightforward and brief, since Indian First Nations in its view already existed in embryo with a potentially full panoply of inherent powers. What it got was a detailed draft act that reads more like enabling legislation than a recognition act, which delegated powers instead of recognizing them, which continued to permit a considerable degree of oversight including disallowance powers as under the current *Indian Act,* and which stressed jurisdictional limits more than the wide range of Indian First Nation powers that the Penner Committee believed already existed. This was the constitutive theory in action, but what was thereby "constituted" bore little resemblance to Indian aspirations or to the *Penner Report* recommendations.

The Penner Committee had called for a new relationship based on rough equality between the federal government and the new Indian First Nation governments it proposed; what it got was the *Indian Act* relationship repackaged. It is unnecessary to go into the details of Bill C–52 since it failed to meet the expectations of the many Indian participants who appeared before the Penner Committee and was supported only by the Assembly of First Nations. While calling its process "recognition," the federal government had only updated the earlier band governance provisions that have appeared in the *Gradual Enfranchisement Act,*[150] the original *Indian Act,*[151] the *Indian Advancement Act,*[152] and in the "advanced" bands provisions in earlier versions of the *Indian Act.*[153]

For instance, to be recognized under Bill C–52 an Indian nation had to meet certain criteria regarding membership codes, appeals, accountability, protection of individual rights, etc., all of which are reasonable and fairly stringent conditions.[154] Nonetheless, the Governor in Council had the power to pass additional regulations regarding recognition criteria that would subject applicant bands to maximum population size limits, governing how and by whom the band referendum for recognition would be held, establishing criteria that would reduce the discretion of the recognition panel concerning when it might judge the recognition criteria to have been met, and restricting the taxation and enforcement powers of Indian nation governments.[155]

The most significant provision related to the power of the Governor in

Council to prescribe "criteria relating to the possession of a land base and evidence of viability in terms of population and economic potential."[156] Despite the fact that this draft act was supposed to apply to all Indians, status or non-status, whether they lived on or off a reserve, this provision gave the federal government power to restrict self-government powers under Bill C–52 to larger, more economically developed groups on a defined land base—in short, what were once referred to under the *Indian Act* as "advanced" bands.

The federal government retained the power to name all the members of the recognition panel and to appoint the chairman, limiting itself only by the requirement to "consult" with Indian representatives and to appoint three Indians.[157]

Moreover, even where the panel may have surmounted all these obstacles and actually recognized an Indian nation, its decision could have been disallowed by the Governor in Council within six months of having been made.[158] Even if not disallowed within the six-month period, the decision to recognize an Indian nation could still be operationally overturned through an additional provision allowing the Minister to appoint an administrator in place of the Indian nation government where he is "of the opinion" that it has "abused its powers, is in serious financial difficulty or is unable to perform its functions."[159] None of the terms is defined. Moreover, the opinion of the Minister is nowhere specifically required to be based on reasonable grounds. Finally, no mechanism for an Indian nation to appeal such a ministerial decision was provided.

In another major departure from the Penner Committee proposals, a recognized Indian nation government under Bill C–52 would not have enjoyed a wide range of powers. Its legislative powers, for example, were limited to the following areas: education; local taxation; charges for public services; voting eligibility and procedures; membership applications; punishment for infractions; and ancillary matters.[160] In the same way, its executive powers were limited to land management; establishing government institutions; community facilities and social services; economic development; educational facilities; and ancillary matters. Additional powers could have been acquired through agreements with the federal and provincial governments. This was not the inherent right to self-government called for by the *Penner Report* and *Partners*.

Furthermore, the *Indian Act* would have ceased to apply absolutely to recognized Indian nations only regarding sections 32 and 33 (sale and barter of produce in the prairies) and 88 (provincial laws of general application).[161] Otherwise, the *Act* would have continued to apply, as would federal and provincial laws except to the extent of inconsistency with Indian nation constitutions, agreements regarding additional powers, treaties, etc., under normal federal paramountcy rules.[162] The status provisions of the *Indian Act* would have continued to apply in any event,[163] thereby allowing the federal government to control indirectly the potential membership of any Indian nations it chose to recognize. In addition, Indian lands would have continued to be inalienable,[164] and Indian nation governments would have been subject to annual reporting requirements regarding their funding.

In summary, despite its virtues, Bill C–52 was not true recognition of Indian self-government; it was delegated Indian band council powers reformulated. It died with the Thirty-second Parliament and was not resurrected.

Difficulties With *Partners in Confederation*'s Association Theory

Partners is based on the assumption that Aboriginal peoples are already part of Canada's constitutional framework, and it devotes itself largely to justifying this view, to defining a space within which they may exercise their residual inherent powers of governance, and to suggesting ways in which those self-governing powers may most effectively be exercised by agreement with the other two levels of government.

It is in many ways a document written from the traditional Canadian pre-1982 constitutional perspective, focused on division of powers between the federal and provincial governments. In this sense it addresses the issues that arise from this perspective and reasons backwards from the *Constitution Act, 1867* to find some way by which the "exhaustiveness" doctrine can be made to accommodate an Aboriginal right of self-government that does not rely on a grant of power from the two orders of government that supposedly exhausted all such powers in 1867. *Partners* finds the conceptual tool it needs in the theory that the unique body of common law that emerged when the settler societies were forced to come to terms with the sovereign presence of Aboriginal nations in North America contained within it the principle of respect for Aboriginal self-governing powers. On this theory, their status as distinct political units has continued into the post-1867 Canadian constitutional period and is reflected, albeit obliquely, in the language of section 35 of the *Constitution Act, 1982.*

On the one hand, this is a fairly conventional account of Canadian constitutional history based on an unarticulated Lockeian notion of the social contract. What is unconventional is the groupist orientation of the social contract theory (in other contexts reflected as the compact theory of Confederation) that implies a sort of like-mindedness on the part of the Aboriginal and non-Aboriginal parties as to the legal and constitutional effect of the treaties and "less formal arrangements" by which they entered into bilateral relations. At root, this notion assumes that tribes and nations in Canada entered the federal union (through the common law) by way of collective consent, rather than by way of individual consent as typically expressed in liberal societies by the exercise of the right to vote. This view seems to discount the political astuteness of Aboriginal peoples who had been making treaties and other less formal arrangements with each other and with other European powers for a long time with no thought of entering into a single political unit. A good example of this is the Covenant Chain of the Six Nations which in no way merged the various members, which included English colonies as well as tribal nations, into a single political unit.[165] It also discounts the fact that treaties and reserves often seem to have been requested by Aboriginal peoples in Canada precisely for the purpose of maintaining a territorial and political distinction between themselves and non-Aboriginal settlers who might otherwise have overwhelmed them through sheer numbers and superior technology. The treaty process undertaken in the Treaty 3 area is a good example of this.[166]

Moreover, this view seems to be based on a particular view of the world that in philosophical terms may conveniently be described as liberal and social contractarian. The application of this type of reasoning is valid only in societies that are liberal and contractarian in nature—in short, in political units that share a similar theory about the underpinnings of that political unit. These are not, therefore, universal concepts that easily cross cultural boundaries into societies that are not organized around liberal values. By assuming that Aboriginal peoples understood the process whereby treaties were made with them, reserves set aside under treaty or otherwise, and other arrangements made that apparently recognized them as distinct political units in terms of liberal contractarian notions is not an unassailable argument.[167]

Partners assumes from the outset that Aboriginal peoples are within the Constitution, and on this basis concludes from the historical evidence that they are within the Constitution. From this perspective, *Partners* could be accused of being a sophisticated exercise in point-missing and begging the very question to be answered.

The other unconventional aspect of the *Partners* theory is the surprising assertion that the conventional account of how Aboriginal peoples as distinct political units came to find themselves within the Canadian federation had merely been forgotten because "the Crown's memory proved more fragile than that of the Aboriginal parties."[168] This is not to say that this version of events might not be true, for Canadian history is nothing if not ambiguous and open to various interpretations, it is only that there is little indication in Aboriginal accounts of the time or in modern Aboriginal testimony that entry into a federal relationship was in their contemplation at that time. The likelier explanation is that it was not contemplated even by the British, colonial, and later Canadian authorities that they were entering into any kind of social compact by these arrangements.

In any event, the main problem with the *Partners* construction is one of perspective. *Partners* argues back from a set of values and from a framework of analysis, both of which are embedded in conventional Canadian constitutional discourse and which assume membership in a common political unit and common jurisdictional concerns. It is trite to note that this is not an Aboriginal perspective, since Aboriginal peoples were not consulted and did not give their formal consent to the constitutional arrangements entered into by the settler societies around them. They were not invited to present their views at the meetings that preceded Confederation, nor were they present when constitutional division of powers issues affecting their rights were litigated in cases such as *St. Catherine's Milling Co. and Lumber Company* v. *The Queen.*[169]

The perspective adopted by the settler societies south of the forty-ninth parallel when they federated beginning in 1776 is equally a non-Aboriginal one and is reflected in the constitutional arrangements into which they entered. The vital difference, however, is that those arrangements viewed the distinct Aboriginal tribal political units more in accordance both with international law recognition principles and with the perspectives of the members of those political units. In short, the pre-constitutional and extra-constitutional status of tribes in the United States appears to accord, in theory at least, with the emphasis placed on the relationship with the United States by the tribes themselves.

Moreover, the legal construction placed on historical events by the American judiciary beginning in the 1830s was closer in time to the actual events in question than is the corresponding construction in *Partners* with respect to Canadian history. It is therefore arguably less informed by subsequent political imperatives and modern intellectual trends in the United States than is the *Partners* construction, and more likely in consequence to reflect a more historically accurate view of things. In short, there appears in retrospect to be a greater likelihood that the American construction of events better reflects a perspective acceptable to Aboriginal peoples. The proof is the continuing insistence by tribes in the United States on the extra-constitutional nation-to-nation treaty relationship as the foundation of their dealings with the United States.

This is not to say, however, that actual practice in the United States is consistent with official rhetoric and legal theory. There is considerable evidence that the extra-constitutional nation-to-nation relationship was honoured more often in the breach than in the observance. As a result, actual conditions in the

United States resemble those in Canada more closely than theory would appear to admit. This is especially the case with regard to the large numbers of landless and unrecognized groups and individuals of Aboriginal racial origins who are recognized neither as tribes nor as Indians.

It seems likely that on philosophical, legal, and historical grounds the *Partners* approach may be a difficult one to maintain in the face of possible assertions by Aboriginal peoples of the primacy of their recognition as separate and distinct political units outside the formal constitutional arrangements of the settler societies that confederated in 1867. A way must be found to harmonize the nation-to-nation perspective held by a significant number of Aboriginal groups and communities and the nation-within-a-nation approach of *Partners*.

In conclusion, the foregoing analysis may be summarized as follows:

1. Recognition even in the domestic context presupposes the acknowledgement by one political unit that another political unit is distinct from itself;

2. Treaties and analogous acts by a political units are in themselves acts of mutual recognition;

3. Bilateral relations between political units are undertaken by way of treaty and similar agreements;

4. A formal merging or sharing of sovereignties is accomplished internationally and domestically by specific agreement or by force (conquest, etc.);

5. It may be possible to imply an informal acquiescence to a merging or sharing of sovereignties that in international terms might be called custom and domestically might be referred to as convention (or common law, the practical equivalent), but such acquiescence must be voluntary and by consent, otherwise it will fall under the heading of force;

6. There has been no convincing rationale offered to show voluntary consent on the part of and from the perspective of Aboriginal peoples.

Implications of Domestic Declaratory Recognition

One consequence of the declaratory theory is that Aboriginal political units will be under no legal or constitutional requirement to join with each other to form larger and more powerful "nations" within the Canadian federation as intended by RCAP. Inherent rights are the "residue" of the original self-governing powers that inhere in a subsisting (or reconstituted or reorganized) group that is the successor to the "historically defined political units" that once exercised those powers in an autonomous fashion.

In fact, *Partners* speaks mostly in terms of communities, not in terms of larger linguistic and cultural nations. This is consistent with history in so far as Aboriginal groups in Canada appear to have operated in units smaller than the Ojibway or Cree nation, for example. *Indian Act* bands will claim with some logic and on the basis of historical precedent that they are the "distinct political units" with the inherent right. This is the current view among the First Nations making up the Assembly of First Nations. This makes it difficult to require Aboriginal communities to regroup in the larger nation format that RCAP will likely recommend.[170]

Thus, just as the declaratory theory deprives the federal and provincial governments of a say in who they will relate to as governments, thereby possibly leading to a confrontation, it also deprives RCAP and Aboriginal nationalists of a justification for requiring larger and more powerful Aboriginal political units. RCAP may rely on good sense and goodwill on both sides of both these issues, but if recent Canadian history is a guide, these are not surplus commodities in the federation at this time.

Another consequence is that the declaratory theory provides no guidance as to who the distinct Aboriginal political units are. Modern Aboriginal communities and populations are generally less distinct and have a considerably diminished capacity to act as political units in their own right. If it were otherwise there would be no present recognition controversies as there are in the United States and in Canada. Relatively isolated *Indian Act* and self-governing Indian bands, Inuit communities, and Métis settlements should qualify as distinct Aboriginal political units. They are what *Partners* refers to as the "central case," namely, groups that constitute a "distinct entity and which possess their own lands."[171]

Other Aboriginal groups that exist as communities and are identifiable as such ought to qualify relatively easily as well. This group would include non-status Indian and Métis communities that exist on Crown or other lands they do not necessarily possess. They are quite close to the "central case." They will generally be found in rural or northern locations.

But what about other groups? How distinct is distinct? This is, of course, the perennial issue of urban groups or of scattered individuals who may wish to come together for the purpose of exercising self-government powers as distinct political units but which do not now enjoy political cohesiveness sufficient to qualify as a "political unit."

Moreover, the *Partners* approach gives Aboriginal political units little guidance on how to organize themselves. They have carte blanche to decide on their own constitutions and citizenship practices with no interference from political units outside themselves. *Partners* recommends but does not call for mandatory written constitutions or inclusive membership lists at the outset. To make such requirements mandatory would be to advocate a constitutive recognition model. However, the federal government, which owes fiduciary obligations to individual Indians as well as to groups, may be forced to prevent the wholesale exclusion of existing or potential members of a self-defining Aboriginal political unit that is exercising its inherent powers in this way. This will mean, as mentioned above, the imposition of a constitutive recognition theory in the membership area.

A further consequence is that the declaratory theory ignores the fact that many of the historically defined Aboriginal political units have been scattered and broken and that many of those remaining now exist as poverty-stricken and factionalized communities suffering from high degrees of social dysfunction. They will require continuing assistance from the other levels of government in order to move forward. The protectorate relationship referred to in connection with the discussion of the *Cherokee Nation* case is more vital in the absence of some formalized mechanism of fiscal transfer and technical assistance than is the uncertain degree of jurisdictional liberty on which the *Partners* approach is premised. Leaving it to notionally "distinct political units" to function as such when many are struggling to conduct themselves as healthy societies appears to be a recipe for various forms of disaster.

To return for a moment to the international analogy, a declaratory theory under such conditions seems tantamount to the indecent rush of European nations to decolonize Africa over the past fifty years that now sees Africa a collection of states in name only. Peoples emerging from colonial conditions need continuing assistance to reorganize themselves into autonomous and functioning political units. The protectorate relationship must therefore continue in abated and gradually diminishing form for an uncertain period while the new entity acquires the practical capacities that it would have had but for the colonial relationship.

Another important consequence of the declaratory approach is the fact that one branch of the federal and provincial governments—the courts—will inevitably have to impose various sorts of conditions on the exercise of Aboriginal self-government. The initial arbiter of the inclusion of the self-governing rights of the Aboriginal peoples within Canada's emerging and emergent Confederation was the judiciary via the common law as described in *Partners*. The ultimate arbiter of the extent of the "residue of powers they originally held as autonomous nations"[172] will once again be the judiciary.

> In cases of conflict between Aboriginal laws and external legislation Aboriginal laws will generally prevail, except in cases where the external laws can be justified under the *Sparrow* standard.[173]

However, judges are typically most responsive to the cultures and assumptions of the dominant society from which they are mostly drawn. Thus, they will likely read *Sparrow,* the legislation, and policy arguments with the concerns of the society from which they are drawn and according to the liberal and contractarian values that predominate in it. Despite its unparalleled nature, the *Sparrow* decision itself is firmly grounded in non-Aboriginal values and perspectives. The same is true of the landmark Marshall decisions of the United States Supreme Court.

Over 150 years ago Mr. Justice Marshall acknowledged openly but indirectly the extent to which he was bound by the current values, perspectives, and "pretensions" of the United States—what he referred to as "the actual state of things." After canvassing many powerful arguments militating against the rightfulness of any exercise of jurisdiction by the United States over the Cherokee Nation, he was forced in the seminal *Worcester* decision to fall back on the fact that his role was constrained by the norms and assumptions of the society of which he was a member and in whose courts he sat as a judge.

> But power, war, conquest, give rights, which, after possession are conceded by the world; and which can never be controverted by those on whom they descend. We proceed then, to the actual state of things, having glanced at their origins; because holding it in our recollection might shed some light on existing pretensions.[174]

Modern judges too will likely fall back on "the actual state of things," and will reason backwards from it to preserve a balance between the "existing pretensions" of the Canadian Constitution as put forward by the federal and provincial governments and the attempts of distinct Aboriginal political units that they be "controverted" because from their perspective they have flowed less from justice than from the threat of "power, war, conquest."

The final and most disturbing consequence of the approach proposed in *Partners* will likely be conflict between Aboriginal political units declaring themselves to be sovereign and their non-Aboriginal partners in confederation. Basically, the declaratory theory deprives Canadian governments of any say in deciding the partners with whom they must enter into bilateral and multilateral relations. They will be concerned because the exercise of inherent powers even in core areas of Aboriginal jurisdiction likely will affect their powers, and they will insist for this reason on imposing a constitutive theory by refusing to recognize Aboriginal jurisdiction that has not been spelled out in agreements.

Thus if distinct Aboriginal political units with the will to do so begin to exercise an inherent right of self-government unilaterally within the existing federal system, they will be able to decide who they are *(Indian Act* bands on reserves come to mind as the most obvious successors to the historically defined political units referred to in *Partners)*, who their membership is, how they will conduct themselves in terms of governance and accountability, and what areas they will regard as "core." In short, like states in the international system, they may simply begin acting like domestic nations and assume recognition from their partners in the federation.

This may have unpleasant and ultimately disappointing consequences for Aboriginal peoples since it is not likely that such a unilateral declaration will be recognized as legitimate by the other, non-Aboriginal political units (or by many Aboriginal persons who may have been excluded from membership in the self-defining distinct Aboriginal political unit). This will lead either to continuing legal disputes and even to conflict of the type already seen in both Canada and the United States unless the Aboriginal political units are content to restrict themselves to the most minimal areas of jurisdiction.

On the other hand, the Aboriginal political units may simply accept to operate under the constitutive theory of recognition imposed on them. They will constitute themselves according to the requirements for formal recognition demanded of them in the ad hoc way that has characterized much of Canadian Aboriginal policy. In this case, the situation will likely resemble the status quo and the notion of the inherent right of self-government may be vitiated. As has been discussed, this is the process underway in the United States as the courts force tribal governments to come to terms with the states around them by allowing state law to regulate more and more of the processes within tribal territory. In the absence of a widely accepted and principled approach to recognition of Aboriginal nations, the victory of the inherent right of Aboriginal self-government in Canada under the *Partners* formulation may be more apparent than real.

Notes

[1]Canada, Royal Commission on Aboriginal Peoples, *Partners in Confederation: Aboriginal Self-Government, and the Constitution* (Ottawa: Supply and Services Canada, 1993).

[2]See "Introduction," *ibid.*, c. 1 at 30ff.

[3]Enacted as Schedule B to the *Canada Act, 1982* (U.K.), c. 11, which came into force on April 17, 1982.

[4]*Partners in Confederation, supra* note 1 at 38:

According to the organic model, the right of self-government would include an *actual* right to exercise jurisdiction over certain core subject matters, without the need for court sanction or agreements with the Crown...[and] also includes a *potential* right to deal with a wider range of matters that lie beyond the core area and extend to the outer periphery of potential Aboriginal jurisdiction. However, this potential right needs to be adapted to the particular needs of the Aboriginal community or communities in question, either by agreement with the Crown or perhaps by arbitral mechanisms established under judicial supervision. [emphasis in the original]

[5]*Ibid.* at 29.

[6]See *supra* note 4.

[7]*Felix S. Cohen's Handbook of Federal Indian Law* (Charlottesville: The Michie Company, 1982) at 19.

[8]25 U.S.C. ss. 461–79. Also referred to as the "Indians' New Deal," this legislation was a watershed event in U.S. Indian policy as it made provision for tribal self-government using inherent sovereign powers, the right to incorporate under U.S. law and to hold tribal property free from mortgage, seizure for debt, etc., Indian preference for BIA jobs and the ending of the allotment policy regarding communally held reservation lands.

[9]*Williams* v. *Lee,* 358 U.S. 217 (1958).

[10]Martin Dixon, *Textbook on International Law* (London: Blackstone Press Ltd., 1990).

[11]Aboriginal organizations with non-governmental organization (NGO) status with the United Nations Economic and Social Council are entitled to attend and contribute to international and intergovernmental conferences, especially the annual Working Group on Indigenous Peoples meetings in Geneva. As of the date of preparing this paper these groups are: Four Directions Council; Grand Council of the Crees (Quebec); Indian Council of South America; Indian Law Resource Center; Indigenous World Association; International Indian Treaty Council; International Organization of Indigenous Resources Development; Inuit Circumpolar Conference; National Aboriginal and Islander Legal Services Secretariat; National Indian Youth Council; and World Council of Indigenous Peoples.

[12]Art. 1 of the 1933 Montevideo *Convention on the Rights and Duties of States.* The fourth criterion is somewhat ambiguous, but likely refers to legal independence in the sense of not being under the control of any other state so as to be able to freely enter into relations with other states unhampered.

The position outlined in *Partners in Confederation* whereby distinct Aboriginal political units may begin exercising their inherent right of self-government in core areas of their jurisdiction without benefit of agreements with the federal and provincial governments argues in favour of the view that Aboriginal nations and communities capable of accessing the inherent right are analogous to international states in the sense of being legally independent from the federal and provincial governments to this extent.

[13]*Mashpee Tribe* v. *New Seabury Corp.* 592 F. 2d (Ist Cir.1979).

[14]In *United States* v. *Joseph* 94 U.S. 614 (1877) the Supreme Court had held certain federal Indian legislation inapplicable to the Pueblo because of their generally "civilized" nature. Fifty years later, the Court reversed itself in *United States* v. *Candelaria* 271 U.S. 432 (1926) by holding (at 441) that the Pueblo Indians were within earlier Congressional legislation referring to "any tribe of Indians."

[15]*Joint Tribal Council of the Passamaquoddy Tribe* v. *Morton* 528 F. 2d 370 (1st Cir. 1975).

[16]336 U.S. 49 (1977).

[17]Canada, Royal Commission on Aboriginal Peoples, *The Right of Aboriginal Self-Government and the Constitution: A Commentary* (Ottawa: February 13, 1992).

[18]*Ibid.* at 11–12.

[19]*R.* v. *Sparrow,* [1990] 1 S.C.R. 1075. The basic holding of this unanimous decision in the words of *Partners in Confederation (supra* note 1 at 31) is that "[T]he section [s. 35] gives constitutional protection to a range of special rights enjoyed by Aboriginal peoples, shielding these rights from the adverse effects of legislation and other governmental acts, except where a rigorous standard of justification can be met."

[20] *Commentary, supra* note 17 at 18–19.

[21] *Partners, supra* note 1 at 36.

[22] *Ibid.* at 21.

[23] *Ibid.* at 29.

[24] *Ibid.*

[25] The 1960 *Declaration on the Granting of Independence to Colonial Countries and Peoples,* G.A. Res. 1514, 15 U.N. G.A.O.R., Supp. (no. 16) at 66 is a good example as it protects the territorial integrity of existing states:

> Any attempt at the partial or total disruption of the national unity and territorial integrity of a country is incompatible with the purposes and precepts of the Charter of the United Nations.

[26] *Partners, supra* note 1 at 37.

[27] *Ibid.* at 47.

[28] R.S.C. 1985, C. I–5. Persons entitled to registration as Indians are identified in s. 6, while those on band lists are referred to beginning in s. 8. Since the amendments in Bill C–31 of 1985, There is no necessary concordance between Indian status and band membership.

[29] *Supra* note 8.

[30] E.g., *Indian Appropriations Act* of 1918, 25 U.S.C. s. 297.

[31] 25 U.S.C. ss. 450–450n, 455–458e.

[32] These figures are from Charles Wilkinson, *American Indians, Time and the Law* (New Haven: Yale University Press, 1986) at 137, note 1, confirmed by documents received by the writer from the Bureau of Indian Affairs.

[33] United States Department of the Interior *American Indians Today,* 3rd ed. (1991) at 9.

[34] Jyotpaul Chaudhary, "American Indian Policy: An Overview" in Vine DeLoria Jr., ed., *American Indian Policy in the Twentieth Century* (Norman: University of Oklahoma Press, 1985) at 21–22.

[35] *Supra* note 7 at 20.

[36] *Supra* note 8.

[37] *Partners, supra* note 1 at 30.

[38] *Ibid.*

[39] *Ibid.*

[40] *Supra* note 16.

[41] A study commissioned by the AFN noted that of the 236 bands that had adopted membership codes under Bill C–31, 49 had band membership eligibility criteria based on the *Indian Act* status provisions, 97 determined eligibility based on blood-quantum requirements for both parents—often 50 percent—while just 90 codes permitted membership where only one parent met blood-quantum requirements. See Stewart Clatworthy and Anthony Smith, *Population Implications of the 1985 Amendments to the Indian Act: Final Report*, December 1992.

[42] U.S. Const., art II, s. 2, cl. 2.

[43] U.S. Const. art 1, s. 8, cl. 3.

[44] *Cherokee Nation* v. *Georgia,* 30 U.S. 1 (1831) at 17.

[45] *Ibid.* at 15.

[46] *Ibid.* at 17.

[47] Article 73 of the United Nations Charter reads as follows with regard to territories in former colonial possessions:

> Members of the United Nations which have or assume responsibilities for the administration of

territories whose peoples have not yet attained a full measure of self-government recognize the principle that the interests of the inhabitants of these territories are paramount, and accept as a sacred trust the obligation to promote to the utmost…the well-being of the inhabitants of these territories and to this end; (a) to ensure, with due respect for the culture of the people concerned, political, social and educational advancement, just treatment and protection against abuse; and (b) to develop self-government, to take due account of the political aspirations of the people and to assist them in the progressive development of their free political institutions according to the particular circumstances of each territory, as peoples and their various stages of development.

[48] *Cherokee Nation* v. *Georgia, supra* note 44 at 16.

[49] *Oliphant* v. *Suquamish Indian Tribe,* 435 U.S. 191 (1978) at 208.

[50] *Partners, supra* note 1 at 29.

[51] *Worcester* v. *Georgia,* 31 U.S. 515 (1832).

[52] E.g., *Washington* v. *Washington State Commercial Passenger Fishing Vessel Association* 443 U.S. 658 (1979): "A treaty, including one between the United States and an Indian tribe, is essentially a contract between two sovereign nations." (Per Stevens J.).

[53] *Supra* note 51 at 593. Justice McLean followed up on this dictum while riding circuit in Ohio for many years in *U.S.* v. *Cisna* 25 F. cas. 22 (C.C.D. Ohio, 1835). He held that the Wyandotte Indians, surrounded on all sides by non-Indians, had become so closely associated with their non-Indian neighbours in commerce and customs as to lose their status as a federally protected and recognized tribe for the limited purpose of the imposition of state criminal law on non-Indians living within the confines of the reservation.

[54] *The Kansas Indians,* 72 U.S. 737 (1867).

[55] *Ibid.* at 755:

> If the tribal organization of the Shawnees is preserved intact, and recognized by the political department of the government as existing, then they are a people distinct from others capable of making treaties, separated from the jurisdiction of Kansas, and to be governed exclusively by the government of the Union.

[56] *Ibid.* at 757.

[57] E.g., *Mashpee, supra* note 13. In addition, in *Washington* v. *Fishing Vessel Association, supra* note 52, the Court denied intervener status to a group of Indians who enjoyed a historic treaty relationship with the United States and which continued to receive treaty benefits. The Court found on the facts that, despite the treaty, that group had never been recognized by the federal government in any other way and could not be recognized by the court as having standing for purposes of the intervention.

[58] See text at note 12, *supra.*

[59] *R.* v. *Sioui,* [1990] 1 S.C.R. 1025 at 1053.

[60] The issues of failure to recognize, loss of status, enfranchisement, Bill C–31, and related matters are discussed in John Giokas & Robert Groves, c. 2, *supra.*

[61] The Supreme Court of the United States is gradually eroding the immunities to state jurisdiction originally affirmed in the *Worcester* decision. It is less and less the case that "Indian country" is an enclave. Much depends now on the answer to the question "Who did what and to whom and where within reservation boundaries" in order to know whether federal, state, or tribal law will apply. An illustration of this approach is provided by the 1973 decision in *McClanahan* v. *Arizona State Tax Commission* 411 U.S. 164 (1973), where the Court upheld the immunity of tribal members from state income taxation for income earned on the reservation, but made the following comment of the new rules for determining tribal immunities more generally (at 172):

> …The trend has been away from the idea of inherent sovereignty as a bar to state jurisdiction and

toward reliance on federal pre-emption...the Indian sovereignty doctrine is relevant, then, not because it provides a definitive resolution of the issues in this suit, but because it provides a backdrop against which applicable treaties and statutes must be read.

Thus, the relevant question in tribal sovereignty cases after *McClanahan* appears to be the extent to which Congress has acknowledged the tribal right to be sovereign by protecting that sovereignty from encroachment by the surrounding states. However complicated this formulation renders modern tribal self-government in practice, it has the virtue of at least preserving the notion of the federal protectorate over the tribes.

[62]*Partners, supra* note 1 at 29.

[63]For a discussion of the Two Row Wampum Treaty see Grand Chief Michael Mitchell, "An Unbroken Assertion of Sovereignty" in Boyce Richardson, ed., *Drumbeat: Anger and Renewal in Indian Country* (Summerhill Press, 1989) 105.

[64]Although on one view the Métis land grants in the *Manitoba Act* could be viewed as fulfilling a treaty or equivalent agreement worked out by the representatives of Canada and the Métis and later put in legislative form and constitutionalized. For arguments to this effect see Paul L.A.H. Chartrand, *Manitoba's Métis Settlement Scheme of 1870* (Saskatoon: University of Saskatchewan Native Law Centre, 1991).

[65]*Partners, supra* note 1 at 21.

[66]*Supra* note 19.

[67]Ch. 20, s.1, 16 Stat. 544, 566 (25 U.S.C. s. 71).

[68]It is difficult to see how Congress can amend the United States Constitution so as to remove the President's judicially sanctioned treaty-making powers without going through the formal amending process. The official explanation is that Congress was merely "interpreting" the treaty power. This is discussed in Russel Barsh, James Henderson, *The Road: Indian Tribes and Political Liberty* (Berkeley: University of California Press, 1980) at 67–69.

[69]The practice on American reservations was for the Indian agent to call the tribe together or, at least, to call the most influential chiefs to meet with him, at which time he would attempt to persuade them to organize themselves through a tribal council to which he could delegate some of his functions. Although some tribal councils might reflect past tribal structures or subdivisions, they would be compelled to be constituted and operated under western democratic principles. Usually the Indian agent would select "progressive" Indian leaders for tribal posts and would oversee tribal council operations with a firm hand. In this practice can be seen the beginnings of the split between traditional and modern factions that bedevils tribal politics today on many American reservations. A brief description of tribal council origins may be found in Vine Deloria Jr. & Clifford M. Lytle, *American Indians, American Justice* (Austin: University of Texas Press, 1983) at 89–99.

[70]The *General Allotment Act* of 1887 U.S. Statutes at Large, 24:389–91 (the Dawes Act) authorized the President to allot reservation land to individuals Indians in specified amounts (160 acres to heads of family, 80 to single persons over the age of eighteen and 40 to single persons under that age) with the remaining "surplus" land to be sold off to non-Indians for settlement. Tribal holdings fell from 152 to 48 million acres as a result. A comprehensive overview of this process and its consequences is provided by Janet A. McDonnell, *The Dispossession of the American Indian 1887–1934* (Bloomington: University of Indiana Press, 1991).

[71]Courts of Indian Offenses were established on reservations in the United States in 1883 under the administrative authority of Secretary of the Interior Henry Teller to eliminate what he described as "savage rites and heathenish practices": *Annual Report of the Secretary of the Interior*, November 1, 1883, reprinted in Francis Paul Prucha, *Documents of United States*

Indian Policy, 2d ed., (University of Nebraska Press, 1990) at 160–62. The Dawes Act individual land allotment policy increased the need for these courts because allotment had broken up traditional family and kinship systems and with them customary methods of dispute resolution.

[72] *Supra* note 54.

[73] *Supra* note 70.

[74] *United States* v. *Kagama* 118 U.S. 375 (1886) at 384°85 upholding the validity of the prosecution for "major crimes" of Indians in the U.S. federal courts—even where the transactions occurred between tribal members, on tribal lands and may already have been dealt with by tribal law.

[75] *Lone Wolf* v. *Hitchcock* 187 U.S. 553 (1903) the Kiowa tribe was forced to accept allotment of their reservation lands in spite of the surrender provisions in the Treaty of Medicine Lodge of 1867 with the United States that called for tribal assent (which had not been given) to such dealings with their lands.

[76] 180 U.S. 261 at 266 (1901). The legislation was to compensate American citizens for "depredations" committed by "any Indians belonging to any band, tribes or nation" that was "in amity" with the United States when the depredations occurred. Payments were diverted from annuities and treaty monies otherwise due to them. Many tribes ended up being so much in debt that the Department of the Interior's civilization program began to be impaired. The legislation and its consequences are described in Sidney Haring, *Crow Dog's Case: American Indian Sovereignty, Tribal Law and United States Law in the Nineteenth Century* (Cambridge University Press, 1994) at 252–58.

[77] *Montoya, ibid.* at 265.

[78] For a history of these policies see John Giokas, "The *Indian Act*: Evolution, Overview and Options for Amendment and Transition," Royal Commission on Aboriginal Peoples, *For Seven Generations: An Information Legacy of the Royal Commission on Aboriginal Peoples* (CD-Rom by Libraxus, Inc., Ottawa, Canada, 1997).

[79] This and other issues relating to whether the Métis are "Indians" in the sense in which the term is used in the Constitution are canvassed in a paper prepared for RCAP: Bradford Morse & John Giokas, "Do the Métis Fall Within Section 91(24) of the *Constitution Act, 1867,*" in Royal Commission on Aboriginal Peoples, *Aboriginal Self-Government: Legal and Constitutional Issues* (Minister of Supply and Services Canada, 1995).

[80] 417 U.S. 535 (1974).

[81] The development, provisions, and aftermath of the *Indian Reorganization Act* are described in detail in Vine Deloria Jr. & Clifford Lytle, *The Nations Within: the Past and Future of American Indian Sovereignty* (New York: Pantheon Books, 1984).

[82] The inherent powers of the tribes were "recognized" in s. 16 where a number of specific powers are listed, but preceded by the phrase "In addition to all powers vested in any Indian tribe or tribal council by existing law...." At least this was the view of the Solicitor for the Interior Department: U.S. Department of the Interior, "Powers of Indian Tribes," *Opinions of the Solicitor: Indian Affairs* (Washington, D.C.: U.S. Government Printing Office, 1946) 445. The opinion concluded (at 447) that "those powers which are lawfully vested in Indian tribes are not, in general, delegated powers granted by express acts of Congress, but rather inherent powers of a limited sovereignty which has never been extinguished." This view is accepted as accurate in legal theory.

At the time it was issued, this opinion was almost revolutionary in its implications (although few people realized it) for it accomplished what the often stormy and acrimonious congressional and Senate hearings on the draft bill had been unable to do: acknowledge the nation status and continuing viability of Indian tribes after up to seventy-five years during which most tribal governments had ceased functioning except as arms of the Bureau of Indian Affairs. Vine Deloria Jr. and Clifford Lytle comment in this connection that "Modern tribal sovereignty thus begins with this opinion...": *The Nations Within, supra* note 81 at 160.

[83]*Partners, supra* note 1 at 36.

[84]*IRA,* s. 16.

[85]*Partners, supra* note 1 at 44.

[86]*IRA* s. 19.

[87]William Canby, *American Indian Law in a Nutshell* (St. Paul, MN: West Publishing Co., 1988) at 21. The reason for this drastic reduction lay in the rapid increase in the population of the United States between 1890 and 1920 from 63 million to 106 million. This created great pressures for land, especially in the west—a phenomenon similar to that which occurred in Canada around the same time when a large number of prairie Indian surrenders were taken by the Crown.

[88]Fred L. Ragsdale Jr., "The Deception of Geography" in Deloria *supra* note 34 at 69.

[89]As described in the 1982 version, *supra* note 7 at 13.

[90]Cohen, *ibid.* at 15, n. 86. Other factors were also relied upon by the Department of the Interior, but they do not appear to have been regarded as anything other than persuasive:

1. The group has received special Congressional appropriations;

2. The group shows social solidarity;

3. The group has Indian ethnological roots;

4. The group history shows tribal roots.

[91]In a legal opinion from 1938, the solicitor for the Department of the Interior was of the view that in the specific case of two remnant bands from the larger Santee Sioux Tribe organized under the *IRA,* they did not enjoy the sovereign powers that flow from capacity as a tribe: *Opinions of the Solicitor, supra* note 82 at 814. This opinion was never given wide distribution or publicity by the BIA.

[92]In fact, a majority had to vote against accepting it or else it would apply. Traditional tribal members often refused to vote in elections of any kind called by the BIA, and so in some cases the *IRA* was "adopted" in this reverse onus situation when it is not clear that a majority of tribal members would have voted for its adoption had the reverse onus test not been used: *The Nations Within, supra* note 81.

[93]For example, an interesting conflict arose around the termination legislation specific to the Menominee tribe and the language contained in its treaty with the United States of one hundred years earlier. Notwithstanding that their lands were no longer held in trust by the federal government or that their members were no longer eligible for federal services as Indians, the members of the Menominee tribe were held to be a tribe for purposes of enforcing their treaty protected relationship with the United States. Thus, de-recognition for purposes of the legislation was accompanied by continuing recognition for purposes of the treaty protected rights. In short, the tribe was recognized for some but not for all purposes: *Menominee Tribe* v. *the United States* 388 F. 2d 998 (Ct. Cl 1967).

[94]25 U.S.C. s. 450b (b).

[95]Some of those contexts have been mentioned and may be summarized as follows: treaties; early Indian legislation modelled on the *Royal Proclamation of 1763* and for the purpose of protecting Indian lands from exploitation (the "Nonintercourse Acts"); early federal

liquor laws to prevent sales of liquor to Indians; Court of Claims legislation regarding compensation for "depredations" by an Indian tribe, band or nation; the 1946 Indian Claims
Commission legislation; the 1934 *IRA*; federal government services to Indians; and for purposes of federal court jurisdiction in proceedings brought by tribes.

[96]*Supra* note 7 at 6. These criteria are not exhaustive, largely because of the inconsistency of official practice. Some federally recognized tribes do not have reservations provided
by the United States (e.g., Passamaquoddy of Maine), others have treaties while being officially unrecognized in terms of federal services for Indians (e.g., Stillaguamish of Washington), while yet others have been "terminated" for some but not all federal purposes and services (Klamath of Oregon hunting and water rights unaffected by termination).

[97]*Partners, supra* note 1 at 30.

[98]*Ibid.* at 44: "Laws passed by an Aboriginal government will take precedence over
conflicting federal laws except where the latter can be justified under the *Sparrow* test."

[99]*Ibid.* at 41–42.

[100]*Ibid.* at 41.

[101]*Ibid.* at 42.

[102]*Ibid.* at 44.

[103]*Ibid.*

[104]*Ibid.* at 45.

[105]See text at note 36 *supra*.

[106]Much of the material for this portion of the chapter is drawn from Rachael Paschal,
"The Imprimatur of Recognition: American Indian Tribes and the Federal Acknowledgement
Process," 66 Washington L. Rev. 209 (1991); William A. Starna, "'Public Ethnohistory' and
Native-American Communities: History or Administrative Genocide?" 53 *Radical History*
126 (1992). The FAP is considered in detail by Professor Barsh in chapter 6 *infra*. This section of the original paper by Giokas has been retained as a valuable part of the comparison
between Canada and the United States.

[107]*Supra* note 15.

[108]*Supra* note 52.

[109]American Indian Policy Review Commission, *Final Report* (Washington, 1977) 1:461,
462.

[110]William Quinn Jr., "Public Ethnohistory? Or, Writing Tribal Histories at the Bureau of Indian Affairs," *The Public Historian* 10, 2 (Spring 1988) 71.

[111]S. 83.6(d).

[112]*Federal Register* 59:38 at 9281.

[113]*Montoya, supra* note 76.

[114]Paschal, *supra* note 106.

[115]*Supra* note 112.

[116]Paschal, *supra* note 106 at 226.

[117]Parliament of Canada, Special Committee on Indian Self-Government, *Indian Self-
Government in Canada* (Ottawa: Ministry of Supply and Services, 1983) [hereinafter, *Penner
Report*].

[118]Committee membership was made up of seven members of Parliament and representatives of three national Aboriginal organizations, the Assembly of First Nations, the Native Women's Association, and the Native Council of Canada. The Committee travelled to all
regions in Canada to hear witnesses, both on and off reserve. In total, 39 of 60 public meet-

ings were held on the road. The Committee also travelled to the United States, to Washington D.C. and to several pueblos in the southwest for comparison purposes.

[119]*Penner Report, supra* note 117 at 53.

[120]*Ibid.* at 55. This was in response to submission from the Native Women's Association and the Native Council of Canada criticizing any notion of allowing current band members—the beneficiaries of discriminatory practices in the past—to determine membership in the future.

[121]*Ibid.* at 56.

[122]*Ibid.*

[123]This concept was proposed by the Association of Iroquois and Allied Indians: *Ibid.* at 55–56.

[124]At that time, in 1951, there were probably fewer than one hundred persons without a band affiliation on the general register.

[125]*Penner Report, supra* note 117 at 47.

[126]*Ibid.* at 43.

[127]*Ibid.* at 59.

[128]*Ibid.* at 57.

[129]*Ibid.*

[130]*Ibid.* at 62.

[131]*Ibid.* at 63.

[132]*Ibid.* at 64.

[133]*Ibid.* at 66.

[134]*Ibid.* at 108–09.

[135]*Ibid.* at 109.

[136]*Ibid.* at 110.

[137]*Ibid.*

[138]*Ibid.* at 122.

[139]*An Act relating to self-government for Indian Nations.* It was introduced for first reading in the House of Commons on June 27, 1984 by the Minister of Indian Affairs, the Hon. John Munro.

[140]*Response of the Government to the Report of the Special Committee on Indian Self-Government* (Indian and Northern Affairs Canada, March 5, 1984) at 2 [hereinafter *Government Response*].

[141]*Ibid.* at 1.

[142]*Ibid.*

[143]*Ibid.*

[144]*Ibid.* at 6.

[145]*Ibid.* at 7, where the response refers to "the importance of seeking concrete results at the community level."

[146]*Ibid.*, where the response refers to future consultations to "ease current administrative constraints."

[147]*Ibid.*

[148]*Ibid.* at 2.

[149]*Ibid.*

[150]S.C. 1869, c. 6.

[151]S.C. 1876, c. 18.

[152]S.C. 1884, c. 28.

[153]R.S.C. 1970 , c. I–6, s. 83.

[154]S. 6.

[155]S. 63.

[156]S. 63(2).

[157]Ss. 42–49.

[158]S. 8.

[159]S. 26.

[160]S. 16.

[161]S. 33–35.

[162]Ss. 40, 41.

[163]S. 36.

[164]S. 13(2).

[165]This is made abundantly clear in Francis Jennings *The Ambiguous Empire: The Covenant Chain Confederation of Indian Tribes With the English Colonies* (New York: W.W. Norton & Co., 1984) where it is evident that the various Indian tribes and nations such as the Delaware, Shawnee, Susquehannocks, and others preserved their liberty from the Iroquois and from the English colonies that were also members of the Chain.

[166]This is made clear in the account provided by Alexander Morris in *The Treaties of Canada with the Indians of Manitoba and the Northwest Territories* (Toronto: Belfords, Clarke & Co., 1880).

[167]This argument is made convincingly by David Williams, "Legitimation and Statutory Interpretation: Conquest, Consent, and Community in Federal Indian Law," [1994] 80 Virginia L. Rev. 403.

[168]*Partners, supra* note 1 at 26.

[169]14 App. Cas. 46 (PC) (1888).

[170]RCAP did make this recommendation in its final report. See Canada, *Report of the Royal Commission on Aboriginal Peoples: Restructuring the Relationship,* vol. 2 (Ottawa, Supply and Services Canada, 1996) part 1, 177ff. and especially at 314–21, under the heading "Rebuilding and recognizing Aboriginal nations." At 236, RCAP concludes as follows:

> The Commission concludes that the constitutional right of self-government is vested in the people that make up Aboriginal nations, not in local communities as such. Only nations can exercise the range of governmental powers available in the core areas of Aboriginal jurisdiction, and nations alone have the power to conclude self-government treaties regarding matters falling within the periphery. Nevertheless, local communities of Aboriginal people have access to inherent governmental powers if they join together in their national units and agree to a constitution allocating powers between the national and local levels.

At 319, it is recommended that the Cabinet decide whether or not to recognize an Aboriginal nation that had complied with certain Constitutional requirements that are discussed in this section. This follows the recommendation, at 236, that "All governments in Canada recognize that the right of self-government is vested in Aboriginal nations rather than in small local communities."

[171]*Partners, supra* note 1 at 44.

[172]*Ibid.* at 36.

[173]*Ibid.* at 37.

[174]*Supra* note 51 at 543.

Chapter Five

Métis and Non-status Indians and Section 91(24) of the *Constitution Act, 1867*

Bradford W. Morse & Robert K. Groves

Introduction

This chapter[1] seeks to explore the key legal and policy issues surrounding the potential application of section 91(24) of the *Constitution Act, 1867* to the Métis and non-status Indian peoples in Canada. It also seeks to correlate the matter of federal constitutional jurisdiction with the recognition of Aboriginal and treaty rights in section 35 of the *Constitution Act, 1982*. The alternative possibilities to obtain clarification are discussed in the final segment.

Section 91(24) speaks to one of the core constitutional issues in Canadian federalism. One might naturally presume that a legal determination of jurisdiction would be followed more or less directly by legislative or executive action. However, the operation of Canadian federalism does not reflect solely the written Constitution. It also reflects, and is motivated by, social and political forces. These forces include entrenched policies and practices, perceptions of financial and political pressure, and intergovernmental understandings and agreements. There are a great many "black letter" legal issues that have been a matter of settled law for some time in Canada, but for which there are few, if any, opportunities for concrete expression. Many of these, not surprisingly to the Métis and non-status Indians in particular, are in the arena of Aboriginal jurisprudence.

To cite only one example, it has been appreciated since at least 1888, if not before, that the underlying ownership by the provinces of lands and resources is subject to federal jurisdiction in relation to the unextinguished title rights of Aboriginal peoples.[2] This understanding was undoubtedly one of the motivations for the federal government's disallowance of certain land laws enacted by the province of British Columbia that attempted to clear the province of Indian interests in 1874. This did not lead to a treaty process, as it had in the Prairies and northern Ontario, although it did lead to the creation of reserves. Laws adverse to Aboriginal interests have been passed by the Legislature of British Columbia on a regular basis without federal interference ever since, and it is only in recent years that the social and political conditions have combined to force the issue of treaty-making back on the active agenda in relation to that province.

The moral of this story is that constitutional law may appear to read plainly in one direction, while the realities of past decisions, actions, and accommodations—often taken with no Aboriginal participation at all—can take a completely different course. The Supreme Court itself often attempts to find a contemporary balance between the written Constitution and the unwritten politics of the federation.[3] This is reflected most recently in its development of a theory to permit significant provincial legislative action in what is otherwise—and in the law— a predominately federal jurisdiction.[4]

It is important, therefore, for the Métis and non-status Indians to understand that even if the scope of section 91(24) jurisdiction was to be clarified— and we are firmly of the view that section 91(24) does include all Aboriginal peoples for at least some purposes—such a legal clarification would not by itself accomplish a revolution in the way that the federal and provincial governments respond to demands for legislative or policy action. That is a matter of policy, or choice, and is beyond what the courts alone can accomplish through such a decision.

This chapter is based upon three distinct elements. The first is a literature review of section 91(24) issues, restricted primarily to the more recent materials developed since the abortive Charlottetown Constitutional Accord of 1992. At that time, governments and Aboriginal groups agreed during the Canada Round of negotiations on a consensus approach on this issue. That consensus is important because it reflected an agreement not about what "should be," but about "what is," namely, that section 91(24) does in fact apply to all three of the Aboriginal peoples listed in section 35(2) of the *Constitution Act, 1982,* yet at the same time that section 91(24) should be amended to confirm this potential understanding so as to remove any uncertainty in the future. It was also agreed at that time to amend section 91(24) to reaffirm the ability of the Alberta Legislature to pass legislation for Métis in that province, subject to potential Parliamentary override. Since the Charlottetown Accord and the October 1992 referendum, relatively little of interest has been published on the question concerning to whom the exercise of section 91(24) authority may affect. It may be that this reflects a diminished interest in the controversy, given the consensus achieved in 1992. This is an unlikely explanation, however, as it is more plausible to assume that it reflects simply a decline in scholarly attention to this important issue. Nevertheless, the Royal Commission on Aboriginal Peoples (RCAP) did conduct specialized research on the matter[5] and discussed the topic at length in its final report.[6]

In addition to a literature review, the case law has been searched and all relevant decisions relating to the issue of the scope of section 91(24) and its meaning for the constituency of the Congress of Aboriginal Peoples (CAP) have been analysed. The results of this search and analysis are summarized in the body of this chapter.

The third and final element of this chapter is a focus on concrete options for action. As a result, this chapter reviews a number of options and makes recommendations.

The Origins of Section 91(24)

There have been two major phases in the history of our contemporary understanding of section 91(24). The first led to the inclusion of this provision in the *Constitution Act, 1867*, while the second concerns how it has been applied since Confederation. For each phase, several motivating causes can be identified.

The Royal Proclamation and Treaty-making

The British conquest of French interests in North America was accomplished in significant measure through alliances with First Nations, with whom the British had already established a pattern of relationships through treaties of peace and trade. Great Britain needed to establish new colonial governments for the territories over which France had relinquished its claims, as well as honour its promises to its Indian Nation allies. Faced with a potential for massive military and administrative expense in managing border wars, insurrections, and even the loss of empire through potential conflicts between settlers and Indian Nations, King George III was advised to use his royal prerogative to reassure the allied Indian Nations and tribes of their rights to their traditional lands and resources, and to prevent colonial governments from exercising any direct jurisdiction over Indian peoples or over any of their lands that had yet to be surrendered through treaties. The result was the *Royal Proclamation of 1763*, a constitutional document whose continuing relevance in Canada is reflected today in section 25 of the *Constitution Act, 1982*.

The *Royal Proclamation* confirmed the "imperial formula" for governing

North America that involved restrictions on the legislative powers of colonial governments in relation to Aboriginal people, and maintenance of a direct "nation-to-nation" relationship between the Crown in Great Britain and the Indian Nations in the Americas. This formula still survives in altered form as the basis for today's law and policy. Since Confederation, however, the role of the British Crown in balancing the interests of, and conflicts between, settlers and Aboriginal peoples has been displaced by the role of the federal government of Canada. Nevertheless, the basic formula remains: settler (now provincial) governments have limited powers to pass laws directly in relation to Indians, and are prevented from signing treaties with them on their own, these powers vesting in the British (and now Canadian) Crown.

Colonial Legislation and Confederation

Between the War of 1812–14 and Confederation, the threat posed by Indian Nations to settlers in the East declined significantly, along with the need for British intervention to arbitrate conflicts. This factor, together with other influences, permitted the replacement of direct imperial control over Indian affairs in Canada with colonial legislative control. Colonial legislative activities increased as a function both of the growing need for lands for settlers, especially after 1814, and of official efforts to "civilize" and "Christianize" Indian peoples. The modern *Indian Act* is still largely inspired by pre-Confederation legislative experiments with the establishment of reserves and defining who are entitled to reside thereon. What is of importance is that the colonial motivation was not, as had earlier been the case with the imperial government, to maintain positive political and economic relations with the Indian Nations. Rather, it was to transform the Indian Nations and the people themselves—with the shorter-term goal of limiting the obstacles that Indians and Indian-occupied land posed for colonial settlement.

During the buildup to Confederation, it is apparent that neither British nor Canadian politicians desired a simple termination of the old imperial formula, at least in the short term. The aspirations for a western and northern expansion of the original Canada, and the military threat of an expansionist American government, meant a renewed need for a central capacity and power to deal with the Indian peoples in border and western regions. Similarly, the cost of dealing with First Nations who had been surrounded and "pacified" in the original colonies that had united to form Canada was something that the new provincial leaders were eager to avoid. As a result, the lapse in the imperial formula witnessed in the mid-nineteenth century was followed by a re-centralization of legislative powers over "Indians and Lands reserved for the Indians" allocated to the new Parliament of Canada. No definition was provided for the term "Indians." Earlier colonial legislation for "Indians" in the Canadas and in Nova Scotia existed as a potential source of definition, but this legislation had more narrow purposes, and even then referred generally to "Indians," their descendants and those living among them, rather than attempting to impose narrow definitions in aid of a broader goal of individual or group assimilation.

There was no legislation in Canada or Great Britain to formally recognize the groups now referred to as "Métis" (as distinct from "Indians") prior to the acquisition of the Hudson's Bay Company (HBC) interests in Rupert's Land and the negotiations with Louis Riel's provisional government in 1870. Most of British North America outside of Canada before 1870 was governed very lightly under the HBC trade monopoly issued through a Royal Charter in 1670, which included executive, legislative, and judicial authority over this massive territory. HBC did not pass legislation specifically for Indian, Inuit, or Métis affairs, but merely operated extremely limited judicial and service-delivery systems. While census records in some areas (such as Quebec) recorded "half-breed" or "Métis" people along with "whites,"[7] this was not consistent, and in other cases HBC and imperial records listed "half-breeds" along with Indians.

In summary, the origins of section 91(24) reflected a number of forces, including the slow evolution of Canada as a self-governing Dominion building on earlier British laws, such as the *Royal Proclamation of 1763*, which established colonial government in much of what became Canada a century later. In addition, there was a continuing British concern to avoid local or provincial government interference in Indian diplomacy (which often involved border or frontier conflicts with other states) and restrict colonial or local capacity to expropriate Indian land interests that could thereby trigger direct conflicts. The result was the centralization of legislative power over all matters affecting Indians and their lands.

At the same time, the new federal government was comprised of leading colonial politicians, many of whom had been involved in earlier efforts to deal with the "Indian" question in the more settled provinces of Ontario, Quebec, and the Maritimes. As a result, it is not surprising that shortly after Confederation, Parliament passed Indian legislation that built on and consolidated earlier legislation, and pursued the same kind of assimilationist goals that guided the earlier legislation. While none of these forces could be said to have clearly contemplated the Métis situation in western Canada, the scope of section 91(24) as including the Métis is suggested by the first federal statute dealing with Indian matters.

All such persons residing among such Indians, whose parents were or are, or either of them was or is, descended on either side from Indians or an Indian reputed to belong to the particular tribe, band or body of Indians interested in such lands or immovable property, and the descendants of all such persons.[8]

Although this provision is obviously not directed to the Métis as a distinct "people" in political, social, and cultural terms, it does readily acknowledge that individuals of mixed Indian and European ancestry can be accommodated within the section 91(24) jurisdiction of the Parliament of Canada.

Confederation to 1982

It is commonly remarked that while section 91(24) quite clearly provides Parliament with exclusive jurisdiction for both "Indians and Lands reserved for the Indians," in fact Parliament has largely chosen over the years to narrow its actual legislative role to "Indians *on* lands reserved for the Indians." This transformation of two broad heads of jurisdiction to one with quite limited effect has been a cause of great frustration to Métis and non-status Indians, as well as to non-reserve Indians and even Inuit,[9] especially since the issue of access to constitutionally protected rights and self-government has emerged since 1982. A brief background on this evolution is therefore useful to an assessment of the jurisdictional scope of section 91(24), as well as to an understanding of the obstacles to reforming federal practice even where federal jurisdictional capacity is confirmed.

From Confederation until the early twentieth century, a key issue for Canada was how to deal with the "Indian Question," including the related "Métis Question," motivated in particular by the course of Canadian western expansion. In some locales the "solution" as far as the Métis were concerned was to absorb them within existing bands or to declare them as bands in their own right. The more common approach, however, was to pursue an individual allotment scheme under the *Manitoba Act* and the *Dominion Lands Act* so as to deny any ongoing collective identity.[10] While a variety of answers were given, the basic goal was never in doubt: Indians and Métis were to be eventually absorbed into the general population. The only issue was how best to accomplish this task at least expense while avoiding overt conflict between settlers and Indian (or Métis) interests. Initially, the imperial formula of central control and mediation between Indian and settler interests crystallized in the spate of treaties signed in the Prairies and northern Ontario, though generally in advance of actual settlement. Once this intensive phase of expansion, settlement, and the formation of local and provincial governments was largely accomplished, however, federal involvement narrowed substantially to focus on the federal obligations tied to treaty promises and the administration of reserves and the resident Indian population pursuant to the precise terms of the *Indian Act*.

All other matters of local government, lands, and resources were left to the provincial legislatures, with the government of Canada retaining ownership of all Crown lands and resources until their transfer to the three Prairie Provinces in 1930.

Métis & Indian: Two Paths to Citizenship

Accommodation was forced upon the federal government for Métis interests, both in Manitoba and in the North-West Angle of Ontario, in the early years after Confederation. In these cases, federal and British legislation recognized Métis (or "Half-breed") interests in traditional Indian title to lands to the extent that the former were allocated land rights in compensation, while the latter were added, as a group, to Treaty 3 and provided with reserves. The *Manitoba Act*'s commitment to land was administered in a manner which resulted in the quick alienation of the lands from the Métis recipients. The *Dominion Lands Act* of 1879 and its subsequent amendments also produced the same result, distributing alienable scrip instead of land. After conflict broke out in Saskatchewan over Métis grievances there and in Manitoba, the Métis scrip system was extended as a regular part of treaty making. From the vantage point of constitutional law, these legislative and executive actions would not appear lawful had those Métis been outside of federal section 91(24) jurisdiction.[11]

Federal practice adhered to its primary goal of clearing Indian title as part of the national scheme of attracting Canadian and European settlement to the West. There was no apparent contemplation of any need to accommodate or provide for persistent or permanent Aboriginal communities. Instead, federal policy as it evolved up to the 1930s was to distinguish amongst "Native" inhabitants by using social tests of their capacity to merge into an agrarian settler society. The Métis, many of whom were already adapted to farming, were generally regarded as early candidates for incorporation, and were therefore compensated as individuals for pre-existing title rights.[12]

Federal policy was no doubt heavily influenced by the views of Treaty Commissioner and later Manitoba Lieutenant Governor Alexander Morris, who noted three types of mixed-ancestry persons in Rupert's Land when writing in 1880:

> The Half-breeds in the Territories are of three classes—first, those who, as at St. Laurent, near Prince Albert, the Qu'Appelle Lakes and Edmonton, have their farms and homes; second, those who are entirely identified with the Indians, living with them and speaking their language, third, those who do not farm, but live after the habits of the Indians, by the pursuit of the buffalo and the chase.[13]

It would seem clear that the federal intent was to see the Métis moved immediately into the general populace, though of course there are many Métis who believe that the arrangements negotiated in Manitoba in 1870 were to protect their collective interests and townships.[14]

In contrast to the federal policy for the Métis, the federal perception was that most Indian groups required greater "protection" and more gradual efforts at socialization, and set aside communal reserves (usually located in areas distant from likely settler interest), to be managed directly or indirectly by agents operating under the *Indian Act*. This collective or communal approach to dealing with Indian Nations was not, however, meant to last indefinitely. Despite the assurances that were sometimes set out in the oral terms of treaties, and as reflected more directly in federal Indian legislation, Indians on reserves were also to be subjected to tests of "civilization" and be encouraged, or forced, to enfranchise into the general populace. The alternative image was that some Indian communities would simply disappear through disease and dwindling numbers. As a result, a hybrid system of individual status or designation emerged. Around a core descent- or kinship-based definition of individual ties to recognized communities (which could theoretically go on forever with in-marriage) were added a variety of social tests for both voluntary and forced removal from official "Indianness."[15] In much of the period of the development of the *Indian Act* the continuity of Indian tribes or bands was simply not seen to be likely beyond three or four generations before these social tests led to the disappearance of collectivities entirely. Until the 1960s it was still confidently hoped that those Indians remaining would gladly enfranchise voluntarily as individuals or en masse as communities in order to attain the many perceived benefits of citizenship.

Therefore the collective or communal approach to land holdings and governance for Indians, in contrast to the more immediate individualized land or money scrip allocations to Métis, cannot be taken to reflect a pre-established distinction between the groups that flowed from section 91(24). The Métis were not treated differently because they were not within section 91(24), any more than individual Indians who were enfranchised ceased to fall under the theoretical jurisdiction of section 91(24). The Métis (and specifically the western Métis) were treated differently because they were seen, as a class, to be socially capable of more immediate absorption. Where individual Indians or entire groups or bands also "met" specific tests of social capacity, as laid out in the *Indian Act*, they too were deemed capable of the duties and privileges of citizenship. They ceased to be "Indians" for the purposes of federal legislation, though not for federal jurisdiction.

As a further reflection on the important distinction between the constitutional head of power and its actual exercise through the *Indian Act*, as well as demonstrating the fluidity across definitional compartments, it is important to note that treaty commissioners frequently gave individuals the option of "taking treaty" or "taking scrip." Those who opted for the former would be entered on the treaty annuity list and henceforth regarded as Indian and a member of the tribe or Nation that was negotiating the treaty in question; those who selected the latter were issued scrip for land or money and subsequently regarded as Métis, with whom the government of Canada needed no longer concern itself.

By 1930 and the end of historic treaty-making in the West, legislative control over lands and resources had been transferred to the Prairie Provinces. While some protective clauses were added to the transfer agreements[16] to assure Indians of a continuing (and treaty-based) right to hunt, fish, and trap on unoccupied Crown lands,[17] as well as an obligation on provinces to transfer Crown lands to Canada to fulfil any outstanding treaty entitlements to reserves, there was no specific reference to the Métis, an issue that has preoccupied courts in the past few years.

The Unravelling of the Policy of Assimilation

Social policy from the 1920s to the 1950s was aggressively assimilationist, as reflected in the legislation and in policy-based bureaucratic campaigns against mixed-blood people generally and any Indians who were deemed to have met any of the various "tests" or presumptions of social capacity set out in the *Act*. A notorious case was that of several thousand people in northern Alberta and Saskatchewan who had managed to settle on Indian reserves, or within Indian communities still awaiting their reserves, often with their relatives, only to be summarily evicted on the grounds of their real or presumed descent from or marriage to scrip-takers.[18] In other cases, any presumption of non-Indian paternity could and was used by federal officials to strip persons of band membership and evict them from reserves, even in the case of families who had resided on reserves for their entire lives.[19]

By 1951 the *Indian Act* became, for Parliament and the civil service, a complete statement of responsibility for Native people. The new *Act* also added to modern discourse the concept of "Indian status," a measure that reduced the capacity of local Indian communities to incorporate new members from outside, making it easier for federal officials to superintend the official "confirmation" of a person's transit between "Indian" and "citizen." Scrip-taking Métis and their descendants were expressly excluded from the *Act*, as were the Inuit, despite having been found to be "Indian" under section 91(24) in 1939.[20]

It is perhaps ironic that just as the assimilation policy was becoming even more fixed in legislative concrete, forces undermining its relevance and legitimacy were simultaneously growing in strength. After the mid-1960s a gradual relaxing, or at least a greater questioning, of assimilationist policy took hold, resulting in a shift in language from "assimilation" to "integration," with no discernable alteration in substantive approaches. After the debacle of the 1969 White

Paper,[21] the federal government was increasingly intervening directly in the social affairs of Aboriginal peoples generally, regardless of "status" under the *Indian Act* or the supposed scope of section 91(24). This trend emerged in the 1970s along with the decline of public support for assimilation, the emergence of aggressive and articulate national and regional Aboriginal organizations, and the related advancement of such concepts as civil liberties, biculturalism, and multiculturalism. By the mid-1970s, the point had been reached where the entire scheme of federal Indian policy—as reflected in the *Indian Act*, the policy of enfranchisement, and the denial of modern relevance for Aboriginal or treaty rights—entered a phase of rapid transformation, culminating in the *Constitution Act, 1982.*

The New Equation: 91(24) in the Context of Section 35

The inclusion of Métis as one of three Aboriginal peoples for whom Aboriginal and treaty rights were recognized and affirmed in the 1982 additions to the Canadian Constitution[22] has created a new equation and altered the traditional approach to issues concerning the scope of section 91(24). The courts, particularly over the last decade, are beginning to deliberate on some aspects of this new equation.

In this part we review the emerging case law in respect of the scope of section 91(24) in order to assist in focusing on a set of key legal policy issues of importance to the consideration of options for potential action in the near term. To this end we examine both the Supreme Court's rulings on section 35 of the *Constitution Act, 1982*—which establish a new context for interpreting section 91(24)—and lower court decisions that more specifically address Métis as well as non-status Indian issues.

Reference re Eskimos

Before turning to section 35 and recent court rulings, it is useful to examine briefly the only major precedent to date for a court reference, one of the available options to clarify the scope of section 91(24). There are two basic ways in which the 1939 reference case, in *Re Eskimos,*[23] is of continuing relevance. First, the reference directly addressed the question of whether or not one of the three Aboriginal peoples now listed in section 35 fell within section 91(24). Second, the case was prompted by Canada's denial of financial responsibility over social programs for Inuit and did not deal with Aboriginal rights or titles directly.

The Nunavik Inuit and their territories were included within the expanded political boundaries of the province of Quebec as a result of the *1912 Quebec Boundaries Extension Act.*[24] The high cost of providing health services and relief payments to this population during the Depression led Quebec to complain that the federal government had responsibility for Eskimos, and should bear the full expense of administering essential services to them. Canada countered with a range of arguments that are familiar to the present debate over the Métis today, with the exception that Canada did not then argue that jurisdiction was severed from financial responsibility in such areas as education, welfare, and health. The Inuit, not surprisingly, were not parties to the reference, nor were they apparently consulted by either government prior to argument before the Supreme Court of Canada.

The following outcomes of the *Reference re Eskimos* decision seem to remain of enduring relevance to any future reference decision.

1. The Court turned to non-legal sources, including anthropological, historical, and linguistic expertise, to examine the "plain intent" of the framers of the Constitution, and also reviewed the correspondence of key drafters.

2. The Court gave particular attention to the records of the Hudson's Bay Company in light of its nominal "governance" over much of the territory concerned in the reference case at the time of Confederation.[25]

3. The Court's conclusion on the plain intent of the framers in using the term "Indians" in section 91(24) was that the term was intended to include the "aborigines" or "aboriginal people" of North America, including those of Rupert's Land.

4. The Court discounted the *Indian Act* as mere federal legislation that cannot define the scope of, or give meaning to, the terms used in the Constitution, although such legislation must be enacted in such a way as to respect constitutional dictates.

These four points will almost certainly have relevance in any future reference case in relation to Métis.

Impact of Section 35

The Supreme Court has not had an opportunity to address Métis legal issues directly, either in the context of section 91(24) or in connection with claims to section 35 rights. It has indicated (in *R. v. Van der Peet*[26]) that a specific fact-based submission would need to be brought forward in order for it to address such issues as whether or how the evidentiary rules it has developed for proof of Indian (or Inuit) rights would be applied to Métis assertions.

However, there are certain interpretive principles regarding section 35 that may shed light on how the Supreme Court (or a provincial or territorial appeal court) would proceed. As a constitutional provision, section 35 must be accorded a substantive and meaningful interpretation. This is the approach the Supreme Court has described as being "purposive." Put another way, it is not open to the courts in Canada simply to describe the inclusion of Métis within section 35(2) as of only rhetorical value, or as being politically revisionist and without real consequence. Regardless of what might have been the intentions of the framers of the *Constitution Act, 1867* regarding Métis, the courts are required now to adapt their interpretation of section 91(24) in light of section 35 and the *Charter of Rights and Freedoms* (and particularly section 25).[27]

In our view, any future reference decision on section 91(24) will have to assume that the framers of the *Constitution Act, 1982,* who used the term "aboriginal peoples" in sections 25, 35, and 37 and included in that term both "Métis" and "Inuit" by virtue of section 35(2), must have been conscious of the Court's own conclusion in 1939 that "Eskimos" were "aboriginal people" and therefore "Indians" under section 91(24) while being "Inuit" rather than "Indians" under section 35(2). Otherwise, section 35 would have read quite differently.[28] Similarly, the effect of drafting the new provisions in this way means that the term "Indians" in section 35(2) is at most a subset of the broader description used in 1867 to delimit Parliament's power. It is of course trite but true to acknowledge that federal and provincial parliamentarians are presumed to know the current law when enacting any alteration to it.[29]

On the basis of this assumption, the Supreme Court might take two broad paths to a judgment. The first path would confine itself to the definitional provision at section 35(2), while the second would examine the substantive "rights" provision of section 35(1).

The Definitional Approach

Like the Supreme Court in 1939, which examined the issue of Inuit inclusion largely from a definitional perspective (as opposed to focusing on Inuit rights), a court facing a Métis reference could choose to focus on the listing of the three Aboriginal peoples in section 35(2) as a matter separate from any particular rights of those peoples. In this way, the Court would have to sort out how the single term involved in the 1867 Constitution ("Indians") relates to the four labels found in the 1982 *Act* ("aboriginal peoples," "Indian, Inuit and Métis peoples of Canada"). It is not our purpose here to examine all the possible arguments in detail, but a broad overview is important to the consideration of strategic options.

As noted above, one major point is the lack of any effort in 1982 by the framers to qualify the reference to Métis in relation to the *Constitution Act, 1867.* In addition, those arguing for Métis inclusion would point to a lack of any explicit exclusion of Métis from the *1867 Act,* to the inclusion of Métis within a confirmatory inclusion clause in the draft legal text of the Charlottetown Accord, RCAP's recommendations on the matter, and the bulk of expert opinion on this topic.

The definitional approach could also involve looking to the second half of section 91(24). The Court has since 1888 referred to the phrase, "Lands reserved for the Indians" as a separate head of power for Parliament. All modern Supreme Court judgements use the phrase "Indian title" as analogous for "Aboriginal title." If it were argued that Métis were not, in 1867, included within the term "Indians," they could not logically have been considered to have any part or interest in "Lands reserved for the Indians." This would mean either that the Métis had no part in the modern concept of "Aboriginal title" as the understanding has been that addressing the issue requires federal involvement due to section 91(24), or that the Métis variation of Aboriginal title is somehow so fundamentally different from the Indian and Inuit version that only provincial participation is required. The latter option would require a colossal recasting of the legal principles that have emerged in Canadian constitutional law over the past century and would call into question the scrip process carried out in accordance with federal legislation.

Separate and aside from evidence of title, or admissions in earlier statutes (such as the *Manitoba Act*) and orders-in-council referring directly to Métis interests in Indian title, this basic argument flounders on grounds of the "purposive intent" principle applied to section 35. It would defeat the assumption of "purposive intent" to prejudge a finding of fact about the existence of any Aboriginal rights at all for Métis persons or groups by arguing that, as "non-Indians," they could never possibly have such rights. Any court that would agree with such an argument would have to accept that the inclusion of "Métis" in section 35(2) was solely the product of a political manoeuvre to garner support for what was then a proposal for constitutional reform, and unrelated to the content of substantive protections set out in section 35(1). In short, any argument that Métis are not "Indians" for purposes of section 91(24) would also have to argue that the section 35(1) reference to Aboriginal rights, or at least the "title end" of the rights continuum,[30] was definitionally exclusive of the Métis, thus rendering the inclusion of Métis within section 35 largely purposeless. Prevailing Canadian jurisprudence invariably states that all constitutional provisions are presumed to have legal meaning, thereby suggesting that including Métis within section 35 must have some legal effects.

The implications of this approach, on its own, would seem confined largely to matters of conflicting laws (such as Alberta's legislation for the Métis settlements, which is discussed in more detail below). It is perhaps for this reason that federal officials have suggested that there is not much to be gained by a reference case in terms of tangible change to the status quo. However, in tandem with *Charter*-based arguments and the introduction of evidence about socio-economic need and disparity, even a narrow definitional clarification could be sufficient to change the landscape of federal policy, particularly where Métis (and possibly to a lesser extent, non-status Indians) are clearly discriminated against in connection with policies, programs and services that are generally available to status Indians and Inuit.[31]

The Substantive Rights Approach
The second approach for a reference court would be to address the question of section 35(1), dealing with the rights of the Aboriginal peoples. Building on the "purposive intent" principle, any court would have to accept that the Métis people must have at least some rights recognized and affirmed in the *Constitution Act, 1982.* Here the question would turn to whether or not the rights concerned, and the related people, fall under provincial or federal jurisdiction.

The Supreme Court has developed a framework for interpreting section 35 rights since 1990 that ties them closely to federal jurisdiction under section 91(24), such that it now appears to be an inescapable conclusion that if and where Métis (or non-status Indians) have section 35 rights, Parliament has the sole mandated legislative jurisdiction to explicitly "regulate" them or to conclude treaties with them. This new element—the relationship between Aboriginal rights and section 91(24), has altered the entire question, and the consequences, surrounding the scope of the latter in relation to Métis or any other group. Whereas in 1939 the reference case turned on "responsibilities" for the basic costs of relief and support payments to Inuit in northern Quebec, after 1982 the question would be broadened to involve constitutionally protected Aboriginal and treaty rights and how, at the very least, access to these rights is to be managed.[32]

The relationship between section 35 and the scope of Parliament's jurisdiction under section 91(24) has not generally been the subject of direct litigation other than in connection with the issue of ascertaining the appropriate tests for valid extinguishment or infringement of Aboriginal or treaty rights through legislation. In its 1997 decision in *Delgamuukw*, however, the Supreme Court has supported the following basic framework:

1. All rights protected by section 35 are by definition within the "core of Indianness" that the Court has stated is exclusively a federal jurisdiction under "Indians" or "Lands reserved for the Indians" in section 91(24). As a result, these rights cannot be expressly affected negatively by provincial legislation.

2. Parliament cannot extinguish section 35 rights after 1982, but may in-

fringe such rights through validly enacted legislation if it is pursuing compelling and substantive objectives, and where its actions are consistent with the Crown's special relationship with, and fiduciary obligations to, Aboriginal people. The courts will assess federal behaviour to see if there has been adequate and effective consultation in advance of the statute being passed, that compensation was considered, and that the least intrusive measure was selected.

3. Provinces, through their normal legislative powers in section 92, may also infringe Aboriginal and treaty rights, but such infringements must also meet the tests of justification. However, provincial laws cannot directly regulate section 35 rights, at least not in any negative manner, nor could provinces ever extinguish Aboriginal or treaty rights.

The Supreme Court has, arguably, indirectly ruled that the inclusion of "Métis" within section 35 necessarily means that Métis rights, including the identification and definition of who is a Métis (since this touches the "core of Métisness") is within exclusive federal jurisdiction under section 91(24).

There are potentially far-reaching consequences for this association between sections 35 and 91(24). For example, the Supreme Court, in *Guerin* v. *The Queen*,[33] has ruled that the Indian interest in lands set aside under the *Indian Act* are the same as Aboriginal title lands, and vice versa.[34] Following this logic, the Alberta Métis settlement lands set aside by provincial law in Alberta could be deemed to be protected and affirmed under section 35, and consequently fall within section 91(24). While the courts would undoubtedly take steps to avoid a full-scale disruption of the Alberta Métis settlements, it might well prove beyond the courts' capacity to bring about an orderly and constitutionally defensible legal change if the effect of this logic was to render constitutionally invalid the special legislative regime that has existed for certain identified Métis communities in Alberta for over sixty years. The Court could, of course, impose a stay upon its decision for a period of time, as it has done on a number of occasions,[35] to allow for possible resolution through negotiations or parliamentary action. It would, of course, be possible for the federal government to accept a transfer of these Métis settlements from the Crown in right of Alberta and for Parliament simply to enact its own legislation that captures the essence of the provincial scheme. Passage of complementary bills by both legislatures could also be a viable strategy,[36] as would negotiating a tripartite land claim agreement that is given added legal force through the enactment of enabling legislation by Alberta and Canada.[37]

The resulting demand for action could also be accommodated in a number of constitutional ways, including section 43 (bilateral) or section 38 (general) amendments under the *Constitution Act, 1982*, as was discussed in detail during the Charlottetown round of negotiations in 1992 that resulted in a short-lived agreement on proposed amendments to resolve this matter.

The direct consequences for change in relation to other rights possessed by Métis or non-status Indians (such as harvesting or cultural rights) may not prove to be as momentous as those involving title, natural resource, or political rights. The response of the federal and provincial governments to the hundreds if not thousands of cases upholding hunting and fishing rights mounted to date by Indian band members or Inuit has been largely administrative and policy based, not legislative. Federal or provincial laws relating to fishing and game have generally been ruled inapplicable to Indians or Inuit where section 35 rights have been established, unless public safety has been an overriding concern in light of the way the harvesting activity was conducted in a particular situation. The statutes concerned have not been held to be generally invalid, as this would force a process of negotiation on new legislation. Instead, administrative changes have followed most of these cases so that charges are no longer systematically laid. In other cases, groups have been asked to negotiate various co-management agreements.

This kind of response is not, of course, unimportant. Métis and non-status Indians, as well as non-reserve Indians, are often seeking just such a level of response to their own interests in harvesting activities, and are particularly frustrated when provincial governments refuse to act with equivalent measures even after successful litigation. In many jurisdictions to date, including the Prairies, Ontario, Quebec, and Newfoundland, only "status" or similarly federally "recognized" Indians (such as the Innu of Labrador, who are still officially non-status Indians although they are largely treated by the government of Canada as if they were registered) and Inuit have been administratively accommodated in relation to fisheries or wildlife legislation. Moreover, only reserve-based Indian organizations and recognized Inuit regional bodies have been involved extensively in co-management negotiations.

Provinces tend to defer to the existing federal regime and particularly the Department of Indian and Northern Affairs Canada (INAC) for "recognizing" Aboriginal people. This regime excludes Métis and non-status Indians, and has no clear procedure for recognizing non-reserve status Indians separately from their nominal bands based on reserve. Since the federal government has not elaborated any formal policy of recognition of Métis, non-status Indian, or off-reserve Indian organizations or community councils, at least in relation to the exercise of section 35 rights, there is, in effect, a recognition "vacuum" that undermines the creation of a policy or administrative response to their successfully asserted rights.

In our view, this problem is not so much in relation to section 35 rights as such. Rather, it is the lack of a federal response to the need for new conventions to be put in place for the recognition both of collective and of individual Aboriginal identity.[38] Such conventions or policies would seem necessarily to involve the explicit exercise of federal jurisdiction under section 91(24), even if, as with the Inuit, it may be policy-based as opposed to being set out in legislation. Any effort by provinces alone to establish such regimes would seem to be beyond their constitutional jurisdiction.

Responsibilities and the Scope of Section 91(24)

A third logical approach to arguing a reference case would be to mount a "responsibility" argument along the lines that Quebec took in 1939. This approach involves asserting that there are meaningful responsibilities flowing from section 91(24) for Aboriginal peoples separate and apart from the particular rights or titles of any specific group or people. This approach would involve asserting that the term "Indians" in section 91(24), alone or in conjunction with the general intention of section 35, compels the federal assumption of a sole or predominant responsibility for the social, cultural, and economic welfare of Métis and non-status and non-reserve status Indians. In essence, this argument deals less with the inclusion of Métis within section 91(24)—which is presumed—but rather with areas of currently denied responsibility, or responsibilities that are assumed to be acceptably "provincial."

There are two broad ways in which a "responsibility" case could proceed. One involves compiling a set of "normal Indian" responsibilities that the federal government has assumed and seeking to have these extended to comparable contexts faced by the Métis, non-status Indians, and non-reserve status Indians. Such an approach would likely require highlighting responsibilities that are not in some integral way tied to Indian lands or residence on Indian reserves, and might then compare them to federal programs or policies applicable to Indian Crown land settlements in some regions and Métis communities also residing on Crown land subject to Aboriginal title.

The second approach would be to broaden the objective to be more inclusive of Indian, Métis, and Inuit interests generally. Instead of comparing "in-group" and "out-group" benefits or entitlements, this approach would seek to have a matter common to all groups declared as inherently falling under the core of "Indianness." A candidate for this sort of inclusion might be primary education of children. The argument would be that "normal" provincial jurisdiction in this area is unfairly applied in cases other than on-reserve residents such that the integrity of Aboriginal communities and societies is undermined through the refusal in most settings to accommodate local cultural and linguistic programming, or other means of supporting Aboriginal primary education.

The distinction between the two approaches is relatively straightforward.

In the first, a pre-established basis for comparative consideration exists in current federal practice. In the second, any matter that is considered integral to the "Indianness" of communal existence could be chosen. In both cases, however, it would be important to argue that as "constitutional Indians," Métis or non-status Indians must fall under federal responsibility in some arena of public policy that is relevant to their "Indianness." The Supreme Court has already upheld the inherent jurisdiction of provinces in relation to laws of general application, such as concerning conservation, labour law, and speed limits.[39] Attention would, therefore, need to be carefully given to the selection of areas that are clearly capable of being argued as falling within the "core of Indianness." These might include education (though not likely post-secondary education), family law in relation to adoption and matrimonial property, municipal governance, public services in Aboriginal languages, cultural protection, certain types of health regulations, and (possibly) some forms of professional accreditation restrictions (such as those restricting or precluding effective access to traditional healing and medicines).

The greatest legal obstacle to success in any pure "responsibility" approach is the strength of the principle of parliamentary sovereignty, namely, that a legislature (or the executive branch of government) cannot be compelled to exercise its jurisdiction solely by virtue of possessing the constitutional jurisdiction to legislate. This is the essential distinction that federal officials and Ministers make when they distinguish "jurisdiction" from "responsibility." While the *Charter*'s guarantees have been invoked to challenge existing legislation and programs, the thrust of this option is not geared toward invalidating distinctions among groups for violating the *Charter*, but rather for asserting a federal failure to fulfil the responsibilities assigned to Parliament and the Government of Canada through section 91(24).

It is important not to underestimate the challenge of framing such a "positive duty" argument. It would require that a court rule that Parliament and the federal government, or either of them, must, as a matter of law, take certain positive acts within its jurisdiction. By way of analogy, it might be noted that some of the greatest political and legal crises in Canadian history have involved just this issue (e.g., denominational and language rights in Manitoba). Even where the constitutional law has been clear on federal capacity and jurisdiction (in the case of remedial legislative powers in the area of denominational rights) or provincial obligations (as with the status of the French language), the courts have been enlisted only to state the law, not to compel legislative action.[40] The closest we have come to stating such a "positive duty" question, other than in the context of *Charter* rights and freedoms, has been where legislation is attacked in an area of integral public governance where legislative action to replace the impugned law is unavoidable.[41]

The Supreme Court of Canada has, in the *Quebec Secession Reference*,[42] outlined a positive duty on federal and provincial governments to negotiate the terms of secession and its aftermath if an appropriate question on this topic ever obtains an acceptable level of voter endorsement. Similarly, the Court has imposed a duty of consultation on the Crown with the Aboriginal peoples concerned before action is taken that infringes upon rights protected by section 35(1).[43] Notwithstanding these advances in the law, the jurisprudence is still unclear as to whether or not the federal and provincial governments, or their respective legislatures, must exercise authority allocated to them by the *Constitution Act, 1867*, as opposed to the judiciary restraining the manner in which such authority has been previously exercised.

Thus, if the courts were to find that the occupation by provincial laws of general application of a federal area of responsibility resulted in the effective "provincialization" of an area that touches the core of "Indianness" and is an important area of public government, with the consequence that it can not be ignored, that might be sufficient to motivate federal occupation of the field.

The other major argument available in a "responsibility" case is to focus on the special fiduciary duty of the Crown to act in the best interests of Aboriginal people. To date the courts have generally ruled on fiduciary obligations only in their "negative" aspect: that is, what obligations the Crown has to Aboriginal people when a specific act of infringement is being taken or being contemplated. The federal government has been particularly concerned to avoid any ruling that a broader "positive duty" is attached to either section 91(24) or to section 35.

At the same time, the Supreme Court has framed the fiduciary obligation in broad terms that do not preclude delivering a ruling of a positive duty to take action. The Court may also be primed to provide a more effective and aggressive form of relief in the face of its pattern since 1982 of calling for negotiated solutions, only to witness continuing governmental avoidance of action. If a clear and publicly supportable argument of positive duty were to be framed in relation to section 91(24), the Supreme Court might be brought to the point of ruling on a positive obligation under the fiduciary principle. However, such a possibility would likely decrease to the degree that a case were framed in overly broad terms. A discrete and carefully circumscribed duty, likely for a specific group, would be more likely of success.

If the experience following the Supreme Court ruling in *Re Eskimos* is any indication, a finding of jurisdiction generally should be followed by the assumption of specific and concrete responsibilities in certain defined areas. In this context, it seems more likely that such an assumption of responsibility would follow in areas where the federal government has been active for other Indians, such as welfare payments and health costs, in comparable circumstances. These areas do not appear to be directly tied to specific Aboriginal rights or titles, but do relate to the identity of Aboriginally predominant communities.

Of the two approaches discussed above, the first has a much higher risk of attracting the intervention of reserve-based organizations such as the Assembly of First Nations (AFN) in opposition to a reference or trial case. The second is more likely to attract a broad coalition of groups—including Inuit and status Indians—in favour of a ruling that finds the federal responsibility expanded, at least as long as the remedy appears to require a sufficient increase in fiscal resources to benefit all, rather than imply a widening of the pool of people chasing too-limited funds.

As a final note on implications, the above general discussion on "federal responsibilities" has often fixed on specific programs and services available to some Aboriginal people, but not to all. Currently, the range of national programs or policies that discriminate against Métis and non–reserve affiliated Indians due to their lack of recognized group or individual status includes post-secondary education assistance and non-insured health benefits.

We understand that at present there is no trial-level litigation underway in relation to post-secondary education assistance in this context, while there is one case being mounted in Labrador on non-insured health benefits in which *Charter* arguments, rather than arguments in respect of the "core of Indianness," are being used.[44]

It is submitted that greater attention should be paid to the second type of responsibility argument—one that involves no necessary competition over the existing division of federal spending.

Directions from the Case Law

Over and above the considerations addressed in broader Supreme Court rulings on section 35, the issue of the scope of section 91(24) in relation to the constituency of the Métis and non-status Indians has emerged over the past decade in a number of specific trial actions. These involve assertions of section 35 rights more directly in connection with the specific harvesting rights provided to "Indians" in the Prairies, as well as in relation to *Charter*-based claims for equal treatment in which section 91(24) arguments have been raised.

In what follows, the rulings as well as key findings and conclusions that have emerged in these three distinct contexts in the recent case law are briefly summarized.

91(24) Status as a Basis for Equal Treatment
Lovelace v. *Ontario;*[45] *Perry* v. *Ontario*[46]
Both these recent Ontario cases have asserted that inclusion of Métis and non-

status Indians within section 91(24) does not lead necessarily to a requirement to treat them as equivalent to band-based organizations for certain purposes. In *Lovelace*, the goal was to acquire access to the proceeds of Casino Rama, while in *Perry*, the goal was equal or equitable treatment under a provincial policy of non-enforcement of provincial wildlife laws. In *Perry*, the application for appeal to the Supreme Court was dismissed, while the Supreme Court heard and rejected the appeal in *Lovelace*.

Results:

1. Inclusion of Métis and non-status Indians in Ontario within section 91(24) (held in *Lovelace* at trial) was found not to be relevant to the issue of the provincial spending power by the Court of Appeal and the Supreme Court.

2. Reserve communities are a legitimate and discrete group for the purposes of remedial action under section 15(2) of the *Charter*, and excluding non-reserve groups is not automatically discriminatory.

3. The mere presence of alleged section 35 rights does not provide the courts with the capacity to order negotiations, whether on an equal basis with reserve groups or on any basis. The Court of Appeal in *Perry* essentially ruled on procedural matters and dismissed the action as moot in light of the cancellation by Ontario of an interim *Wildlife Act* enforcement policy that only accorded First Nations with negotiation status. In *Lovelace* the Supreme Court acknowledged the severe deprivation faced by Métis and non-status Indian communities resulting from many years of discrimination, but concluded this was not a sufficient foundation to disrupt a scheme to share casino profits exclusively among First Nations who are also desperately needed economic advancement.

Section 35 Assertions by Non-status Indians or by Métis

R. v. Fowler;[47] *R. v. McPherson;*[48] *R. v. Morin and Daigneault;*[49] *R. v. Powley*[50]
These four cases all involve assertions of harvesting rights unattached to assertions about falling under federal section 91(24) jurisdiction, or, in the Saskatchewan case *(Morin)*, the term "Indian" in the *Natural Resources Transfer Agreement*. In all four cases, in New Brunswick, Ontario, Manitoba, and Saskatchewan, the accused were acquitted.

Results:

1. Métis have the Aboriginal right to hunt where no evidence is clearly established that the right has been extinguished by scrip or otherwise *(McPherson)*.

2. Lower courts have no jurisdiction to rule that laws are generally invalid, or to order new regulations or the registration of Métis. The courts can only read down constitutional exemptions from statutes *(McPherson)*.

3. Lack of Indian status is not a bar to entitlement under section 35 where there is evidence of a substantial connection to the Indian community, such as potential entitlement to status *(Fowler)*.

4. Scrip descent is not relevant to fishing rights, since title and rights are distinct. Métis "similarly situated" as Indians do not permit distinctions between them in federal Fisheries Regulations *(Morin)*.

5. Métis have hunting rights on Crown lands under section 35 in Ontario in their traditional areas (not tied to treaty), and a reasonable approach to determining Métis entitlement at a minimum includes self-identification and community recognition or acceptance by a Métis organization *(Powley)* and may also require proof of descent from the Métis community resident in the area at the requisite time *(Powley at trial)*.

Only the *Powley* case has been appealed, yet the New Brunswick, Manitoba, and federal governments have not moved to establish co-management arrangements or other schemes to give effect to the decisions beyond the individuals acquitted.

Claims to Be *"Indian"* within the Natural Resources Transfer Agreement

R. v. Grumbo;[51] *R. v. Ferguson;*[52] *R. v. Desjarlais;*[53] *R. v. Blais*[54]

These four cases all involve an assertion, whether by a Métis or by a non-status Indian, of entitlements to hunt without a provincial licence by virtue of being "Indian" within the meaning of the *Natural Resource Transfer Agreement (NRTA)* in the Prairies. What is common to them is that they all attempt to rely upon the use of the term "Indian" in the various *NRTAs* of 1929 that acquired constitutional force through the *Constitution Act, 1930*,[55] in which Indians were assured the right to hunt and fish on unoccupied Crown lands.

Results:

1. The 1978 Saskatchewan Court of Appeal decision in *Laprise*[56] is no longer a binding precedent in Saskatchewan because it interpreted a constitutional provision solely in light of the *Indian Act* of the day *(Grumbo)*.

2. The *NRTAs* only protect "pre-existing" rights, therefore trials must establish whether Métis rights survived to 1930 in order to be protected *(Grumbo)*.

3. Métis who meet a social test of descent and "following the Indian mode of

life" are "non-Treaty Indians" within the meaning of the *NRTA*s and the 1927 *Indian Act*, and therefore are permitted to hunt without a licence *(Ferguson, Desjarlais)*.

4. Manitoba Métis are not included within the meaning of "Indian" in the *NRTA* since they are not within the definition of "Indian" in the 1927 *Indian Act*, and so would have been directly mentioned if they were intended to be included *(Blais)*.

5. The *NRTA* only speaks to existing rights, with Métis hunting rights having been extinguished by the *Manitoba Act (Blais)*.

The Court of Appeal in *Blais* distinguished *Blais* from *Powley* on the grounds that there was no "historical linkage" between the accused, the community, and the area where the hunting took place.

As can be seen, it is far from clear that a general trend is apparent nationally. The courts are clearly struggling with how to balance the apparent inclusion of Métis and non-status Indians within section 35 and the existing framework for systematic exemptions from wildlife restrictions for status Indians. In these cases, as well as in those dealing directly with section 35 rights, the lower courts tend to look to social tests of "Indianness" in order to determine entitlement, with the alternative of looking at straight political membership in descent or kinship groups being less prevalent, particularly in the Prairies. This orientation reflects the absence of a collective recognition policy or framework available to the courts for dealing with non–*Indian Act* based groups, and the failure of the lower courts to consider the implications of recognition for the development of a doctrine of Aboriginal rights. These issues are thoroughly canvassed throughout this book.[57]

Assessment

Our review of the constitutional rulings of the Supreme Court as well as other recent case law gives rise to a number of issues of importance in deciding on an approach to clarification of section 91(24).

Goals and Impacts

First, anyone seeking to clarify the scope of section 91(24) must carefully analyse the goals to be achieved by such an effort. This will require an assessment of the likely impacts, which are discussed in summary form in the next part. As shown by the cases reviewed above, efforts to use section 91(24) inclusion as a basis for equal treatment with reserve-based groups have been few, and so far unsuccessful.

In connection with assertions of section 35 rights, the lower court cases to date have tended to proceed on the logic that if a person is "Indian" within section 91(24), he or she has a right. This may be contrasted with the Supreme Court of Canada's emerging logic: If a group or person has a right, the exercise of the right and the person fall within section 91(24).[58]

Finally, it should be added that harvesting cases by Métis and non-status Indians seem to place the courts in the position of having to import a wider social test of "Indianness." While this orientation seems to flow as much from judicial concerns with social equity in often-mixed Indian/Métis rural and remote settings, it carries with it the danger that large groups of Métis and Indians could be restricted from having access to section 35 rights and section 91(24) federal jurisdiction simply by virtue of contemporary lifestyles. At the same time, status Indian groups and individuals escape such restrictions regardless of where they live and how "modern" their current lifestyle may be, solely by virtue of statutory kinship connection to federally recognized communities. Aside from the double standard being imposed here, this point has relevance for both the options selected for dealing with section 91(24) and for the kind of federal responsibility sought.

Who are the "Métis"?

A final major issue disclosed from the constitution and case law to date more directly relates to the question "Who are the Métis?" The determination of which Aboriginal people are to be accounted as "Métis" or indeed "Indian" for the purposes of section 35 has been a significant and growing issue since 1982 and has involved what may be described as a "two-front" challenge.

On the Métis side of the question, the definition of Métis is a matter of often heated division between the Congress of Aboriginal Peoples (CAP) and the Métis National Council (MNC), with the latter associating the reference to Métis in section 35 solely and exclusively to descendants of the Red River and other Métis who were involved in the scrip system, although this may be shifting somewhat in light of the MNC's decision to intervene in supporting the Métis defendants in the *Powley* case. By way of contrast with the MNC approach, CAP has self-identifying Métis affiliates in the Northwest Territories, in Labrador, and in Ontario, as well as affiliates with significant Métis-identifying populations in Quebec. These constituents do not rely upon a connection to the Red River Valley or the scrip system as a core component of their Métis identity. As discussed below, in the absence of a political resolution of this issue, either between the Aboriginal groups concerned or between them and governments, the courts are increasingly entering the fray of defining who is entitled to be called Métis, with considerations of lifestyle, self-identification, and community recognition, as well as established government recognition of communities all playing a role.[59]

In relation to the Congress's non-status as well as its non-reserve status Indian constituency, a similar struggle, if less open, embraces the Assembly of First Nations and reserve-based First Nation communities. In this case, a core issue is what criteria or tests can or should apply to establish a reasonable connection between individuals accessing a section 35 right and the collectivity whose right is being accessed? As section 35 rights are necessarily collective in nature, or at the very least have an essential collective dimension, the primary issue becomes who decides who is entitled?

In our view, both these issues are less concerned with section 91(24) and its scope than the absence of any national recognition policy in relation to section 35.[60] While it seems clear that any such recognition system would necessarily be federal because of the presence of section 91(24), the challenge becomes how to motivate federal action to take steps for implementation. To date, the federal government has shown little interest in proceeding in this direction, with the exception of the rather general commitment set out in its response to RCAP's final report in its *Gathering Strength* policy initiative to work with provinces and Aboriginal organizations on the recognition of Aboriginal governments. This commitment can, of course, be interpreted in any number of ways, but would not seem to preclude a continuation of the current "province-by-province" approach of the tripartite self-government policy advanced by Ottawa since 1985.

It is not our purpose here to explore this issue in detail other than to highlight three features of the debate:

1. An attempt to resolve the scope of section 91(24) in relation to the Métis on a comprehensive basis will likely involve having to define, and defend, collective boundaries as between Métis and Indian, and possibly, between Métis and Inuit.

2. The assertion of collective boundaries will likely be of most relevance to a court when they are based on an historical and distinctive cultural association tied to a natural community or society that has traditionally used a generally defined territory for a long time. As a result, a generic or "pan-Métis" approach to determining recognition or identity may prove less than useful to settling any question of the scope of section 91(24), particularly if the question is expressed in relation to the exercise of a specific right under section 35.

3. The boundaries between "Indian" and "non-Indian" will necessarily implicate the non-status Indian population in grappling with collective identities and organizational structures that are tied to traditional boundaries of relevance to section 35 rights, as well as with determining individual entitlements to membership in such communities. Since many if not most

non-status Indians have natural descent and cultural ties to status and reserve-based First Nation organizations, this question would not seem to be answerable in isolation of the latter.

Diverse Impacts & Implications

Before turning to the major options for clarifying section 91(24), in this part we examine the likely impacts or implications for Métis and non-status Indian communities across Canada from a regional perspective.

The North

No major impacts of a ruling on section 91(24) would likely be felt in any of the three territories, but some adjustments to federal justifications for discretionary programs like health care and post-secondary education might follow, particularly for Métis in the Northwest Territories and for non-status Yukon First Nation members. A favourable decision would also confirm federal jurisdiction, which currently rests upon a policy basis only tied to authority over territories. Confirming federal jurisdiction might also give added comfort to the federal policy decision to negotiate land claims settlements with those Métis communities that are excluded from First Nations negotiations tied to historic treaties.

British Columbia

The British Columbia government is currently involved in a tripartite process with Métis groups in the province, so the major impact for a section 91(24) case might be felt in relation to the substance of those talks and the linkage between them and the British Columbia treaty process. It should be noted that the British Columbia situation provides an opportunity to challenge federal practice and law in relation to treaty-making in this regard. The federal legislation in place for the British Columbia Treaty Commission (BCTC)[61] defines "First Nation" as any "aboriginal group or organization, however mandated, within its traditional territory." As a result, the Métis groups involved (all of them now affiliates of the MNC) might be able to clarify section 91(24) by way of seeking to be added formally to the BCTC process, such as by applying formally for funding and then contesting any exclusion.

The Prairies

For Métis, the most significant and possibly critical impact is in relation to the legal validity of Alberta Métis settlement legislation. At the same time, the contemporary Alberta legislation has a fairly broad definition of Métis that the courts might find acceptable.

The Alberta and Saskatchewan courts seem disinclined to regard scrip as having a bearing on harvesting rights, particularly for Métis or non-status Indians who are reliant on traditional foods. The considerable number of Indians in the Treaty 8 area who took scrip in order to avoid settling on agricultural reserves, the great social overlap involved as in northern Saskatchewan, together with the many thousands of "bandless" status Indians, makes this a prime area for a section 91(24) responsibility case.[62]

A treaty rights implementation or harvesting co-management case for treaty descendants (status and non-status) would have particular impact within Treaty 8 (and to a lesser extent Treaty 6), given the incapacity of band-based structures to claim the thousands of persons involved lacking membership. Such a case would address section 35 implementation and "responsibility" issues, rather than the definitional scope of section 91(24).

The impact of a section 91(24) case on responsibility would likely be felt most intensely in Manitoba and Saskatchewan by virtue of the numbers of people affected.

Ontario

Because of the treatment of the "Métis" in Treaty 3,[63] at least those in the North-West Angle, Ontario might provide one of the easiest cases for the assertion that Métis are "Indians" within section 91(24) on definitional grounds alone.

Any section 35–based assertion of Métis or non-status Indian entitlements and related section 91(24) jurisdiction would have potentially significant impacts on treaty harvesting rights and title interests in northwest and northern Ontario. The key question here would be the failure of the federal and Ontario governments to agree, after 1905, on a way to settle Métis land claims and grievances. A major question for the courts would be whether Métis and non-status Indians constitute a "group" with unsettled title and harvesting claims following the precedent of the "Half-breed" adhesion to Treaty 3, or are more or less subject as individuals to the discretion of Indian band decisions about membership or access to harvesting rights protected under treaty. This approach is implied in the history of the Robinson Huron and Robinson Superior Treaties and has been pleaded in some recent cases. Regardless of which way the courts were to proceed, significant changes would be called for, but the most disruptive to current *Indian Act* bands and Tribal Councils would be in relation to having Métis and non-status Indians found to be claimants on their collective rights. Therefore they might be likely to support a more "stand-alone" assertion of both rights and federal obligation. While the decision of First Nations not to intervene in the *Powley* case before the Ontario Court of Appeal was surprising and left this matter unaddressed, one can anticipate that the issue will receive attention by the Supreme Court of Canada on appeal.[64]

The impact on non-indigenous Métis from other origins (e.g., scrip Métis from Saskatchewan living in Toronto) would not likely be great except in the case of a successful "responsibility" case or reference. However, a responsibility case that tries to reach this growing category of Aboriginal people, seeking full "portability" of demands upon federal responsibility, would face additional, and perhaps unnecessarily risky, hurdles.[65]

Quebec

Quebec was the province that mounted the first "responsibility" reference on section 91(24) over sixty years ago, and, interestingly, Quebec might possess one of the most significant impacts of a modern section 91(24) case on Métis. Considerable pressure would be placed on the courts to find a dividing line between Métis and Indian, and Aboriginal and non-Aboriginal, in a totally "scrip-free" context. This is partly because of the long history of intermarriage of French and Indian people in the province, which was, after all, the longest to be involved in the fur trade, and the existence of 16,000 self-identified Métis today. It is unclear what definition of "Métis" was in the minds of those individuals when they chose to self-identify as such in the 1996 census in Quebec, however, it presumably was not based upon a connection to the Métis culture and language of Manitoba.

A section 91(24) case would be of equal if not of greater relevance to the many non-status Indians in the province. It is they who have experienced long-term alienation from reserve communities, sometimes dating from before the establishment of reserves. As with some parts of Ontario and the Atlantic, a key consequence would be that the courts would be invited to comment on questions of "sufficient" connection to Indian collectivities, whether in terms of descent and self-identification, or in terms of social distance from non-Aboriginal people.

The relative size of the *soi-disant* Métis and non-status Indian population in Quebec, at least according to census figures, together with the general lack of land cession treaties south of the Cree and Naskapi territories, means that section 35 as an approach is of potentially greater relevance in this province than in Ontario. Since no question is involved about treaties having implied that federally recognized Indian chiefs had discretion to include, or exclude, such persons, the focus would be more purely placed on the nature of an acceptable boundary between such non-status groups and the wider populace.

Maritimes

The Atlantic provinces face no real impact regarding a Métis section 91(24) case, but there are possible implications for self-identified Métis if this self-identification amounts to an implied abandonment of rights in common with Mi'kmaq or

Maliseet where Métis, as a collectivity, are not found to have any independent collective existence.[66]

It should be added that the only Supreme Court of Canada case to date to address tests of connection by individuals to collective treaty entitlements was in Nova Scotia. In *Simon*,[67] the Court simply noted that membership in a band was sufficient, but not necessary, to establish entitlement. Therefore in this region, the main section 91(24) issue is to establish a clear group-based entitlement to benefit from treaty or title-based rights. A second step, in relation to section 91(24), would be to call for some guidance about which level of government has jurisdiction to regulate or negotiate in relation to such rights, a matter that has been sidestepped in recent Crown forestry access demands in New Brunswick, since the province chose to restrict negotiations to *Indian Act* bands, an approach so far uncontested in court.

Newfoundland/Labrador

The people represented by the Federation of Newfoundland Indians (FNI) and the Labrador Métis Nation (LMN) would likely face major impacts of any section 91(24) case. For the Mi'kmaq of the FNI, inclusion within federal jurisdiction under section 91(24) has been accepted by the Crown for the purposes of a Federal Court action, with the Crown arguing simply that it is not obliged to take any action at all in relation to those within its jurisdiction. However, pressure on the scope of section 91(24) in relation to "responsibility" and the fiduciary obligations of the Crown would likely have a unique impact on the Newfoundland Mi'kmaq case (which is now in out-of-court discussions since the appointment of Hon. Marc Lalonde in the spring of 2002 to seek a potential resolution for the recognition of the Mi'kmaq involved.

The impact on the Labrador group, which has taken on the self-identifying label of "Métis," would be more distinctive. The Labrador Métis Nation is the sole group in Canada claiming to be of predominately Inuit and non-Aboriginal descent, as well as having formed a unique and separate society. The key issue for this society would be whether or not the term "Métis" includes any contemporary group of Aboriginal descendents of mixed ancestry who see themselves as distinct from other groups in Canada, or also requires some other distinguishing features. In the LMN case, one of the questions is whether or not the Métis, to have section 35 rights as a collectivity, must have emerged as a distinctive society prior to the date of sovereignty. This is also the case for asserted Métis title rights in British Columbia and northern Ontario. Otherwise, it might be argued, with ramifications in other areas of Canada, that Métis only have such rights as are allowed them by some independently defined "core" group of Aboriginal people, in this case Inuit. In other words, those communities who continue to define themselves as Inuit would be entitled to determine the identity and the scope of the rights of those Métis who trace their Aboriginal ancestry to their Inuit forebears. Conversely, if the latter "core" group cannot establish their own societal boundaries as sufficiently autonomous, the implication is that the courts will be invited to define tests of connection that are more objective.

Procedural Options for Clarifying 91(24)

In this part of the paper, a synoptic overview of the major options available for a litigation strategy to clarify the complex of issues surrounding section 91(24) is provided.

A Reference Case

The basic concept underlying a reference case simply implies the negotiation by an Aboriginal community or association of a question in the nature of a constitutional reference to the courts. The federal government, if it agrees, would make a reference to the Supreme Court of Canada, whereas provinces and territories are only able to mount reference cases to their courts of appeal.

Background

- Precedent in 1939 Inuit Reference case (followed by federal agreement to exercise responsibility for Inuit).

- Offered to MNC/NCC in 1985 by federal Attorney General and Justice Minister John Crosbie.

- Mooted since early 1990s by both NCC/CAP and MNC.

- May be of some interest to the governments of the Northwest Territories, Ontario, the Prairie Provinces, and similar "high impact" jurisdictions.

Pros

- Fastest way to a clarification of scope and implications of section 91(24).

- Offers a procedurally "inclusive" approach since all parties with an interest could intervene.

Cons

- Possible lack of "pen" control on what question(s) are put, particularly important to definition of Métis (scrip versus non-scrip) and what implication questions are set.

- Doubtful that non-status Indian issues would predominate, and may be sidelined.

- Does not allow for a "context-rich" factual setting to be made, though evidence about specific issues and settings are permitted. The absence of a trial setting containing a specific factual situation with oral evidence led through direct examination of witnesses makes any section 35–based approach less certain than a more simple definitional approach, or one asserting a clearly defined area of responsibility.

A Trial Action

As illustrated here, there are numerous trial actions that address section 91(24) to some degree, but none to date has proceeded past provincial superior courts. Nevertheless, a trial action affords the plaintiff much greater control over the factual nature of a case, which as discussed above, largely determines whether section 91(24) will be addressed in a definitional fashion, as a consequence of a section 35 rights assertion, or in relation to a particular arena of responsibility.

Pros

- If mounted as a test case with federal/provincial funding, provides plaintiff with greater "pen control."

- May involve other groups as interveners, but not as full parties (e.g., reserve-based groups, provinces, Aboriginal rights coalitions, etc.).

Cons

- All cases to date have lacked sufficient financing and coordination of broadly stated mandates or consensus issues.

- Counsel for individual plaintiffs at trial necessarily seek the best short- or mid-term solution for their clients, not for a wider cause or objective. Therefore waiting for a "good" trial action in which to intervene may not result in success, as opposed to mounting a trial action directly.[68]

- Trials involve a lengthy and uncertain process in getting to the Supreme Court (perhaps as much as 10+ years), and most are settled or abandoned before getting that far.[69]

Policy Change (and Possible Legislation)

This broad approach involves mounting a political lobby for federal policy change, whether through legislation or another means. This approach offers a potentially secure and completely negotiated solution where constitutional reform is on the table for First Ministers as part of a broader negotiation process as in the past, but otherwise involves a sustained (three to five year) commitment to continuous work to mount a solid political case and have it supported to the point of being accepted by Cabinet and Parliament. Over the past decade, the following policy milestones have been set within this approach.

- The proposed Charlottetown Accord contained a proposed constitutional amendment (section 91(24)A), which set a new standard of debate over the issue by confirming that Métis are within section 91(24).

- The NCC's "Aboriginal Authorities Act" in 1993, which was formally accepted as a basis for legislative action in 1993 by the outgoing Conservative government.

- The Royal Commission recommended new recognition legislation.

- *Gathering Strength* made a commitment in 1998 to "recognition" consultations.

Pros

- Better chance of controlling outcomes than a trial or reference action, if the intergovernmental or constitutional approaches are taken, but necessarily involves constant bargaining and trade-offs with those involved in the process.

- Most flexible approach, which could involve intergovernmental, constitutional, or legislative action, or all three.

- A negotiated approach would allow for consensus to build and be reflected in agreement with all stakeholders involved.

Cons

- The federal government holds essential control over all policy initiatives, and a federally controlled approach may want to narrow issues to avoid any direct "flow-through" call on responsibility as a result of an accepted "jurisdiction."

- Cannot force governments to engage in negotiations.

- Quasi or full constitutional processes face political opposition from those concerned about Quebec, as has been the case since 1992.

- Legislation could be a negative, and tied to the "squeakiest wheel" group, unless national recognition legislation is involved.

Recommendations

The first necessary step for a strategy to clarify section 91(24) is to identify the goals that are sought before a decision can be taken on specific options for seeking clarification of section 91(24). The following are key questions that may assist in achieving this consensus.

1. Is the primary goal to achieve certainty for Métis, or also for all or specific groups of non-status Indians as well? The issues and outcomes may be quite different for these two broad categories, and distinctions between the two categories would need to be made.

2. Is the goal to support a particular definition of Métis? If so, which one? This will have definite consequences for the selection of any test case or the framing of a reference, as well as for any of the policy options discussed.

3. Is the objective to achieve a specific, tangible outcome such as:

   • access to specific section 35 rights? If so, which ones?

   • access to specific statutory or non-statutory entitlements or benefits? If so, which ones?

   • a change in the exercise of federal responsibility or jurisdiction, such as in connection with self-government policy?

   • to extend the scope of section 91(24) to include an "obligation to act" in certain circumstances, whether based on a fiduciary argument or on some other basis, such as the *Charter*?

4. Is the achievement of clarity about section 91(24) related to a specific plan of implementing a new regime (such as stated in the NCC's "Aboriginal Authorities Act" or as set out in various clauses of the Charlottetown Accord)?

To formulate a consensus on action, clear goals must be uppermost in mind. We note in particular that many of the issues that are involved necessarily embroil either or both of the MNC and AFN, and some also involve the Inuit Tapirisat of Canada and its constituents.

We regard a process to generate consensus on the Aboriginal side as being more important and relevant than legal, academic, or government views about the meaning or scope of section 91(24). The real issue appears to be perceptions of differential treatment, implications for change, and financial stakes in the status quo, rather than with purely "jurisdictional" questions.

The key "hidden" issue of section 91(24) is not its scope or Parliament's obligations to act, but what role is left or to be found for Aboriginal organizations, regional associations, and nations? What is the Aboriginal jurisdiction and responsibility? The Royal Commission spent some effort in advancing the view that the essential unit for action was the Aboriginal nation, transcending boundaries of legislated status and residence. Accepting this perception leaves unresolved how constitutional federal jurisdiction under section 91(24) can relate to a universe containing section 35-protected rights and Aboriginal nationhood.

Conclusions on Options for Clarification

Aside from the issues identified above, the clearest and cleanest option for clarity about the nature and scope of section 91(24) would be a reference case in which a senior level government agreed to develop a jointly framed reference with relevant regional and national organizations. The problem lies in asking judges to arbitrate what they may tend to characterize as essentially political and intergovernmental disputes, although interpreting constitutional language clearly falls within the purview of the judiciary.

The option of seeking change through constitutional, intergovernmental, legislative, or policy-based action seems the best mix overall from the vantage point of involvement in controlling outcomes, but lacks a clear venue to initiate consensus. At present, there does not appear to be any interest or motivation to engage in such policy initiatives. Therefore, this option appears to be unrealistic in the short term and may require being framed in tandem with a court action.

The trial action option, while it is least advantageous in relation to time, cost, and content concerns, is also the one that reflects some level of grassroots commitment to change. If carefully framed and well funded, and if successful, a trial action provides the initiator with greater control of the wider political climate. The action can be abandoned at any time if it is not a case involving criminal charges, and abeyance can be offered as an inducement to negotiation.[70]

What is crystal clear from the experience of the last three decades at least is that the basic question considered in this essay refuses to disappear. It is also apparent that it is unlikely to be answered at present unless litigation is pursued.

Notes

[1]This chapter was originally a paper prepared in 1999 to provide critical information and guidance on these issues to the leaders of the Congress of Aboriginal Peoples and its provincial and territorial affiliates. It has been revised for a more general audience.

[2]In *St. Catherine's Milling & Lumber Co.* v. *The Queen* (1888), 14 App. Cas. 46 (PC).

[3]*Reference re Secession of Quebec*, [1998] 2 S.C.R. 217 [hereinafter *Quebec Secession Reference*].

[4]The Supreme Court's decision in *Delgamuukw* v. *B.C.*, [1997] 3 S.C.R. 1010, illustrates this in ruling that despite sole federal legislative capacity to legislate for "Lands reserved for the Indians," which since B.C.'s union has included most of the province, the provincial legislature nevertheless had and has the right to pass legislation for the general "advancement" of the province, including extensive forestry, mining, and settlement developments. This accommodation reflects an obvious political reality: 130 years of legal, social, and political

development affecting an entire province will not be ruled illegal simply on the basis of an obvious breach of the written Constitution. Instead, the "law" will be adaptively and even retroactively interpreted to maintain legitimacy for the overall political structures, while advancing modern accommodations between contending interests. This balancing act is best expressed by the Court itself in its closing remark: "Lets face it, we are all here to stay."

[5]Bradford W. Morse & John Giokas, "Do the Métis Fall Within Section 91(24) of the *Constitution Act, 1867?*" and Don McMahon & Fred Martin "The Métis and 91(24): Is Inclusion the Issue?" in Royal Commission on Aboriginal Peoples, *For Seven Generations* (Ottawa: Libraxus CD-ROM, 1996).

[6]Canada, *Final Report of the Royal Commission on Aboriginal Peoples: Restructuring the Relationship*, vol. 2 (Ottawa: Supply and Services Canada, 1996).

[7]Hudson's Bay Company (HBC) census records around the time of Confederation showing "Eskimo" tabulations listed with those of "Indians" was a point noted by the Supreme Court in a 1939 reference case in favour of finding that 91(24) included the Inuit, with the implication that "half-breeds"[sic] were not so included. See *Reference re Whether the term "Indians" in s. 91(24) of the B.N.A. Act, 1867, includes Eskimo Inhabitants of Quebec*, [1939] S.C.R. 104 [hereinafter *Reference re Eskimos*].

[8]*An Act providing for the Organization of the Department of the Secretary of State of Canada, and for the Management of Indian and Ordnance Lands*, S.C. 1868, c. 42, s. 15.

[9]It is important to appreciate that the Inuit, particularly in Quebec and Labrador, have generally experienced a similar lack of access to the range of federally funded community support and individual program benefits as non-reserve status Indians. While communal and institutional support is now provided by the Government of Canada, this has come fairly recently and often is tied to wider comprehensive land claims processes or agreements. As recently as 1988, DIAND attempted to advance the view that Inuit south of the 60th parallel were as much a provincial responsibility as were Métis and non-status Indians.

[10]It is interesting to note the subsequent adoption of this strategy by the U.S. government regarding Indian tribes to expedite assimilation and free up land for white settlement through the *General Allotment (Dawes) Act of 1887.*

[11]If, as appears plain, Métis fell within 91(24) due to their rights in "Lands reserved for Indians," it is difficult to see how it could be argued that they are nevertheless not "Indians" under s. 91(24). Not all commentators agree with this interpretation. For a contrary view, see Bryan Schwartz, *First Principles, Second Thoughts: Aboriginal Peoples, Constitutional Reform and Canadian Statecraft* (Montreal: Institute for Research on Public Policy, 1986). This latter view appears to underscore at least one recent ruling on Métis hunting rights: *R. v. Blais*, [1998] 4 C.N.L.R. 103 (Man. Q.B.), confirmed by the Manitoba Court of Appeal at (2001), 198 D.L.R. (4th) 220.

[12]The degree to which half-breed scrip allocations "in exchange for Indian title" also extinguished Métis rights to fish, hunt, or trap is being litigated in a new trial ordered by the Saskatchewan Court of Appeal in *R. v. Grumbo* (1997), reported at [1998] 3 C.N.L.R. at 172.

[13]Alexander Morris, *The Treaties of Canada with the Indians of Manitoba and the North-West Territories* (Toronto: Belfords, Clarke & Co., 1880, reprint Saskatoon: Fifth House, 1991) at 294.

[14]This argument is made by the Plaintiffs in *Dumont et al. v. R.*, a long-dormant case in Manitoba that has now been revived and slated for early trial action. The Congress of Aboriginal Peoples, which is a co-plaintiff in Dumont with the Manitoba Métis Federation, has argued as well that the *Manitoba Act's* provisions constitute a treaty within s. 35 of the *Constitution Act, 1982.* Paul Chartrand argues in his book *Manitoba's Métis Settlement Scheme of*

1870 (Saskatoon: University of Saskatchewan Native Law Centre, 1991), that the s. 31 lands are to be viewed as providing for both collective and individual interests on the model of the earlier Indian enfranchisement colonial legislation.

[15]For Métis, the degree of group identity and the use of kinship for determining individual status under federal rules only accommodated a "one-generation" linkage, as illustrated in the allocation of scrip to only the "children of the half-breed heads of families" accounted for at the time of any particular federal Scrip Commission's operations. Thereafter, in effect, the "Métis" ceased to exist as a distinct legislated category.

[16]The *Natural Resource Transfer Agreements* of 1929. These agreements were confirmed by British legislation so as to amend the Constitution of Canada in *The Constitution Act, 1930,* R.S.C. 1985, Appendix II, No. 26, s. 1.

[17]For an example of the impact of these provisions and their interaction with treaties, see e.g., *R.* v. *Horse,* [1988] 1 S.C.R. 187; *R.* v. *Horseman,* [1990] 1 S.C.R. 901; and *R.* v. *Badger,* [1996] 1 S.C.R. 771. The Manitoba Court of Appeal has recently declared that these harvesting rights do not apply to the Métis *qua* Indians in *R.* v. *Blais, supra* note 11.

[18]This trauma took over a decade and a royal commission to rectify on grounds of equity—a process that was only partially successful. This episode is briefly described in Richard Daniel, "A History of Native Claims Processes in Canada," prepared for the Research Branch, DIAND, 1980 at 24 & 25. For an account of its severe impact on one such community see John Goddard, *The Last Stand of the Lubicon Cree* (Vancouver: Douglas & McIntyre, 1991).

[19]See *Tuplin* v. *The Registrar of Indians, Graham Tuplin* v. *Registrar, Indian and Northern Affairs Canada* (indexed as *Tuplin* v. *Canada (Indian and Northern Affairs),* [1999] 1 C.N.L.R. 268 (P.E.I. Sup. Ct.), where a trial de novo was ordered so that the trial judge could assess whether or not the oral history of Aboriginal custom adoption is relevant to the appellant's claim of membership in a Mi'kmaq band based on his father's membership from the point of his adoption at infancy by custom in 1890, and if relevant, in what form it may be adduced.

[20]See *Reference re Eskimos, supra* note 7. The reasons why the Inuit were excluded from the *Act* and not provided any parallel legislation for communal or individual recognition remains a largely unexplored question of potential relevance. It is possible, though only speculative at this point, that federal administrators felt that Inuit were somehow, like Métis, "different" from Indians in relation to their need for collective protection from "civilization" during the process of assimilation. No efforts were made to negotiate treaties, set aside discrete lands, or establish trust accounts to administer. However, a form of registration was established involving the issuance of a letter-number identification scheme to individuals.

[21]Sally Weaver, *Making Canadian Indian Policy: The Hidden Agenda 1968–70* (Toronto: University of Toronto Press, 1981).

[22]S. 35(1) and (2) of Part II of the *Constitution Act, 1982,* are as follows:

RIGHTS OF THE ABORIGINAL PEOPLES OF CANADA

35(1) The existing aboriginal and treaty rights of the aboriginal peoples of Canada are hereby recognized and affirmed.

(2) In this Act, "aboriginal peoples of Canada" includes the Indian, Inuit and Métis peoples of Canada.

[23]*Re Eskimos, supra* note 7.

[24]*The Quebec Boundaries Extension Act,* S.C. 1912, c. 45.

[25]Of interest is that European and HBC characterizations of Inuit along the Labrador peninsula as far south as the Lower North Shore adjacent to Anticosti Island as "Indians" was persuasive for the Court, and that within five years after Confederation the Prime Minister

was intervening to provide for relief payments to destitute "Eskimo half-breeds" in several of Quebec's Lower North Shore communities. It is likely that by the Depression-era controversy over the Nunavik Inuit in the Ungava, this southern population became absorbed into Innu or non-Native communities, moved further north and east into Labrador proper—now the heartland of the Labrador Métis Nation and its Inuit descendent communities—or a combination of both.

[26]*R. v. Van der Peet,* [1996]2 S.C.R. 507.

[27]ABORIGINAL RIGHTS AND FREEDOMS NOT AFFECTED BY THE CHARTER

25. The guarantee in this Charter of certain rights and freedoms shall not be construed so as to abrogate or derogate from any aboriginal, treaty or other rights or freedoms that pertain to the aboriginal peoples of Canada including

(a) any rights or freedoms that have been recognized by the Royal Proclamation of October 7, 1763; and

(b) any rights or freedoms that now exist by way of land claims agreements or may be so acquired.

[28]To our knowledge, at no point in the drafting process was a clause ever proposed that drew an explicit distinction between s. 91(24) "Indians" and s. 35 "aboriginal peoples," though such a clause is relatively simple to craft. Moreover, the text of s. 35 is virtually identical to the draft proposed by the Native Council of Canada, the Inuit Tapirisat of Canada, and the National Indian Brotherhood in separate submissions to the Joint Special Parliamentary Committee on the Constitution, which formed the basis of the amendment. The working papers and agreements on drafting of the Aboriginal organizations concerned, therefore, may also become of importance in any reference case in the future along with the Hansard record of the Committee's hearings and deliberations. Finally, any records or written arguments relating to the proposed deletion of "Métis" from the draft s. 35 clause in early 1981 would be relevant as well, particularly if those documents alleged a concern about the implications for interpreting s. 91(24).

[29]For a detailed analysis of these basic principles see Ruth Sullivan, *Statutory Interpretation* (Concord, ON: Irwin Law, 1997).

[30]In *Delgamuukw v. British Columbia,* [1997] 3 S.C.R. 1010, and *R. v. Adams,* [1996] 3 S.C.R. 101, the Supreme Court ruled that title was on one end of a continuum of rights, with other rights such as harvesting for food, etc., at different points on that continuum that may or may not be as tied to actual possession of land. This "continuum" framework makes it much harder now to argue that only some rights of Métis were intended to be acknowledged as recognized or affirmed in 1982, whether still "existing" or not, as opposed to others that have been defined consistently as "Indian title" by the Court itself and in constitutional statutes such as the *Manitoba Act.*

[31]Not that such programs are always or only restricted to these classes. Some legislative entitlements (taxation exemptions) are solely available to status Indians with property situated on reserves. Other benefits, like non-insured health benefits, are non-statutory and have been extended since 1988 to Inuit as well as status Indians, and also Labrador Innu Nation members (who are neither registered nor formed as bands under the *Indian Act).*

[32]It is, of course, arguable in light of the burgeoning *Charter* jurisprudence, such as *Hunter v. Southam Inc,* [1984] 2 S.C.R. 145, that Parliament and the Crown in right of Canada owe a general obligation not merely to respect constitutionally protected rights, but also to take positive measures to make such rights meaningful and effective.

[33](indexed as *Guerin v. Canada),* [1984] 2 S.C.R. 335.

[34]For further information, see e.g., Richard H. Bartlett, *Indian Reserves and Aboriginal*

WHO ARE CANADA'S ABORIGINAL PEOPLES?

Lands in Canada: A Homeland (Saskatoon: University of Saskatchewan Native Law Centre, 1990).
[35]A recent example of such a stay involving eighteen months is *Corbiere* v. *Canada (Minister of Indian and Northern Affairs)*, [1999] 2 S.C.R. 203.
[36]As has been done, for example, by the enactment of the *Indian Lands Agreement (1986) Act, S.C. 1988; Indian Lands Agreement Confirmation Act, 1989*, S.O. c. 26.
[37]For a recent example see the Nisga'a Treaty that was appended to federal and provincial enabling statutes: *Nisga'a Final Agreement Act*, S.C. 2000, c. 7, and *Nisga'a Final Agreement Act*, S.B.C. 1999, c. 2, respectively.
[38]It should be noted that the Supreme Court of Canada has created the new term of "Aboriginality" in the context of its s. 15(1) *Charter* analysis of the *Indian Act* in *Corbiere* v. *Canada (Minister of Indian and Northern Affairs)*, supra note 35.
[39]See Jack Woodward, *Native Law* (Toronto: Carswell, 1994, as revised) chapter 4, "Provincial Powers and Responsibilities" for a comprehensive listing and description of these cases.
[40]A review of the Manitoba Schools question dealing with s. 93 of the 1867 Constitution, *Reference re Public Schools Act (Man.), s. 79(3), (4) and (7)*, [1993] 1 S.C.R. 839, may be of use in framing a responsibility case on s. 91(24). Since minority education rights have been so integral to the nature of Canadian federalism, a case focusing on Métis or Indian minority education rights could also enlist wider public acceptance and support.
[41]This seems to be the case with the Indian elections system in the case of *Corbiere* v. *Canada*, supra note 35. Here the Federal Court, Trial Division, ordered legislative action to replace an illegal restriction on non-residents' voting rights while the Federal Court of Appeal preferred to avoid ruling the legislation invalid, which would have forced Parliament to replace it, and instead exempted the band in question from the legislation. The Supreme Court declared the subsection *ultra vires* but stayed the effect of its decision for eighteen months to allow the government to consult First Nations and for Parliament to amend the *Act*.
[42]*Quebec Sucession Reference*, supra note 3.
[43]See *R.* v. *Sparrow*, [1990] 1 S.C.R. 1075.
[44]Notice of such an action was filed in Federal Court by the Labrador Métis Nation over two years ago.
[45]*Lovelace* v. *Ontario*, [1998] 2 C.N.L.R. 36 (Ont. C.A.), aff'd [2000] 1 S.C.R. 950.
[46]*Perry* v. *Ontario*, [1998] 2 C.N.L.R. 79 (Ont. C.A.), leave to appeal to S.C.C. refused 152 D.L.R. (4th) vi.
[47]*R.* v. *Fowler*, [1993] 3 C.N.L.R. 178 (N.B. Prov. Ct.).
[48]*R.* v. *McPherson*, [1994] 2 C.N.L.R. 137 (Man. Q.B.).
[49]*R.* v. *Morin and Daigneault*, [1998] 1 C.N.L.R. 182 (Sask. Q.B.).
[50]*R.* v. *Powley*, [1999] 1 C.N.L.R. 153 (Ont. Prov. Ct.), [2000] 2 C.N.L.R. 233 (Ont. Sup. Ct.), aff'd [2001] 2 C.N.L.R. 291 (Ont. C.A.). Appeal to the S.C.C. accepted, [2001] S.C.C.A. No. 256, n. 48.
[51]*R.* v. *Grumbo*, [1998] 3 C.N.L.R. 172 (Sask. C.A.), rev'g [1996] 3 C.N.L.R. 122 (Sask. Q.B.).
[52]*R.* v. *Ferguson*, [1993] 2 C.N.L.R. 148 (Alta. Prov. Ct.), aff'd [1994] 1 C.N.L.R. 117 (Alta. Q.B.).
[53]*R.* v. *Desjarlais*, [1996] 3 C.N.L.R. 113 (Alta. Q.B.).
[54]*R.* v. *Blais*, [1997] 3 C.N.L.R. 109 (Man. Prov. Ct.), [1998] 4 C.N.L.R. 103 (Man. Q.B.), aff'd (2001), 198 D.L.R. (4th) 220 (Man. C.A.). Leave to the S.C.C. accepted, [2001] S.C.C.A. No. 294, n. 52.
[55]*The Constitution Act, 1930*, S.C. 1930, c. 26, Schedule (1) Manitoba, s. 13; Schedule (2) Alberta, s. 12; Schedule (2) Saskatchewan, s. 12; Schedule (4) British Columbia, s. 13.

For example, s. 12 of Schedule (2) Alberta reads:

> In order to secure to the Indians of the Province the continuance of the supply of game and fish for their support and subsistence, Canada agrees that the laws respecting game in force in the Province from time to time shall apply to the Indians within the boundaries thereof, provided, however, that the said Indians shall have the right, which the Province hereby assures to them, of hunting, trapping and fishing game and fish for food at all seasons of the year on all unoccupied Crown lands and on any other lands to which the said Indians may have a right of access.

[56]*Laprise,* [1978] 6 W.W.R. 85 (Sask. C.A.). *Laprise* held that the *NRTA* provision on Indians should be interpreted the same as the *Indian Act, 1927,* despite the fact that the *NRTA* was a constitutional instrument. *Laprise* also involved the conviction of a non-treaty Indian, despite the plain inclusion of non-treaty Indians under the 1927 version of the *Indian Act.*

[57]See the introduction, and especially c. 2, 3, 4, and 6.

[58]*R.* v. *Fowler,* [1993] 3 C.N.L.R 178 (N.B. Prov. Ct.). See also *R.* v. *Chevrier,* [1988] O.J. No. 1792 (Ont. Dist. Ct.), online: QL (CJ).

[59]See c. 3 and 8, where the question of Métis definition is fully canvassed.

[60]See c. 2, *supra,* for a full discussion of this issue.

[61]*The British Columbia Treaty Commission Act,* S.C. 1995, c. 45, s. 2.

[62]Prior to the 1990s, DIAND rebated Alberta for certain social welfare expenditures for off-reserve Indians in northern Alberta. Alberta could be interested in a test case on responsibility to reinstate such an arrangement or a more self-governing equivalent.

[63]See c. 3. In addition, there is a group of descendents of the Métis or "half-breed" and listed adherents of the Robinson-Superior Treaty of 1930—today's "Red Sky Métis Nation"— that were struck from band lists in the 1885–1890 period who are seeking an accommodation from both the federal and provincial government. Interestingly, federal correspondence of the period describes the group as "provincial Treaty Indians" for whom the province should be responsible, since the treaty in question was pre-Confederation and the individuals concerned were deemed by Ottawa not to be members of Indians bands governed by the then extant 1888 *Indian Act.*

[64]See also c. 3, *supra.*

[65]It should be noted that fully portable entitlements under federal policy is now provided for in the case of health and education support so long as the First Nation concerned is supportive. In this case, the issue would likely boil down to a *Charter*-based argument involving comparing socio-demographically identical persons discriminated against solely on grounds of status.

[66]We note that some of the oldest references to the term "Métis" occur in the Atlantic—in both Acadia and the Gaspé, dating to the early-mid 1600s. However, we know of no sustained emergence of a distinct "Métis" community. See also *R.* v. *Chiasson,* discussed in c. 8, text accompanying note 103, *infra.*

[67]*Simon* v. *The Queen* (indexed as *R.* v. *Simon*), [1985] 2 S.C.R. 387.

[68]The Congress of Aboriginal Peoples has experience with trying to mount such a trial action in relation to Métis land claims. However, this case (now styled as *Dumont et al.* v. *The Queen)* has not advanced to trial in twenty years. Almost a decade was devoted to a federal motion to strike out the statement of claim, culminating in a dismissal by the Supreme Court, [1990] 1 S.C.R. 279.

[69]The Crown has abandoned almost all cases involving a successive win at trial and appeal for an Aboriginal plaintiff in an effort to avoid any kind of national precedent.

[70]We would caution, however, that this approach has to be sustained over time. The *Dumont et al.* case was initiated in 1981 with this objective of "levering" negotiation in mind.

Chapter Six

Political Recognition

An Assessment of American Practice[1]

Russel Lawrence Barsh

In Canada, the *Indian Act* confers discretionary authority on the Minister of Indian Affairs to "constitute new bands" of Indians, or to divide or amalgamate existing bands. Rarely exercised, this power has neither been the subject of ministerial regulations nor of interpretive litigation. It is likely to meet more challenges, however, as Canada pursues its policy of negotiating agreements recognizing the right of individual Indian groups to "self-government." It is useful in this regard to remind the reader of some basic points that were covered in earlier chapters.

Canada's policy of negotiating modern treaties is based on the recognition that an inherent right of self-government is vested in the "aboriginal peoples of Canada" under section 35 of the *Constitution Act, 1982*. As discussed in chapter 4, the central problem for Canada is to identify which *specific* groups constitute "peoples" or "nations" entitled to a distinct legal status and a negotiated political relationship with Ottawa and the provinces.

If history is a guide, Ottawa will eventually look to the United States for inspiration. Our neighbour to the south instituted a modern process of recognition in the implementation of the 1934 *Indian Reorganization Act (IRA)*. Like section 35 of the *Constitution Act, 1982,* the *IRA* reversed a long-standing policy of dismantling Indian nations following the original, incomplete project of negotiating treaties.

In the United States as in Canada, the era of non-respect for treaties led to the breakdown of traditional forms of self-government and dispersal of peoples from their customary territories. When the United States restored respect for the collective political rights of Indian tribes in 1934, many tribes were no longer made up of the same clans and families. Others had never signed treaties. The United States spent decades making case-by-case determinations of eligibility to benefit from the *IRA*, but there is no reason to suppose (as considered in chapters 2 and 4) that "federally recognized Indian tribes" represent all of the Indigenous groups entitled to self-government. Canada now faces the same problem. Despite the significant constitutional differences that exist between our two countries, their similar social and historical contexts invite a comparison.

The conceptual point of reference for comparison is the "recognition" of distinct Indigenous nations for the purpose of self-government negotiations. The constitutional entrenchment of the inherent rights of "aboriginal peoples" in 1982 parallels the legislative affirmation of the inherent powers of "Indian tribes" in the *IRA* in 1934. In both cases, the confirmation of distinct legal status led to political negotiations and the emergence of a new class of governments.

The discussion of the United States's Federal Acknowledgment Process (FAP) in this chapter lays bare the pitfalls of allowing bureaucrats to devise policies and procedures for recognition without judicial guidance. In Canada, we are at a crossroads in conceptualizing and implementing the idea that distinct Aboriginal peoples entitled to self-government can be newly constituted, and recognized, whether by the judicial, executive, or legislative branches of government.

The Royal Commission on Aboriginal Peoples (RCAP) recommended that autonomy be conferred on "nations" rather than the administratively constituted "bands" currently recognized as political entities under Canadian law, which the Commissioners concluded are too small.

> The problem is that the historical Aboriginal nations were undermined by disease, relocations, and the full array of assimilationist government policies. They were fragmented into bands, reserves, and small settlements. Only some operate as collectivities now. They will have to reconstitute themselves as nations.[2]

The Commission did not indicate how "nations" could be identified in practice, although it opposed the American fascination with "blood quantum" standards.

> We believe strongly that membership in Aboriginal nations should not be defined by race. Aboriginal nations are political communities, often comprising people of mixed background and heritage. Their bonds are those of culture and identity, not blood. Their unity comes from their shared history and their strong sense of themselves as peoples.[3]

In an internal policy document circulated shortly after the June 1997 election extended the Liberals' mandate in Parliament, the Department of Indian Affairs and Northern Development (DIAND), now Indian and Northern Affairs Canada, proposed that eligibility for self-government will depend, among other things, on the practical size, geographical proximity, and "national identity" of Indian groups.[4]

DIAND concurred with the Commission's recommendation that the core requirement be "a common heritage including a common history, language, cultural traditions, political consciousness, laws, governmental structures, spirituality, ancestry, homeland or adherence to a particular treaty."

The federal government has not responded to RCAP's recommendation that guidelines for recognition be agreed between Ottawa and Aboriginal representatives at national meetings convened by the Prime Minister. The *First Nations Governance Act* would exclude questions about the internal membership of those "First Nations" that are already recognized as "Indian bands" under the *Indian Act*, but offers no new approach to the recognition of other Aboriginal political entities.

What guidance can Canadians derive from the American experience? The following study was based on: formal decisions taken by the Bureau of Indian Affairs on the legal status of individual Indian groups from 1935 to 1996; internal documents of the Bureau obtained under Freedom of Information Act requests and retrieved from the National Archives; and testimony of federal officials who drafted and applied the current federal standards, taken from *Greene* v. *Babbitt*, the first successful federal court challenge of a denial of recognition. What emerges is a picture of American bureaucratic incrementalism, ineptitude, and political sensitivity, which have resulted in shifting thresholds and inconsistent decisions for more than sixty years.

Recognition and Reorganization

"Recognition" has had the same meaning in American Indian law as in international law: the formal decision to establish a relationship with another government. For more than a century, federal courts viewed the recognition of particular groups as distinct "Indian tribes" as a political act, the exercise of which was entrusted to the discretion of the executive.[5] Indian groups were usually identified as political entities by treaty, or by having lands or funds set aside for their exclusive use. The same was true in Canada.

By 1900, American policies aimed at breaking up reservations and promoting assimilation had led to growing confusion and conflicts regarding the legal status of individual Indians and their communities. Most of the disputes that reached federal courts involved local efforts to impose taxes on Indian farms, or the prosecution of non-Indians for selling liquor to Indians they believed were emancipated.[6] The courts eventually took a more activist posture, loosely defining "tribe" as "a body of Indians of the same or a similar race, united in a community under one leadership or government, and inhabiting a particular though sometimes ill-defined territory,"[7] and warning Congress against any future attempt to "bring a community or body of people within the range of [federal] power by arbitrarily calling them an Indian tribe."[8] Significantly, the courts' concern at that time was protecting citizens from being transmuted involuntarily into legally restricted Indians; today, the dispute is over claims by citizens that they have been arbitrarily deprived of Indian status.

There were few benefits to being a "tribe" in the early years of this century, but this changed in 1934 with the adoption of the *IRA* and the extension of many New Deal social programmes, such as the Civilian Conservation Corps, to Indian reservations. New Deal Indian Commissioner John Collier felt that Indians had suffered from too much emphasis on individualism and assimilation. His solution was to restore collective economic and political institutions and rebuild collectively owned reservation land bases.

Eligibility to form self-governing Indian communities was limited to "tribes residing on the same reservation."[9] In their enthusiasm to promote the new programme, the Bureau's field staff often bent this rule, with Collier's approval. In Washington State, for example, they found very few people living on the Puyallup reservation, most of which had been sold, and a community that was at best "very loosely integrated."[10] The Nooksacks had no reservation at all, and were deemed "progressive" because they were employed in the region's logging camps and mills.[11] The Bureau's field agents repeatedly sought advice from solicitor Nathan Margold and staff lawyers Felix Cohen, Kenneth Meiklejohn, and Charlotte Westwood.

The Miami Tribe in Oklahoma was problematic, for example, because it no longer had any land in trust, 90 percent of its members had less than one-fourth Indian blood, and half of its members lived outside of the state. Nearly a month after Collier authorized an election on the proposed Miami constitution, Margold raised a "serious question" about their eligibility as the regulations stated that "there must be a currently existing group distinct and functioning as a group in certain respects."[12] Bureau field staff confirmed that tribal activity had ceased by 1920, only to reappear in the late 1930s in response to the possible economic benefits of *IRA.*[13] Based on these facts, the solicitor's office recommended rejecting the Miami tribal constitution, but the "front office" worried about consistency—"Some of the adverse circumstances [the solicitor] mentioned have been ignored when other tribal groups have been under consideration."[14] In the end, the Miami were authorized to proceed.

In New England and the South, however, Collier formally adopted a policy of neglect, reasoning that the self-identified Indian tribes of these regions were merely "folk groups" with "a certain amount of Indian blood mixed with a large degree of blood other than Indian," i.e., African-American, which "have never had an explicit relationship to the Federal government" but instead "have lived amidst the general population for hundreds of years—and have made their social and economic adjustments as human beings and as citizens not under the guardianship of the United States."[15]

"Miscegenation with the surrounding population has gone on for so long and has been so extensive that it would be impossible to determine the degree of blood" of these people, Collier explained, and "there is also grave doubt" that any of them could establish one-half Indian blood as required by the *IRA*. In view of the Bureau's limited budget, it was best to ignore these "folk groups" and not "jeopardize the work with those Indians already under Federal guardianship." Thus the Bureau jettisoned scores of historical Indian communities, largely on surmise and without supporting research. Many of these northeastern and southeastern communities subsequently regained their Indian tribal status, beginning with litigation launched by the Passamaquoddy tribe of Maine in 1972,[16] but the status of many others remains in dispute.

Cohen purported to synthesize Bureau recognition practice in his "Handbook of Federal Indian Law," originally prepared in 1941 as a Bureau office manual. In it, he suggested following considerations which, singly or jointly, have been particularly relied upon in reaching the conclusion that a group constitutes a "tribe" or "band":

1. That the group has had treaty relations with the United States.

2. That the group has been denominated a tribe by act of Congress or Executive order.

3. That the group has been treated as having collective rights in tribal lands or fund, even though not expressly designated as a tribe.

4. That the group has been treated as a tribe or band by other Indian tribes.

5. That the group has exercised political authority over its members, through a tribal council or other governmental forms.[17]

In the absence of any of these factors, Cohen suggested resort to "ethnological and historical" evidence. Cohen's formula remained the only official guidance in recognition matters for another thirty-five years.

Politics Behind the New Criteria

Policy debates in the public arena mask the real interests behind many administrative decisions, which can be narrowly bureaucratic—for example, reallocating power and funds among departments, strengthening a department's influence, perpetuating bureaucrats' jobs, or making their work easier.[18] Policy debates also mask government efforts to appease elected politicians, as in decisions to construct public works. It is important to look behind the official discourse.

By 1945, the rush to "reorganize" Indian tribes had been replaced by growing Congressional pressure to "terminate" the very same tribes, and integrate Indians into the American mainstream. There was little cause for concern about recognizing "new" tribes until 1971–1974, when the Nixon and Ford administrations were confronted by two revolutions in American Indian law.[19] The Supreme Court revived the land claims of Indians located within the original thirteen states, although they had never been under federal supervision,[20] raising the question of such groups' entitlement to federal Indian benefits and tribal self-government. In the second legal revolution, a federal court in Washington State ruled that tribal signatories to five mid nineteenth-century treaties reserved the right to harvest up to half of that state's commercial fishery.[21] The problem was that one-third of the tribal signatories were landless and had never "organized" under *IRA.*

Washington State's congressional delegation immediately asked the Bureau to clarify its criteria for "recognition." An initial reply in January 1974 stated that while a land base is not required by law, "we have consistently construed [the *IRA]* as limiting formal organization under that Act to those tribes that are reservation-based."[22] Several months later, the Bureau responded in greater detail, reaffirming the applicability of the 1942 Cohen formula regardless of the existence of a land base.[23] Meanwhile, the Bureau submitted a supplemental budget request for work on "recognition, organization, and tribal regulation" for thirteen landless Northwest tribes.[24] By June, letters recognizing five of the tribes had been drafted and were on the commissioner's desk.

On June 20, 1974, the Office of Management and Budget (OMB) unexpectedly "passed back" the Bureau's supplemental budget request, citing the financial burden of any increase in the number of federally recognized tribes.[25] All status-clarification work was suspended while the Commissioner's staff weighed the implications of the OMB pass-back. One option they considered was announcing that the Commissioner lacks authority to recognize any new tribes. The solicitor's office was asked for a legal opinion, and added to the confusion by arguing that while the Commissioner could not "recognize" any new tribes, he nonetheless had both the authority and duty to "acknowledge" pre-existing political relationships with tribes such as treaty signatories.[26]

There was growing political pressure on the Commissioner to draw the line against "new" tribes, not only from the Washington State congressional delegation, but at least one tribe that was opposed to sharing the treaty fishery more widely.[27] Finally one of the landless tribes, the Stillaguamish, applied for a Federal court order directing the Bureau to make a decision about its status. In October, Bureau staff recommended that the Commissioner "bite the bullet," even at the risk of a dispute with the Secretary and OMB.[28] Cautiously, he asked the Secretary to recognize the Stillaguamish as a trial balloon, while arguing that the Cohen formula was not "adequate" for clarifying the status of other groups.[29] The solicitor's office was assigned the task of developing alternative criteria and procedures.[30]

The Secretary did not act on Stillaguamish until ordered to do so by the federal court in September 1976.[31] He made no decisions on other landless tribes, pending the results of the review by the Solicitor.[32] Assistant Solicitor Scott Keep was assigned to the recognition review; at the same time he was the Bureau's liaison with George Dysart, the lawyer representing the United States in the Northwest treaty fishing litigation.[33] In a memorandum that Keep continues to withhold on the grounds of lawyer-client privilege, he advised Dysart to argue that an Indian group can only be recognized if it is a socially and culturally cohesive "community" exercising political authority over its members—not based on the Cohen formula, but rather on the 1901 *Montoya* case.[34] Dysart made this argument in proposed findings of fact and conclusions of law he submitted later that year to federal judge George Boldt.[35]

While Dysart was advocating a new recognition formula in federal court, the Bureau's chief of tribal operations, Les Gay, had prepared draft regulations to standardize recognition criteria and procedures, based on the Cohen formula.[36] Les Gay's draft was "trashed," however, on the advice of the solicitor's office— presumably because it was inconsistent with the memo prepared by Keep.[37]

During the same period, Indian tribes "terminated" by Congress in the 1950s and 1960s were lobbying aggressively for the restoration of their legal status. OMB was opposed to restoration, complaining that it was costly, there were no clear benefits to the Indians (other than validating their "social identity"), the criteria were race-based, and as a whole there was "no agreed-upon long-range Indian policy."[38] OMB nevertheless asked the Interior Department in 1976 "to develop criteria for restoring Federal recognition to terminated Indian tribes," and an options paper was under review within the Interior Department by February 1977.

The options paper recommended that restoration criteria should be different from recognition criteria "since the terminated tribes were previously recognized and have already met those requirements."[39] One option was to require merely the "existence of an ongoing identifiable community of Indians," descended from the terminated tribe and located in the same vicinity. The other option was to require proof that the contemporary community is "cohesive," that it "performs self-governing functions," that "widespread use of their aboriginal language, customs and culture" continues, and the group suffers from poor socio-economic conditions warranting renewal of federal responsibilities. The latter approach was ultimately adopted.[40]

The problem of landless, terminated, and unrecognized tribes was meanwhile also taken by the American Indian Policy Review Commission, which concluded in 1977 that "there must be a valid and consistent set of factors applied to every Indian group which seeks recognition," and an independent office to screen applications.[41] Applicants would be required to meet any one of seven tests: "historic continuance as an Indian tribal group," a tribal council or some other structure for exercising authority over its members, relationships with other Indian tribes, collective rights to land or funds (including claims judgment awards), or designation as a tribe in a treaty, an act of Congress, or in state or local law.[42] In effect, the Commission combined the Cohen formula with the Keep formula.

Regulations governing the "acknowledgement" of Indian tribes were finally promulgated in 1978. Authority was sought for the "management of all Indian affairs" to the Secretary of the Interior and the Bureau.[43] The Keep model was adopted, essentially as Dysart had argued it to the Boldt court.

Although there are seven criteria for petitioners to satisfy, the majority of decisions have revolved around two of them, which refer to the continuous existence of "a distinct community," and the continuous exercise of "political influence or authority."[44]

The existence of effective leaders implies the existence of a group of followers, and the maintenance of an organized group implies that there are individuals who initiate collective decisions. The two criteria therefore overlap.

The original Federal Acknowledgment Process (FAP) regulations did not define "distinct community" further than to suggest that geographical proximity and intermarriage could be used as indicators. Scholarly criticism led to the adoption of an expanded definition of "community" as part of 1994 amendments to the regulations.[45] Indicators now include intermarriage, "significant social relationships connecting individual members," "significant rates of informal social interaction which exist broadly among the members of a group," "a significant degree of shared or cooperative labor or other economic activity," strong patterns of social isolation or discrimination, and distinctive ritual or cultural activities involving a significant proportion of the group.

In 1979, Judge Boldt signed an order drafted by Dysart that adopted the Keep formula, and found that five landless Northwest Indian treaty tribes were ineligible to exercise treaty fishing rights.[46] This vindicated Keep's FAP regulations, which could now be justified as a codification of existing law. Three tribes moved unsuccessfully to reopen Boldt's 1979 decision.[47] At the time of this writing, the Bureau's Branch of Acknowledgment and Research (BAR) has approved 16 petitions for acknowledgment and denied 15; Congress had intervened and recognized or restored the status of 10 petitioners; 33 petitions are either under active consideration by BAR or are fully documented and ready for review; and 160 petitions are deemed not ripe for evaluation because they are incompletely documented.[48]

Even after eliminating the large backlog of incompletely documented petitions, BAR has taken twenty-three years to act on half of its docket.

Crafting the Regulatory Scheme

Attempts to rationalize the FAP criteria sociologically actually began long after they were implemented, as was revealed when the first chief of BAR, "Bud" Shapard, testified in the *Greene* case.[49]

> Well I was, I guess I was a primary drafter. I drew from all sources, got a lot of people's comments, we took all the comments that we could get, and comments that had been written with inside the department about the regulations, and anything else like that we could come up with, and tried to come up with something that would work.[50]

Shapard was assisted by Assistant Solicitor Scott Keep, who appears to have been the major source of ideas for the criteria.[51] Shapard knew only one anthropologist, George Roth, who had done his doctoral thesis on the Indian reservation where Shapard had been recreation director a few years earlier. Shapard recruited Roth as BAR's anthropologist and entrusted him with elaborating the criteria in practice.[52]

Shapard originally understood the goal of BAR was to be "neutral" and reject "phony groups" that were clearly ineligible for recognition as tribes.[53] He moreover believed that neutrality would be ensured by his employees' concern for their professional reputations.[54] Although draft technical reports were routinely sent to Scott Keep and staff in the Secretary's office, Shapard recalled nothing more than changes in the "wording" of supporting arguments as opposed to the conclusions.[55]

Shapard nevertheless concluded after leaving the Bureau that the criteria were "too subjective" (especially with regard to the concepts of "community" and "political influence"), "very paper-oriented," and too dependent on the survival of written documentation.[56] He was surprised that "there were fewer frauds out there," more shades of grey, and groups that had characteristics "we weren't even looking for [but we] should have been looking for."[57]

Shapard has denied that the evidentiary threshold was raised once it became apparent that "there were fewer frauds out there" than he or his staff had imagined, accusing BAR and the petitioners of launching an arms-race of spiralling documentation.[58]

In 1983, however, BAR's former chief of tribal operations, Les Gay, was hired as a consultant to evaluate BAR. He wrote to Shapard:

> Part of our problem is that when we drafted the regs originally we were damn strong Indian advocates. The entire concept of the regs arose from my desire to recognize those Eastern groups which I felt had been shafted. The "Passama-quoddys" were the Indians that lit my fuse. It couldn't be done administratively so regs was the only course available. Then you came on board and we bent over backwards with our advocacy. ...Our advocacy got us in to a box you won't get out of unless you become hard nosed!![59]

Scholarly critiques of BAR have focused on the growing research burden on petitioners. This has been attributed to failure to define key concepts, failure to fix thresholds for proof, and a preoccupation with documentation.[60] "Efforts to compensate these insecurities have involved bulk rather than clarity."[61] BAR has also been accused of a bias towards groups that resemble reservation tribes in terms of their geographical and social boundedness, and of conflicts of interest.[62]

Validity and Application of the Criteria

After several years of professional work for BAR and some of the petitioners, anthropologist Susan Greenbaum posed a number of theoretical issues about "community" which she felt had been sidestepped in BAR's decisions.

> How many different forms do authentic communities take? How varied are the structures around which communal relations are established and maintained? ...Is there a qualitative difference between Indian "tribes" and other ethnic communities? Is it relevant to make such a distinction? Similarly, do we know whether or not the recognized Indian tribes would all qualify as communities? ...If community is a continuous variable, i.e., a group can have more or less of it, then how much does it take to get recognized as a tribe?[63]

Greenbaum criticizes the idea that the petitioners can be placed along a single continuum from relatively traditional and cohesive to assimilated and detribalized. "Tribal" societies were not necessarily all homogeneous, harmonious, or sharply bounded. Likewise, centres of ethnic identity and interaction exist even within urbanized societies. Most groups are characterized by fuzzy boundaries, and most individuals have multiple affiliations whether they live in "tribes" or in cities. Moreover, "if telephones and automobiles have altered the effects of distance on relationships, then why must people live together in order to have a community?"[64]

In the past, anthropologists and sociologists never found it useful to ask whether a community existed; they focused their research on describing and comparing the ways communities functioned internally and in relation to others. Hence there is no academic literature from which BAR could derive a more precise definition of the threshold. As a consequence, BAR has taken an ad hoc approach in decision-making with confusing and apparently inconsistent results.

Several prominent anthropologists have testified at congressional hearings that BAR's decisions reflect a fallacious idealization of the "tribe" as a socially closed, endogamous, physical settlement.[65]

What emerges from a close scrutiny of BAR's reasoning in these cases is, in fact, even more fallacious and disturbing: a preoccupation with race. In order to appreciate this conclusion, it will be necessary first to explore the ways in which BAR staff have defined and applied criterion "b," the requirement that there be a "distinct community."

What Is a "Community"?

In his testimony in the *Greene* case, Roth described "community" in terms of "some substantial body... of social connectedness and social distinction," taking account of landlessness, economic migration, and other factors which may affect the ability of a group to interact. He admitted that comparative data on the sociology of long-recognized reservation tribes do not exist,[66] hence he had no standard for comparison. The only sociological model of a "community" used by BAR refers to a "core group" of active families, surrounded by "concentric circles" of relatively peripheral ones. Roth purportedly seeks evidence that the peripheral members are linked to the core, but not necessarily with each other.[67]

The judge in *Greene* also heard from William Sturtevant, curator of North American ethnology at the Smithsonian Institution, who said that he would look for "networks of communication" including "how much people know about other people..., [w]hen they see them, what they see them for, what they know about them," all which may change over time.[68] "The group can continue..., whereas the cultural features, the behavior, the way of being, changes."[69]

What is distinctive about the group's activities today may not even be of Aboriginal origin, and the group may differ from its non-Indian neighbours only insofar as its consciousness of common ancestry and historical ties to a territory.[70]

The members of contemporary Indian communities are generally active in non-Indian communities and organizations as well as their own.[71]

Indicators of Social Cohesion

Until the mid-1980s, BAR placed a great deal of probative weight on the persistence of a core settlement inhabited by at least some members of the group.[72]

Roth testified in *Greene* that a settlement merely creates a presumption of cohesion, and is not a condition for a community to exist.[73]

Geography continues to be invoked in ways that suggest its residual hold on BAR thinking. In its favourable report on the Mohegans, BAR stressed that about half the members lived within a 10-mile radius until 1941, and 7 percent still do so today.[74] Likewise, BAR commented favourably on the fact that the Snoqualmies, albeit lacking a core settlement after 1914, mainly still resided within their historical territory.[75] According to BAR's Miami decision, however, mere proximity (as opposed to a settlement) proves nothing.[76]

Direct evidence of recent and ongoing social interaction has been required in all cases, but the quantity and nature of interaction that has been required varied considerably. Traditional ceremonies, ritual, and language were typically absent, or restricted to a small number of families. Participation in pan-Indian pow-wows, weddings and funerals of Indian kinfolk, and annual tribal meetings was sufficient evidence of social cohesion in most cases.[77]

Annual family and tribal reunions were insufficient in the Miami case, however; the annual reunion "does not establish that a cohesive community exists, since by its nature it brings together many individuals who rarely interact with each other otherwise."[78]

In the Samish case, core families actually did practice traditional religion, and the tribe had dedicated a ceremonial site in the 1980s that was recognized by nearby reservation tribes, but Roth dismissed this as insufficient evidence of cohesion.[79]

BAR's assessments of social interactions are generally couched in quantitative terms such as "much" or "little," but the underlying data are either qualitative or derived from very small samples. In Samish, Roth interviewed eleven tribal members (2 percent of the total), of whom five stated that they attended tribal meetings. He reported that there was "limited" interaction and that "most" Samish were inactive.[80]

Samish oral history was disregarded as biased. Yet the favourable decision on the Snoqualmies was expressly based on the group's own oral history.[81]

In the Miami case BAR meticulously calculated the percentage of tribal members who attended meetings and social events, and concluded that it was too low, while rejecting the group's ethnographic research as "not systematically gathered... often anecdotal in nature... [and] obtained from key informants."[82]

Only one petitioner thus far has submitted a random survey of its members as evidence of social interaction—the Samish.[83] BAR rejected the results as biased, arguing that the proportion of respondents that reported having served on or worked for the tribal council was higher than it should have been. When cross-examined in *Greene,* however, BAR staff were unable to explain how they had come to this conclusion. In any event, they insisted that surveys have little validity.

Hence when petitioners quantify, BAR rejects quantitative methods in favour of qualitative ethnography; when petitioners do ethnography, they may be criticized for being non-quantitative. At the fundamental level of methodological validity, then, the process lacks consistency. If quantitative methods were uniformly adopted, moreover, BAR would be forced to establish quantitative thresholds, which would undermine its discretion.

Consistency in the interpretation of social dynamics is also lacking. BAR has generally sought evidence of a "core group," for example. The BAR field report on the Samish observed:

> I was unable to identify a distinction made by members concerning a core or fringe membership. Generally anyone of Samish Indian blood is considered to be a member regardless of the participation in tribal affairs, association with other members or marriage patterns.[84]

BAR inferred from this data that no Samish core group existed. When the Tunica-Biloxi made the same comment about the absence of a core group, however, BAR used it as evidence of social cohesion.[85]

Similarly, the only recent collective activity BAR could document for the Jamestown Klallam was pursuing land claims, and this was used as cogent evidence of social cohesion and political authority.[86] In the Samish and Snohomish cases, BAR used similar data to argue that the groups were organized "solely for claims purposes."

BAR has sometimes drawn inferences from political dynamics within the group. A struggle for leadership of the Mohegans in the 1970s was considered strong evidence of social cohesion, even though the extent of broad, grassroots involvement in the conflict was never assessed.[87]

In the Snoqualmie case, cohesion was inferred from the existence of an outspoken tribal "chief" in the period 1914–1956, although the extent of his actual power or authority was not determined.[88]

BAR lacks internal guidelines for the intensity or breadth of its own ethnographic fieldwork. There are no interview protocols, nor any standards for the reliability or recording of data.[89]

There has been no protocol for resolving interpretive disputes between BAR staff and petitioners' researchers.[90]

Inferences from Genealogy

Interpretations of social interaction data have been haphazard, in part because the dispositive factor has been genealogy. From the beginning, BAR has been preoccupied with intermarriage and blood quantum. Race has been used to reject groups that would have satisfied the "community" test sociologically. Moreover, BAR has used its discretion to set higher racial quotas for some of the applicants.

BAR argued that the Samish were "unable to retain a distinction from surrounding communities" because of widespread intermarriage with non-Indians in the late 19th century. The Samish had also absorbed a number of Indians from other Northwest tribes. A group of such "diverse backgrounds," BAR concluded, is "well outside the concept of a tribal community."[91] Similar conclusions were drawn in Snohomish.[92] Yet the neighbouring Snoqualmies were deemed to be sufficiently cohesive and distinct because they had generally married other Indians of any background as opposed to whites until 1900, and subsequently adopted a blood-quantum requirement for membership.

> The blood degree of the Snoqualmie membership as a whole provides evidence of the maintenance of a community. A blood degree requirement for membership in a group establishes a requirement for the maintenance within the group as a whole of at least a minimal degree of social ties, since it is a measure of how close kinship ties of a given individual are with other members of the tribe. The higher the blood degree of an individual, the higher the number of relatives that individual is likely to have within the tribe and the closer his relationship to them.[93]

BAR similarly stressed the fact that the Mohegans had been a "closely related group" before 1900, albeit today 98 percent of the members are related only to the fourth degree or less.[94]

In other cases, BAR justified high rates of marriage outside the group. Among the Jamestown Klallam, marriage outside the tribe was an "old pattern," and among the Timbi-Sha Shoshones, exogamy was actually evidence of "group consensus" and cohesion since it had been customary aboriginally.[95] Exogamy was understandable in the case of the Tunica-Biloxi because they are a very small group.[96] Most exceptional of all is Poarch Creek, which actually had its origins in a so-called "half-blood" town of the Creek Nation.[97] If a group consisting exclusively of the descendants of mixed marriages can become a distinct tribe, how can BAR maintain that mixed marriages are incompatible with being a community?

The Requirement of Continuity

The original FAP regulations were drafted in the present tense: "inhabits a specific area or lives in a community viewed as American Indian." BAR nonetheless always required proof of social cohesion throughout history, from first contact to the present.[98] This increased the burden of research and documentation by an order of magnitude, and led to disputes over the permissible length of gaps in the historical record, or of "fluctuations" in the activity of groups. Many petitioners experienced significant dispersal in the period between the two world wars. BAR regarded this as fatal to some groups' petitions and justifiable in others.[99]

One proposal to ease the burden on petitioners has been to set a baseline for historical continuity at 1871, the year that the United States ceased making treaties with Indian tribes, while Shapard has suggested a baseline of 1934.[100]

The 1994 revised regulations require continuity "from generation to generation," which implies taking a snapshot of cohesion every twenty to forty years.

Consistency with Tribal Restoration Standards

BAR decisions not only are inconsistent with each other, but inconsistent with standards applied to the eligibility of terminated tribes for restoration.

The Interior Department supported the restoration of the Klamaths in Oregon, for example, upon the following evidence of "cohesion" and the "widespread use" of Aboriginal culture:

> Through the efforts of their committees, the tribe held meetings and pursued their treaty claims in court. They also had associations to handle the affairs of their local cemeteries. They elected officers and committees to conduct business. The general membership continued to meet on Memorial Day each year, and at other times as certain celebrations were held, or other matters of importance would come to their attention. ...An annual Pow Wow is held each year on Memorial Day. The general membership have formed cemetery committees to maintain the graves of their people and their elders. Classes are held so the culture, traditions and language of the tribe can be maintained and passed onto the youth. Vision walks, a tribal tradition, are being taken by members of the tribe.[101]

It may be argued that terminated tribes should be held to a lower threshold because they were previously recognized. At least one-fifth of the groups which are under review by BAR are descended from treaty signatories, however.[102]

Reforms of mainly procedural nature have been debated in Congress for more than a decade and an advisory council has been established to recommend solutions for California, source of one-fourth of the total FAP caseload.[103]

In one recent round of proposals, Arizona Senator John McCain, a long-time senior player in the Committee on Indian Affairs, championed a bill that would have created an independent presidential commission to act promptly and decisively on petitions.[104]

Most petitioners favour a more court-like, adversarial process in which government experts can be cross-examined, but the Bureau is steadfastly opposed.[105]

Although the National Congress of American Indians (NCAI) has joined the appeal for "a fair and predictable process," it demands "basic assurances to the recognized tribal community regarding their rights."[106] Petitions should not be "rubber-stamped," nor the substantive criteria weakened. "If the gates were opened to all applicants," NCAI told Congress, "the significance and solemnity of the relationship could be diminished."

At the same time, a growing number of petitioners have simply won their status through special legislation. The Interior Department has opposed these measures on the grounds that they bypass FAP and thereby create inconsistency.[107]

The Persistent Issue of Race

BAR's fascination with blood quantum as an indicator of a group's social cohesion and cultural authenticity merits closer attention. It raises problems of constitutional law as well as issues of validity in social science.

Until 1934, "Indians" were defined by lineal descent and by their personal choice of maintaining "tribal relations."[108] *IRA* introduced a new category of "persons of one-half or more Indian blood," reflecting Congressional interest in the welfare of Indians who no longer resided on reservations because they had lost their lands or their communities had been dismantled.[109]

When the issue of blood-degree arose within tribes in the 1930s, the Bureau took the position that there was no federal minimum quantum and that "persons having a very minute degree of Indian blood were... entitled to be enrolled provided they were born into, affiliated with, and recognized by the tribe."[110] It was for the tribe, not the Bureau, to determine whether blood-degree should be a condition of membership.

IRA was enacted more than twenty years before the Supreme Court ruled in *Brown* v. *Board of Education* that the Fourteenth Amendment prohibits racial distinctions. In 1974, the Supreme Court dismissed a challenge to the constitutionality of section 12 of the *IRA*, ruling that Indians are a political rather than racial classification, based on historical relationships between the United States and Indian tribes.[111] The use of race to establish a person's legal status as an Indian is therefore constitutionally suspect—unless the distinction is made by his or her own tribe.[112]

Shapard did not recall considering the use of blood quantum as an indicator of cultural orientation after the original regulations were drafted, and was surprised to learn that Roth had included it in some FAP decisions.

> When I first started writing the regulations, I was a strong proponent of a blood quantum and then the Solicitor's Office informed me that, we simply couldn't do that. And so, that's the only discussion I ever remember, once we discarded that, then it was strictly a descendency thing as far as I was concerned.[113]

In his *Greene* testimony, Roth recognized that "the real issue is who people interact with," but then admitted that the principal measure of interaction he had explored in the Samish case had been "genealogical distance."[114]

He could not identify any publications on the validity of inferring a child's cultural orientation or interactions from mixed ancestry. An academic expert called to testify in Roth's defence was also unable to recall any published studies correlating intermarriage with social interaction, and conceded that his views were "theoretical statistical" rather than based on empirical research.[115] Other expert witnesses were emphatic that genealogical ties have far less impact on the child's identity and behaviour than actual contacts and attachments while growing up.[116]

The administrative law judge in *Greene* rejected racial standards, but the Assistant Secretary of the Interior defended them in her final determination that the Samish are, indeed, an Indian tribe.[117]

Why is the Bureau insistent on equating race with culture? One explanation—at the level of policy—is the convenience of using race as a tool to keep the size of the service-eligible population of Indians in check. The FAP regulations grew from OMB's 1974 pass-back of funding for "new tribes," and the same administration had been experimenting with using both blood-degree and reservation-residency as ways of limiting tribal members' eligibility for federal services.[118]

The Future: A New Paradigm

The federal acknowledgment process has replaced Cohen's legal and historical criteria for tribal existence with sociological and racial tests. In so doing, FAP has undermined the legal security of all U.S. Indian tribes. Signing a treaty or accepting a reservation set aside by an act of Congress is an irreversible historical fact. But social behaviour, cultural manifestations, and blood-degrees change over time, opening the possibility of tribes being challenged on the grounds that they are no longer Indian enough.

Tribal status confers material benefits that, like other public benefits, are protected from arbitrary confiscation by the Due Process Clause of the Fifth Amendment.[119]

The FAP regulations were drafted to circumvent this constitutional shield: they speak it terms of whether a tribe still "exists." If a tribe has ceased to "exist," it arguably enjoys no constitutional protection. The Samish were confronted with this argument in *Greene*. As a treaty signatory, they felt they had no need to meet the FAP criteria. The court disagreed, although it ruled that the Samish had a right to a full-dress adversarial hearing on the merits of their case.

When the FAP criteria were adopted, it was generally assumed that their application would be restricted to vetting "new" Indian tribes. Leaders of recognized tribes felt secure, and undoubtedly many of them felt that raising the threshold for federal recognition would protect the interests of the existing club. It now appears that this was an error of judgement. As the Samish had argued, the FAP criteria represented a broad, paradigmatic shift in the solicitor's office, which eventually might be applied retroactively.

In 1987, the Burns Paiute Tribal Council was advised that its new constitution would be approved solely on the understanding that it is not a "tribe," but rather "a community of adult Indians residing on a reservation." As such, they would lack any inherent sovereignty, and could exercise only those powers of self-government delegated to them by Congress.[120] Interestingly, the Burns Paiutes were denied eligibility for *IRA* in 1946, but in 1967 the solicitor found that they were indeed "a cohesive unit" characterized by "ethnological and historical unity" and thus could adopt an *IRA* constitution.[121] A group might satisfy the "community" criterion and deserve recognition, then, without gaining a right to self-government. Unfortunately few tribal leaders were alert to the dangerous implications of the Burns Paiute case.

Six years later, Congress was told that the Bureau had a general policy of distinguishing between historic and non-historic tribes.[122] Only the former could legitimately exercise full powers of territorial sovereignty; the latter are restricted to powers delegated to them by the Bureau when it approves their constitutions. A list was attached, identifying twenty-one "examples" of non-historic tribes.[123]

In a recent case, several Lac Courte Oreilles challenged the decision of the Bureau to revoke a 1992 tribal constitutional election on the grounds that non-resident members of less than one-half Indian blood had been allowed to vote.[124]

Eligibility to vote on the original tribal constitution had been limited to reservation residents and nonresidents of one-half or more Indian blood, pursuant to the definition of "Indian" in the *IRA.* The tribe subsequently allowed its members to move away without losing the right to vote. According to the Bureau, however, constitutional amendments must be adopted by the same kind of electorate as the original constitution, meaning that the nonresident members would need one-half or more Indian blood. The constitutional amendment in question would have removed blood quantum as a criterion for tribal membership. The real dispute, then, is over the Bureau's new racist ideology.

The Lac Courte Oreilles are not exceptional in demographic terms. Nearly all U.S. tribes have experienced a combination of population growth, declining blood quanta, and emigration. If the Bureau prevails in the courts, tribes will have more difficulty amending their constitutions to accommodate these demographic trends, and the proportion of kinfolk within each tribe that can safely claim Indian status will continue to shrink.

Lessons for Canada

Lessons can be gleaned from common experience. Implementation of the *IRA* in the United States required a process for recognizing the Indian tribes who would be acknowledged as capable of entering into "government-to-government" political relations with the federal government of the United States. In Canada, the constitutional recognition of "aboriginal peoples" with undefined "aboriginal and treaty rights" in section 35 of the *Constitution Act, 1982* has necessitated a similar process for identifying all Aboriginal peoples, regardless of their current status under the *Indian Act.* Canada faces the same kind of challenge that the United States faced in 1934 under the *IRA.*

In its final report published in 1996, RCAP recommended that the Prime Minister invite Aboriginal and government leaders to a national forum to discuss and agree on national guidelines for a "nation"-recognition framework. The Prime Minister and Parliament have not acted upon this recommendation. As a result, the development of a Canadian recognition process has proceeded bureaucratically, in a characteristically slow and incremental fashion. In the United States, similarly, the recommendations for an independent tribunal to expedite the modern recognition process have not been adopted. Both countries' procedures have been marked by a combination of vague standards, arbitrary procedures, and agonizing delays.

The main issues of principle in the United States are also beginning to arise in the Canadian courts. The Supreme Court of Canada (S.C.C.) has vacillated in its approach to the characterization of Aboriginal peoples. While it has clearly adopted a racist characterization of "Indians" and "Indian bands" when reading the *Indian Act*, it has also appreciated the fact that Aboriginal and treaty rights are not created by Parliament but arise from the actual course of dealings between the Crown and the people and group that were found on the land. Furthermore, the Court has used "culture" as a criterion for determining the existence and scope of Aboriginal rights, which implies that culture is also a criterion for Aboriginal peoples.[125]

Notes

[1]Unless otherwise indicated, the archival documents cited in the text were obtained by the Samish Indian Tribe from the Bureau of Indian Affairs through the Freedom of Information Act; copies are available from the author. "Jackson Papers" refers to the personal papers of Senator Henry M. Jackson at the University of Washington, Seattle. "NARA" refers to documents in the National Archives, Record Group 75 (Indian Affairs); within this record unit, CCF refers to the Central Classified Files, which are organized by Indian Agency and subject matter, and Entry 1011 refers to the "Records Concerning the Wheeler Howard Act." The author represented the Samish Indian Tribe in the administrative and judicial proceedings described in the text.

[2]Royal Commission on Aboriginal Peoples, *People to People, Nation to Nation* (Ottawa: Minister of Supply and Services, 1996) at 25–26.

[3]*Ibid.* at 26.

[4]DIAND, "A Strategic Framework to Support Sustainable First Nation Governments" [June 1997] at 2. In the possession of the author.

[5]*United States* v. *Holliday,* 70 U.S. 407, 419 (1865); *United States* v. *Candelaria,* 271 U.S. 432, 439 (1926); *United States* v. *John,* 437 U.S. 634, 650 (1978). In 1871 Congress forbade the making of any further treaties with Indian tribes. This pre-empted the President's means of extending recognition to new tribes; thereafter, recognition was essentially by legislation alone.

[6]E.g., *United States* v. *Holliday,* 70 U.S. 407 (1866); *United States* v. *Rickert,* 188 U.S. 342 (1903); *Perrin* v. *United States,* 232 U.S. 478 (1914); *United States* v. *Nice,* 241 U.S. 591 (1916).

[7]*Montoya* v. *United States,* 180 U.S. 261, 266 (1901). The *Montoya* case arose under the 1891 Indian Depredations Act, thus the issue was not whether someone was an Indian, but whether the claimant had been victimized by "a band, tribe, or nation in amity with the United States" for whom the national government had accepted political responsibility.

[8]*United States* v. *Sandoval,* 231 U.S. 28, 46 (1913).

[9]Section 16 of *IRA,* now codified as 25 U.S.C. 476. Under section 19 of the *Act,* "Indian" was defined as "persons of Indian descent who are members of any recognized Indian tribe" and were residing on an Indian reservation on June 1, 1934, as well as all other persons "of one-half or more Indian blood." Thus some *IRA* benefits could be claimed either on the basis of political affiliation or on the basis of race.

[10]O.C. Upchurch, Superintendent, Tulalip Agency, to Commissioner of Indian Affairs, February 8, 1936, File 9698A, and George P. LaVatta, Field Agent, to Commissioner of Indian Affairs, November 8, 1938, File 9698, NARA, Entry 1011. There were more than 300

Puyallups on the Agency records, but LaVatta found only five of them on the reservation. The rest were "scattered throughout the Pacific northwest," mainly in urban areas. "[M]ost of these Indians think, act and live as individuals instead of as a group or tribe." They were nonetheless approved for tribal organization under *IRA* section 16. So, too, were the Suquamish, although only 10 percent of them could be found on the reservation. LaVatta, Memorandum to Mr. Meiklejohn, March 28, 1940, File 9698, NARA, Entry 1011.

[11]George P. LaVatta, Field Agent, to Commissioner of Indian Affairs, March 19, 1938, File 9698, NARA, Entry 1011. Some uncertainty remained as to the status of the Nooksacks until 1971, however, when the Solicitor's Office held that they satisfied the so-called Cohen criteria for recognition as an Indian tribe. Op.Sol.Int. M–36833 (August 13, 1971).

[12]Nathan A. Margold, Solicitor, Memorandum to the Commissioner of Indian Affairs, December 13, 1938, NARA, CCF, Quapaw Agency, File 10652.

[13]H.A. Andrews, Superintendent, Quapaw Agency, to A.C. Monahan, Regional Coordinator, February 15, 1938; same to the Commissioner, January 31, 1939. NARA, CCF, Quapaw Agency, File 10652.

[14]William Zimmerman, Assistant Commissioner, Memorandum to Daiker, April 18, 1939; Kenneth Meiklejohn, Assistant Solicitor, Memorandum to [Division of] Indian Organization, February 25, 1939; and Oscar L. Chapman, Assistant Secretary of the Interior, to H.A. Andrews, August 16, 1939. NARA, CCF, Quapaw Agency, File 10652.

[15]Typed "Memorandum" signed "Collier," April 22, 1936, NARA, Entry 191 (Office Files of Joseph McGaskill), Box 9, File "Study—Lousiana Indians."

[16]*Joint Tribal Council of the Passamaquoddy Tribe* v. *Morton,* 388 F.Supp. 649 (D.Me. 1975), affirmed on appeal, 528 F.2d 370 (1st Cir. 1975). But the United States did not contest the Passamaquoddies' claim that they were racially and culturally Indian.

[17]*Handbook* (1942 ed.), at 140–141. Cohen's criteria were applied as recently as 1972, when the Bureau concluded that the Sauk-Suiattle and Upper Skagits of Washington State were "recognized" because a cemetery had been purchased for them under authority of a 1913 act of Congress. John O. Crow, Deputy Commissioner of Indian Affairs, to Representative Lloyd Meeds, June 8, 1972.

[18]Russel Barsh, "The BIA Reorganization Follies of 1978: A Lesson in Bureaucratic Self-Defense," *American Indian Law Review* 7(1):1–50 (1980), and "Progressive-Era Bureaucrats and the Unity of Twentieth-Century Indian Policy," *American Indian Quarterly* 15(1):1–17 (1991).

[19]Indeed, there was no official list of recognized Indian tribes at the Bureau's central office as late as 1966, when Patricia Simmons, a long-time employee working in tribal enrolment, was asked to compile a list of tribal groups "based on a review of the files." She relied chiefly on whether there was any recent record of correspondence with the group. *Greene* v. *Babbitt,* Hearing Transcript, 347–349.

[20]*Oneida Indian Nation* v. *County of Oneida,* 414 U.S. 661 (1974).

[21]*United States* v. *Washington,* 384 F.Supp. 312 (W.D.Wash. 1974).

[22]Senator Henry M. Jackson to Secretary of the Interior, December 7, 1973; Morris Thompson, Commissioner of Indian Affairs to Jackson, January 15, 1974, Jackson Papers, Box 47, File 9.

[23]LaFollette Butler, Acting Deputy Commissioner of Indian Affairs to Senator Jackson, June 7, 1974, Jackson Papers, Box 47, File 9; Morris Thompson, Commissioner of Indian Affairs, to Lloyd Meeds, Chairman of the House Subcommittee on Indian Affairs, April 10,

1974. Checklists using the Cohen criteria had already been distributed to Bureau personnel assigned to reviewing the status of Northwest groups.

[24]Doyce Waldrip, Bureau of Indian Affairs, to Commissioner of Indian Affairs, "Progress Report on Issues involved in implementing U.S. v. Washington," April 23, 1974. The total request was for $1.5 million.

[25]*Greene* v. *Babbitt,* Deposition of Reid Chambers, December 26, 1993, at 14–17 [hereafter Chambers dep.]; David H. Getches, Native American Rights Fund, to Senator Jackson, April 29, 1975. The Bureau was given an additional $125,000 later that year for the "recognition" of Northwest tribes but remained paralysed. Les Gay, [Tribal Operations,] to Ted [Krenzke], October 3, 1974. But in 1976, OMB was again recommending a moratorium on recognizing any more tribes, as well as a gradual phase-out of federal benefits. Howard G. Borgstrom, Interior Branch, Natural Resources Division OMB to Mr. Mitchell, April 19, 1976, at 4.

[26]Reid Chambers, Associate Solicitor—Indian Affairs, to Solicitor, "Secretary's Authority to Extend Federal Recognition to Indian Tribes," August 20, 1974. Chambers later advised Senator Jackson that a treaty was still "a prime indicator of recognition." Chambers to Jackson, May 2, 1975, Jackson Papers, Box 58, File 6.

[27]David H. Getches, Native American Rights Fund, to Senator Jackson, September 4, 1974, Jackson Papers, Box 47, File 8, and "Memorandum to the files Re: Federal recognition for tribes in Western Washington, Feb 12, 1975" [referring to pressure from the Tulalip Tribes].

[28]Les Gay, [Tribal Operations,] to Ted [Krenzke], October 3, 1974.

[29]Morris Thompson, Commissioner, to Lewis A. Bell, Everett, February 18, 1975; Kent Frizzell, Solicitor, to Bell, February 26, 1975.

[30]"[T]he law with respect to recognition is unclear and standards and procedures…have never been established. Accordingly, this Office has undertaken a general legal study of the concept of recognition in order to aid in the development of such standards." Kent Frizzell, Solicitor, to Jackson, May 22, 1975, Jackson Papers, Box 58, File 5.

[31]The decision was worded ("acknowledge that the Stillaguamish Tribe of Indians is an Indian tribe and extend to it federal recognition") in such a way as to dodge the issue of authority to recognize any new tribes. Kent Frizzell, Acting Assistant Secretary of the Interior, to David H. Getches, Native American Rights Fund, November 1, 1976.

[32]Indeed, after press reports that the Passamaquoddies had been recognized, the Ford Administration went to great lengths to deny it. Howard G. Borgstrom, Interior Branch, Natural Resources Division, OMB, to Mr. Mitchell, "Article in Post on Federal Recognition of Maine Tribes," May 11, 1976.

[33]Chambers dep. at 14–17; *Greene* v. *Babbitt,* Deposition of Scott Fitzmorris Keep, December 17, 1993 [hereafter Keep dep.] at 81–86.

[34]Keep dep. at 116–119. The Miami Tribe unsuccessfully sought a Federal court order to disclose the text of this memorandum. *Miami Nation of Indiana* v. *Babbitt,* 887 F.Supp. 1158 (N.D.Ind. 1995).

[35]Dysart subsequently objected to recognition of the Duwamish Tribe, which the Bureau had concluded satisfied the Cohen formula, contending that it would undermine his arguments to the court. George D. Dysart, Assistant Regional Solicitor, Portland, to Donald R. Wharton, Division of Indian Affairs, "Duwamish Fishing Rights," August 23, 1977.

[36]*Greene* v. *Babbitt,* Deposition of John A. Shapard Jr., December 18, 1993 [hereafter Shapard dep.] at 107, 135.

[37]*Ibid.* 135. Shapard speculated that the rejection of Les Gay's draft had come from Associate Solicitor Reid Chambers. *Ibid.* at 9 and 109. However, Chambers recalled defending the Cohen formula against a "more restrictive" approach urged by Dysart, and he had assumed that his views were upheld by the lawyers he supervised. Chambers dep. at 4–5, 8–9, 19–21, 25, 59, 72–74, 80–83, 104–105. He left government in 1976.

[38]Susan Kemnitzer, Natural Resources Division OMB, Memorandum to the Director, "S. 2801, Siletz Restoration Act," March 29, 1976.

[39]Raymond V. Butler, Acting Commissioner, to Legislative Counsel, "Restoration of terminated Indian tribes," February 25, 1977.

[40]"Statement of Hazel E. Elbert, Acting Deputy Assistant Secretary for Indian Affairs, Department of the Interior, Before the Hearing of the Committee on Interior and Insular Affairs, U.S. House of Representatives, on H.R. 1344," October 17, 1985.

[41]*American Indian Policy Review Commission Final Report* (Washington, D.C., 1977), at 479. Established by an act of Congress, the Commission consisted of Congressmen and Indian leaders.

[42]*Ibid.* 481–82. Legislation implementing these recommendations was introduced in 1978, but set aside after the Bureau promised to address the Commission's concerns administratively. See *Recognition of Certain Indian Tribes: Hearing on S. 2375 Before the Senate Select Committee on Indian Affairs,* 95th Congress 2d Session (1978). Since the Bureau had already decided internally to discard the Cohen criteria, it could not allow Congress to legislate Cohen in S. 2375.

[43]25 U.S.C. 2 and 9; 43 U.S.C. 1457.

[44]25 C.F.R. 83.7(b) and (c).

[45]William A. Starna, "The Southeast Syndrome: The Prior Restraint of a Non-Event," *American Indian Quarterly* 15(4):493–502 (1991); Russel L. Barsh, "Federal Acknowledgment of Indian Tribes: A Challenge for Anthropologists?" *Practicing Anthropology* 10(2):2 (1988); Jack Campisi, *The Mashpee Indians: Tribe on Trial* (Syracuse: Syracuse University Press, 1991).

[46]*United States* v. *Washington,* 476 F.Supp. 1101 (W.D.Wash. 1979), affirmed 641 F.2d 1368, 1371 (9th Cir. 1981) (noting that Dysart's proposed findings and conclusions had been adopted verbatim by the district court).

[47]See "Order Denying Motion by Duwamish, Snohomish and Steilacoom Indian Tribes to Reopen Judgment Under Rule 60(b)," *United States* v. *Washington,* No. 9213–R, Subproceeding 93–2, U.S. District Court, Western District of Washington, January 23, 1995.

[48]"Summary Status of Acknowledgment Cases as of February 6, 2001," available from BAR's web page www.doi.gov/bia/bar. In addition, one petitioner was recognized by Secretarial action without any findings by BAR (Ione Band of Miwoks), and one regained its status through a court-ordered hearing before an administrative law judge (Samish). Two other rejected petitioners have tried to overturn BAR's findings in court. One failed, *Miami Nation of Indiana* v. *Babbitt,* 112 F.Supp.2d 742 (N.D.Ind. 2000), and the other, involving the Ramapough Mountain Indians, a small community of Afro-Indian families in northern New Jersey with documented roots to the eighteenth century, is still in litigation.

[49]*Shapard dep., supra* note 36 at 7; "anybody in the branch could have done it," *ibid.* at 8.

[50]*Ibid.* at 8.

[51]*Ibid.* at 9–10; also see 107–9, 115–16, 119, 121, 135. Shapard described his task as one of "compromise" in which "We ended up making a camel…sorta by committee." *Ibid.*

133–134.

[52]*Ibid.* 59, 135–36. Shapard noted that he did not supervise what Roth was doing because of his own lack of expertise. *Ibid.* 68, 88–89, 123. "I'm not sure how George does whatever he does." *Ibid.* 83.

[53]The same criteria and procedures were followed even in cases where there was evidence that the group had once been recognized by a treaty or legislation, however. *Shapard dep.* at 21–22, 53–54.

[54]In actuality, there was no peer review of BAR research other than informal circulation of drafts within the office. *Ibid.* 23–25.

[55]*Shapard dep.* at 26–29. Shapard noted pressure from other Bureau employees who, as members of Indian tribes, opposed the recognition of more tribes. *Ibid.* 28, 31–33, 101–3, 114.

[56]"By my count the 1978 original regulations contained 35 phrases that required a subjective determination by the evaluator and the petitioner. The 1994 revised…regulations …more than doubled the areas that required a subjective determination." Shapard quoted in *House Report No. 103–782,* 103rd Congress 2d Session (1994) at 16. Also see *Shapard dep.* 15–19, 40, 87, 101.

[57]*Shapard dep.* 39, 101. "I realize [now] I wasn't smart enough to write the regs." *Ibid.* 18.

[58]*Ibid.* 29, 47.

[59]Les Gay to Bud Shapard, January 1983 [holograph letter]. Gay had already retired, but was given a short-term contract to evaluate BAR.

[60]Rachael Paschal, "The Imprimatur of Recognition: American Indian Tribes and the Federal Acknowledgment Process," *Washington Law Review* 66(1):209–228 (1991); Susan Greenbaum, "Federal Acknowledgment and the Quest for Tribal Community," Paper presented at the annual meeting of the American Society for Ethnohistory, Chicago, November 4, 1989; "Written Testimony before the Senate Committee on Indian Affairs, May 23, 1995, Submitted by Christine Grabowski, Ph.D." Shapard estimated that it cost BAR an average of $250,000 to process each case and noted that the output had dropped from 1.3 to 0.5 decisions per year. House Report 103–782, *supra* note 56 at 16.

[61]Greenbaum, "Federal Acknowledgment," *ibid.* at 10. BAR recently decided that its staff will engage in no collateral research whatsoever, and prepare no internal technical reports. "Changes in the Internal Processing of Federal Acknowledgment Petitions," 65 *Fed.Reg.* 7052 (February 11, 2000). This change will increase the research burden on petitioners, while rendering BAR's own thinking more obscure.

[62]Grabowski, "Written Statement," *supra* note 60.

[63]Greenbaum, "Federal Acknowledgment," *supra* note 60 at 4.

[64]*Ibid.,* at 7.

[65]*Federal Acknowledgment Process: Hearing Before the Senate Select Committee on Indian Affairs,* 100th Congress 2d Session (1988), at 42–52, 98, 129, 178; *Federal Acknowledgment Administrative Procedures Act of 1989: Hearing on S.611 Before the Senate Select Committee on Indian Affairs,* Part 2, 101st Congress 1st Session (1989), at 168, 176, 183. Aboriginally, Indian groups usually overlapped; the social insularity of contemporary reservation Indian tribes is a consequence of federal laws and policies. Grabowski, "Written Testimony," *supra* note 60 at 7.

[66]*Greene* v. *Babbit,* No. Indian 93–1, Proceedings Held before David Torbett Adminis-

trative Law Judge, August 22–30, 1994 [hereafter Greene hearing], at 663–65.

[67]*Ibid.* 728; *Shapard dep.* 83. *Mashpee Tribe* v. *New Seabury Corp.*, 592 F.2d 575, 583, cert. denied 444 U.S. 866 (1980), refers to this model approvingly.

[68]*Greene hearing*, at 42, 59–62, 74–75, 78. A community "tends to be broader in membership than a group of people related by marriage," he added, "and more permanent and broader in its interests than a social club or professional association." *Ibid.* 41.

[69]*Ibid.* 66.

[70]*Ibid.* 66–67, 71, 125–26, 149. On the salience of kinship in modern Indian communities, also see the testimony of Dr. Wayne Suttles at 223–24, and of Dr. Anthony Paredes at 298–99.

[71]*Ibid.* 69–70. In the Pacific Northwest, at least, Indian communities were never isolated socially. *Ibid.* 200 [Suttles].

[72]This factor was present in the Grand Traverse, Jamestown Klallam, and Poarch Creek cases, all of which resulted in positive decisions; and its absence was underscored in the negative recommendations on Samish, Snohomish, and Tchinouk. Paschal, "Federal Acknowledgment," *supra* note 60 at 224.

[73]*Greene hearing*, at 618–619, 755. The Bureau's expert witness, Dr. Anthony Paredes, was more emphatic about the significance of an actual settlement. *Ibid.* 307–309.

[74]Summary Under the Criteria and Evidence for Final Determination for Federal Acknowledgment of the Mohegan Tribe of Indians of the State of Connecticut, March 7, 1994 [hereafter *Mohegan*], at 12–14.

[75]Summary Under the Criteria and Evidence for Proposed Finding for Federal Acknowledgment of the Snoqualmie Indian Tribe, April 26, 1993 [hereafter *Snoqualmie*], at 8, 11–12. Nearly identical facts were deemed insignificant in the Samish case, however.

[76]Summary Under the Criteria and Evidence for Final Determination against Federal Acknowledgment of the Miami Nation of Indians of the State of Indiana, Inc., March 7, 1994 [hereafter *Miami*], at 7.

[77]Recommendation and summary of evidence for proposed finding for Federal acknowledgment of the Grand Traverse Band of Ottawa and Chippewa Indians, October 3, 1979 [hereafter *Grand Traverse*], at A19; Recommendation and summary of evidence for proposed findings for Federal acknowledgment of the Death Valley Timbi-Sha Shoshone Band of Indians of California, February 9, 1982 [hereafter *Timbi-Sha Shoshone*], at A22; Recommendation and summary of evidence for proposed finding for Federal acknowledgment of the Tunica-Biloxi Indian Tribe of Louisiana, December 4, 1980 [hereafter *Tunica-Biloxi*], at A14, A19, A23; Recommendation and Summary of Evidence for Proposed Finding for Federal Acknowledgment of the Narragansett Indian Tribe of Rhode Island, July 29, 1982 [hereafter *Narragansett*], at 10; *Snoqualmie* at 9, 11–13, 18; *Mohegan* at 12–15. In *Snoqualmie* and *Mohegan*, BAR even excused evidence that participation in these activities had declined since the 1950s.

[78]*Miami* at 22.

[79]*Greene hearing*, at 855–578, 1051, 1055. Since regaining their legal status in 1996, the Samish have hosted a number of large potlatches and conducted several "burnings," ceremonies for feeding ancestral spirits.

[80]*Ibid.* 579–80.

[81]*Snoqualmie* at A3. Scarcely three years later, BAR criticized the use of oral historical evidence by the Duwamish, who had employed the same anthropologist as the Snoqualmies.

[82]*Miami,* Technical Report, at 12.

[83]*Greene hearing,* at 551–52, 977–82. Snohomish conducted surveys and extensive standardized interviews in preparing its response to an adverse Proposed Finding, but this material has not yet been submitted to BAR. Shapard did not recall his staff ever attempting quantitative research of their own. *Shapard dep.* 90–91.

[84]Lynn Forcia, "Technical Report."

[85]*Tunica-Biloxi* at 3, A24.

[86]Recommendation and summary of evidence for proposed finding for Federal acknowledgment of the Jamestown Band of Clallam Indians of Washington, May 16, 1980 [hereafter *Jamestown],* at A16–A17.

[87]*Mohegan* at 121–65. Samish had a similar conflict in the 1970s, but Roth interpreted it as a sign that there were really two distinct groups, "Indian descendants" and real Samish. *Greene hearing,* at 581.

[88]*Snoqualmie* at 11, 14. Ironically, the Snoqualmies split into two hostile groups shortly after this decision, leading to litigation and an award of punitive damages against a former chairman. There are now two councils, operating out of separate offices.

[89]Grabowski, "Written Testimony," *supra* note 60 at 5; *Shapard dep.* 41–49.

[90]Roth was entrusted with resolving differences of interpretation between himself and petitioners' anthropologists. *Shapard dep.* 49, 85, 129; also Greenbaum, "Federal Acknowledgment," *supra* note 60 at 12.

[91]Recommendation and Summary of Evidence for Proposed Findings Against Federal Acknowledgment of the Samish Indian Tribe, October 27, 1982 [hereafter *Samish],* at 4, 6, 11–13, 16–17. Note the insertion of the term "tribal" as a qualifier of "community." Obviously a "tribe" is mono-ethnic!

[92]Recommendation and Summary of Evidence for Proposed Finding Against Federal Acknowledgment of the Snohomish Tribe of Indians, Inc., March 16, 1983 [hereafter *Snohomish],* at 10–11.

[93]*Snoqualmie* at 13.

[94]*Mohegan* at 11, 15.

[95]*Jamestown* at A23; *Timbi-Sha Shoshone* at G9.

[96]*Tunica-Biloxi* at A23. BAR subsequently argued in *Miami,* Technical Report, at 6–7, that the geographical dispersal of the Timbi-Sha and Tunicas was offset by their high degree of marriage inside the group.

[97]Recommendation and summary of evidence for proposed finding for Federal acknowledgment of the Poarch Band of Creeks of Alabama, December 29, 1983 [hereafter *Poarch Creek],* at 1. The Poarch Creeks' anthropologist had been Dr. Paredes, who paradoxically later testified in *Greene* that mixed marriages inevitably erode community solidarity. *Greene hearing,* at 300–302, 317.

[98]*Chambers dep.* 88–89. BAR imported the phrase "historical times to present" from 25 C.F.R. 83.7(a), which requires evidence that the group has been "identified as American Indian" throughout history.

[99]Compare *Samish* at 11, and *Snohomish* at 12–13, with *Mohegan* at 11–12, *Grand Traverse* at A14–A15, *Tunica-Biloxi* at A18, *Poarch Creek* at A31, and *Timbi-Sha Shoshone* at A16, A20.

[100]S. 479, introduced by Senator John McCain in the 104th Congress; *Shapard dep.* 20, 22, 124.

[101]Wilford G. Bowker to Deputy Assistant Secretary—Indian Affairs (Operations), "Klamath Restoration Bill—H.R. 3554," April 1, 1986.

[102]*House Report 103–782, supra* note 56 at 16.

[103]Public Law 102–416, 106 Stat. 2131 (October 14, 1992). Thus far the advisory council has argued that California Indian societies were more disrupted, and less studied than tribes elsewhere, making it more difficult for them to satisfy the FAP criteria. "Testimony of Stephen V. Quesenberry, California Indian Legal Services, on S. 479, Before the United States Senate Committee on Indian Affairs, May 23, 1995."

[104]*Congressional Record* S3283 (February 28, 1995).

[105]"Formal adjudicatory proceedings [are] inappropriate for complex, research-based decisions of this nature," and would ultimately involve increased delays and expenses. "Statement of Michael Anderson, Deputy Assistant Secretary-Indian Affairs, Department of the Interior, Before the Senate Committee on Indian Affairs on S. 479," July 13, 1995, at 4. The situation remained unchanged at the time of my most recent opportunity to meet with the staff of the Senate Committee on Indian Affairs in June 2000.

[106]"Prepared Statement of Gaiashkibos, President, National Congress of American Indians, Before the Senate Committee on Indian Affairs, July 13, 1995," at 1.

[107]E.g., Roy H. Sampsel, Deputy Assistant Secretary of the Interior, to William S. Cohen, Chairman, Senate Select Committee on Indian Affairs, September 27, 1982 [regarding Cow Creek]; Kenneth L. Smith, Assistant Secretary of the Interior, to Morris K. Udall, Chairman, House Committee on Interior and Insular Affairs, October 25, 1983 [regarding Grande Ronde].

[108]*Elk* v. *Wilkins,* 112 U.S. 94 (1884); 25 U.S.C. 182–185 (regarding lineal descent and the severance of tribal relations).

[109]25 U.S.C. 479; 1 Op.Sol.Int. 1026 (January 29, 1941).

[110]J.M. Stewart, Chief, Land Division to H.E. Bruce, Superintendent, Potawatomi Agency, March 2, 1935. NARA, Potawatomi Agency, File 4598. Bureau personnel themselves were wary of the accuracy of blood-degrees appearing on tribal rolls. E.g., H.A. Andrews, Superintendent, Quapaw Agency to Commissioner of Indian Affairs, September 13, 1934 [Bessie Elliott]. NARA, Quapaw Agency, Box 4, File 39587. Sturtevant echoed this concern in the *Greene* case. *Greene hearing,* at 106–107.

[111]*Morton* v. *Mancari,* 417 U.S. 535, 554 (1974). S. 12 granted preference in civil service appointments to "Indians," interpreted by the Bureau as meaning the members of Indian tribes. A more recent application of this principle is *Rice* v. *Cayetano,* 120 S.Ct. 1044, 528 U.S. — (2000) (eligibility to vote for members of Hawaii state board entrusted with Native Hawaiian affairs cannot constitutionally be limited to persons of Indigenous Hawaiian ancestry).

[112]The Supreme Court has concluded that Indian tribes are not bound by the Bill of Rights and can discriminate among their members in ways that would be impermissible for the Federal or State governments. See *Santa Clara Pueblo* v. *Martinez,* 436 U.S. 49 (1978).

[113]*Shapard dep.* 94; also 95–97, 128. Personally, Shapard still believed that blood-quantum was a useful indicator, 125–26; Chambers stated that he would not have approved a blood-quantum test in the FAP regulations. *Chambers dep.* 109.

[114]*Greene hearing,* at 713–15, 717.

[115]*Ibid.* 318, 322, 328–33, 335. The only study he recalled was Deward Walker Jr., "Measures of Nez Perce Outbreeding and the Analysis of Cultural Change," *Southwestern*

Journal of Anthropology 23(2):141–58 (1967), which merely proposed the usefulness of pursuing research along these lines.

[116]*Greene hearing*, at 105–9, 130–33 [Sturtevant], and at 864–67, 912–14, 998–99 [Dr. Yvonne Hajda]. For an excellent critical review of race and identity see Susan Greenbaum, "What's in a Label? Identity Problems of Southern Indian Tribes," *Journal of Ethnic Studies* 19(2):107–26 (1991).

[117]Assistant Secretary of the Interior-Indian Affairs, Final Determination To Acknowledge the Samish Tribal Organization As a Tribe, November 8, 1995, at 6–7.

[118]See *Morton* v. *Ruiz,* 415 U.S. 199 (1974).

[119]*Greene* v. *Babbitt,* 64 F.3d 1266 (9th Cir. 1995); Delaware Tribal Business Committee v. Weeks, 430 U.S. 73 (1977). Even Congress, if it resolves to terminate the legal status of an Indian tribe, must do so in clear and unambiguous terms. *Menominee Tribe* v. *United States,* 391 U.S. 404, 412 (1968).

[120]Ross Swimmer, Assistant Secretary—Indian Affairs, to Alfred S. Kennedy, Chairman of the Burns Paiute Tribal Council, August 18, 1988; Hazel E. Elbert, Deputy to the Assistant Secretary—Indian Affairs, to Senator Mark O. Hatfield, September 20, 1988.

[121]Op.Sol. M36759 (November 16, 1967), reversing 2 Op.Sol.Int. 1394 (May 31, 1946).

[122]Wyman Babby, Acting Assistant Secretary—Indian Affairs, to Rep. George Miller, Chairman, House Committee on Natural Resources, January 14, 1994. The Bureau also contended that residence on a reservation is required for the members of "non-historic tribes" to vote in tribal elections.

[123]One group that was not identified as "non-historic" was the Tulalip Tribes, despite the fact that Keep had cooperated with their lawyers and was familiar with their history. As Superintendent Raymond H. Bitney reminded the Commissioner by letter of November 28, 1953, "There is no Tulalip Tribe has never has been." Rather, Tulalip was organized as "a community group...of the people with Indian blood who reside on the Tulalip Reservation." It was on this basis that the United States successfully opposed Tulalip participation in the Indian Claims Commission process. ICC Docket 262, dismissed January 13, 1958.

[124]*Sandra Thomas* v. *United States,* No. 96–C–828, U.S. District Court for the Western District of Wisconsin. Pleadings obtained courtesy of Tracey Schwalbe, attorney for the plaintiffs.

[125]These issues get further attention in chapter 8, where the authors consider the application of the test for proof of Aboriginal rights to the case of a Métis right of self-government.

Chapter Seven

When Is a Métis an Indian?

Some Consequences of Federal Constitutional Jurisdiction over Métis

Dale Gibson

Introduction

Although the Supreme Court of Canada has not yet ruled on the question, there seems little doubt that the Parliament of Canada's jurisdiction with respect to "Indians and Lands reserved for the Indians" under section 91(24) of the *Constitution Act, 1867* extends to the Métis.[1]

The view of the Royal Commission on Aboriginal Peoples (RCAP) and most academic opinion supports this view. In the writer's opinion, the evidence upon which this conclusion is based is quite sufficient to put the matter to rest,[2] although there is certainly room for further academic research into the meaning of "Indians" under section 91(24).[3]

On that assumption, this chapter addresses the second stage of the section 91(24) question: what are some of the *consequences* of federal jurisdiction over the Métis?

Not every consequence of that assumption will, or could possibly, be examined here, of course, but three implications of major importance will be considered:

1. Unconstitutional *discrimination* against Métis people by the federal government;

2. The *fiduciary duty* owed to Métis people by the federal government; and

3. Overlapping *provincial jurisdiction* with respect to Métis people.

258

The chapter will conclude with a brief examination of the jurisdictional implications of section 35 of the *Constitution Act, 1982,* and the relationship between section 91(24) and section 35 in terms of litigation strategy.

Federal Discrimination Against Métis

The Government of Canada discriminates against the Métis people in many ways. Two examples of such discrimination will be examined to illustrate the general problem, as well as to indicate the type of constitutional relief I believe to be available. In both cases section 91(24) is important to the analysis.

Unequal Treatment of Métis Displaced from Primrose Lake Weapons Range

In 1953–1954 the Government of Canada established, at the behest of the United States government and in cooperation with the governments of Alberta and Saskatchewan, an air weapons testing range in a 4,500 square mile (11,650 km²) area in the northern part of those provinces. This necessitated the removal from that vast territory of all humans who either lived there or used the area for trapping, logging, hunting, fishing, or gathering. A high proportion of those displaced were Aboriginal persons, both Indian and Métis. The lifestyles of the Indian and Métis persons affected were substantially identical.

Although some compensation was paid to all who were displaced, it was far from adequate, and it was significantly less for Métis than for registered Indians. Complaints about the inadequacy of compensation eventually led to consideration by the Indian Claims Commission, under the federal government's Specific Claims Policy, of claims for supplementary compensation by displaced Indians from the Canoe Lake Cree Nation and the Cold Lake First Nation. The Commission recommended that substantial additional compensation be paid,[4] and the Government of Canada has accepted and acted on that recommendation.[5]

Representatives of Métis people displaced by the weapons range requested similar treatment in communications to the Indian Claims Commission, the Minister of Indian Affairs and Northern Development, and the Prime Minister of Canada, but no such relief was forthcoming. The Indian Claims Commission pointed out that its jurisdiction does not extend beyond claims on behalf of Indians, and the federal government adopted its traditional stance that Métis are not its responsibility.[6]

Litigation commenced against these federal authorities on behalf of Métis displaced from the weapons range is based, in part, on a claim that discrimination between the plaintiffs and the Indians to whom the government has agreed to give extra compensation violates section 15(1) of the *Charter of Rights and*

Freedoms by discriminating on the basis of race and ethnic origin. In order to succeed in a discrimination claim, those who assert it must establish that the group that has been discriminated against is comparable in all relevant respects to the group that has been favoured. In this case, the government will likely take the position that the displaced Métis are not comparable to the displaced Indians because Parliament's special jurisdiction over Indians under section 91(24) of the Constitution is not applicable to Métis.

The position adopted by RCAP and others who contend for the application of section 91(24) to Métis is therefore crucial to this aspect of the Primrose Weapons Range case. Since that position is constitutionally strong, in my opinion, prospects seem good for the Métis claimants.

Discrimination Against Métis Descendants Re *Indian Act* Status

Sections 6(1)(a) and 6(1)(f) of the *Indian Act* entitle persons to be registered under the *Act* if, among other things, they or their parents were so entitled immediately prior to April 17, 1985. The pre-April 1985 legislation set out a number of entitlement qualifications based on ancestral connections, along with a few overriding *dis*qualifications. One of those disqualifications applied to "a descendant of a person" who "has received or has been allotted half-breed lands or money scrip."[7]

This, I submit, is discrimination on the basis of race or ethnic origin. While it is true that not everyone who accepted Métis land or scrip was Métis, the majority probably were, so the exclusion has a disparate adverse impact on Métis people, and is therefore discriminatory.[8] In any event, the Supreme Court of Canada has held that discrimination on the "analogous" ground of marital status violates the equality guarantee entrenched in section 15 of the *Charter*,[9] and it seems probable that the courts will also treat discrimination based on family status, such as the "descendant" provision of the pre-1985 *Indian Act*, in a similar fashion if called upon to do so.

If an equality-based *Charter* challenge to the Métis disqualification were brought before the courts, the government could be expected to raise at least three lines of defence.

1. That the equality guarantees in section 15 of the *Charter*, which did not come into force until April 17, 1985, cannot be used to attack the Métis disqualification provision, because that provision was repealed simultaneously with section 15 coming into effect;

2. That there are relevant differences between Métis scrip-takers and other Aboriginals that justify treating them differently; and

3. That even if the Métis disqualification is discriminatory it is justifiable under section 1 of the *Charter*, as a "reasonable limit" in a "free and democratic society."

None of these defences would be likely to succeed.

The equality guarantee of the *Charter* would be applicable, in my opinion, because even though the *explicit* reference to Métis scrip disappeared from the *Indian Act* the same moment section 15 came into force, it remained *operative* thereafter through the legislative device of "incorporation by reference" in the statute. A very recent decision of the Federal Court of Canada, Trial Division, ruled (subject to possible justification under section 1 of the *Charter* or section 35 of the *Constitution Act, 1982)* that section 15 of the *Charter* voided a provision of the *Indian Act* that, like sections 6(1)(a) and 6(1)(f), had the adverse impact of perpetuating a loss of status (birth-band membership in that case) that was initially inflicted long before section 15 was in operation.[10] A similar conclusion would seem likely here.

Alternatively, the provision could be attacked as a violation of the equality guarantees of the *Canadian Bill of Rights, 1960,* which was in force before April 1985,[11] or of freedom of association and expression under the *Charter*, which were also constitutionally entrenched before 1985.[12]

The defence that the descendants of Métis scrip-takers are relevantly different from the Indians who are granted status under section 6 of the *Indian Act* could be met, as in the weapons range situation, by showing that both groups are "Indians" within the meaning of section 91(24) of the Constitution.

The third possible defence—that the Métis disqualification is a "reasonable limit" on *Charter* rights—would also fail, in my opinion. Those who rely on the reasonable limit defence must show, among other things, that there is a "rational connection" between the purpose of the limit and the restriction of *Charter* rights. In this case, the apparent purpose of the restriction was to extinguish possible Métis claims of Aboriginal title to land.[13] Since status under the *Indian Act* does not, in itself, entitle anyone to land rights, there is no rational connection between that purpose and disqualifying Métis scrip-takers and their descendants for *Indian Act* status. Moreover, there was so much fraud and maladministration involved in the distribution of Métis land and scrip that it would be ludicrous to rely on their receipt as a "reasonable" justification for anything.[14]

I conclude, therefore, that the discrimination against the descendants of Métis scrip-takers under section 6 of the *Indian Act* stands a good chance of being struck down by the courts if challenged under section 15 of the *Charter*. If so, the number of persons entitled to the medical and other benefits currently available to status Indians under the *Indian Act* would expand dramatically.

Federal Fiduciary Obligation to Métis

Another extremely important ramification of federal jurisdiction over Métis under section 91(24) of the Constitution is that the special "fiduciary," trust-like obligation that the Government of Canada owes to all Aboriginal persons includes the Métis. This duty has been described as follows by the Supreme Court of Canada.

> The Government has the responsibility to act in a fiduciary capacity in respect to Aboriginal peoples. That relationship is trust-like, rather than adversarial, and contemporary recognition and affirmation of Aboriginal rights must be defined in light of this historic relationship."[15]

If the federal government's responsibility for "Indians and Lands reserved for the Indians" under section 91(24) of the *Constitution Act, 1867* embraces all Aboriginal peoples, including the Métis, as asserted at the outset of this chapter, it follows that this fiduciary obligation is also owed to the Métis. The Royal Commission on Aboriginal Peoples concluded that this is so.

> Does the fiduciary obligation apply to Métis peoples? It appears that it does. It will be recalled, first, that the Supreme Court of Canada was careful in *Sparrow* to describe it as a duty owed to Aboriginal peoples, not just to Indian people, and the court did this with full knowledge that section 35(2) now defines Aboriginal peoples to include Métis. Moreover, it seems clear that although section 91(24), enacted in 1867, refers expressly only to Indians, that term embraces *all* Aboriginal peoples, including the Métis."[16]

The implications of applying the federal fiduciary duty to the Métis are suggested in the following comment by RCAP.

> What does the fiduciary obligation entail? It certainly means that the governments must do nothing that would interfere with the free exercise of existing Aboriginal rights. That negative obligation clearly applies to both federal and provincial governments. There is good reason to believe that at least the federal government, in which section 91(24) vests authority over Aboriginal matters, also has a positive obligation to take steps necessary to the full realization of existing Aboriginal rights....
>
> Although the full implications of the federal government's positive obligations respecting existing Aboriginal rights cannot be catalogued, it is possible to speculate about some of them. Where there are Métis groups with whom treaties or claim settlements were never completed, it seems clear that the government of Canada is obliged to initiate negotiations. If the exclusion of Métis groups from treaty or settlement negotiations in which they should have been included has resulted in harm to Métis

interests, the government of Canada is probably obliged by its fiduciary duty to compensate Métis groups for such harm. If the realization of a particular Métis Aboriginal right requires legislative enactment, Parliament may well have an obligation to enact suitable legislation. While the courts may not be empowered to order Parliament to fulfil a legislative obligation, they clearly have the power to order compliance with the Constitution by the Crown and its subordinates. Even Parliament may be subject to declaratory rulings of the courts, which can have a powerful political impact."[17]

Provincial Jurisdiction Not Diminished

The province of Alberta has taken major steps to provide benefits for the Métis people of that province. Eight Métis settlements, established on Crown land set aside for that purpose by the provincial government, provide a land base for many Alberta Métis, and self-government is gradually evolving under the umbrella of provincial legislation: the *Métis Settlements Act*[18] and related statutes and regulations.

Concern is sometimes expressed that federal jurisdiction over Métis might imply that provincial authorities have no such jurisdiction, and that provincial initiatives like Alberta's *Métis Settlements Act* would therefore be nullified. In the writer's opinion, this is not a significant problem.

It has long been acknowledged as a basic principle of Canadian constitutional law that although the various heads of jurisdiction bestowed on the Parliament of Canada and the provincial legislatures by the *Constitution Act, 1867* are all stated to be "exclusive," they are in fact overlapping in nature. This is a consequence of the fact that most heads of jurisdiction, both federal and provincial, are expressed in general words of sweeping import, and that most legislative topics therefore have aspects falling under both federal and provincial jurisdiction. To deal with this situation, the courts have developed an approach called the "dual aspect doctrine," according to which each order of government may deal with those aspects of a particular legislative subject which fall within its purview. The federal and provincial statutes may continue to function side-by-side unless they are mutually inconsistent. If there is an inconsistency, the federal legislation prevails, but only to the extent of the inconsistency.[19]

The *Métis Settlements Act* of Alberta and similar provincial laws and arrangements designed to benefit the Métis population of a province are valid exercises of provincial power in relation to such undoubted areas of provincial competence as "the management and sale of the public lands belonging to the province" [section 92(5)]; "property and civil rights" [section 92(13)]; and "matters of a merely local or private nature" [section 92(16)]. Since nothing in the provincial legislation conflicts with federal legislation, there is no reason to fear that it would be overridden.

What If the Assumption Is Wrong?

As noted earlier, this chapter is rooted in the assumption that Métis are "Indians" within the meaning of section 91(24) of the *Constitution Act, 1867*, and are within the jurisdiction of the Parliament and Government of Canada for that reason.

While legal support for that assumption appears to be strong, it must be acknowledged that it cannot be considered unassailable until it has been upheld by the Supreme Court of Canada. What if the assumption turns out to be wrong?

Even in that case all would not be lost, because in the writer's view the constitutional recognition and affirmation in section 35 of the *Constitution Act, 1982* of the existing aboriginal rights of the Aboriginal peoples of Canada, including the Métis people, leads to many of the same conclusions as the assumption that Métis are "Indians" under section 91(24).

Section 35 is unequivocal: it recognizes, affirms, and places beyond legislative tampering the existing aboriginal rights of Canada's Aboriginal peoples, specifically including the Métis. While the Supreme Court of Canada has decreed that the protected aboriginal rights of Indians must be traceable to times before European contact,[20] this clearly cannot mean, given the inclusion of Métis people in section 35(2), that the Métis are ruled out. Whether the courts eventually decide that Métis aboriginal rights are an exception to the general rule, or alternatively that they are protected because of the ancestral linkage of all Métis to pre-contact Aboriginal peoples, there can be no doubt that Métis possess all aboriginal rights that were not lawfully extinguished before 1982.

This means, in the writer's opinion, that Métis are in much the same constitutional position, for practical purposes, as if section 91(24) applied to them. Consider the fiduciary duty of governments towards the Métis, for example. Whether that duty is founded on section 91(24) or on the more fundamental basis of aboriginal rights, it continues to be owed to Métis people by both federal and provincial governments.

Consider the two examples of anti-Métis discrimination outlined above: denial of additional compensation for Métis persons removed from the Primrose Lake Weapons Range, and denial of *Indian Act* status to descendants of Métis scrip-takers. In both cases the rights taken away—traditional harvesting rights in the one case, and full association with one's Indian heritage in the other—derive from fundamental aboriginal rights, which the Government of Canada must respect whether or not section 91(24) is relevant.

Conclusion

Having suggested that *both* section 35 and section 91(24)—the latter being a stepping-stone to reliance on equality rights under section 15 of the *Charter*—

are major constitutional buttresses for the Métis, I will conclude with a few thoughts about their interrelationship.

It is imperative, in my view, that litigation be commenced very soon to obtain definitive rulings from the courts confirming the fundamental constitutional rights of the Métis. The wounds have festered too long already. Some ask whether it would be better for such litigation to be based on section 35 or on section 91(24). In my opinion, that question creates a false dichotomy; it would not be wise to consider the two approaches to be mutually exclusive alternatives.

"Either/or" thinking can be misleading, and sometimes tyrannical. The Government of Canada, for example, tries to force Aboriginal people into separate groups: "Indian," "Métis," "Inuit." It demands that those who are not of Inuit origin must be *either* Indian or Métis, not both, despite the reality that many people who are "Indians" within the meaning of section 91(24) are *also* Métis. To force a choice in those circumstances is both illogical and unjust in my opinion.

Similarly, I think it would be both illogical and unwise to suppose that a choice must be made between litigating on the basis of section 35 and doing so on the basis of section 91(24). These guarantees can and should be used *together*, and in conjunction with section 15 where appropriate, to fashion the strongest *combined* legal arguments possible to advance Métis constitutional rights. While the precise nature of those arguments, and whether they should all be raised in a single legal action or in several concerted proceedings, are matters that must be left to the lawyers entrusted with conducting the litigation, it is clear that when the Métis go to court to vindicate their historic rights they should be armed with *every* constitutional argument available.

Notes

[1]Although the chapter addresses Métis interests expressly, much of it is equally relevant to the situation of non-status Indians.

[2]Canada, *Report of the Royal Commission on Aboriginal Peoples: Perspectives and Realities,* vol. 4, (Ottawa: Supply and Services Canada, 1996) at 209. The author discloses that he penned the following passage for the Commission.

> We are convinced that all Métis people, whether or not they are members of full-fledged Aboriginal nations, are covered by section 91(24). There are several reasons for that conclusion. The first is that at the time of Confederation, use of the term "Indian" extended to the Métis (or "halfbreeds" as they were called then). This can be seen, for example, in section 31 of the *Manitoba Act, 1870* and in section 125(e) of the *Dominion Lands Act 1879,* both of which made provision for land grants to "halfbreed" persons ("Métis" in the French versions)...in connection with the "extinguishment of *Indian* title" [emphasis added]. The Supreme Court of Canada held as early as 1939 that Inuit ("Eskimos") are included within the scope of section 91(24) because the section was intended to refer to "all the aborigines of the territory subsequently included in the Dominion,"[5] and there is every reason to apply the same reasoning to Métis people. Most academic opinion supports the view that Métis are Indians under section 91(24),[6] and a recent commis-

sion of inquiry in Manitoba reached the same conclusion.[7] We support this view.

Footnotes included in the passage were:

"5. *Re the term 'Indians,'* [1939] S.C.R. 104; 2. D.L.R. 417 at 433 per J. Kerwin.

6. Peter W. Hogg, *Constitutional Law of Canada,* 3d ed. (supplemented) (Scarborough, ON: Carswell, 1992); C. Chartier, "'Indian': An Analysis of the Term as Used in Section 91(24) of the *B.N.A. Act"* (1978) 43 Sask. L. Rev. (1978–79) 37; and Bradford W. Morse & John Giokas, "Do the Métis Fall Within Section 91(24) of the *Constitution Act, 1867?"* in *Aboriginal Self-Government: Legal and Constitutional Issues* (Ottawa: RCAP, 1995). A contrary view was expressed by Bryan Schwartz in *First Principles, Second Thoughts: Aboriginal Peoples, Constitutional Reform and Canadian Statecraft* (Montreal: Institute for Research on Public Policy, 1986), p. 245.

7. Public Inquiry into the Administration of Justice and Aboriginal People, *Report of the Aboriginal Justice Inquiry of Manitoba,* Volume 1: *The Justice System and Aboriginal People* (Winnipeg: Queen's Printer, 1991).

[3]A graduate student could be kept quite busy, for example, scanning the excellent Javitch American Indian collection at the University of Alberta Library for nineteenth century usages of the word "Indian."

[4]Indian Claims Commission, *Primrose Lake Air Weapons Range Report,* August 17, 1993.

[5]E.g., "Settlement Agreement, May 20, 1997, between Her Majesty the Queen in Right of Canada and Canoe Lake Cree Nation and Members of Canoe Lake Cree Nation"

[6]Affidavit of Ambrose Maurice, filed July 10, 1998 in *Maurice et al.* v. *Indian Claims Commission et al.,* Federal Court of Canada Court No. T –1356–98.

[7]S. 12(1)(a)(ii) of the pre-April 1985 *Indian Act.*

[8]"Adverse impact" discrimination has been held to violate s. 15 of the *Charter: Eldridge* v. *British Columbia* (1997) 151 D.L.R. (4th) 577 (S.C.C.).

[9]*Miron* v. *Trudel* (1995) 124 D.L.R. (4th) 693 (S.C.C.).

[10]*Steinhauer-Anderson* v. *The Queen et al.,* F.C.T.D., Court No. T–1874–92; February 19, 1999, unreported.

[11]A discriminatory provision of the *Indian Act* was struck down on that ground in *R.* v. *Drybones* (1970) 9 D.L.R. (3d) 473 (S.C.C.).

[12]In the *Steinhauer-Anderson* case, note 10 *supra,* the "marrying out" provisions (s. 12(1)(b) and s. 14) of the former *Indian Act* were declared to violate the *Charter* freedoms of association and liberty, even though they had been repealed when the *Charter* came into force, since the loss of *Indian Act* status they had caused continued to affect the Plaintiff after 1985.

[13]As the extract from the RCAP report quoted in note 2 *supra* points out, the original Métis land allotment and scrip provisions under the *Manitoba Act* and the *Dominion Lands Act* were aimed at the "extinguishment of Indian title."

[14]For a brief overview of this maladministration, see RCAP, *supra* note 2 at 334ff. Those who rely on the "reasonable limit" defence must show, in addition to a "rational connection," that the restriction impairs the *Charter* right as little as reasonably possible, and that it is not disproportionate in an overall sense to the goal of the legislation: *R.* v. *Oakes* (1986) 26 D.L.R. (4th) 200 (S.C.C.). It is unlikely that the Métis descendant disqualification could meet those tests. The *Oakes* case also established that to satisfy s. 1 of the *Charter* the purpose of the restriction in question must be "pressing and substantial," and it is doubtful, in light of its sordid history, that the extinguishment of Métis title could be said to have ever served such a goal.

[15]*R.* v. *Sparrow* (1990) 70 D.L.R. (4th) 385, at 408 (S.C.C.).

[16]Note 2 *supra,* at 294–95, footnote omitted.

[17]Note 2 *supra,* at 295–96. The author discloses that he authored this passage and the foregoing one for the Commission.

[18]*Métis Settlements Act*, revised to January 10, 1999, R.S.A. c. M–14.3. The Alberta Legislature has even gone so far as to provide a degree of constitutional entrenchment for some of these Métis benefits by providing, in the *Constitution of Alberta Amendment Act, 1990*, R.S.A. c.C 22.2, s. 5, that the Legislature will not amend or repeal the *Métis Settlements Land Protection Act*, alter or revoke the letters patent for Métis settlement land, or dissolve the Métis Settlements General Council, without the agreement of the Métis Settlements General Council.

[19]See P. Hogg, *Constitutional Law of Canada* (Toronto: Carswell) looseleaf edition, #15.5(c).

[20]*R. v. Van der Peet* (1996) 137 D.L.R. (4th) 289 (S.C.C.).

Chapter 8

Defining "The Métis People"

The Hard Case of Canadian Aboriginal Law

Paul L. A. H. Chartrand & John Giokas

Introduction

In chapter 3, a review of Canadian law and policy led to the conclusion that defining "the Métis people" at the uncertain boundary of Indian definition is doomed to fail. All rational criteria for defining the membership of human groups, including style of life, kinship, and "blood quantum," have been put beyond functional reach by the irrational administration of the federal government's definition of "Indian." This chapter maps out a journey from the boundary of the federal government's definition of "Indian" to the positive core of section 35 Métis identity. This approach assumes that justice is more likely to be done by recognizing the distinct rights of Indian and Métis people in this way.

It is sometimes said that hard cases make bad law. Better decisions are likely to result from inquiries that proceed from the known to the unknown, from the certain to the uncertain, from the core to the periphery. The question of defining the Métis people and their rights is *res integra,* without precedent or principle. At the time of writing, there are no decisions of the Court dealing with Métis claims to Aboriginal rights.[1] Consequently, there are no precedents available, and no principles that have been derived from a line of decided cases. The definition of "the Métis people" in section 35 is the hard case of Canadian Aboriginal law, and the aim of this chapter is to contribute to the question of Métis definition by focusing upon the central case of the Aboriginal right of self-government of "the Métis people." Several reasons suggest this approach.

Judicial Method

The Court will decide only the law that is needed to settle the merits of each case, based upon the facts available to the court. There has been no reference case asking the Court to define "the Métis people" in section 35. The rights in section 35 are those that are vested in "the aboriginal peoples of Canada" mentioned therein. Accordingly, the constitutional meaning of "the Métis people" in section 35 will develop in the courts as the rights protected by section 35 are defined judicially.

At the present stage of development of the law of Aboriginal rights, it is evident that different kinds of rights are vested in different kinds of communities.[2] The community designated by the expression "the Métis people" will be identified, in time, in relation to the kind of right it possesses. Like all definitions of human groups, this is inevitably circular.

There are two decisions, *Blais* and *Powley*, from the appeal courts of Manitoba and Ontario respectively, that will be heard by the Supreme Court of Canada, likely in 2003. Each of these cases involves issues that, at best, lie at the boundary of the question of defining the Métis for purposes of section 35.

Blais[3] raises the question of whether Métis persons are included within the meaning of "Indians" who are entitled to hunt for food under the terms of the 1930 *Natural Resources Transfer Agreements (NRTA)*. These *Agreements,* which were given constitutional status under the *Constitution Act, 1930,* operate only in the Prairie Provinces. The *NRTAs'* "game laws paragraph" deals with the entitlements of individuals and will not resolve the question of identifying "the Métis people" that has *Aboriginal* rights or other rights protected by section 35. If the Court comments on the Aboriginal rights of the Métis at the time of enacting the *NRTAs*, those rights will not fill the ambit of the rights recognized and affirmed by section 35, and therefore will not provide a comprehensive definition of "the Métis people" in section 35.

Powley[4] involves a defence to a prosecution under Ontario wild game hunting regulations based upon a claim to Métis Aboriginal rights in section 35. A resolution of this claim can decide that the claimants have section 35 rights to hunt moose, but will not decide the broader question of defining "the Métis people" in section 35. The claim is based upon the alleged rights of residents in a small community in Ontario, not upon a claim of the rights of a "people" or a "nation" that might comprise the entire scope of section 35. Furthermore, the facts reveal a classic "boundary" case where the defendants' ancestors were members of a local Indian band defined by the *Indian Act*, who were enfranchised.[5] The Court will be faced with references in the lower courts to "the Métis people," but with no reasoning that ties the defendants' immediate community to a "people." The courts showed less interest in examining the features of the claim-ants' community, in which an alleged Aboriginal right was vested, than in the personal antecedents of the defendants, who relied on remote "Métis" ancestors for their claim to a Métis identity.

The *Powley* case is a classic "hard case" not only because the Court has no previous cases and principles of its own to guide it (it has the views of the lower courts), but also because it begins to address the question of Métis definition at its boundary, not at the core. The historic and geographical core of the Métis people lies within the Prairie Provinces, where "Riel's people" struggled for and gained recognition in political and military actions over a long period of time.[6] *Powley* deals with the alleged rights of a small community.[7] The case cannot de-cide the law applicable to the definition of the entire "Métis people" in section 35.[8]

A focus on the question "Who has the Aboriginal right of self-govern-ment" attempts to tackle this problem by focusing upon what is assumed to be the broadest category of community comprised by the term "the Métis people." Such an inquiry can be expected to shed light on the question of identifying the Métis communities *within* "the Métis people" whose rights are recognized in section 35. The analysis below will demonstrate that a proper application of the principles relating to the interpretation of section 35 identifies only *one* Métis people with an Aboriginal right of self-government.

In summary, asking who has the Métis Aboriginal right of self-government can be expected to produce the broadest possible judicial definition. This is be-cause the judicial approach will define the Métis according to the process of finding who has Métis rights, and the right of self-government is generally un-derstood to be vested in a large, historic "nation" or "people" rather than in small communities with the kinds of Aboriginal rights that the courts have already found to exist in small Aboriginal communities.[9] This approach aims to contrib-ute to the evolving judicial definition, which will not be resolved in cases now before the courts.

Section 35 and Aboriginal Right of Self-government

The existence of the Aboriginal right of self-government has not yet been settled by the existing case law, but an inquiry into the meaning of a "nation" that has an Aboriginal right of self-government is supported by a variety of sources that are relevant to judicial decision-making, including the following.

- The current federal policy recognizes that section 35 protects an Aborigi-nal right of self-government.

- The Royal Commission on Aboriginal Peoples (RCAP) argued that the common law recognizes an Aboriginal right of self-government that was vested in "Aboriginal nations" conceived as sub-entities of the "peoples" in section 35.

• There is express support from the United Nations for the approach of RCAP, including recognition that Canada ought to meet its international obligations to respect the human right of self-determination of all peoples by implementing the recommendations of RCAP.[10]

The RCAP Definition of an Aboriginal "Nation"

RCAP identified the attributes of an Aboriginal "nation" that, it argued, had an Aboriginal right of self-government protected by section 35. This provides a useful conceptual frame of reference for the Court, which considers the views expressed by Royal Commissions in the process of judicial reasoning.[11]

The RCAP concept of an Aboriginal "nation" with a right of self-government was the same as the Aboriginal "nation" that RCAP recommended should be recognized by federal policy as entitled to enter into "nation-to-nation" or intergovernmental relations with the Government of Canada and other governments. This recommendation suggests that a similar judicial definition should be considered because it would be feasible.

The RCAP concept of an Aboriginal "nation" is a useful conceptual reference because it facilitates the task of explaining why the popular idea of "race" and the process of ethnogenesis are inadequate conceptual tools for the judicial analysis required in defining "the Métis people."

Judicial Decisions Tested against the Concept of Recognition

Any decision of the Court that identifies a community that has rights vested in "the Métis people" will be highly controversial. Governments, which have a duty to respect constitutional rights and make them effective, thereby incurring political and economic costs, will be interested. Métis persons, communities, and political representative organizations will be interested. There exists a high level of emotional and political attachment to Métis nationalism in western Canada, where there is a history of political and military struggles against colonial and Canadian authorities and settlers since the early 1800s. Many others have recently adopted the label "Métis" in making their claims to Aboriginal rights, as reviewed in chapter 3. They will be interested. The question of Métis identity directly raises some of the most controversial issues about the legal recognition of group rights generally, and Aboriginal rights in particular, in Canada. The public and the media, which has a significant influence on public opinion, will be interested.

Judicial decisions on the question of Métis rights will be particularly controversial because the Court will be deciding issues that direct political processes failed to resolve, as was reviewed in chapter 1. Decisions on Métis definition will raise questions about the appropriate constitutional functions of the executive, legislative, and judicial branches of government, and test the limits of justiciability.

For the above reasons, it will be useful to test the merits of the judicial decision against a standard that is external to the law created by the judges themselves.[12] The concept of recognition, which was considered in earlier chapters, provides a useful conceptual frame of reference, particularly because the concept applies to intergovernmental relations which are at issue in the case of an Aboriginal right of self-government.

The Historic Métis "Nation" Provides the "Core"

The question of defining "the Métis people" in section 35 is essentially a task of construing a term of the Constitution of Canada. Accordingly, the interpretive principles that have been adopted by the Court in constitutional cases must guide the analysis. The results of this analysis require an historical inquiry to identify a "people" with a history of Crown-Métis relations. A reference to the established historiography, of which the courts may take judicial notice, identifies the historic "Métis nation" of western Canada as the people with a well-known history of Crown-Métis relations. This establishes a solid factual and legal "core" which is useful in weighing the merits of boundary cases.

Although it is beyond the scope of this chapter to inquire into the facts upon which a contemporary claim may be made, a comparison of the Métis National Council (MNC) definition of "nation" that was adopted in recent political negotiations with governments, with the RCAP definition sheds some light upon the application of the emerging doctrine of Aboriginal rights to the "hard case" of defining the Métis people in section 35.

Interpretive Approach and Principles

The 1982 amendments to the Constitution of Canada not only introduced a new provision that expressly recognized and affirmed the rights of the Aboriginal peoples of Canada, it also heralded a significant shift in the locus of constitutional decision-making power. The Court has described the shift made by the 1982 amendment as one that transformed the Canadian system from a system of parliamentary supremacy to a system of constitutional supremacy.[13] The courts now have a more significant role in constitutional policy-making because of their duty to interpret the text of the Constitution.

The judicial approach to the interpretation or construction of section 35 requires attention to three factors:

1. general principles of constitutional interpretation,

2. principles relating to Aboriginal rights, and

3. the purposes behind section 35 itself.[14]

General Principles of Constitutional Interpretation

In the *1985 Manitoba Language Rights Reference,* the Court explained its perspective on interpreting a constitution.[15]

> The Constitution of a country is a statement of the will of the people to be governed in accordance with certain principles held as fundamental and certain prescriptions of the powers of the legislature and government. It is, as section 52 of the *Constitution Act 1982* declares, the "supreme law" of the nation, unalterable by the normal legislative process, and unsuffering of laws inconsistent with it. The duty of the judiciary is to interpret and apply the laws of Canada and each of the provinces, and it is thus our duty to ensure that the constitutional law prevails.

In cases following the *Manitoba Language Reference,* the Court has found a number of these fundamental constitutional principles. In the *Quebec Secession Reference,* the Court explained that the constitutional texts enumerated in section 52(2) of the *Constitution Act, 1982* "are not exhaustive," and that the Constitution "embraces unwritten, as well as written rules."[16] In particular, there are underlying constitutional principles that "animate the whole of our Constitution" including:

* federalism,

* democracy,

* constitutionalism and the rule of law, and

* respect for minorities.[17]

The Court explained the role of these principles in the process of constitutional interpretation.

> The principles assist in the interpretation of the text and the delineation of the spheres of jurisdiction, the scope of rights and obligations, and the role of political institutions. Equally important, observance of and respect for these principles is essential to the ongoing process of constitutional development and evolution of our Constitution as a "living tree," to invoke the famous description in *Edwards* v. *Attorney-General for Canada.* ...As this Court indicated in the *New Brunswick Broadcasting Co.* v. *Nova Scotia (Speaker of the House of Assembly),* [1993] 1 S.C.R. 319, Canadians have long recognized the existence and importance of unwritten constitutional principles in our system of government."[18]

The Constitution is unlike ordinary statutes; it is not the direct work of Parliament but represents the results of the political action of diverse actors. These results include political compromises and pacts between peoples. The resultant terms in the text of the Constitution are intended for the protection of the people concerned, who may comprise a numerical minority which needs constitutional protection for its interests against the results of democratic rule of the majority. This constitutional function of protection is reflected in the principle of judicial interpretation which posits that judicial interpretation "ought not to be allowed to dim or to whittle down the provisions of the original contract upon which the federation was founded...."[19]

This general interpretive principle was initially adopted in 1932 to interpret the *Constitution Act, 1867*. It recognized that "the preservation of the rights of minorities was a condition on which such minorities entered into the federation, and the foundation upon which the whole structure was subsequently erected."[20]

In the *Aeronautics* case in which the Privy Council formulated this principle, the minorities and their bargains were the provinces upon entering Confederation. The principle has also been applied in a case dealing with religious minorities.[21] It applies to the constitutional "bargain of Confederation" entered into between the Métis and Canada which led to the creation of the province of Manitoba in 1870.[22]

Another principle articulated in the 1985 *Big M Drug Mart* case is that the Court must favour interpretations that accord with contemporary "appreciations" and "reassessments."[23]

Principles Relating to Aboriginal Rights

As a result of the *Constitution Act, 1982,* the Court has been assigned, or on another view perhaps has undertaken, the role of designing a new constitutional and Aboriginal rights jurisprudence that is based upon Canadian history, culture, and experience. The Court explained in general terms in the *Sparrow* case that the political history behind a constitutional provision has interpretive significance in finding the purpose of a provision.

> It is clear, then, that s.35(1) of the *Constitution Act 1982*, represents the culmination of a long and difficult struggle in both the political forum and the courts for the constitutional recognition of aboriginal rights. The strong representations of native associations and other groups concerned with the welfare of Canada's aboriginal peoples made the adoption of s. 35(1) possible and it is important to note that the provision applies to the Indians, the Inuit and the Métis. Section 35 (1), at the least, provides a solid constitutional base upon which subsequent negotiations can take place...[24]

Aboriginal rights are based in history, but the history of Crown-Aboriginal political relations is not only the source of Aboriginal rights. That history also reveals the interests that are judicially recognized in contemporary terms as legal rights. In theory, legal rights are judicially "found," or created, by identifying the interests that, for reasons of law and justice, require legal protection.[25]

In principle, the law of Aboriginal and treaty rights finds the source of these rights in the political relations between "the Crown" and the Indian "nations."[26]

The Purposes Behind Section 35

In the *Sparrow* case, the Court said that section 35 is not just a codification of the case law that had accumulated by 1985; section 35 "calls for a just settlement for aboriginal peoples."[27]

In the *Van der Peet* case, decided in 1996, the Court discussed one of the fundamental purposes of section 35, that of "the reconciliation of the preexistence of distinctive Aboriginal societies with the assertion of Crown sovereignty."[28] The Court also explained how the judicial process transforms historical, social, and political interests of the Aboriginal peoples into contemporary legal interests.

> In order to fulfill the purpose underlying section 35(1)—i.e., the protection and reconciliation of the interests which arise from the fact that prior to the arrival of Europeans in North America Aboriginal peoples lived on the land in distinctive societies, with their own practices, customs and traditions—the test for identifying the Aboriginal rights recognized and affirmed by section 35(1) must be directed at identifying the crucial elements of those pre-existing distinctive societies."[29]

The reconciliation of the interests of the Aboriginal peoples in Canada with the sovereignty of Canada is expressed constitutionally in the fiduciary relationship which the Court has found to exist between the Crown and Aboriginal peoples.[30]

In *Sparrow*, the Court considered the purposes of section 35, and in respect to the affirmation of Aboriginal rights, stated that previous cases "ground a general guiding principle for section 35(1)."

> That is, the Government has the responsibility to act in a fiduciary capacity with respect to aboriginal peoples. The relationship between the Government and aboriginals [sic: Aboriginal peoples] is trust-like, rather than adversarial, and contemporary recognition and affirmation of aboriginal rights must be defined in light of this historic relationship.[31]

The fiduciary relationship reflects the principle of protection which the

Crown owes to the interests of Aboriginal peoples when it asserts its sovereignty. In Canadian law, one effect of this new relationship is that the legal authority of Aboriginal people to determine the nature and scope of their own public interest is now constrained by the constitutional relationship assumed by the Crown,[32] wherein constitutional sovereignty is shared. According to recent jurisprudence, the protection afforded by section 35 proscribes government actions purportedly undertaken under its legislative power in section 91(24), unless infringement can be justified and reconciled with the federal duty of protection. [33]

In the *Quebec Secession Reference*, the Court considered Aboriginal and treaty rights and stated that "the protection of these rights… whether looked at in their own right or as part of the larger concern with minorities, reflects an important constitutional value."[34] Accordingly, "…it is clear that the principle [of protecting Aboriginal and treaty rights] has equal weight with other underlying constitutional principles."[35]

The above principles relating to the protection of minorities and the rights of Aboriginal peoples indicate the political and constitutional significance of the Aboriginal peoples as historic nations within the Canadian federation. The principle that the terms under which the provinces agreed to join the Canadian federation must be respected applies equally to the terms under which Aboriginal peoples agreed to join the federation, where the facts support the existence of such agreement.

If an Aboriginal right of self-government is protected by section 35, then the federal principle is engaged in interpreting section 35 because "it is only by sharing sovereignty that the relationship between Aboriginal peoples to the nation-states in which they live can move to one that is fundamentally federal rather than imperial."[36] The political character of Aboriginal nations or "peoples" and their status as political entities within the Canadian federation is an emerging aspect of the doctrine of Aboriginal and treaty rights in section 35.[37] In the *Sioui* case,[38] the Court stated that "Indian nations were regarded in their relations with European nations which occupied North America as independent nations," and the Court characterized relations with the Indian tribes as *sui generis,* falling between the kind of relations conducted with sovereign states and the relations such states had with their own citizens.

Application to the Meaning of "The Métis People"

The interpretive approach that has been reviewed shows that the Court now has the constitutional role of designing a new constitutional and Aboriginal rights jurisprudence that is based upon Canadian history, culture, and experience. Judges and lawyers are no longer allowed to look exclusively or primarily to the history and culture of the British for inspiration for the development of Canadian rights; the "patriation" of the Constitution in 1982 mandates the Court to develop a truly North American jurisprudence, a doctrine that recognizes and affirms the historical foundations and cultures of Canada, including the histories, cultures, and philosophies of the Aboriginal peoples of Canada.[39]

The Historic Métis Nation

The "Métis people" in section 35 must be defined in light of the purposes of recognizing Aboriginal rights. Aboriginal rights are *history-based* rights vested in *communities*.[40] In *Sioui*, the Court referred to a political relationship between the Crown and independent Indian "nations."[41] The descendants of these historic nations comprise the "Indian peoples" recognized in section 35 today. By the same reasoning, and in accordance with the principles reviewed above, today's "Métis people" is the people descended from the historic nation that had political relations with the Crown.

In the *Manitoba Language Reference*, the Court identified the *Manitoba Act, 1870* as "the culmination of many years of co-existence and struggle between the English, the French, and the Métis in Red River colony" and acknowledged the attempts of Riel's provisional government to unite the various political segments of the community.[42]

In another case involving interpretation of the Constitution of Manitoba, it was stated that the Métis in Red River in 1870 were "apprehensive about the transfer of their homeland to Canada and viewed the prospects of immigration from Ontario as a threat to their culture and way of life, indeed to their very survival as a people."[43]

The Court has found that culture is an important interest that is protected in the form of Aboriginal rights. Survival as a people is logically the basic goal of the Aboriginal right of self-government, whether the right is explained on the basis of culture or otherwise.

An examination of the established historiography, of which the courts may take judicial notice,[44] reveals that there has been only one historic group of "Métis people" that was self-governing: the Métis of western Canada.[45] Canada did not exercise effective constitutional authority over the Métis nation until at least 1870, with the agreement of the Riel Provisional Government to join the Canadian federation. This was based upon the "bargain of Confederation," that Riel called "the Manitoba Treaty," some terms of which are reflected in provisions of the *Manitoba Act, 1870*.[46]

If the Constitution is "a statement of the will of the people to be governed in accordance with certain principles held as fundamental and certain prescriptions of the powers of the legislature and government,"[47] as the Court has held, then the true constitutional meaning of "the Métis people" in which is vested an Aboriginal right of self-government is the people whose collective will is material to the political and constitutional legitimacy of the Constitution. The collective will of the Métis people recognized in section 35 is material to the legitimacy of the fundamental rules of the Constitution which are to govern them within Canada. Those rules acquire legitimacy in part because the forebears of the Métis people were historically active in generating the constitutional norms that govern us today.

It takes time to develop a distinct society, a "new people." History shows that, although many mixed-blood communities emerged at the boundary of the advancing "frontier" with the Aboriginal world, only in the Canadian northwest did there occur political action of the kind that challenged the assertion of Crown sovereignty, and that made clear the distinction between a "new people" and the Indian societies.[48] The emergence of the "Métis Nation" out of Red River was essentially a four- or five-generation process that took place in the first and into the second half of the nineteenth century. It is in the nature and intensity of Crown-Métis relations during that period that can be found the historical basis for the existence of a "new people," distinct from Indians, that emerged within the Indigenous world and territory. This new people challenged Canada's assertion of sovereignty, and that today invites a just constitutional "reconciliation" of competing historical sovereignties grounded in section 35. There is no historical evidence of similar facts concerning any other "mixed-blood people" that challenged the sovereignty of Canada.[49]

Aboriginal rights can serve the ends of justice in the case of a people with a history that challenges the moral and political legitimacy of Canadian sovereignty. The significance of political action in generating constitutional rights is evident in the factual background of section 31 of the *Manitoba Act,* and in the background of the enactment of section 35, section 35.1, and the former section 37 in the *Constitution Act, 1982.* Constitutional rights often result from the actions of many actors; they reflect cooperative political action and compromise. The unwritten constitutional principle of democracy suggests that in appropriate cases, constitutional provisions ought to be construed to encourage such developments. The Court's interpretation of section 35 in the *Sparrow* case reviewed above[50] also encourages political action and negotiations. The Constitution, then, is to be interpreted as a national document which recognizes and confirms the results of historical political action, and which encourages future democratic political action and compromise within Canada.

The historic Métis nation of the North West, or "Riel's people," was the only group that was able to organize a civil government, to defend itself against Canadian intrusion, to make its place within the economic niches of the West along with the Indian nations,[51] and to insist that Canada not annex the West without dealing with it. The Métis nation has the symbols associated with this history, including "Falcon's Song," the "national anthem" proclaiming military victory against settlers in 1816, a distinctive flag, unique languages, music, and art, and the well-known symbol of its economic culture, the Red River cart. It is the Métis nation which is mentioned in the Constitution, in the terms of the *Manitoba Act, 1870,* and whose rights were recognized in statutes and orders-in-council from the early 1870s until well into the twentieth century.[52]

Constitutional provisions must be interpreted, not in isolation, but read together with the text of the entire Constitution. Accordingly, the meaning of "the Métis people" in section 35 is informed by the meaning of section 31 of the *Manitoba Act 1870,* which is a part of the Constitution of Canada[53] and which expressly recognized the Métis people. Applying this general principle to section 35 identifies the Métis people who negotiated terms of a "bargain of Confederation" in 1870, some of the terms of which are memorialized in provisions of the *Manitoba Act, 1870.* [54] Section 31 of that *Act* provided for a gradual land settlement scheme for the Métis in the Red River region. That agreement, including the amnesty to all Red River residents and the performance of section 31, was not implemented according to its spirit and intent. The Métis are today seeking the assistance of the courts in legitimizing the exercise of Canadian sovereignty over them, which was gained by the agreement of 1870, by requiring respect for the "bargain of Confederation" under which the Métis agreed to join Canada.[55]

The Test for Proof of an Aboriginal Right of Self-government

The purpose of this analysis is to identify "the Métis people" with an Aboriginal right of self-government that is protected by section 35. Although Aboriginal rights have their source in history, they exist legally as contemporary rights and will be claimed by existing communities. The current test applied by the courts in Indian cases requires social continuity between the claimant and the historic communities. Aboriginal rights are in their nature group rights, and the general test for proof of Aboriginal rights was stated as follows in the leading case of *Van der Peet:* "In order to be an Aboriginal right an activity must be an element of a practice, custom or tradition integral to the distinctive culture of the Aboriginal group claiming the right."[56] Cultures are reflective of group norms, institutions, and behaviour, not of idiosyncratic personal characteristics of individuals.

Van der Peet is also the leading case on the test for continuity between the contemporary and the historic community from which the Aboriginal rights are claimed. The Court stated that although a practice may change over time, there must be evidence that it has an historical relationship to "pre-contact" times. A claimant group is not required to provide evidence of continuous activity linking the contemporary and historic communities; interruptions will not defeat evidence that the source of the right lies in historical practice.[57] The Court left open the important question whether an Aboriginal right disappears from discontinuity of practice or usage, the "use it or lose it" idea.[58]

An Aboriginal right of self-government is vested in an Aboriginal community that can prove descent from an historic "people" that exercised self-government at the time that Canada asserted constitutional authority over the territory and assumed a fiduciary relationship with the Aboriginal people.

A community maintains itself by means of societal institutions that are not born and do not die, unlike the individuals comprising the community. Proof for the Aboriginal right of self-government requires factual evidence of societal institutions that link the contemporary community to the historic community. Aboriginal self-government is vested in the group, and it is the group's identity that is at issue, not the identity of its members. The members of a self-defining community are identified by the rules or practices of the community.

Characterizing the Contemporary "Nation" Claiming the Right of Self-government

RCAP proposed a scheme of federal recognition legislation to identify an Aboriginal nation entitled to exercise a right of self-government, and to enter into political relations with Canadian governments.[59] An independent tribunal would recommend to the Cabinet which applicant nations to recognize. The conditions for recognition included the creation and subscription of the claimant group to a constitution that included a definition of its existing members and also rules of membership to govern the continuation of the group. This would identify the members of the Aboriginal nation in a new "nation-to-nation" relationship within Canada.

In chapter 3, the RCAP argument recognizing an Aboriginal right of self-government in section 35 was criticized for being based upon the declaratory theory of recognition; in practice, it had to be acknowledged that unilateral attempts at group self-identification leading to the exercise of self-government would be resisted by Canadian governments, who would want a say in the rules for selecting Canadian citizens as members of an Aboriginal self-governing nation. This latter factor reflects the constitutive theory of recognition. The final recommendations of RCAP, requiring approval of the federal Cabinet on decisions to recognize an Aboriginal "nation" entitled to enter into "nation-to-nation" relations with Canadian governments, illustrated the tension between the two competing theories and the difficulty of trying to reconcile principle with power. RCAP adopted the term "nation" to mean a people that has the right of self-determination at international law.[60]

> An Aboriginal nation is a sizeable body of Aboriginal people with a shared sense of national identity that constitutes the predominant population in a certain territory or collection of territories.[61]

A "nation" is of sufficient size to operate as a self-governing entity; its identity and governing authority attaches to a traditional homeland territory. A nation which chooses to exercise its Aboriginal right of self-government is free to exercise its jurisdiction over its members extra-territorially. The RCAP definition of a nation is adopted for present purposes.

On Race and Ethnogenesis

The idea of "race" is very persistent in Canada but its meaning in popular thought and language is elusive. RCAP made clear the point that an Aboriginal people with an Aboriginal right of self-government protected by section 35 is not merely a race of people identified by birth. An Aboriginal people is a dynamic social and political entity with a special constitutional status today that is identified by history, culture, and its community features.

The *Charter of Rights and Freedoms*, in section 15, recognizes race as a constitutional category that defines persons for purposes that are quite distinct from the purposes of section 35. These and perhaps other reasons have led to widespread confusion about the character of an Aboriginal people entitled to the special status recognized in the Constitution. The debate has been contentious, and in the political arena, at times pernicious. It is therefore appropriate to emphasize the following point made by RCAP.

> Aboriginal peoples are not racial groups; rather they are organic political and cultural entities. Although contemporary Aboriginal groups stem historically from the original peoples of North America, they often have mixed genetic heritages and include individuals of varied ancestry. As organic political entities, they have the capacity to evolve over time and change their internal composition.[62]

The courts have no British precedents to guide them in understanding the emergence of the Métis people and the identity of its contemporary descendant communities. Faced with the necessity of crafting a truly Canadian jurisprudence based upon Canadian history, the judges have examined the learning of both historians and social scientists in their search for principles and facts upon which they may erect a doctrine of Métis rights. One of the processes that has been considered to explain the emergence of the Métis people is the formation of an ethnic identity, or "ethnogenesis."

In the *Powley* case,[63] which dealt not with the claim of a people to Aboriginal self-government but to the right of the people in a small community in Ontario to kill moose for food, the Ontario Court of Appeal delivered certain opinions about the identity of a contemporary and a historic Métis community. The opinions expressed in this case are a convenient focus for the present discussion of race and ethnogenesis.

The two defendants in *Powley*, whose immediate ancestors were non-status Indians descended from members of a local Indian band defined by the *Indian Act*, asserted a Métis identity based upon their descent from a local community of "mixed-blood" people who had not been recognized as Indians by the Crown or the local Ojibway at the time a treaty was entered into with the Ojibway in 1850.[64] It appears that their ancestors had accepted, at the time of the treaty, the benefit usually provided by the Crown in respect to the possessory interests in the lands occupied by settlers in advance of surveys.[65] Subsequently, the Powley ancestors had been accepted into the local Objiway band as status Indians.[66] The Court of Appeal upheld the decision of the lower courts which judicially recognized them as members of a Métis community, although the Crown had not recognized them as Aboriginal people in 1850.[67] The descendants of remote Métis ancestors who had enjoyed membership in Indian bands for a period of time were entitled to rely upon a "Métis" Aboriginal right to hunt moose for food in a defence against a prosecution for infringing the Ontario game hunting laws.

In the Court of Appeal, Justice Sharpe commented on the history of "mixed-blood" communities in the Great Lakes area, and observed that "in the late 1700s, the mixed-blood families began to evolve into a new and distinct people through a process known as ethnogenesis."[68] According to historians and social scientists, however, evidence of ethnogenesis by itself is not sufficient to prove the existence of a new ethnic group. The ethnic community that results may not survive as such. Ethnic formation is not issued a one-time, fail-proof guarantee once it undertakes the path of ethnogenesis. The fragile new ethnic community may not survive the inflow of new arrivals.[69] Historians who had written about the "mixed-blood" communities in the area considered in the *Powley* case, well before the case was conceived, had concluded that this was the case. The inchoate new ethnic community had disappeared around 1850 following the signing of the local treaty with the Ojibway.

The court saw things differently. Guided by the *Van der Peet* pronouncements on the test of continuity, the Ontario Court of Appeal agreed with the lower court judge that, although the "mixed-blood" community had been invisible since 1850, it had not legally disappeared.[70] In the face of such a significant difference between the historical conclusion and the legal fiction, is the concept of ethnogenesis a compelling rationale for extending judicial recognition to a group of people who were not recognized by the executive government in 1850? A fuller elaboration of the relationship between the idea of ethnogenesis and that of race will assist the discussion.

Groups of persons who are descendants of a recognizable group of ancestors that are viewed, by outsiders, as distinct from the observers, are often called a "race" of people. One connotation of the term "race" focuses on the biological character of the members of the group. In *Powley*, for example, Justice Sharpe used the term "Métis" in reference to a "racial" group which he described as "unions between Scottish employees of the Hudson's Bay Company and Native [sic: Aboriginal] women produced another strain of Métis children."[71]

This comment reflects what professional scholars have called a widespread folk belief that Métis identity is based on mixed personal antecedents,[72] an idea supported by the etymology of the French term. However, the concept of race, whatever its legal content, has no biological significance.[73] The concept belongs, not to the realm of science, but to the realm of ideas. The purposes of using the concept are not scientific but political. The concept of race has a social meaning, which is used for political purposes.[74]

The following extract from a recent publication on the subject of Métis identity by two prominent scholars addresses the complex relationship between the idea of "race" and ethnogenesis.

> The mixing of so-called races and ethnic groups has been going on since time immemorial. In fact, most of the world's people are of mixed ancestry, and while this sharing of genes has contributed to great variation within the human species, it may or may not give rise to a new ethnic group. Persons of mixed white and aboriginal ancestry do not necessarily form a distinct and separate people. Indeed, it is time to acknowledge the racist origins of such a classification based solely on biological differences.[75]

The principles for interpreting section 35, which were reviewed above, indicate that the source of Aboriginal rights lies in the political relationship between the Crown and historic nations. The source of Aboriginal rights is not to be found in racist ideologies which attempt to classify human beings into biological categories.

At least some of the confusion evident in debates that rely on the terms "race" and "ethnogenesis" can probably be explained by the primary importance that is widely placed upon "blood" over such factors as residence, kinship, adoption, or other factors as a determinant of "belonging" in a community.

The utility of the concept of ethnogenesis and its application to complex social processes is the subject of debate amongst social scientists. According to one commentator,

> ...when ethnicity has come to refer to everything from tribalism to religious sects,

from City men in London to the shifting identities of Shan and Kachin, from region-
alism to race, it is difficult to see that it has any universal utility either as an analytical
tool or as a descriptive one.[76]

The concept of ethnogenesis is too fragile and ambiguous an idea to meet,
all by itself, as the Court in *Powley* appeared to accept, the task of defining an
historic people in the Constitution of Canada.[77]

Section 15 of the *Charter of Rights and Freedoms* includes the social construct of race. The Court has found that section 15 prohibits unequal treatment
of individuals under law that are based not on merit, but on personal characteristics such as race.[78] Individuals who are not part of an Aboriginal community
with Aboriginal or treaty rights protected by section 35 but who have personal
characteristics that have the potential of subjecting them to discriminatory actions prohibited by section 15, such as "Aboriginal ancestry" or "racial origins,"
are protected from discrimination by section 15. In addition, such persons are
entitled to the benefits of discretionary government programmes and laws intended to remedy their historic disadvantage.[79] But this has nothing to do with
the Aboriginal and treaty rights protected by section 35.

In Canada and elsewhere, the modern state has created communities where
common citizenship is viewed as the primary determinant of "belonging" to the
political community. Aboriginal rights are often confused with citizenship rights,
particularly in places like Canada where common citizenship is thought to pre-
empt official state recognition of ethnic communities.

Aboriginal people have Aboriginal rights, based upon the purposes behind
section 35 of reconciling the pre-existing social and political integrity of their
ancestral societies. They also have citizenship rights, as members of a community
organized around the concept of citizenship. The popular idea that all Canadians
should have the same rights fails to recognize this.

In conclusion, section 35 recognizes the existence, not of individuals united
by externally defined features which make them vulnerable to discriminatory
actions, which is the work of section 15 of the *Charter*, but rather of social and
political communities descended from historic "aboriginal peoples." This meaning reflects the meaning of ancestral rights in section 35[80]; it reflects the true
meaning of "existing" Aboriginal and treaty rights, the purpose of which is to
give legal protection to interests that were identified in historical political relationships between the Crown and Aboriginal people.

The alternative approach, which views Métis identity as a pan-Indian identity, is based upon a new interest that is not founded upon previous Crown-
Aboriginal relationships. Legal claims that are being made under a pan-Indian
label, under the term "Métis," reflect the consequences of the *Indian Act*, which

fulfilled its policy goal of dismantling the original Indian nations. Under the *Act*'s definition scheme, all Indian nations were treated as fungible entities—one was the same as another; ancestral community links did not matter.

Applying the Test of a "Nation" to a Contemporary "Métis People"[81]

As previously noted, RCAP made the following recommendation in its final report in 1996 on the identification of a modern claimant to the Aboriginal right of self-government: "An Aboriginal nation is a sizeable body of Aboriginal people with a shared sense of national identity that constitutes the predominant population in a certain territory or collection of territories."[82]

In principle, the features of a "nation" adopted by RCAP are the same as the features of a "people" with a right of self-determination at international law. These are here adopted as the definition of the contemporary claimant community that is entitled to ancestral or Aboriginal rights gained by the historic Métis nation in relations with the Imperial and Canadian Crown in the nineteenth century.

There is only one such historic Métis nation that was self-governing: "Riel's people," the Métis of western Canada.[83] Claims to the Aboriginal right of self-government will be made by contemporary communities which can prove continuity with this historic nation.

In addition to the questions of fact mentioned above, which are required for proof of the Aboriginal right of self-government, the identity of a proper claimant to the Aboriginal right of self-government vested in "the Métis people" in section 35 will depend in part on the resolution of some open legal questions. In other words, the law has not yet been decided on these material points. Some tentative comments are offered on some of these issues.

Some Difficulties in the Current Doctrine of Aboriginal Rights

The Métis as an Aboriginal People

Some commentators have criticized the express inclusion of "the Métis people" among the Aboriginal peoples of Canada by those who negotiated the 1982 constitutional amendments. They have argued that the Métis people in Red River, for example, can not be characterized as an "aboriginal" people because the Métis, conceived as a new people emerged from Indian ancestors and newly arrived non-Indians, were not here at the "Aboriginal" time that might be judicially adopted to define Indians.[84] Because the Métis people is recognized as one of the

Aboriginal peoples of Canada in the Constitution,[85] the law must adopt a date as the relevant beginning which includes the Métis.

In the French version of the Constitution, which is equally authoritative as the English, the term "droits ancestraux" is used to characterize the section 35 rights. Accordingly, the Métis have rights derived from the ancestral rights resulting from the political activities of their ancestors; there is no reason to require that the ancestral relations with the Crown all date to one mystical "Aboriginal date" that excludes the Métis people.[86]

The purpose of section 35 recognition is to affirm Aboriginal and treaty rights; an "original date" which will define the Métis as being "ab-original," ought to be adopted as the date for proof of Aboriginal rights.

The question of identifying a relevant date for proof of Métis rights is complicated by the results of the *Van der Peet* decision, which established two different dates for proof of different kinds of Aboriginal rights in Indian cases. Scholars have criticized the conclusion of the Court on this point, and have shown that it is not supported by either precedent or principle.[87] In *Van der Peet*, the Court recognized that one of the results of its conclusion on the date for proof of Aboriginal rights would be to give the back of the hand to the idea that the Métis people has Aboriginal rights. It therefore took pains to state that it left open the question whether the rights of "the Métis people" in section 35 could be defined by applying the "pre-contact date" for proof of Aboriginal rights that the Court adopted in that case.[88] The other date in issue is the date the Court established for proof of Aboriginal title, a subset of Aboriginal rights, which is not the date of "contact" with Europeans but the date the Crown asserted sovereignty.

The "transition date" proposed by Professor Slattery as the common date for proof of Aboriginal title and Aboriginal rights, if adopted, would contribute to a rational and principled development of the law of Aboriginal rights generally, and as it pertains to the Métis people in particular. [89] Here the transition date is called the "original date" to emphasize the function of the word in defining the Métis as an Aboriginal people.

The original date is set at the time that the Crown undertook to protect the interests of an Aboriginal people upon its assumption of constitutional authority. The Métis people is an "ab-original" people because it is descended from a people that existed at the "original date," which the law establishes as the time when the Crown assumed governmental responsibility for the particular Aboriginal people in question, and a fiduciary relationship was established.[90] This applies in the core case at issue, where the Aboriginal right claimed is a right of self-government. The Crown assumed a fiduciary's duty to protect the group interests of the Aboriginal people which the self-governing Aboriginal nation had previously protected by itself.

Turning to the historical facts, the Métis people at Red River existed when Indian treaties were signed in western Canada. The Métis people were dealt with at the time that the Crown assumed governmental responsibility in respect to the interests of all the Aboriginal peoples in this particular geographic region, and there is no reason to twist the logic of Indian cases to suit a "later arrival."[91] In fact, the Métis were expressly recognized and dealt with separately in respect to their Indian title, so it is not necessary to look for a reason to establish a different date for proof of Métis rights.[92] There seems to be no reason to do other than to assert only one important date to mark the start of the constitutional relationship which will reconcile the existence of two distinct political and legal systems.[93]

This leads to a consideration of certain remarks by Chief Justice Lamer, also in *Van der Peet*, concerning the approach to the reconciliation of a pre-existing Aboriginal society with Canada's claims to political and constitutional hegemony over the Aboriginal people and their territory: "To reconcile aboriginal societies with Crown sovereignty it is necessary to identity the distinctive features which need to be acknowledged and reconciled with the sovereignty of the Crown."[94] It is this reasoning that seems to have influenced the Chief Justice in conceiving the idea that a different date from the assertion of Crown authority was required for proof of certain Aboriginal rights. It seems to be evident, however, that the existence of pre-existing, self-governing Aboriginal societies had to be reconciled with Crown sovereignty by addressing the competing sovereignty of the Aboriginal societies. It is the competing political and military authority of Aboriginal nations that, in fact, had to be reconciled with the newly asserted power and authority of the Crown.

In the case of "the Métis people," Canada's attempts to assert its sovereignty over the Métis homeland in 1869 were quickly rebuffed by Métis people who possessed the capacity to do so, and the West only joined Canada once an agreement had been negotiated, as a bargain of Confederation, with the local Métis who challenged Crown sovereignty. It was not the culture of the Métis, but the collective political will to resist Canada, coupled with the power to do so, that had to be reconciled with Canada's annexationist ambitions. The fiddle music and food production methods of the Métis were no threat to Canada in 1869–70. The Métis capacity to form a civil government and to defend its exercise of political authority over its homeland *was* a threat to Canada's unconscionable attempt to assert sovereignty without the agreement required by the law of the Constitution.

An alternative theoretical option is to argue that the Métis do not have

Aboriginal rights but only treaty rights. The political agreement reached between the representatives of the Métis and Canada in 1867, some terms of which are memorialized in section 31 of the *Manitoba Act, 1870,* is arguably a constitutionally protected "bargain of Confederation" and a treaty within the meaning of section 35.[95] The weight of judicial opinion in Métis cases to date, however, does not support the proposition that the Métis people do not have Aboriginal rights, although some of those cases appear, on the facts, to involve non-recognized Indians and not Métis people.

Does "Inherent" Mean the Right Disappears with the People?

An important open question is the "use it or lose it" issue, that is, whether an Aboriginal right is legally irredeemable when a custom, practice, or tradition has effectively been abandoned. In the case of an Aboriginal right of self-government, that possibility will have to be balanced against the implications arising from the fiduciary obligation of the Crown. Presumably, in the case of a self-governing Aboriginal people, the fiduciary relationship means that, upon the assertion of Crown sovereignty, the Crown assumed, in law, the duty to protect the "public interest" of an Aboriginal nation, which must include its continued existence. If the "people" ceases to exist in the sense that there are no continuing societal institutions to sustain its existence, the question must arise whether its disappearance is causally related to a breach of the fiduciary duty of the Crown. If this is the case, does the Crown now have an obligation to assist the reconstitution of the "people" by descendants of the historic nation? Or does an "inherent" right of self-government inhere in a people and disappear with the people? This issue was raised and expressly left open in the *Van der Peet* case.[96]

The RCAP final report did not deal with this issue. It recognized that past policies had resulted in disintegration of Aboriginal "nations" and recommended that the Crown adopt a policy of assisting Aboriginal people to constitute or reconstitute themselves into nations with the features of identified above. Such nations would then be "recognized" as having the legal capacity to enter into political and legal relations with other governments, that is, to exercise an Aboriginal right of self-government.

The Relationship between Local Communities and the Larger Métis "Nation"

Another open question concerns the relationship between the territorially small Aboriginal communities in which are vested certain types of Aboriginal rights related to the user of land, such as hunting and fishing rights, and the larger "people" in which is vested the Aboriginal right of self-government.[97] Any Court decisions that recognize *any* kind of Aboriginal right of "Métis" communities will have significant political consequences on the politics of representation of these communities, and on the subsequent development of the right of self-government.

Definitions of Political Representative Organisations

In 1979 the Native Council of Canada (NCC) officially endorsed a number of statements on behalf of "the Métis and unregistered Indian people of Canada."[98] In *A Statement of Claim*, the NCC identified the Métis nation in these terms: "The Métis people developed as a distinct national group in the Canadian west."

In respect to its unrecognized Indian constituents, it stated, *inter alia*, that "federal Indian legislation was never based on a simple racial classification. As a result government has always recognized many mixed blood people as status Indians and, therefore, as parties to treaties with the Crown."

As mentioned in chapter 1, in 1983 the Métis National Council (MNC) split from the NCC to provide special representation for the Métis people. Subsequently, the NCC restyled itself the Congress of Aboriginal Peoples (CAP). Currently, MNC claims to represent only members of "the Métis nation," whereas CAP claims to represent non-status Indians and those who have recently taken on a "Métis" identity. MNC provincial affiliates predominate in the three Prairie Provinces. Both organizations have provincial political affiliates in British Columbia and Ontario. Only CAP has members who call themselves Métis in all provinces and territories.

Congress of Aboriginal Peoples

The constituency of the Congress of Aboriginal Peoples identifies itself mainly on the basis of their "exclusion from policies and programs for other Aboriginal peoples."[100] Essentially, CAP's constituency consists of persons and groups who view themselves as Aboriginal people but who are excluded from official recognition and its benefits. CAP does not directly assert that it represents the descendants of the Métis nation of western Canada.

CAP does not try to define the Métis people. It describes its Métis constituency as being comprised of various groups of persons.

> These persons, who may or may not be entitled to status under the *Indian Act*, are Métis culturally, historically and for purposes of constitutional recognition. Some of this group are a distinctive mixed blood population, others are closely identified with the history and culture of the French/Cree Métis in southern Manitoba and central Saskatchewan in the 1860's. [sic]
>
> A third group identifies themselves [sic] in terms of specific Tribal connections but are collectively distinct as social communities (e.g., Bush Cree/Métis; "Bay-Métis" in

Northern Ontario, and Gwitchin [sic: Gwich'in] Métis in the northern McKenzie). Specific objectives of these groups vary considerably, but usually include claims settlements in connection with related bands/Inuit settlements (the MNNWT and LMA), claims settlements for small groups of Métis in Ontario and joint initiatives for programs, services and self-government for rural and urban groups, usually in common with rural and urban non-status and status off-reserve Indians.[101]

This constituency of non-recognized persons and groups is at the definitional boundary of Indian and Inuit definition. The CAP constituency describes itself in terms that are reflected in the approach to Métis definition adopted by Professor Gibson in chapter 7, that is, persons who wish to associate with their Indian heritage, and who wish to gain access to government services made available to recognized Indian and Inuit people.

The CAP approach attracts persons who view Métis identity as a preferred label for self-identification for a variety of reasons. Some espouse a pan-Aboriginal identity equivalent to the pan-Indian movement in Canada and the United States.[102] The term "Métis" is a convenient label for this pan-Aboriginal identity, on account of the ease with which the etymological connotation of "mixed blood" can be applied to anybody with any Aboriginal ancestry.

The personal ambivalence or confusion about a Métis identity leads some claimants to plead alternative identities in court. For example, in *R. v. Chiasson*, a New Brunswick case, the defendant claimed Indian identity on account of an eighth-generation unnamed Indian ancestor who lived 280 years earlier. In the alternative legal process, he claimed membership in an organization called la Nation Indien/Métis du Nouveau-Brunswick. The provincial court judge in the case rejected the defendant's arguments, stating,

> There is no history in the eastern provinces, in the Maritimes, of a treaty, pact, convention or agreement with the Métis, as far as I know, in contrast, for example, as to what we find in the western provinces. [translation][103]

In the *Chiasson* case, Judge Arsenault stated that the courts ought to recognize Métis rights as being vested in a group that historically engaged in political relations with the Crown. This is consistent with the approach that has been developed in this chapter and is also evident in the approach the MNC has proposed.

Métis National Council

In 1984, in the course of the First Ministers' conferences that tackled the meaning of section 35, the MNC proposed the following amendment to section 35(2) to particularize the meaning of the reference to "the Métis people" in section 35(1) in order to attain recognition of the Aboriginal right of self-government.[104]

> And whereas from the earliest contact between Indians and Europeans, it was govern-

ment policy to legally recognize persons of mixed ancestry as Indians if they lived and [sic] like Indians and as non-Indians if they lived in the non-Indian community;

and whereas in the Northwest of Canada where the fur trade was carried, on [sic] a separate people emerged who established themselves in separate communities, identified themselves as Métis and asked to be dealt with as an aboriginal people separate from Indians;

and whereas the Government of Canada agreed in 1870 and 1879 to legally recognize these people who elected to identify themselves as Métis as a separate aboriginal people while still recognizing other persons of mixed ancestry in the Northwest of Canada as Indians;

and whereas since one century has elapsed during which a number of additional persons of aboriginal ancestry have come to identify themselves as Métis and have been accepted by the Métis community;

Now therefore the Government of Canada and the provincial governments hereby agree as follows:

1. That the term "Métis" in section 35(2) of the *Canada Act, 1982* [sic], is identified as follows:

Firstly, all persons who are descendants of those Métis who received land grants and/or [sic] Scrip under the provisions of the *Manitoba Act, 1870* or the *Dominion Lands Act, 1879.*

Secondly, other persons of aboriginal descent who identify themselves as Métis and who have been or are accepted by the Métis community.

2. A Métis community is any group of Métis people who can trace their ancestry to those Métis who were legally identified and dealt with as Métis under the two *Acts* referred to in subsection 2 above.

In the October 1992 draft Métis Nation Accord in the Charlottetown Accord, the following definition was proposed.[105]

Whereas in the Northwest of Canada the Métis Nation emerged as a unique Nation with its own language, culture and forms of self-government;

And whereas historically the Métis Nation has sought agreements with Canada to protect its land and other rights;

And whereas Métis were formally recognized in the *Manitoba Act 1870* and the *Dominion Lands Act;*

And whereas the existing aboriginal and treaty rights of Aboriginal peoples including the Métis are recognized and affirmed in the *Constitution Act 1982;*

And whereas the Métis Nation, Canada and the Provinces agree that it is just and desirable to recognize the contribution made by the Métis to the Canadian federation and further agree that measures are necessary to strengthen their place within the Canadian federation;

And whereas the Métis people of Canada have contributed and continue to contribute to the development and prosperity of Canada;

And whereas the Métis Nation, Canada, and the Provinces agree that it is necessary and desirable to set out their respective roles and obligations to each other;

NOW THEREFORE the representatives of the Métis Nation, Canada and the Provinces hereby agree to enter into an Accord in the following terms;

1. Definitions

For the purposes of the Métis Nation and this Accord,

a) "Métis" means an Aboriginal person who self-identifies as Métis, who is distinct from Indian and Inuit [sic: people] and is a descendant of those Métis who received or were entitled to receive land grants and/or [sic] scrip under the provisions of the *Manitoba Act 1870,* or the *Dominion Lands Act,* as enacted from time to time.

b) "Métis Nation" means the community of Métis persons in subsection a) and persons of Aboriginal descent who are accepted by that community.

This definition was part of a package of proposals which included express constitutional recognition of the Aboriginal right of self-government, and which had been negotiated with First Ministers by MNC as the recognized representatives of the Métis nation. The Charlottetown Accord did not become part of the law of the Constitution, as reviewed in chapter 1, and MNC has continued to tackle the question of Métis definition for purposes of section 35.

MNC is now consulting its membership on the following definition which was proposed at the organization's annual meeting in Vancouver in June 2001.[106]

1. "Métis" means a person who self-identifies as Métis, is of Historic Métis Nation ancestry, and is accepted by the Métis Nation through the Acceptance Process.

2. "Acceptance Process" means the process to accept applications for registration on the Métis Nation Register, as established herein, and administered by the respective MNC provincial governing members jointly with the MNC, all as amended from time to time.

3. "Historic Métis Nation" means the Aboriginal people then known as Métis or Half-Breeds who resided in the Historic Métis Homeland.

4. "Historic Métis Nation Homeland" means the area of land in west central North America used and occupied as the traditional territory of the Métis, or Half-Breeds as they were then known.

...

7. "Métis Nation" means the Aboriginal people descended from the Historic Métis Nation which is now comprised of all Métis Nation Citizens and is one of the "aboriginal peoples of Canada" within the meaning of section 35 of the *Constitution Act 1982*.

8. "Métis Nation Citizen" means a person whose name is on the Métis Nation Register.

The following features of these definitions reflect the analysis in this chapter.

1. "Mixed ancestry" is not the foundation of the identity of the Métis people; many other people have mixed ancestry.

2. Unique economic, social, and political circumstances in northwestern North America gave rise to an Indigenous people that was distinct from the ancient Indigenous peoples of the area, who are now called "Indians."

3. The new Indigenous people was recognized by colonial authorities and Canada.

4. The contemporary Métis communities that descend from the historic Métis nation have accepted as members persons not themselves descended from the historic Métis nation.

The MNC definitions, surprisingly, focus on defining individuals rather than the nation itself, but it is nevertheless clear that the nation is conceived as an organic social and political community, which maintains its identity through time and generations, and not as an aggregation of individuals united by a concept of racial ancestry. Another salient feature is the weight or value placed upon birth in the community to determine if a person belongs to the community.

MNC has been recognized since 1983 as the political representative of the Métis nation of western Canada by actions of the federal government, including invitations to participate in various national Aboriginal initiatives, and by the Prime Minister of Canada in exercising his constitutional duty to invite "representatives of the Aboriginal peoples" to the First Ministers' conferences on Aboriginal constitutional reform of the 1980s.

The membership of the MNC consists of regional or provincial political representative organizations; it is not an organization of Métis persons, but of political organizations that represent Métis communities. Its membership has shifted from time to time since its creation. It included an organization from the Northwest Territories for a time, and now includes the Métis Nation of Ontario, which has members in communities that were formerly hotbeds of hatred against the Métis of the West.

The Métis settlements of Alberta, the only communities recognized as Métis today in provincial law, were originally set up in 1938 for impoverished Cree people who had been enfranchised with Métis scrip. The settlements are not members of MNC, although many of the residents of the settlements identify as Métis and participate in MNC politics.

The shifting membership of MNC illustrates the dynamic character of political representation, and the overwhelming ambivalence and confusion about Métis identity in Canada. It also shows that the task of identifying the contemporary Métis people with a right of self-government is not a straightforward project.

Conclusion

"The Métis people" in section 35 will be defined by the Court in cases that decide which communities have the rights protected by section 35. The assumption that section 35 affirms a right of Aboriginal self-government draws support from federal policy, the RCAP (1996) recommendations, and the opinion of United Nations bodies, as well as from scholarly works. The fundamental human right of self-determination, in its domestic reflection in the form of the Aboriginal right of self-government, supports the approach, based upon the review in chapter 3, which moves away from the boundary of Indian definition.

Each of the Indian peoples, or "First Nations," has its own right of self-determination and of self-government, and the term "Métis people" must not be interpreted in a manner that would make Métis rights parasitic upon Indian rights. A central thesis in chapters 3 and 8 is that the interpretation of section 35 ought to do justice to all the Aboriginal peoples that are recognized by the provision. Moving away from the irrational boundary of Indian definition as maintained by past federal law and policy is better than using that definition as a foundation for the judicial recognition of new claimants to Aboriginal rights under the term "the Métis people." Persons of Aboriginal ancestry who wish to associate with their Indian heritage may become members of their ancestral community, where they are accepted by that Indian community.

An inquiry into the definition of "the Métis people" in section 35 leads to the conclusion already reached by historians, namely, that in Canadian history there has been only one ancestral "Métis nation" that was self-governing, and whose recognized historical existence reveals the long and difficult struggle for the protection of the rights that are now affirmed by section 35, according to the Court's view of the purpose of section 35. This historic nation is "Riel's people" of western Canada, whose history includes negotiations that led to the birth of Manitoba, and military encounters with both Indians and colonial and Canadian authorities, which crystallized their distinct identity as a unique people.

A just interpretation of section 35 requires attention to the need to revise, and perhaps expand, the category of "Indians," while "the Métis people" is better confined to a category that can rationally be distinguished from the Indian category. Moving towards this positive core of Métis identity means abandoning not only the conceptual boundary of Indian definition, but also the idea that Métis rights are derived from the rights of Indians. In particular, Métis persons have no claim to participation in the benefits of Indian treaties. The idea that Métis persons can claim treaty benefits only arises if the erroneous assumption that "Métis" means "mixed blood" is adopted.

The true construction of the term "the Métis people," following accepted judicial analysis, recognizes the evolution of the Métis people as an exceptional phenomenon that responded to a unique set of social, political, and economic stimuli in western Canada during the nineteenth century.

It is necessary to recognize the distinction between the racial category comprised of individuals of Aboriginal ancestry who are entitled to affirmative action remedies under section 15 of the *Charter of Rights*, and the historic nation whose group rights are recognized in section 35. The purposes of the two constitutional provisions are quite distinct, and the membership of the two categories must not be conflated. This distinction reflects the broad experience in other countries, where "mixed blood" or *mestizo* people are not viewed as part of the Indigenous population.

It is not possible, on the present state of the law and without a factual inquiry that is beyond the scope of this chapter, to offer a definite conclusion about the identity of "the Métis people" with an Aboriginal right of self-government. However, some useful observations may be drawn from an examination of the CAP and MNC approaches to Métis identity and definition.

The "pan-Aboriginal" approach to Métis identity emphasizes a "mixed blood" ancestry linked to any Indian family anywhere in Canada. This approach would legitimize in law the effects of the policy of dismantling Indian nations and would therefore be inconsistent with Canada's international obligations to respect international law, which recognizes the equal right of self-determination of all peoples. It fails to recognize the exceptional circumstances which gave rise to the Métis people in western Canada, and would fail to reflect the long and wide experience of other countries where the "mixed blood" or *mestizo* people are not regarded as a separate Indigenous people, but are either part of the general population or part of the Indigenous nations. The geographically proximate case is the United States, where "mixed blood" people, including many belonging to the kinship networks of the Métis nation, are part of Indian tribes or part of the general American population.

The project of building a Métis definition at the irrational boundary of federal Indian definition legitimizes the results of the federal policy of dismantling ancient Indian nations, and emphasizes the subsequent integration of Aboriginal families and individuals into Canadian society. This approach asks about the identity of the individual, as if Aboriginal rights belonged to individuals as

Charter rights do. It fails to ask persistently, as it ought, about the identity of the Aboriginal *community* to which a claimant belongs, and without which the individual has no Aboriginal rights. By focusing on individuals and searching for an Indian ancestry, the courts, in this approach, view all Indian nations as fungible; one is the same as the other. The result would be to ascribe constitutional status to the idea that the group identity derived from an ancestral link to an Indian nation has no constitutional relevance; any descendant can trade in an ancient link to a particular Indian nation by relying on a new pan-Aboriginal sense of Métis identity. This approach, which is evident in many cases reviewed in chapter 3, is inconsistent with the basic purposes of section 35, which aims to respect the distinctive value of each Aboriginal nation.

There are over one hundred cases now making their way through the courts under the name of self-styled Métis claimants. Whatever definition the Court adopts will be the correct legal answer, but it is bound to be a politically contentious decision. One result that can be anticipated is significant turmoil over the question of the legitimacy of political representation.

The definition of "the Métis people" is the hard case of Aboriginal law in Canada. The decisions of the Court will reverberate across Canada and beyond, as did the events at the ill-fated Battle of Batoche in 1885, where the rattle of the newly invented Gatling Gun being used on the hapless Métis heralded the modern era, where small arms fuel worldwide violence rooted in ethnic and civic nationalisms.

In these circumstances, it is useful to have a frame of reference to test the merits of the judicial decision that lies outside the realm of judicial invention. The concept of recognition, straddling both law and policy, offers a useful frame of reference against which to judge the answers of the judges. An approach has been proposed where judicial recognition follows historic recognition by the Crown. This approach moves away from the boundary of federal Indian definition, and does not legitimize the dismantling of Indian nations. It moves towards the positive core of Métis ancestral identity. Moving away from the boundary of federal Indian definition is just, for it respects the history and heritage of the Métis people and the Indian people alike. It pays due regard to the history in which the Métis people set for themselves the conditions under which they were prepared to assert their distinct identity. It eschews the notion that modern claimants might base their claims to a status and rights in the Constitution of Canada upon their own contemporary assertions and not upon the claims that are brought through them by their ancestors who fought for these rights. The courts ought to heed the voices of the ancestors in deciding on the nature and scope of ancestral rights, and who has them.

Notes

[1]The Court has decided the *Dumont* case, *infra* note 55, which involved a preliminary issue in an action seeking a declaration about Métis constitutional rights to land, not Aboriginal rights. Although there are no Court decisions on Métis Aboriginal rights, there is a large number of lower court decisions, and over one hundred cases now across Canada styled as Métis cases. The point in the text is simply that the Court has no previous decisions of its own to guide it, and few principles from English law.

[2]Brian Slattery, "Making Sense of Aboriginal and Treaty Rights" (2000) 79 Can. Bar Rev. 196.

[3]*R. v. Blais,* [2001] 3 C.N.L.R. 187 (Man. C.A.), leave to appeal to the Supreme Court of Canada granted: [2001] S.C.C.A. No. 294 n. 52.

[4]*R. v. Powley,* [2001] 2 C.N.L.R. 291 (Ont. C.A.), leave to appeal to the Supreme Court of Canada granted: [2001] S.C.C.A. No. 256 n. 48.

[5]*Ibid.,* at 332. "The respondents' ancestors were among those who moved to the reserve. They accepted the benefits of the treaty and acquired status as band members. The respondents' Métis ancestor, Eustace Lesage, left Sault Ste Marie with many other Métis in the 1850s and joined the Batchewana Band, with the result that his descendants' membership in the band community was thereafter controlled by the *Indian Act.* In 1918, Steve Powley's grandmother, Eva Lesage, lost her band membership by marrying a non-Indian, with the result that her descendants are not band members and the respondents cannot benefit from the band's communal rights," per Sharpe J.

[6]The history includes skirmishes in Red River with the first European settlers early in the 1800s, political resistance to the Hudson's Bay Company's attempts to monopolize the fur trade, political and military action, including the creation of a civil government in 1869–70, which gave rise to the birth of Manitoba in an historic "bargain of Confederation," continued resistance to Canadian intrusions in regions further west, which resulted in legal and practical recognition of some Métis rights, and culminated in the final military encounter at Batoche on South Saskatchewan River in May, 1885. This history is recorded in a voluminous literature; see e.g. works cited in note 45 *infra.*

[7]*Powley, supra* note 4, at 329.

[8]This is expressly emphasized by Sharpe J. in the Ontario Court of Appeal in *Powley, ibid.* at 315; "It is impossible to define the rights of an entire people within the confines of one case. As the record in this case amply demonstrates, claims of Aboriginal rights are intensely fact specific, and involve close, careful and detailed scrutiny of events long past. Recognition of a right on one set of facts does not necessarily mean that the right will be made out on the next set of facts. We must guard against the temptation to pronounce broadly upon all possible aspects of the rights of the Metis people and should instead confine ourselves to what is necessary for the resolution of the case before us." This is a technique of legal analysis, which distinguishes cases on their facts. Accordingly, statements in the court of appeal, such as those relating to "the Métis Nation" at 299 (para. 18) are not part of the legal decision because the facts involved a small community in the geographical vicinity of Sault Ste Marie.

[9]See RCAP's definition of Aboriginal "nation," *supra* at 276, and especially Canada, *Report of the Royal Commission on Aboriginal Peoples: Restructuring the Relationship,* vol. 2 (Ottawa: Supply and Services Canada, 1996) c. 3.

[10]See Ted Moses, "Self-Determination and the Survival of Indigenous Peoples, in Aikio & Scheinin, eds., *infra* note 60 at 155, esp. at 172–75, for a discussion of these United

Nations commentaries, and citations.

[11]See *supra* note 9.

[12]For a critique of circular legal reasoning, see Felix Cohen, "Transcendental Nonsense and the Functional Approach" (1935) 35 Columbia L. Rev. 809.

[13]In the *Quebec Secession Reference* case, as cited in Joffe, *infra* note 35 at 173 and note 16. For a severe condemnation of the doctrine of parliamentary sovereignty in respect to Indian policy, see Menno Boldt, *Surviving as Indians: The Challenge of Self-government* (Toronto: University of Toronto Press, 1993) at 9.

[14]*R. v. Sparrow*, [1990] 1 S.C.R. 1075, where the Court stated:

> The approach to be taken with respect to interpreting the meaning of s. 35(1) is derived from general principles of constitutional interpretation, principles relating to aboriginal rights, and the purposes behind the constitutional provision itself.

[15]*Reference Re Language Rights Under the Manitoba Act, 1870*, [1985] 1 S.C.R. 721 at 745.

[16]*Reference Re Secession of Quebec*, [1998] 2 S.C.R. 217, 161 D.L.R. (4th) 385, 228 N.R. 203, 37 I.L.M. 1342 at para. 32 S.C.R.

[17]*Ibid.* (para. 32).

[18]*Ibid.* (para 52).

[19]*Re The Regulation and Control of Aeronautics in Canada*, [1932] Appeal Cases 54, at 70. (Privy Council), rev"g [1930] S.C.R. 663. RCAP relies on this authority in its interpretation of s. 35 of the *Constitution Act, 1982*, in its final report, *supra* note 9 at 194.

[20]The extract from the *Aeronautics* case was quoted with approval by the Court in *Re British North America Act and the Federal Senate* (1979), 30 N.R.271, at 287. In the *Reference Re Adoption Act*, [1938] S.C.R. 398 at 402, Duff C.J. referred to the "basic compact of Confederation."

[21]*Re Education Act*, [1987] 1 S.C.R. 1148, at 1173–74, per Wilson J.

[22]Paul L.A.H. Chartrand, *Manitoba's Metis Settlement Scheme of 1870* (Saskatoon: University of Saskatchewan Native Law Centre, 1991) at 5.

[23]*R. v. Big M Drug Mart*, [1985] 1 S.C.R. 295 at 335.

[24]*R. v. Sparrow, supra* note 14 at 1105.

[25] The Court identifies the nature of the interests at stake in construing constitutional provisions: *Hunter* v. *Southam*, [1984] 2 S.C.R. 145, at 157; sub nom *Dir. of Investigation and Research, Combines Investigation Branch* v. *Southam* (1984), 41 C.R. (3d) 97, at 112. The interpretation of s. 35 requires the identification of the interests of the Aboriginal peoples, and "the Métis people" is identified by finding in history, a "people" having interests of the kind that was recognized and affirmed in s. 35. The capacity of the Crown to infringe those interests are restrained by the principle of protection in the fiduciary relationship.

For a discussion of the function of common law Aboriginal rights in protecting the interests of Indigenous peoples, see Jeremy Webber, "Beyond Regret: Mabo's Implications For Australian Constitutionalism" in Duncan Ivison, Paul Patton & Will Sanders, eds., *Political Theory and the Rights of Indigenous Peoples* (Cambridge University Press, 2000) c. 4, p. 60.

In *Oyekan et al.* v. *Adele*, [1957] 2 All E.R. 785, at 788, Lord Denning M.R. stated:

> In inquiring, however, what rights are recognised, there is one guiding principle. It is this: The courts will assume the British Crown intends that the rights of property of the inhabitants are to be fully respected. Whilst, therefore, the British Crown, as Sovereign, can make laws enabling it compulsorily to acquire land for public purposes, it will see that proper compensation is awarded to every one of the inhabitants who has by native law an interest in it; and the courts will declare the inhabitants entitled to compensation according to their interests, even though those interests are of a kind unknown to English law: see *Amodu Tijani* v. *Southern Nigeria (Secretary)* [1921] 2 A.C. 399; *Sakariyawo Oshodi* v. *Mariano Dakolo* [1930] A.C. 667.)

[26]Brian Slattery, "Making Sense of Aboriginal and Treaty Rights," [2000] 79 *Can. Bar Rev.* 196.

[27]*R.* v. *Sparrow, supra* note 14 at 1105–1106.

[28]*R.* v. *Van der Peet,* [1996] 2 S.C.R. 507 at 548, 550.

[29]*R.* v. *Van der Peet,* [1996] 4 C.N.L.R. 177 at 200 (S.C.C.).

[30]See generally Leonard Ian Rotman, *Parallel Paths: Fiduciary Doctrine and the Crown-Native Relationship in Canada* (Toronto: The University of Toronto Press, 1996).

[31]*R.* v. *Sparrow, supra* note 14 at 1108.

[32]The law of the constitution has emerged from early English principles: *R.* v. *Keyn* (1876) 2 Ex.D.63, at 236–37, per Cockburn C.J. The constitutional result of a Crown assertion of sovereignty vis-à-vis the interests of an Aboriginal people does not have the same result as the duty of allegiance which, in traditional English law, binds individual subjects to loyalty to the Crown. The new relationship is one where sovereignty is shared. P.H. Russell, "Aboriginal Nationalism and Quebec Nationalism: Reconciliation through Fourth World Decolonization" (1997) 8:4 *Constitutional Forum* 110, at 116.

[33]*Sparrow, supra* note 14 at 1109.

[34]*Supra* note 16 at para. 82 S.C.R.

[35]Paul Joffe, "Assessing the *Delgamuukw* Principles: National Implications and Potential Effects in Quebec, (2000) 45 *McGill Law Journal,* 155, at 166, and see also the view of Peter Russell, *supra* note 32 at 165, 166 therein.

[36]Russell, *supra* note 32 at 116.

[37]Professor Slattery has proposed an "organic" model of the Constitution which seems to suggest the same approach. The model has three main features: 1) It is rooted ultimately in Canadian soil rather than in Europe, while acknowledging the important influences of Great Britain and France; 2) It subscribes to a pluralist conception of the sources of law and authority, viewing the Crown as the constitutional trustee of coordinate spheres of jurisdiction rather than their exclusive source; 3) It rejects the positivist view that our most fundamental laws are embodied in legislation and are grounded ultimately on the sovereign's power to command obedience. The model portrays the law as immanent in our collective practices and traditions, which, in turn, reflect more basic values and principles.

In summary, the organic model views the Constitution as: indigenous to Canada rather than an alien import; complex in nature rather than monistic; and fundamentally customary in nature rather than composed simply of positive law. According to Professor Slattery, the model "encourages us to recognize the diverse roles that Indian, Inuit and Métis peoples have played in the formation of this country, and its Constitution. It suggests that Aboriginal peoples should be viewed as active participants in generating the basic norms that govern us—not as people on the fringes, helpless victims, or recipients of constitutional handouts from the government or the courts, but as contributors to the evolution of our Constitution and most fundamental laws." Brian Slattery, "The Organic Constitution: Aboriginal Peoples and the Evolution of Canada" (1995) 34 Osgoode Hall L.J. 101 at 111, 112.

[38]*A.G. Quebec* v. *Sioui,* [1990] 1 S.C.R. 1025 (S.C.C.)1043 at 1053.

[39]For a contemporary appeal to the idea that justice suggests that Canadians ought to adopt an image of Canada as a multinational North American country that respects its Indigenous or North American foundations, see Paul L.A.H. Chartrand, "Aboriginal Self-Government: Towards a Vision of Canada as a North American Multinational Country" in J. Oakes & R. Riewe, *Issues in the North,* vol. II (Winnipeg: Canadian Circumpolar Conference and Department of Native Studies, University of Manitoba, 1997) 81. See also Slattery, *supra* note 37.

[40]S. 35 recognizes and affirms existing Aboriginal and treaty rights. In the case of each

category of rights, their origins are in the history of the political relations between the Aboriginal peoples and the Crown. Prof. Brian Slattery argues that one of the two main sources of the doctrine of Aboriginal rights is "a distinctive body of custom generated by intensive relations between indigenous peoples and the British Crown..." in "Making Sense of Aboriginal and Treaty Rights" (2000) 79 Can. Bar Rev. 196 at 199. Will Kymlicka discusses history based agreements as sources of group-differentiated rights of national minorities in *Liberalism, Community and Culture* (Oxford: Oxford University Press) 116ff.

    [41]*Sioui, supra* note 38.

    [42]*Reference re Language Rights Under the Manitoba Act, 1870,* [1985] 1 S.C.R. 721, at 731; (1985), 19 D.L.R. (4th) 1, at 9; (1985), 35 Man.R. (2d) 83, at 91; (1985), 59 N.R. 321 at 329; [1985] 4 W.W.R. 393.

    [43]*R.* v. *Forest,* [1977] 1 W.W.R. 363 at 374–75 (Man. Co. Ct.) per Dureault Co.Ct.J. A similar view is expressed by the historian W.L. Morton, who states that in negotiating with Canadian representatives in 1870, the Métis "aim was to make such terms with Canada as would enable the people of the North-West to control its local government in the early days of settlement, and would allow them to possess themselves [sic], as individuals and as a people, enough of the lands of the North-West to survive as a people...." W.L. Morton, ed. *Manitoba: The Birth of a Province* (Winnipeg: Manitoba Record Society Publications, 1984) at xvi. Interestingly, historians have concluded that the inchoate "mixed-blood" ethnic community in Ontario, from which the plaintiffs in Powley claim descent, had not survived the onslaught of local immigration twenty years earlier.

    [44]Cases are generally decided on the basis of the facts proved in court, but judges are permitted to "take judicial notice" of facts that are so notorious or uncontroversial that evidence of their existence is unnecessary. See *Public School Boards' Association of Alberta* v. *Alberta (Attorney-General),* [2000] 1 S.C.R. 44 at 47, per Binnie J.

    [45]See particularly the scholarly analyses in the following two publications: Jacqueline Peterson & Jennifer Brown, eds., *The New Peoples: Being and Becoming Metis in North America* (Winnipeg: University of Manitoba Press, 1985); T. Binnema, G.J. Ens & R.C. Maclead, eds., *From Rupert's Land to Canada* (Edmonton. University of Alberta Press, 2001). Other historical accounts of the Métis in the Canadian West may be found in, among many others, W.L. Morton, *Manitoba: A History* (Toronto: University of Toronto Press, 1957), J.K. Howard, *The Strange Empire of Louis Riel* (New York: Houghton-Mifflin Co., 1952), Marcel Giraud, *The Metis in the Canadian West,* trans. George Woodcock, 2 vol. (Edmonton: University of Alberta Press, 1985); G.F.G. Stanley, *The Birth of Western Canada: A History of the Riel Rebellion* (Toronto: University of Toronto Press, 1960); W.L. Morton, ed., *Manitoba: The Birth of a Province* (Winnipeg: Manitoba Record Society Publications, 1965).

    [46]Chartrand, *supra* note 22 at 127–37.

    [47]*Re Manitoba Language Rights, supra* note 42 at 745 S.C.R.

    [48]Dickason in Brown, *supra* note 45.

    [49]See Peterson in Brown, *supra* note 45 and c. 3 *supra.*

    [50]*Sparrow, supra* note 14.

    [51]See the more recent literature which analyses the factors that allowed the rise of a new people, including John Foster, "Wintering, the Outsider Adult Male and the Ethnogenesis of the Western Plains Metis" in Peterson & Brown, *supra* note 45 at 179; and Heather Devine "Les Desjarlais: The Development and Dispersion of a Proto-Metis Hunting Band, 1785–1870" in T. Binnema *et al., supra* note 45 at 129.

    [52]These statutes and orders are reviewed in Percy Hodges & E.D. Noonan, *Saskatchewan Metis: Brief on Investigation into the Legal, Equitable and Moral Claimes [sic: claims] of*

the Metis People of Saskatchewan in Relation to the Extinguishment of the Indian Title (Saskatoon, Saskatchewan Archives Board, Premier's Office, R–191, Box 1, P–M2, 1943.)

[53]S. 52(2), Constitution Act, 1982, and Schedule, Item 2.

[54]See Chartrand, supra note 22.

[55]See Dumont v. Canada (Attorney General), [1987] M.J. No. 108, where the court dismissed the application of the Attorney General of Canada to strike out the plaintiff's statement of claim. The Manitoba Court of Appeal, [1988] M.J. No. 327, [1988] 3 C.N.L.R. 39. The order of the Court of Appeal was subsequently set aside by the Supreme Court of Canada, [1990] S.C.J. No. 17, and the action was allowed to proceed to trial. See Dumont v. Canada (Attorney General) M.J. No. 57 (Oliphant J.) allowing motions of the plaintiffs to amend their statement of claim and the defendants to adjourn the trial date which had been set for May 13, 2001.

[56]R. v. Van der Peet, [1996] 2 S.C.R. 507, [1996] 4 C.N.L.R. at 201 (para. 41).

[57]Ibid. at 206 (para. 65).

[58]Ibid. at 205–6 (para. 63). Lamer C.J. noted the trope used by Brennan J. in the Australian High Court case of Mabo v. Queensland [No 2] (1992), 175 C.L.R. 1 at 60, on this point, "…when the tide of history has washed away any real acknowledgement of traditional law and any real observance of traditional customs, the foundation of native title has disappeared. A native title which has ceased with the abandoning of laws and customs based on tradition can not be revived for contemporary recognition." It may be emphasized that an aboriginal right of self-government is not the same as a native title right that was the subject of comment by Brennan.

[59]See c. 1 supra at 33ff.

[60]The implications of the right of self-determination for the construction of s. 35 deserve a full examination that is beyond the scope of this work. See Paul Joffe, supra note 35 for a scholarly discussion of the subject. Some informative recent works on the significance of the right of self-determination for Indigenous peoples include Royal Commission on Aboriginal Peoples, Canada's Fiduciary Obligations to Aboriginal Peoples in the Context of the Accession to Sovereignty by Quebec, vol. 1, International Dimensions by S. James Anaya, Richard Falk & Donat Pharand (Ottawa: Canada Communication Group–Publishing, August 1995); Grand Council of the Crees, Sovereign Injustice: Forcible Inclusion of the James Bay Cree and Cree Territory into a Sovereign Quebec (Nemaska, Eeyou Astchee, Canada: Grand Council of the Crees, October 1995); S. James Anaya, Indigenous Peoples in International Law (New York: Oxford University Press, 1996); Pekka Aikio & Martin Scheinin, eds. Operationalizing the Right of Indigenous Peoples to Self-Determination (Turko, Finland: Abo Akademi University. Institute for Human Rights, 2000).

[61]RCAP, supra note 9, c. 3 at 178. In Powley, supra note 4 at 335, the Ontario Court of Appeal correctly noted that the RCAP definition of individual Métis persons (in Vol. 4, c. 5, p. 203) was not for the purpose of proving common law rights but for the different purpose of political recognition by the federal government.

[62]RCAP supra note 9, c. 3 at 177.

[63]Powley, supra note 4.

[64]Ibid.

[65]Ibid. at 299–300 (para. 23): "In 1852, the Crown made lands available for sale to the Metis inhabitants of Sault Ste. Marie at a favourable price." This is the equivalent of the settler rights recognized in s. 32 of the Manitoba Act, 1870. On s. 32, and the difference between aboriginal group rights recognized in s. 31 of the Act and individual rights of settlers, see Chartrand, supra note 22 at 19–21.

[66]*Powley, supra* note 4.

[67]*Ibid.* at 299 (para. 22).

[68]*Ibid.* at 298 (para. 18).

[69]See Jacqueline Peterson, "Many Roads to Red River: Métis Genesis in the Great Lakes Region 1680–1815" in J. Peterson & J. Brown, *supra* note 35, 37, where it is concluded that this is what happened to the Sault Ste Marie area "mixed-blood" population.

[70]*Supra* note 4 at 331–32 (para. 135, 136). The creation of the legal fiction of community continuity relied upon a view which took account of "severe prejudice and discrimination inflicted upon the Metis," which, in the Court of Appeal's view, entitled the Superior Court judge on appeal to take this "historically disadvantaged situation of the Metis into account when assessing the continuity of their community." However, the Court of Appeal relied upon evidence, at 331 (para. 135), concerning the Métis people in western Canada. This is contrary to the law established in the Supreme Court of Canada, which requires that aboriginal rights be based upon local conditions relevant to the claimant community.

[71]*Powley, supra* note 4 at 298. The word "strain" has a biological and not a social meaning. The *Concise Oxford Dictionary of Current English,* H.W. Fowler & F.G. Fowler, eds., 8th ed. (Oxford: The Clarendon Press, 1990) defines it as meaning "a breed or stock of animals, plants, etc."at 1204; the *Gage Canadian Dictionary* (Toronto: Gage Publishing Ltd, 1983) defines it as "a line of descent; race; stock; breed.," at 1110.

[72]*Supra* c. 3, text accompanying note 4.

[73]See e.g., Ashley Montagu, *Man's Most Dangerous Myth: The Fallacy of Race,* 6th ed. (Walnut Creek, CA: Altamira Press, 1997). A basic tenet of racist thinking is that physical differences such as skin colour or nose shape are intrinsically and unalterably tied to meaningful differentials in basic intelligence or "civilization": Joe R. Feagin & C.B. Feagin, "Racial and Ethnic Relations" in Juan F. Perea *et al., Race and Races: Cases and Materials for a Diverse America* (St. Paul, MN: West Group, American Case Book Series, 2000) at 56.

Here is an example of this view applied to "mixed-blood" people in western Canada in the nineteenth century: "My criterion for distinguishing a halfbreed from an Indian is not colour, hair or morals, for these all fail in pointing out your man at times. I take the nostrils. The pure Indian, whose blood has never been polluted by Europeans, has a large distended nostril, all of those who have any portion of European blood, have their nostrils contracted in proportion to their approximation to Europeans": John E. Foster, "Missionaries, Mixed-Bloods and the Fur Trade" *The Western Journal of Anthropology* (1972) 3:1, p. 94, at 112–13.

[74]"...[T]here is no distinctive biological reality called 'race' that can be determined by objective scientific procedures. The social, medical and physical sciences have demonstrated this fact... Human populations singled out as 'races' are simply groups with visible differences that Europeans and European Americans have decided to emphasize as important in their social, economic, and political relations," in Feagin & Feagin, *supra* note 73 at 57.

[75]Jennifer Brown & Theresa Schenk, "Métis, Mestizo and Mixed-Blood" in Philip J. Deloria & Neal Salisbury, eds., *A Companion to American History* (Malden, MA, and Oxford: Blackwell Publishers, 2002) at 231.

[76]Karen I. Blu, *The Lumbee Problem: The Making of an American Indian People* (New York: Cambridge University Press, 1980) at 219.

[77]The tangled web of such cross-cutting identities is illustrated by the seven "typologies" identified by Robert K. Thomas, in Peterson and Brown, *supra* note 45, 243, at 248–50. See also the confusion identified by an eminent scholar, the late John Foster, in attempting to account for the multiplicity of groups made up of "mixed-blood" persons with various ante-

cedents, in "The Métis: The People and the Term" in A.S. Lussier, ed., *Louis Riel and the Métis* (Winnipeg: Pemmican Publications, 1979) p. 77.

[78]*Corbiere* v. *Canada*, [1999] 3 C.N.L.R. 19. An analysis of the judicially constructed notion of "Aboriginality," its relationship to the other judicial notion of "human dignity" for purposes of s. 15, and the concepts behind the category of "Indians" in s. 91(24) of the *Constitution Act, 1867*, which the Court has also characterized as a "racial" concept, invites a thorough and critical analysis that is beyond the scope of this work.

[79]*Lovelace* v. *Ontario*, [2000] 4 C.N.L.R.145.

[80]See Alan Cairns, *Citizens Plus: Aboriginal Peoples and the Canadian State* (Vancouver: University of British Columbia Press, 2000), where the distinction does not seem to be addressed.

[81]Contrary to what often seems assumed by commentators, the text of s. 35 does not require the construction that there is more than one Métis people. The plural would be required to refer to the aggregation of the three categories even if there were only one "people" in each of the three categories of Indian, Inuit, and Métis. Manifestly, there are many "Indian" peoples, on any definition of the word, but, as a matter of textual construction alone, the plural form of "peoples" where it appears at the end of the three categories signifies nothing about whether either the singular or the plural form applies to any one category preceding the noun. The same would be true if either Indian or Inuit had been inserted in the current place of the word "Métis" next to the term "peoples." The term "Métis" does not require the plural construction merely because it is the next-door neighbour of the term "peoples." *Contra*, C. Bell, "Who are the Métis People in Section 35(2)? (1991) Alta. L. Rev. 351, at 355. In *Powley, supra* note 4 at 314, Sharpe J. stated: "It is clear from the text of s. 35 that the Métis peoples of Canada had, as of the date of the enactment of the section, "existing" rights, and that those rights have now acquired constitutional protection." It appears from this statement that the court intended to express a view only about the effect of s. 35, and not about whether there is one or more Métis peoples, an issue which the court did not directly consider.

[82]RCAP, *supra* note 9, c. 3, at 178. In *Powley*, the Ontario Court of Appeal correctly noted that the RCAP definition of individual Métis persons (in vol. 4, c.5, p. 203) was not for the purpose of proving common law rights but for the different purpose of political recognition by the federal government, *supra* note 4 at 335.

[83]*Supra* note 45 and c. 3.

[84]For example, Bryan Schwartz states that "The Métis are certainly indigenous to North American—they came into being as a distinct people on this continent. But they are not aboriginal in the same sense as the Indian and Inuit; they were not here from the beginning...." *First Principles: Constitutional Reform with Respect to the Aboriginal Peoples of Canada, 1982–1984* (Kingston: Institute of Intergovernmental Relations, Queen's University, 1985) 188, at 228.

[85]See Catherine Bell, "Métis Constitutional Rights in Section 35(1)" (1997) 36 (1) Alta. L. Rev. 180.

[86]This approach, which recognizes the positive value of Metis political action, may be compared to the approach of the court in *Powley*, which seems to aim to develop a theory of Métis rights based upon liberal sympathy for the disadvantages suffered by some Métis people. The latter approach belongs to the realm of *Charter* interpretation, not to s. 35 rights.

[87]See Slattery, *infra* note 89.

[88]*R.* v. *Van der Peet*, [1996] 4 C.N.L.R. 177 at 207.

[89]See Brian Slattery, "Making Sense of Aboriginal and Treaty Rights" in (2000) 79 Can. Bar Rev. 196, esp. 215–20.

[90]*Ibid.* at 218.

⁹¹In *Powley, supra* note 4, the Court took the view that the law decided in Indian cases required to be changed to accommodate the later emergence of the Métis people.

⁹²In constitutional theory, when the Crown assumes governmental responsibility for the protection of the "public" or group interests of an Aboriginal group, and the law imposes a fiduciary relationship for that end, the Aboriginal people owe a legal duty of allegiance to the Crown. See *supra* note 32. In 1885, Louis Riel was hanged for treason, which assumes a duty of allegiance to the Crown, so it appears that the original date must precede 1885, unless the charge of treason was constitutionally flawed. The question seems not to have been raised in the appeals from Riel's conviction.

⁹³See J.C. Smith, "The Concept of Native Title" (1974) 24 University of Toronto L. J. 1.

⁹⁴This paragraph in the *Van der Peet* case is typical of the reasoning which attaches significance to distinctive cultural features: [1996] 2 S.C.R. 507 at 554 (para. 57) per Lamer C.J.

⁹⁵See Paul Chartrand, *Manitoba's Métis Settlement Scheme* (Saskatoon: University of Saskatchewan Native Law Centre, 1991) at 127–37. The Court has held that s. 35 treaties can include implied terms based on the relations between the parties and underlying assumptions: *R. v. Marshall*, [1999] 4 C.N.L.R. 161 at 186–87.

⁹⁶*Van der Peet, supra* note 28.

⁹⁷ *Prima facie*, the concept of "subsidiarity" might prove to be a useful conceptual tool to define this relationship. The principle of subsidiarity, not well known in Canada, is found in the Maastricht Treaty of the European Union of 1992. For a discussion of the origins of the term, see M. Wilke & H. Wallace, "Subsidiarity: Approaches to Power-Sharing in the European Community" (1990) Royal Institute of International Affairs. Discussion Paper No. 27. See also the series of articles about subsidiarity in (1993) 3:3 *National Journal of Constitutional Law*, pp. 301–427.

⁹⁸Native Council of Canada, *A Statement of Claim Based On Aboriginal Title of Métis and Non-Status Indians* (Ottawa: Native Council of Canada, February, 1980) at (i).

⁹⁹The federal government recognizes and negotiates land claims with Métis representatives in the Northwest Territories, where there is no provincial authority upon which to foist responsibility for the claims of the Métis people. Elsewhere, the federal government disputes the legal claims of the Métis people, and mounts vigorous legal defences.

¹⁰⁰The information about CAP and its constituency is from its web site at www.abo-peoples.org/.

¹⁰¹*Ibid.*

¹⁰²The *Indian Act* definition is an example of a pan-Indian identity. See Canada, Report of the Royal Commission on Aboriginal Peoples: Looking Forward, Looking Back, vol. 1 (Ottawa: Supply and Services Canada, 1996), c. 9, 255 at 277ff. For a discussion of the pan-Indian movement in the U.S.A., see Hazel W. Hertzberg, *The Search for an American Indian Identity: Modern Pan-Indian Movements* (Syracuse. N.Y. Syracuse University Press. 1971)

¹⁰³*R. v. Chiasson*, [2002] 2 C.N.L.R. 220. N.B. Prov. Ct. at 228. [Cite in English]

¹⁰⁴First Ministers' Conference on Aboriginal Constitutional Matters. Métis National Council. *Métis National Council Draft Constitutional Accords on Métis Self-Identification and Enumeration* (Ottawa: March 8 and 9, 1984.) Document: 800–18/019

¹⁰⁵Canada, Report of the Royal Commission on Aboriginal Peoples: Perspectives and Realities, vol. 4 (Ottawa: Supply and Services Canada, 1996), c. 5, appendix 5D, at 377.

¹⁰⁶This information is available on the MNC web site at www.metisnation.ca/. It may be noted that the MNC annual assembly is not a meeting of Métis individuals, but a meeting of the provincial representative organizations that comprise the MNC.

Chapter Nine

Conclusion

Paul L. A. H. Chartrand

This book has analysed constitutional questions of recognition, definition, and jurisdiction concerning the Aboriginal peoples of Canada.

The law of the Constitution requires the federal government to implement a principled and defensible policy of recognition of all the Aboriginal peoples who are mentioned in section 35 of the *Constitution Act, 1982,* including the Indian, Inuit, and Métis peoples. This means replacing the *Indian Act,* which was unilaterally established to administer the lives of Indians on Indian reserves, as defined by federal policy, and adopting a new system of recognition which respects the law of the Constitution. Case law striking down provisions of the *Act* is beginning to show its potential to dismantle the *Act.*

An alternative to reactionary, incremental change by government officials is the establishment of a national political process which sets the guidelines for the recognition of the Aboriginal peoples who would be parties to modern negotiations and agreements on Aboriginal self-government. The Aboriginal peoples are already recognized, by the former section 37 and by section 35.1 of the *Constitution Act, 1982,* as having a special status and role in constitutional change. They must also be partners in implementing the legislative changes required by the 1982 constitutional amendments.

Such a process was recommended by the Royal Commission on Aboriginal Peoples (RCAP), which emphasized that legitimate government policy and legislative action concerning the interests of Aboriginal peoples must be conducted only with the effective participation of the Aboriginal people affected. To date, the federal government has not responded to these recommendations. Proposed federal legislation responding to judicial findings of constitutional invalidity respecting the current *Indian Act* avoids questions of membership and definition. RCAP proposed that the original Indian treaties and the Métis "bargain of Confederation" negotiated with the entry of Manitoba into the Dominion represent an important part of the organic constitution of Canada and ought to be the subject of modern negotiations and agreements for lasting political and legal relationships between the historic nations of Canada. In addition, the Aboriginal peoples without a treaty history must also engage in treaty negotiations and relations to legitimize the exercise of constitutional authority over them. Constitutional principles expounded by the Supreme Court of Canada describe the constitution of Canada as comprised of rules and principles representing the consent of the governed. Accordingly, the group consent of the Aboriginal peoples is required to complete the process of "patriation" of the constitution as a truly North American foundation for the exercise of constitutional power and authority in Canada. The recognition and affirmation of the rights of the Aboriginal peoples is a national commitment to this process and to this constitutional ideal.

The process of recognizing the potential partners in Confederation, that is, the "Aboriginal nations" entitled to exercise the Aboriginal right of self-government in Canada, faces some significant challenges. The "ab-original" nations which the Europeans encountered in what is now Canada have been changed by the effects of time and government policies that aimed to dismantle them and replace them with immigrants. Indian and Métis communities have been affected by time and other factors that promote the personal integration of their members into the general Canadian population.[1] The idea of merging Aboriginal people into the general Canadian population, however, is no longer a constitutionally valid option in Canada, given the 1982 recognition and affirmation of the "aboriginal peoples" and their rights.

In the absence of a coherent federal recognition policy, the Métis and non-status Indians are turning to the courts to assert their rights and to demand government action on the 1982 constitutional recognition and affirmation of their existence and their rights. Emerging constitutional jurisprudence suggests the likelihood of success in litigation aimed at finding that the government has obligations to recognize the Métis people and their rights, and to act to protect these rights and make them effective.

The difficult constitutional question of Métis definition was addressed. Some have attempted to define the Métis people at the boundary of Indian definition, as if Métis people were "almost Indians" who could be identified as Aboriginal people according to their cultural or other similarity or propinquity to Indians. The federal government's own scheme for defining "Indians" in the *Indian Act* puts beyond reach the prospect of arriving at a rational definition of

"Métis" at the boundary of Indian legislated definition. The better prospect is to move away from the Indian boundary and towards the positive core of Métis identity. This approach is also more likely to do justice to Indian people, by avoiding results that might tend to infringe on Indian community interests. In principle, section 35 must be construed so as to do justice to all the Aboriginal peoples whose rights it recognizes.

A move to the positive core of Métis identity in section 35 was attempted in an analysis that focused upon the identification of the Métis community that is entitled to an Aboriginal right of self-government. This is an issue that has not yet come before the courts. The cases to date, including two cases to be heard early in 2003 by the Supreme Court of Canada, concern Métis claims to common law Aboriginal rights to use lands for subsistence purposes and the interpretation of the term "Indians" in the game laws paragraph of the Natural Resources Transfer Agreement between Canada and the Prairie Provinces, which is part of the *Constitution Act, 1930*.

Although not established in the emerging Aboriginal rights jurisprudence, the Aboriginal right of self-government is accepted as part of current federal policy; it has also been argued by scholars and by RCAP, and has received support of the United Nations as an exercise of the right of self-determination. A constitutional recognition of the Métis among the Aboriginal peoples must be interpreted according to fundamental principles and values of the Constitution.

This eliminates the idea that the Métis people means people of "mixed" personal antecedents, or that the term can be interpreted by reference to personal sentiments derived from association with a "pan-Indian" identity. "The Métis people" entitled to exercise political rights within Canada that are recognized and protected by the law of the Constitution must be distinguished from persons of Aboriginal ancestry who are entitled to the benefits of affirmative action undertaken pursuant to section 15, the equality provision of the *Charter of Rights and Freedoms*. These two groups are often wrongly conflated in discussions on the constitutional meaning of "the Métis people."

The jurisprudence on Aboriginal rights, and scholarly opinion, suggests that the source of Aboriginal rights is in the history of Crown-Aboriginal relations. This history identifies the interests that are meant to be protected today by the law of the Constitution in section 35. Furthermore, Aboriginal rights are not only history-based rights, but group rights. Accordingly, an inquiry into Métis rights begins with the identification of the Métis community to which a claimant belongs, not with an inquiry about the claimant's personal antecedents, a direction that has often been undertaken by lower courts.

The conclusion that "the Métis people" in section 35 refers to the descendant communities of the historic Métis nation of the West, or "Riel's people," which has a well documented role in struggling for its rights against Canadian intrusion in western Canada, is supported by historians and social scientists, by federal legislation and practice, by the Constitution of Canada, and by judicial observations. It is a history of which the courts may take judicial notice. There is no need for revisionist historical inquiries, but only tentative comments are possible on the current state of development of the law of Aboriginal rights concerning the identification of the contemporary Métis "people" entitled to the Aboriginal right of self-government.

Recognition theory is based upon the notion that two discrete political entities enter into a political relationship with one another. As discussed in chapter 4, in such situations one entity has no interest in the internal composition or membership of the other. The citizenship rules of one state are not the business of other states, subject to observance of international human rights standards. Recognition theory is helpful to explain some aspects of the domestic relationship between Aboriginal "nations" with some internal political autonomy. It is less helpful in dealing with the fact that Aboriginal people are citizens of Canada, as well as theoretical members of an Aboriginal nation that gets recognized. This dual status is behind some of the challenges that lie in the path of recognition of Aboriginal nations. It also raises some difficulties related to questions of defining both the nations and their members.

The American experience with government "recognition" of Indian tribes with whom it agreed to enter into political relations as "domestic, dependent nations" provides some valuable lessons for Canada, which now faces a situation very similar to the American experience with the modern recognition process initiated by the 1934 *Indian Reorganization Act*. The main lesson is that the matter of recognizing the Aboriginal peoples, the descendants of the historic nations upon whose ancient homelands Canada has been built, is a task of tremendous national importance that must not be left in the hands of civil servants. The process must be conducted with solemnity, and according to agreed upon, legislated, and widely respected standards, and appropriate executive protocols.

The adoption and implementation of a process of recognition of the Aboriginal peoples of Canada and their rights, a process that is just and conforms to the constitutional commitment of 1982, faces a diverse range of significant challenges.

One challenge concerns the size of feasible self-governing nations. Most Indian bands and Inuit and Métis communities would, according to the RCAP analysis, be too small, and would need to constitute themselves as larger political aggregations. This national reconstitution process faces challenges presented by interests that favour the status quo in these communities. This presumed tendency towards the status quo is reinforced by judicial decisions on Aboriginal rights. The cases are finding rights that are vested in small, local communities, not in large "nations."

On the other hand, if a process of national reconstitution aimed at the establishment and recognition of a relatively large Aboriginal nation, it would likely encounter the political resistance that is sure to meet any proposal to introduce a new entity with significant political power and authority. In particular, the "inflexible federalism" experience to which Harry Daniels referred in the foreword suggests that provincial rights, interests, and power will trump the rights, interests, and power of Aboriginal nations. Provincial boundaries may be expected to continue to contain any Aboriginal ambition for the establishment and recognition of Aboriginal nations, the territorial scope of which would transcend provincial boundaries.

To fit within the Canadian federal system, Aboriginal nations must confront all the established orders of government—federal, provincial, and municipal. Canada, as a member of the United Nations, has a duty to protect human rights, and arguably then has a duty to protect the human right of self-determination of Aboriginal peoples against provincial interests, and to oversee the implementation of Aboriginal orders of government. On the other hand, Canada's obligations extend to the protection of the human rights of all its citizens and persons within Canada, including the members of the Aboriginal nations. The implications complicate the question of federal recognition of Aboriginal self-governing authority. RCAP proposed that the *Charter of Rights and Freedoms* applies to the citizens of Aboriginal nations, and that section 25 of the *Charter* provides a constitutional mechanism for reconciling the political authority of an Aboriginal nation with the individual rights of its citizens.

The significance of provincial power and its creation, municipal power, is a reminder of the imperial and federal formulas which aimed to concentrate political authority in respect to Aboriginal relations at the centre, away from the influence of local interests inimical to Aboriginal interests. The evolution of Canadian politics has resulted in a concentration of federal executive power, and this is now a significant feature in assessments of policy change. Just as one is not likely to buy a dog that might bite, governments are loath to adopt policies that might cause political problems. This is a likely explanation for the failure of governments to adopt recommendations for the creation of independent tribunals to oversee the implementation of Aboriginal policy, such as the RCAP recommendation that an independent tribunal be established to make recommendations on the recognition of Aboriginal nations. In theory, Aboriginal nations can and must use the economic advantages of urban areas and build Aboriginal institutions there. This means that Aboriginal people will be moving to the cities as real communities, and not as marginalized individuals.

There is no doubt that to succeed, Aboriginal nations will have to aggregate their resources in the towns and cities, and gain access to the social and economic advantages of urban places, including jobs and markets. Because cities have been built by the takers and intruders, it does not mean that cities must forever be foreign to Aboriginal institutions. Aboriginal resources can be aggregated to build hospitals, schools, and other social institutions in urban places. The urban Aboriginal population can join the "core" Aboriginal nations, as new or old members, and strengthen the human resources base from the current reserve communities. The idea of self-determination means self-definition, and in the vision of RCAP, an Aboriginal nation is free to accept new members. On this view, the Aboriginal population shift to urban areas is only a political challenge to the recognition of feasible Aboriginal nations.

The real challenge is that Canada seems happier to accommodate the needs of marginalized Aboriginal individuals in cities than to accommodate the building of strong Aboriginal communities there.

The recognition of Aboriginal nations challenges the status quo, and there is much power and influence in the status quo. Power must be redistributed to permit Aboriginal peoples to gain access and control of the resources required to create functional sub-state social and political entities. Canada was formerly known as the Dominion of Canada; it is a challenge to move from dominion over Aboriginal peoples to a condominium in which power and authority are distributed to allow both shared rule and self-rule.

One of the greatest challenges to the constitutional recognition of the Aboriginal peoples is the result that the courts decide the meaning of its terms. Even if the courts were to decide that Aboriginal nations have a right to decide their own rules of membership, they would make decisions that would define the nations themselves. The political legitimacy of judicial definitions of Aboriginal nations is the great challenge. Not only are the Aboriginal peoples forced by political weakness to accept that their most fundamental rights are being defined by courts on which they have never had a single member; they are faced with the prospect of being screened at the door of political negotiations and participation by judicial decisions. The task of recognizing and defining the Aboriginal peoples must be legitimized by setting up specialized tribunals with representation from Aboriginal peoples, as RCAP proposed. The federal government has not acted on this recommendation, but there will be no justice or political resolution of the questions of recognition and definition without legitimate decision-making processes.

The failures of the Canadian government in taking action that reflects the constitutional recognition and affirmation of the Aboriginal peoples of Canada and their rights in the 1982 amendment are compounded by the positive actions that government lawyers take in litigation. The executive arm of government has a positive duty to protect the rights of the Aboriginal peoples. Yet when Aboriginal people attempt to take important issues to the courts, they are met at every turn with unconscionable obstructionist and delaying tactics by government lawyers. These tactics are significant drains on the public treasury, and on the well of the spirit of reconciliation of Aboriginal peoples. The Crown must act in court in a manner that is consistent with the fiduciary relationship that the Crown has with Aboriginal peoples. As mentioned above, the best solution is the establishment of specialized tribunals that can adopt fair and equitable procedures.

The inequity in the present Crown approach is revealed in the following extract from an action undertaken by the Congress of Aboriginal Peoples and Harry Daniels following the conference which generated the core of materials presented in this book.

> I would remind the Crown, …that unreasonable difficulty ought not to be thrown in the way of procedures in which claimants, acting *bona fide*, bring questions of great importance to the courts in order to obtain declaratory relief.[2]

Notes

[1] The Aboriginal people of the Far North, the Inuit, have been less affected by these factors, and are participants in federal negotiations and agreements on land, cultural, and governance issues.

[2] *Harry W. Daniels, Leah Gardner and the Congress of Aboriginal Peoples* v. *R.* Docket T–2172–99, Neutral citation: 2002 FCT 295; Vancouver, B.C. March 15, 2002, *Reasons for Order.* John A. Hargrave, Prothonotary.

Index

312